MW00466225

SIMPSON

IMPRINT IN HUMANITIES

The humanities endowment
by Sharon Hanley Simpson and
Barclay Simpson honors
MURIEL CARTER HANLEY
whose intellect and sensitivity
have enriched the many lives
that she has touched.

The publisher and the University of California Press Foundation gratefully acknowledge the generous support of the Simpson Imprint in Humanities.

WAR AND RELIGION

WAR AND RELIGION

EUROPE AND THE MEDITERRANEAN FROM
THE FIRST THROUGH THE TWENTY-FIRST
CENTURIES

Arnaud Blin

 UNIVERSITY OF CALIFORNIA PRESS

University of California Press, one of the most distinguished
university presses in the United States, enriches lives around
the world by advancing scholarship in the humanities, social
sciences, and natural sciences. Its activities are supported by
the UC Press Foundation and by philanthropic contributions
from individuals and institutions. For more information, visit
www.ucpress.edu.

University of California Press
Oakland, California

© 2019 by The Regents of the University of California

Library of Congress Cataloging-in-Publication Data

Names: Blin, Arnaud, author.
Title: War and religion : Europe and the Mediterranean from
    the first through the twenty-first centuries / Arnaud Blin.
Description: Oakland, California : University of California
    Press, [2018] | Includes bibliographical references and index. |
Identifiers: LCCN 2018033189 (print) | LCCN 2018034560
    (ebook) | ISBN 9780520961753 | ISBN 9780520286634
    (cloth : alk. paper)
Subjects: LCSH: War—Religious aspects—History. | Religion
    and politics—Europe—History. | Religion and politics—
    Mediterranean Region—History. | Mediterranean
    Region—History. | Europe—History. | Mediterranean
    Region—Politics and government. | Europe—Politics and
    government.
Classification: LCC BL65.W2 (ebook) | LCC BL65.W2 B55 2018
    (print) | DDC 201/.727309—dc23
LC record available at https://lccn.loc.gov/2018033189

Manufactured in the United States of America

26 25 24 23 22 21 20 19
10 9 8 7 6 5 4 3 2 1

To Kimberly, Margaux, and Emerson

For six thousand years war
Has pleased the quarrelling peoples
And God has wasted his time making
The stars and the flowers

—Victor Hugo, *Les chansons des rues et des bois*

CONTENTS

ILLUSTRATIONS

CHRONOLOGY

72/73 CE	Siege and fall of Masada, Israel
312	Constantine's epiphany at the Milvian Bridge outside Rome
ca. 400	Saint Augustine develops just war doctrine
499 (or 508)	Clovis converts to Catholicism
622	Muhammad and the Hegira
636/637	Muslim armies defeat the Byzantines at Yarmouk and the Sassanians and Qadisiyya
732	Muslims stopped at Poitiers
751	Muslims defeat Chinese at Talas
800	Charlemagne emperor
786–809	Hārūn al-Rashīd and the Golden Age of Islam
1071	Byzantines crushed by Alp Arslan at Manzikert
1095	Council of Clermont: Pope Urban II launches First Crusade
1099	Crusaders enter Jerusalem
1187	Saladin wins at Hattin, retakes Jerusalem
1204	Sack of Constantinople by crusaders
1209–44	Albigensian Crusades
1212	Christian victory at Las Navas de Tolosa, Spain
ca. 1270	Saint Thomas Aquinas revives just war doctrine
1396	Christian army routed by Ottomans at Nicopolis

1410	Teutonic Knights defeated at Grünwald-Tannenberg
1419–36	Hussite Wars
1453	Fall of Constantinople
1492	Muslims and Jews expelled from Spain
1517	Luther posts his ninety-five theses
1555	Peace of Augsburg between Catholics and Lutherans
1560–98	French Wars of Religion
1571	Holy League defeats Ottomans at Lepanto
1588	Spanish Armada repulsed by England
1618–48	Thirty Years' War
1648	Peace of Westphalia
1648–54	Khmelnytsky uprising, Ukraine and Belarus
1656 and 1712	Villmergen wars in the Swiss Confederacy
1702–10	*Camisard* uprising in southern France
1736–47	Nader Shah seeks to unify Islam
1913–22	Turkish genocide of Armenians, Assyro-Chaldeans, and Pontic Greeks
1924	Atatürk abolishes the Caliphate
1979	USSR invades Afghanistan
1979	Iranian Revolution
2001	9/11 terrorist attacks

ACKNOWLEDGMENTS

Not many publishers would have taken the risk of accepting a manuscript on a topic as complex and sensitive as this one, and so the first person I must thank is Reed Malcolm of the University of California Press. Reed believed in the project from the start and entrusted me with bringing it to fruition. From there, he followed the process from beginning to end, encouraged me when I needed it, and helped me clear the obstacles that popped up along the way. Without Reed, this book might never have taken off, and it would have had difficulty landing when it had. The editorial team at the University of California Press was professional to the core and ensured that the transmutation from manuscript to book was a smooth process. Archna Patel steered me efficiently and patiently through the process as Cindy Fulton took the book through the various stages of production. The final draft of the manuscript had the good fortune of being entrusted to Peter Dreyer for copyediting. Peter's extraordinary depth of knowledge, formidable experience, and uncompromising rigor no doubt contributed dramatically to elevate the quality of the text.

Great thanks must also go to Kristie Bliss and Gérard Chaliand. The job of the historian is to make sure that his or her material is not too difficult to digest, and, to this end, form is as central as substance. Kristie painstakingly read the various iterations of this long manuscript. Her mastery and love of the English language, as well as her tireless attention to detail, enabled me to steer clear of stylistic pitfalls and to resist excessive digressions. She made sure I kept the text as fluid as possible, essential given the bulk of information.

Gérard Chaliand is one of the few people on earth with the breadth of knowledge, as well as the command and capacity, to evaluate a topic as multifaceted and extensive as this one so thoroughly. Gérard's detailed comments, suggestions, and criticisms were invaluable, and his intellectual support was much appreciated. My thanks also go to the anonymous evaluators whose acute and penetrating comments helped make this text a lot more focused and solid than was the case with the initial draft. Last, but not least, my sincere thanks to Nicolas Rageau who, once again, worked his cartographic magic and brought life to the complex maps I asked him to produce.

My beloved wife, Kimberly, provided much needed emotional support, as well as the indispensable technical expertise needed in this digital age, which lost me long ago. Thank you also to our two children, whose high spirits and good humor allowed me to decompress and recharge my oft-depleted batteries on a daily basis.

Lastly, I would like to thank my high school history teacher and lifelong friend Nooman Kacem, who many years ago instilled into a young lad an unquenchable thirst to explore the past and an unrelenting desire to discover and comprehend some of its mysteries. His voice was an omnipresent and reassuring companion during this journey.

Introduction

Of all the animosities which have existed among mankind, those which are caused by a difference of sentiments in religion appear to be the most inveterate and distressing, and ought most to be deprecated.

—George Washington

The goal of religious wars is the purification of the city through the elimination of the ideas that pollute it.

—Élie Barnavi

On October 28, 312, on a river overpass outside Rome, in the midst of a violent battle for supremacy in the Roman Empire, the emperor Constantine I experienced a spiritual epiphany.[1] Or so legend has it. Whether the epiphany actually took place at that particular moment or was injected into the narrative later by the emperor and his hagiographers we'll never know. In any case, Constantine's victory that autumnal day at the Milvian Bridge was epochmaking. For subsequently, having eliminated his rivals, the now uncontested monarch declared Christianity to be the official religion of the empire, thus changing the course of history.

Fast forward thirteen hundred years, to 1648. We are now in Münster and Osnabrück, where the sound of cannons, which had deafened the greater part of Europe for several decades, has suddenly given way to the buzzing of negotiation: whether on foot, horse, or carriage, diplomats from all over the continent are scurrying to the German province of Westphalia, where they will formalize the treaties marking the end of the Thirty Years' War, a religious conflict that has ravaged much of Europe. In doing so, the plenipotentiaries will rewrite the rules and norms of international relations, in the process creating a new European order that will effectively flush out religion from politics.

During those thirteen centuries between the battle of the Milvian Bridge and the Peace of Westphalia, the many wars that rocked and shaped Europe, the Mediterranean, and the greater Middle East were in one way or another driven or influenced by religion, thus forming a continuum that lasted roughly until the turn of the eighteenth century. This book proposes to retrace the origins of this long history, from its timid beginnings around the first century CE, with the advent of the great new monotheistic religion, Christianity, to the accords of Westphalia, followed by the various manifestations of religious violence that came to define the international political order from 1650 until today. The events described in these pages thus form a single narrative, which essentially revolves around the regions where the Abrahamic religions took hold, though on occasion these events take us beyond Europe and the Mediterranean to America, for example, where the Spaniards, after rolling back the Muslims from the Iberian peninsula, pursued their global crusade.

For centuries, religion and war seem to have cohabited without necessarily feeding on each other. Two developments, however, were to change all that: the emergence first of Christianity and then of Islam and the political empowerment of their religious institutions. Both religions began as small, marginal sects, which eventually spread around the Mediterranean. By the seventh century, all of the area that had formerly comprised the empires of Alexander the Great and Rome was either Christian or Muslim. By then, Judaism, which had courageously fought the Roman onslaught in the first century and laid the foundations from which Christianity and then Islam sprang, was politically all but powerless—one reason, paradoxically, that it was able to survive. Two other monotheistic religions, Manichaeism and Zoroastrianism (which has also survived), which had taken root in Persia, were equally pushed to the sidelines. Manichaeism failed in its attempt to supplant Zoroastrianism as the state religion of Persia, and Zoroastrianism itself was driven out of the equation when the Sassanian dynasty that ruled Persia was annihilated by the Muslim armies that overran the empire between 636 and 642.

The provocative historian, Yuval Noah Harari, summarizes best the singular dynamics of monotheism and its impact on global history:

> Monotheists have tended to be far more fanatical and missionary than polytheists. A religion that recognizes the legitimacy of other faiths implies either that its god is not the supreme power of the universe, or that it received from God just part of

the universal truth. Since monotheists have usually believed that they are in possession of the entire message of the one and only God, they have been compelled to discredit all other religions. Over the last two millennia, monotheists repeatedly tried to strengthen their hands by violently exterminating all competition. It worked. [. . .] Henceforth, the monotheist idea played a central role in world history.[2]

People who want to compel others to adhere to their beliefs and adopt their myths are naturally drawn to acquire the practical means to do so, which brings us to the second part of the equation: the political empowerment of religious institutions. Politics is primarily concerned with power: how to win it, how to keep it, how to manage it, how to project it, how to protect it, how to increase it, and how to pass it on. The use of force is a tool of power, and war is one of the principal ways of wielding it. As the Prussian thinker Carl von Clausewitz famously stated two centuries ago, war, in the end, is nothing but "an act of force to compel our enemy to do our will."[3]

In a nutshell, then, the belief in a universal truth fosters a compelling desire to share this truth with others, which naturally attracts those with this desire to power and prompts them, once in the saddle, to use the traditional instruments at the disposal of those who wield power, including force. "If you have discovered the truth will you not want to live in a world governed by that truth?" James Laine asks. "Which, in turn, begs another question: 'Is not the story of religion inseparable from political and military history?'"[4]

ARE RELIGIONS INHERENTLY VIOLENT?

Recent events linked to the radicalization of religion and its central role in the latest waves of terrorism have largely altered our perception of the violent nature of religion. Today, it is not uncommon to hear that religion as such is inherently violent and the source of most conflicts in history. Is this true?

The first thing one should point out is that the history of war is long, varied, and, so to speak, very rich. If one looks at the most violent conflicts in history, or rather, those that caused the greatest destruction, many were not exclusively, or even remotely, religious in nature. Among the most violent wars to date, the American Civil War and World Wars I and II were essentially political affairs. The Thirty Years' War, on the other hand, started as a religious conflict before becoming a political one, and although there was a strong religious element to the Taiping Rebellion in China (1850–64), with its twenty to seventy million casualties, it exacerbated tensions that were not completely religious in nature.

This quick assessment illustrates an important point: while religion may have been a significant factor in a number of armed conflicts throughout history, it has not been an exclusive one.[5] To this we may add that its role in fueling or fostering war has largely been dictated by historical circumstances, rather than by an inherent propensity on the part of religious leaders or believers to generate violence. Religion has in some instances merely contributed—in varying degrees—to a political conflict: "Religious participation," says Ara Norenzayan, "cements social ties and builds group solidarity. But when groups are in conflict, this solidarity translates into the willingness to sacrifice to defend the group against perceived enemies."[6] In other instances, religion has been at the root of a conflict or its principal driver, as will be amply demonstrated in this volume. More often than not, religion also helped contain or avoid violence or provided moral restraints on the use of force. Finally, from a global perspective, religions taken as a whole have in many instances had little or no impact on the decisions that were made to go to war or on how it was waged.

Another key point is that religions evolve. Christianity, for example, started with a strong pacifist message and an intransigent attitude toward war and even military service. Circumstances, however, pushed the church to adopt an increasingly flexible attitude, leading first to the development of the doctrine of just war and later to the call for holy war. Over the past century or more, the Catholic Church has gone back to its pacifist roots and shifted away from holy war, albeit without abandoning its acceptance of just war ethics.

The elements that pushed for this change in attitude can be traced to the evolution of Christian doctrine, to the development of an institutionalized church that became a player in power politics, to pressure from an exogenous religious force, Islam, and finally to the emergence of the modern secular state. Thus, in the thousand-plus years that separate Jesus Christ and Pope Urban II, Christians saw themselves transformed from a small, fringe pacifist sect that shunned anything remotely linked to military activity to the church that gave rise to the powerful religious-military orders created in the twelfth century to wage and support holy war. However, this evolution left room for differing, sometimes directly opposed, attitudes to cohabit. Jesus's pacifist message and example remained the core of Christian thought and practice, but just war and holy war nevertheless became integral to Christian doctrine and practice.

In a way, the contradiction paved the way for both the Reformation and the Counter-Reformation. Within Protestantism, movements like the Quakers, in particular, revived and proclaimed Jesus's original message of uncompromising peace, but the doctrine of just war was later given a new lease on life by Protestant theologians such as Reinhold Niebuhr. Though holy war has ceased to be an effective element of Western policy since the seventeenth century, it has survived to this day as a symbolic instrument, regularly brandished through the discourse on war, as exemplified by the tone of the debates that surrounded the reaction, most notably in the United States, to the events of 9/11. The path taken by Anabaptists, a Protestant group, was more radical still: after supremely violent beginnings and much soul-searching, they made an about-turn and adopted pacifism as their creed.[7]

Although it also has a pacifist strand that cohabits with its traditions of just war and holy war, these being more intimately related for Muslims, Islam has been much more consistent in its attitude to war. Its general approach to organized violence is similar to what has come to be adopted in the West, in China, India, and elsewhere, namely, a dual attitude that reflects the violent nature of international politics, on the one hand, and the hopefully peaceful internal workings of society, on the other. Much like Western political philosophy, Islamic thought on the matter understands the inherent distinction between the need to keep and promote social peace within one's political entity and the need to prepare for war against other, competing entities.

Both in the Islamic world and the Western world, the dual nature of politics came to a head when the real nature of competitive politics was pitted against the desire by many to create or recreate a political space that would encompass all the religious brethren under one political roof. For Muslims, that roof came to be known as the Grand Caliphate, and its proponents included such powerful and respectable figures as Saladin and Suleiman the Magnificent. Closer to us, the likes of Osama bin Laden and Ayman al-Zawahiri, among others, have publicly stated their desire to recreate the caliphate, in defiance of all probability. For Western Christians, the desire to unify Western Christianity manifested itself through the dream of recreating a new, Christian, Roman empire, embodied in Charlemagne in the eighth century and the Spanish and Holy Roman emperor Charles V in the sixteenth. That dream did briefly come about in the Holy Roman Empire, but it became the focal point of religious conflicts that destroyed half of Europe in the seventeenth century and enabled the rise of the modern secular state and, with it, the demise of the dream of unifying the Christian world under one banner.

Although the most violent conflicts in history are not exclusively religious, there is one element that seems to be omnipresent in the most gruesome wars: ideas, or, if one prefers, ideology, or, to use the older terminology, opinion. When wars involve more than political, territorial, or personal elements, the violence often escalates uncontrollably, causing mayhem and, more often than not, indiscriminate civilian deaths. The great Swiss strategist of the early nineteenth century Antoine-Henri de Jomini pinpointed the major characteristics of these wars, underlining the fact that religious and political dogma are both conducive to formidable bursts of violence, and that religion can both be a cause and a pretext for war: "Although originating in religious or political dogmas, these wars [of opinion] are most deplorable; for, like national wars, they enlist the worst passions, and become vindictive, cruel, and terrible. The wars of Islamism, the Crusades, the Thirty Years', War, the wars of the League, present nearly the same characteristics. Often religion is the pretext for obtaining political power and the war is not really one of dogmas. The successors of Muhammad cared more about extending their empire than about preaching the Quran, and Philip II, bigot as he was, did not sustain the League in France for the purpose of advancing the Roman Church. [. . .] The dogma sometimes is not only a pretext, but is a powerful ally; for it excites the ardor of the people, and also creates a party. [. . .] It may, however, happen, as in the Crusades and the wars of Islamism, that the dogma for which the war is waged, instead of friends, finds only bitter enemies in the country invaded; and then the contest become fearful."[8]

All in all, the pacific dimension of religion, which at times seems to dominate its outlook on human affairs (one thinks of Jesus's message) has not prevented religions, including Christianity, from generating conflicts. Nor has religious conflict arisen solely from fringe fanaticism fueled by radicalized or isolated individuals or groups. In many instances, church authorities have instigated wars and even taken part in them. The religious-military orders of the Middle Ages embodied the bellicose attitude that characterized the church at the time. In some instances, as with the Teutonic Knights, the orders devoted all their energies to waging imperialistic wars against nations that for the most part, like Poland in this case, shared their religious beliefs.

In the medieval Western world, the understanding and practice of war essentially combined Germanic military culture with Christian morals and theology. The Christian dimension affected not only society's approach to war but strategies and tactics as well. Hence, the classic pitched battle whose outcome is decided by the judgment of God, understood to be the culminating point of a war. It must therefore take place in an open field where all sides fight on equal ground so that God's decision is untainted by extraneous elements. In many ways, this conception ran counter to all strategic principles, and in practical terms, generals had to compromise between strategic expediency and moral constraints. But generally, the rules were clear. The fight was straightforward, one force against another, and might the worthiest men win, with this worthiness defined in both military and moral terms.

During the Hundred Years' War, for example, the English believed in the biblical injunction that any divided people will perish. Since France, at the time, was divided, it should perish. For the English King Henry V, his resounding victory at Agincourt (1415) thus signaled that God recognized the legitimacy of his claim to the French throne. But interpretations can suit one's desires, and for the hapless French knights who survived the day, the religious interpretation of the crushing loss meant something else: that God had punished the soldiers for their sins. Of course, the war found its denouement in the most religious manner when a young shepherd, Joan of Arc, claiming to act upon God's direct guidance, proceeded to roll the English back out of France.

Wars between Christians conformed to a set of norms that was more or less adhered to by most states and armies, but wars against extraneous non-Christian elements evidently loosened these moral constraints—God, regardless, was on the side of the Christians—thus expanding one's strategic and tactical outlook. Richard Lionheart, for one, fought as "unchristian" a war as any when he attempted to reconquer Jerusalem in the name of Christ, all the while showing himself the most pugnacious and ruthless of all the Crusader commanders. A little later, when Crusader armies rampaged through Constantinople and all but destroyed the city in 1204, they showed little restraint toward their Christian Orthodox brethren. Wars fought before God and awaiting His judgment were less violent, it seems, than those that were fought in His name.

ARE SOME RELIGIONS MORE BELLICOSE THAN OTHERS?

The question of the bellicosity of religion can be tackled from an analytical perspective—with one central question: *what causes a religion to foster violence and war?*—or a historical one, which looks at the various manifestations of religious wars in all their conjectural complexities and their changing nature, without disregarding the effects that religion may have had on mitigating violence and preventing or limiting armed conflicts. The second approach, which is concerned as much with effects as with causes, is, on the surface at least, more approachable, though it is largely conditioned by the fact that wars, even wars of religion, do not occur in a religious vacuum, since many elements independent of religion come into play. In sheer magnitude and frequency, it will come as no surprise to the reader that, historically, two religions in particular have been at the root of a majority of significant conflicts: Islam and Christianity. Discussing violence in African religions, Nathalie Wlodarczyk underlines an important point in this regard:

> Unlike some of the other world religions, however, African Traditional Religion has rarely been the cause (real or proclaimed) of wars. Because of the lack of central doctrine and, therefore, hierarchy and institutions, it has never become the powerful tool for state conquest that Christianity or Islam have become. Although traditional religious explanations for misfortune have helped legitimize the cause of many insurgent groups, and aided their recruitment, this has tended to be on a smaller-scale than state-sponsored warfare.[9]

Islam was committed to violence almost from the very beginning, and violence has remained a part of its makeup, including its message. Of course, as we are often reminded, Islam is not only about violence, and a significant part—indeed, the great majority—of its teachings have little or nothing to do with violence. Some, as with Christianity, are chiefly concerned with peace. By separating the world (in tune with the political and geopolitical realities) between the inner society and the outside world, Islam attempts to reconcile the contradictions between the world of peace and the world of violence, contradictions with which Christian theologians also grappled.

Islam, much like Christianity, also developed a strand of pacifism, and its central message is one of peace. However, its universal character permits and even encourages violence in order to suppress those who fall outside its realm. The term "jihad" is open to interpretation, but the claim that it does not encourage physical violence toward non-Muslims, particularly nonbelievers, is altogether misleading. The fact that the prophet Muhammad and his immediate successors founded not only a religion but also a state has meant that, from the beginning, Islam has been enmeshed with politics. Contrary to Christianity, where internal conflicts within the religion, some very violent, have been due to theological or dogmatic disputes, internal conflicts in Islam typically stem from the bitter disagreement over the succession of Muhammad that has ripped Muslim followers into two principal, bitterly rival camps, the Sunnis and Shiites (a third camp, of lesser importance today, being the Kharidjites).

In the West, historically, the institutions of the state predate Christianity by several centuries, and Christianity was first proclaimed a state religion three centuries after Jesus Christ. This chronological and institutional hiatus at the inception has defined the relationship between politics and religion in the Christian West that continues to this day. The increasingly violent misunderstandings that prevail today between secularized Christian majorities and Muslim minorities, most notably in western Europe, find their source in the respective historical developments of Christianity and Islam in their relationship to political power. And while Christianity has on various occasions and for long periods of time been associated with political and state power, it has followed a path of its own. In Islam, the paths have been traced by the double helix of the Shiite and Sunni traditions, but on a singular track, where religion and political governance have been intermeshed with each other. This fact in and of itself is at the heart of the difficulties that Muslim countries, particularly Arab ones, have had with political modernization.

In essence, there are three mechanisms through which religion interacts with political power. At one extreme, a theocracy exercises absolute political power. At the other end, in what is sometimes referred to as "caesaropapism," the secular ruler claims to have absolute authority over religious matters. In between, we find secular and religious authorities overlapping in their exercise of political power.[10] The Western world has essentially exercised religious-political power in the second and third realms. Islam has exercised it over the whole spectrum, with religious and political authority often in the hands of the same individual. The fact, supported by any historical survey of conflicts, that Islam and Christianity are the champions of bellicose behavior among religious practitioners does not imply that other religions are not, or are less, violent, or less conducive to violent conflict. All it says is that either Muslims or Christians (or parties claiming to be such), or both, have been the principal belligerents in the vast majority of the wars in recorded history of which religion was one of the main causes. This points to the main determinants of religious bellicosity.

These determinants are the ones that James W. Laine identifies in his analysis of religion and power, and are concerned with the fundamental character of a religion as inclusive or exclusive, as rooted in and limited to a particular group or universal in vocation. *Inclusivism* implies that the overarching religion accepts other religions under its umbrella. *Exclusivism* implies that a religion holds to an exclusive Truth or God and thus excludes the existence of another Truth or God. That this Truth is valid for all people, independent of their position in space and time, is what leads to universalism, the opposite, then, of particularism, for which different people may have different belief systems.[11]

Judaism, for example, is exclusivistic but not universalistic. At the other end of the spectrum, Buddhism is inclusivistic and, through the Four Noble Truths, universalistic, much like Greek religion during the age of Alexander or Hinduism in the age of Ashoka, which, in the latter two cases, fostered a religious pluralism that went beyond mere tolerance of varying religious creeds. Zoroastrianism, the first of the monotheistic religions, was exclusivist but not quite universalistic, though it was less particularistic than Judaism, since it remained rooted in Iranian culture, unlike Manichaeism, which, like Christianity and Islam, was both exclusivist and universalistic (incidentally, the Latin word *catholicus*, "Catholic," which surfaced in the second century CE and came to designate the Roman church, is derived from the Greek word for "universal": *katholikos*.)

Universalism is one of those concepts that are complicated to define but easy to understand. Garth Fowden's simple definition is as good as any and sufficiently clear for our purposes: "A universalist culture or religion is one that is accessible to all human beings and tends to be accepted by them eventually, whether or not it actively proselytizes or has yet penetrated the geographical area they inhabit."[12]

Tolerance, then, is not really the issue here and exclusivist-universal monotheistic religions may be tolerant of other religions. The caliphates of the Golden Age of Andalusia or the Ottoman Empire were famously tolerant of other religions . . . as long as they did not challenge the political order. That said, Muslim Spain was without a doubt much more tolerant than Catholic Europe at the same time, and when Ferdinand and Isabella took control of all of Spain in 1492, they promptly showed all non-Catholics the door if they refused to convert, starting with the Jewish communities of Spain, which had until then been an integral part of the society.

Christendom, for the most part, did tolerate Jewish communities, though often grudgingly, even if these became regular targets of popular resentments or political maneuvering when scapegoats were sought. But tolerance of minorities, which often have secondary social and legal status, is one thing and recognition of other exclusivist-universal religions is quite another, a fact that we tend to forget in our pluralistic and somewhat tolerant societies (though the challenges to our secular culture by radical Islamists are changing our outlook, as was evident during the 2016 U.S presidential campaign, among other examples).

In essence, then, as pointed out earlier, it is basically impossible for one group that is convinced it holds the universal truth to cohabit equally with another group that holds another truth to be universal. Such religions might cohabit with one another in a political environment where religion and politics were almost totally disconnected, and thus under the umbrella of a suprapolitical structure that supersedes them, as evidenced in contemporary liberal democracies, or, for that matter, in secular dictatorships (though when these crumble, religion tends to come back in full force in the resulting political struggles, as it did in the former Yugoslavia, Egypt, Iraq, Tunisia, and Libya). Such cohabitation is both ideologically and practically impossible, however, in societies where the frontier between religion and politics is less clear-cut. And in fact, they pose serious problems in a society such as France, where secularity *(laïcité)* functions as a meta-religion of sorts,[13] and attacks to it by radical religious groups are seen as a challenge.

RELIGIOUS IDENTITY

Identity is an important element of this story. The modern world, which revolves around the primacy of the individual and liberty, has highlighted the difficulties inherent in defining one's identity when our attachments to a particular community have become increasingly tenuous, creating many of the problems that contemporary societies are facing today. Today's religious conflicts are in many ways related to this crisis of identity, with extremists forcefully rejecting the very core of the individualistic creed that defines modernity, which entire regions are at odds with and reject more or less openly.

Obviously, we are talking here mainly about the modernity emerging from the West, a movement that took hold in the fifteenth-century Italian city-states and was to steer history in a new direction by defining what it is to be an unshackled individual.[14] Indeed, today, modernized or modernizing Confucian societies—Japan, China, or Vietnam—continue to privilege the community over the individual, the latter having little purpose outside a social setting. In the past, though, an individual's identity was irremediably tied to a linguistic, ethnic, and religious community, including in Europe.

During the Middle Ages and the Renaissance, Europe was equated with Christendom. For Muslim outsiders, however, Europeans were either Romans (Byzantines) or Franks (Westerners). For most, the world was divided into one's own world, namely, the world inhabited by co-religionists, and the "outside world" where few dared go, an accepted fact that explains the success of Marco Polo's account of his life at the court of Kublai Khan. Likewise, when Ibn Battuta, the great Moroccan traveler of the fourteenth century, undertook his long journey, his intention was to visit all the "known world," specifically the Muslim world (though he did venture to southern Russia and Constantinople). When, at about the same time, the Tunisian historian Ibn Khaldūn made the first attempt to write a global political history, his scope was strictly limited to the Muslim world, his vision of the "Frankish world" being essentially ahistorical. Outside of what seemed to be two planets whose tips touched ever so slightly in southern Spain and Portugal, the rest of the world was perceived by both Christians and Muslims as a hodgepodge of heathens of various kinds, whose souls, at least from the Christian standpoint, could potentially be saved through more or less forceful conversions (Islam, on the other hand, does not advocate forced conversion). Indeed, when lone Christian ambassadors such as John Plano Carpini (1245–47) or William of Rubrouck (1253–55) were sent, the one by Pope Innocent IV, the other by the French king Louis IX (Saint Louis), to the courts of the Mongol rulers who reigned over half of the Eurasian continent, they naïvely endeavored to convert their hosts and were genuinely surprised at being politely rebuffed.[15] Evidently, these emissaries were misled by the wishful thinking of a time when, owing to the popular and enduring legend of Prester John, the Mongols were thought ready to embrace Christianity and eagerly defend it with their bows and arrows against the Turks.

The point here is that for the greater part of the Middle Ages, the Renaissance and even modern times, the world was essentially compartmentalized, with communication between different worlds left to a few merchants, even fewer embassies, and, at various times, armed conflicts, invasions, and wars. Although recently historians have attempted to show that the world may then have been less compartmentalized than once thought, most notably by Henri Pirenne, it still remained very much so.[16] Therefore, the "other" or "others" were perceived with great suspicion, often justified in an environment that was altogether violent, so that when two worlds met, they often clashed. For the most part, both Islam and Christianity fed on this suspicion, whether because they felt either threatened or empowered to expand their influence, or both. Religion and power being intermeshed in the Christian and the Muslim worlds, it was only logical that religious and political authorities colluded to instigate wars with what was essentially considered to be the arch-enemy. King François I of France committed the ultimate political crime in the eyes of his European peers when he allied himself with the Ottomans in the sixteenth century to curtail Habsburg hegemony in continental Europe. And although (southern) Christian Europe presented a united front against the Ottomans at Lepanto in 1571, François had broken the mold. With him, international politics became increasingly guided by political exigency rather than by religious considerations. During the Thirty Years' War, which began less than half a century later, Protestant Sweden allied with Catholic France formed the winning coalition, even though the conflict was a struggle between Protestants and Catholics.

RECONCILING THE WORLD OF GOD AND THE WORLD OF MEN

War is omnipresent in some of the earliest writings we have, including the Victory Stele of the Akkadian king Naram-Sin (ca. 2250 BCE); what is perhaps the earliest work of fiction, the epic *Gilgamesh* (2100 BCE), which pairs man's heroic deeds in war with his search for eternal life (treating the two main themes of this book); and the epic poem "The Battle of Kadesh" (ca. 1295 BCE), with the first written international agreement. These early writings treat war as a spiritual journey in which man overcomes his own shortcomings by defeating his enemies. Though war is depicted as a positive outlet for man to display such qualities as courage, loyalty, and heroism, one can already find in these emotional texts the tension between man's quest for social peace and his recourse to violence, even if committed in order to achieve and protect peace.

From the earliest times, it seems, religion served as the go-between connecting the ideals of a peaceful social environment with the realities of violent conflicts that pervaded an anarchical geopolitical environment. By distinguishing between the world of God and the world of men, religion similarly placed at the forefront of its concerns the contradictions that pit our ideals and aspirations against our instincts and desires. One of the principal attributes of religion is to demarcate the profane from the sacred, inasmuch as war, like feasts, straddles the two domains. War is both a catalyst of progress and a scourge capable of annihilating the greatest human accomplishments. As such, it transcends humankind, and its irrationality is better elucidated by divine explanations than by rational interpretations. Its impact is almost too formidable to bear.

This fact is exemplified by the difficulties we encounter in rationalizing war in the secular age. The literary production that followed World War I and World War II points almost unanimously to the absurdity of war. But even then one finds poignant depictions of trench warfare, most notably those of Ernst Jünger, that redirect us to the epic of Gilgamesh by underlining the dual nature of war. Our rational minds are confused by, and even incapable of comprehending, the simultaneous abomination and exhilaration of war:

> What was that about? War had shown its claws, and stripped off its mask of coziness. It was all so strange, so impersonal. We had barely begun to think about the enemy, that mysterious, treacherous being somewhere. This event, so far beyond anything we had experienced, made such a powerful impression on us that it was difficult to understand what had happened. It was like a ghostly manifestation in broad daylight.[17]

Along with love, war is the great theme of fiction writing. From the Iliad to *War and Peace* to *Catch-22*, war has been the central character in masterpieces of world literature. While fiction exalts the emotional, and at times passionate and irrational dimension of war, historians have traditionally considered it to be an integral part of foreign policy and one of the guiding threads of history. Thus war embodies at the highest level the perpetual conflict between passion and reason, between individual emotions and political expediency, between good and evil, between the civilized and the barbarian. It is only recently, in the past century and a half or so, that other factors, such as economics, social change, or climate, have been considered to be greater drivers of history, taking precedence over military conflicts, now often considered an effect of these stronger forces rather than independent of them.

Just as war has occupied center stage in fictional and historical texts, it has also permeated religious writings. From the beginning, theologians and students of religion also had to grapple with the significance of war, its role in the global scheme of things, its relationship to individuals and religious communities, its moral ramifications. In essence, theologians had to explain what such a horrific event might signify in a world created by God, who presumably desired peace and stability for His (or Her) children.

For this reason, war is omnipresent in the foundational texts of the great religions. For those religions that are revealed, the issue of war has a significance that goes beyond the symbolic and historical context within which the religion appeared. This significance is not only strong, it is long-lasting and has very practical effects. In the classical Jewish tradition, for example, war is justified as a preemptive tool to fend off adversaries bent on destroying the Jewish people. Far from being a symbolic interpretation of events concerning only the inhabitants of Judea twenty-five hundred years ago, this view of war and the use of force have persisted through the centuries. Today, in the twenty-first century, preemption has been a cornerstone of Israel's strategy to fend off hostile nations like Iran and Pakistan (or, previously, Iraq) that might launch, or threaten to launch, nuclear weapons against its territory.[18]

Generally speaking, war holds a significant place in religious writings of various traditions. As a consequence, it is an issue that has been discussed at much greater length, and one might even argue, more thoroughly, by theologians than by philosophers. If one looks at the Christian tradition, war has been a constant source of interest and an issue that in many ways has defined Christianity and what it means to be a Christian. From Jesus to Saint Augustine, from Thomas Aquinas to Reinhold Niebuhr, the question has never ceased to be debated. If one goes back to the Old Testament, war is ever-present, as is its justification. Indeed, nowhere perhaps are the Old Testament and New Testament more at odds than on the topic of war, a contradiction one also finds in other religious traditions. Both war and its absolute rejection have always been present in the religious debate, with each side able to justify its position, often with the aid and support of scripture. In essence then, what do the foundational religious writings say, or not say, about war? And is this important, or not so important?

One of the most common arguments advanced today to "explain" violent jihadist activity rests on the supposedly bellicose nature of the Quran. More generally, this type of argument raises the fundamental problem of the role of sacred texts in instigating or justifying physical violence. The type of answers one might provide evidently rests on one's idea, belief, or opinion about the nature of violence and how it is related to religious beliefs. In essence, at the two ends of the spectrum, one finds those who believe that the violence found in scripture can be a genuine trigger of real violence and, at the other end, those who feel that scripture is but a pretext used by those who, regardless of what is written, are bent on violence. Michael Walzer famously showed how one passage of the Bible, Exodus 32, which grapples with holy war, was interpreted and used in very different ways by Saint Augustine, Saint Thomas Aquinas, and John Calvin.[19]

Generally, given the complexity and inherently contradictory nature of the attitude of religion to war, it is important to remember the context in which the texts appeared. With the exception of the Quran, the foundational religious texts all surface at around the same time. Though the evolution of religion was a long process, the third century BCE was a watershed that saw several empires gradually abandon sacrificial religious practices to adopt the religions of salvation and enlightenment that have endured to this day. Among these religions of salvation and enlightenment that emerged through the centuries, some of which have come to be known as "universal religions," and some as "religions of the book," we find Zoroastrianism, Judaism, Buddhism, Jainism, Hinduism, Manichaeism, Christianity, and later Islam.

These religions of salvation and enlightenment often overlapped with the earlier sacrificial religions, from which they also sometimes evolved. The new religions also developed into several branches, with varying degrees of longevity. Although the new religions sometimes retained certain sacrificial elements of the earlier religions, for example, in their cuisine or festive practices, they almost always abandoned one of the centerpieces of the traditional sacrificial religions: the sacrificial dimension of violence. In this respect, the break between traditional and modern religions, though the latter may have retained a symbolic element of earlier practices, was an important one indeed. In practice, when armies that belonged to different religious cultures clashed, one traditional-sacrificial, one not, the gap between them was nowhere so profound as in their differing attitudes to violence. A striking example of this cultural clash occurred between the Spaniards and the Mexicans during the conquest of Mexico in the sixteenth century. Though the Spaniards may have invoked the Virgin Mary before each battle, they were appalled by the sacrificial dimension of the Aztecs' fighting strategies and general attitude to war. The Aztecs, in turn, were shocked and repulsed by the Spaniards' strategy of annihilation.

The purging of sacrificial violence from war and, more generally, from society, was thus one of the characteristics that distinguished the earlier forms of religious life from the religions of salvation and enlightenment that gradually—and with varying speed—came to replace them in the West, East, Middle East, and the Indian subcontinent. Within the new religions, then, violence was understood first and foremost as the manifestation of power through the collective use of force, the principal question being whether this use of force—or sanctioned violence—was morally acceptable or not, and under what circumstances.

From the beginning, this moral attitude to sanctioned violence posed a challenge to the philosophers, historians, and theorists who expounded the first theories of politics and policy at the very same time that these religions were emerging. Thus, we find Kautilya, Sun Tzu, Liu Ja, Su Ma Tsien, and the Greek and Latin philosophers and historians all developing principles of governance that sought to resolve the tension between political expediency and moral demands. At the same time, theologians grappled with the moral justification or condemnation of war as understood within a strict theological framework. In both cases, though, the use of force was essentially understood as a means to resolve problems with other peoples, be they—those people— defined in terms of denomination, ethnicity, or nationality, and not as a tool for religious or political governance. Liu Ja, the third-century (BCE) Confucian counselor to the first Han emperor, Gaozu (Liu Bang), summed up this fundamental attitude: "If the Tang and Wu kings conquered the throne through violence, they kept it through gentleness: only the judicious usage of military and civilian means can ensure the sustainability of dynasties."[20] In the West, the durable underlying tension between theologians and political theorists on the issue of war broke open with Machiavelli at the turn of the sixteenth century, when the Florentine thinker forcefully disengaged political thought from moral and theological considerations, thereby opening the gates to the formal divorce of church and state in the seventeenth century. At around the same time, Spanish theologians sought to resolve the complex humanitarian questions that arose with the conquests of entire continents and the subjugation of millions of people. As a result of this introspective reflection on the moral consequences of imperialism, they revived the old Christian just war theory and used it as the foundational pillar of the *jus gentium*, or law of nations, now called international law, a process that came to fruition in the mid-seventeenth century with the Dutch theologian and diplomat Hugo Grotius, who had been witness to the most horrendous religious conflicts.

For jurists and political theorists, then, war can only be comprehended as an element of political action, one that can or must be controlled, because it can be best exploited if it is controlled, or because only by controlling it can one mitigate its effects on nations and peoples. Religion, on the other hand, has no such limits, and war forms an integral part of its discourse, at least until Jesus of Nazareth, whose uncompromising attitude to any kind of violence, as well as his refusal to be implicated in any manner in politics, broke the mold for good. Jesus's attitude not only determined his own destiny, it also created an insoluble dilemma for Christianity, which theologians have been struggling with to this day.

Most religious writings from the formative period of the great universal religions bear similar attitudes to war and peace. As with the epic texts mentioned earlier, the foundational religious texts of the first millennium BCE, all of which precede the first political writings, produced beginning in the fifth century BCE, deal extensively with the issue of war and peace. This fact has often been used by those who argue that religion is inherently violent, even though this argument tends to confuse the treatment of violence with the condoning of violence. While religions unanimously condemn the killing of other human beings—this interdiction forming one of their basic precepts— all make room for the morally acceptable fact of collective violence committed for some higher good. In this respect, the ethics of the individual is clearly distinguished from the ethics of a community, a people, or a state. Only in Islam is such a distinction not as clear-cut, hence the whole debate about the meaning of jihad as a personal or collective act. Even in Hinduism and Buddhism, where the ethics of noncruelty and nonviolence rank especially high, there is space for ethically justified war, as in the Bhagavad Gita, for example, in which the climactic segment of the text, the Battle of Kurukshetra, is accompanied by a penetrating discussion on the ethics of war.[21] Within the Sino-cultural realm, religious identity has been much less robust than in other parts of the world. For this reason, one expert suggests, "Their religious identity unclear, the Chinese have been less prone than their Western counterparts to religious warfare."[22]

WAR, RELIGION, AND THE SACRED

Attitudes to war create three camps: those who seek to end it once and for all; those who accept it as a fact of life and seek to work with it or around it; and, finally, those who exalt it. The first two camps view war as a rational phenomenon and focus principally on the intrinsic nature of the individual (whether fundamentally aggressive or malleable) or the nature of politics (whether fundamentally rooted in an endless struggle for power, or susceptible to being reformed). Followers of Immanuel Kant envisage a global transformation to general peace based on reform of the system. Machiavelli, Clausewitz, and the so-called realists stress the perennially unchanging nature of international power politics. Both camps view war as essentially political in nature, and thus as predominantly rational. Neither perceives how much war throughout history has often been much more than a rational endeavor, how much it has been intertwined with the sacred. This aspect of it, grossly underscored by political thinkers as well as historians, ultimately shows war and religion to have more in common than is generally assumed.

Although viscerally allergic to all things religious for the most part, writers like Friedrich Nietzsche and Ernst Jünger who have romanticized and exalted war have resurrected the sacred dimension that characterized it at various times in the past. Hitler himself, though not known to have had much sympathy for religion, used a variety of religious symbols, beginning with the infamous reversed swastika (a common Hindu, Buddhist, and Jain symbol) to instill a sacred character into his violent enterprise.[23]

In what circumstances does war take on the characteristics of the sacred? Roger Caillois pointed to the fascinating similarities between war and religious celebrations For Caillois, both are parentheses in which one transcends the realities of daily life to project oneself into another world, a world of transgressions where the fundamental rules of life are turned upside down, and where one will not suffer punishment, whether by the state or by God, for having transgressed these rules. War, Caillois says, "possesses to a significant degree the character of the sacred: she seems to forbid that we examine her objectively. She paralyses critical examination. She is formidable and overbearing. We damn her, we exalt her. We hardly study her."[24]

In war, as in religious ritual, individuals are extracted from their social setting and thrown into a communal environment. Everyone's place is blurred, and other rules apply, which often erase those one usually plays by. Extracted from their quiet—and often tedious—daily lives and thrown together with others like them, individuals can transgress their daily norms, in what is often an act of religious proportions. One lives for such daunting, exhilarating moments that push one to discover who one really is, and which one cherishes—or sometimes abhors—for the rest of one's life. These are times of "excess, violence, and outrage," Caillois observes. However, both religion and war can in certain circumstances lead to unpunished destruction, including, in war, destruction of what is most precious: life. They are both a time of waste; indeed, of absolute waste, of food, of resources, of people. Wars are like festivals and religious celebrations, which "open the doors to the world of the Gods, and man is transformed into a God and attains superhuman existence."[25]

In these moments, the individual is ejected from society and thus comes face to face with the only element that is above society: God. In war, individuals fight and risk their own lives—and often those of their families—for a higher purpose that makes one's self seem irrelevant, aside from one's contribution to victory. War is often absurd in its purpose, and tragic beyond what is acceptable; its justification is found above political interests. We see this even today in our secular societies when the so-called national interest proves insufficient to justify the use of force in certain instances, politicians having to juggle with religious concepts such as just war to get public opinion to support what it is they want to do. This state of mind is authentically religious in the sense that

> War, no less than the festival, seems like the time of the sacred, the period of divine epiphany. It introduces man to an intoxicating world in which the presence of death makes him shiver and confers a superior value upon his various actions. He believes that he will acquire a psychic vigor—just as through the descent to the inferno in ancient initiations—out of proportion to mundane experiences. He feels invincible and as if marked by the sign that protected Cain after the murder of Abel.[26]

War thus bestows on the combatant an aura that gives him or her a sense of superiority to those who did not fight and did not kill. In a sense, he (or she) is graced with a divine mandate to transgress the basic rules of life in society, for only God, in a sense, can allow, tolerate, and reward what the laws of all nations prohibit. For this reason, war is generally regarded with much uneasiness in secular societies—with a few exceptions, like Nazi Germany, though one might argue that that was not a secular regime. It is much more acceptable and accepted in societies where religion has more traction, even where religious teaching promotes a message of peace.

The sense of communion with God that comes through a violent act sanctioned by war is something we have become reaccustomed to in the new age of radical terrorism. Although we see this as an attribute that concerns a tiny minority of marginal religious fanatics who have been "brainwashed," this type of attitude—which appears foreign to us—has characterized many soldiers and combatants through the ages, across many cultures and regions. It is an attitude that is not necessarily linked to the teachings of a particular religion, which may or may not justify violence in certain instances, but rather one that sees war as the paroxysmal link between man and the sacred.

In this sense, war is effectively the ultimate, paroxysmal transgression of modern societies, whereas paroxysmal religious celebrations were the transgressions of primitive societies: "taking into account the nature and development of modern society, only one phenomenon manifests comparable importance, intensity, and explosiveness, of the same order of grandeur—war."[27] The fact that it is war, and not violence per se, that makes this link possible is fundamental, because only war can give the individual this sense of acting as part of a community of souls. When "self-radicalized" individuals or small groups of individuals perpetrate terrorist acts, they always see their action as part of a grander scheme, indeed, of a "war." This explains why terrorism is a phenomenon so different from serial or mass killings perpetrated out of a grudge or by reason of mental illness; even if both may act in similar fashion, terrorists always have more in common with traditional soldiers.

THE SCOPE AND FOCUS OF THE BOOK

Although the history of war and religion crystallized around the Mediterranean at a time when the great monotheistic universalistic religions emerged, its scope extends beyond this realm. Still, the greater Mediterranean region (extending to northern and central Europe) has for centuries been the central pivot of religious warfare, and it is with this that the bulk of this book will be concerned. Although our journey will also briefly take us beyond the greater Mediterranean, it is essentially in the Middle East and Europe that the story unfolds. This is where the conditions came together that transformed what might otherwise have been constrained religious violence into all-out wars, and where power struggles became inextricably linked to religious conflicts. In essence, this volume will focus almost exclusively on the Abrahamic religions, Judaism, Christianity, and Islam, while touching on the religions of Iran, Zoroastrianism and Manichaeism, which may have influenced them in one way or other or interacted with them at some point in history. Since history does not occur in a vacuum, the religious conflicts that involved one or several of these religions did extend to geographical areas beyond their traditional theater, and we will follow such extraneous manifestations wherever they occurred. Thus, I will only make passing references to religious conflicts involving other faiths, including Hinduism, Buddhism, and traditional African religions. In this respect, this book does not purport to be an authoritative volume on all wars of religion throughout history. Nor, within the already broad topic it proposes to address, is this book a mere catalog or survey of unrelated or loosely related events. Rather, this volume presents an uninterrupted historical narrative of events, peoples, and individuals that begins in antiquity, leads right up to the turn of the eighteenth century, and, in a diluted form, runs through to the twenty-first century.

Before delving into the topic, which to my knowledge has not yet lent itself to academic expertise, I should perhaps say a word about my intellectual background. My academic interests in religion probably date back to my freshman year at Georgetown University, a Jesuit institution that offered classes in theology in its core curriculum. Although I eventually veered toward history and political science, the interest remained vivid, and, while pursuing my graduate studies in these areas, I decided to enroll in a master's program on religion. At the time, the early 1990s, this choice baffled my friends, few of whom then saw any link between international politics and religion, something that would quickly change in the following decade. Despite the excellent grounding in theological matters I may have gained during this formal exposure to the study of religion, it would be a stretch to claim that I am an expert in this matter. I am, and have become during the past quarter century, a historian of war (which I prefer to the restrictive term "military historian"), with a subexpertise in the history of terror and terrorism, an area that touches upon the theme of religious violence.

The consequence, of course, is that my approach, my intellectual references, and perhaps my style and my vocabulary may contrast with those of a scholar of religion or a theologian. The basic engineering of this text is that of a historian of war, politics, and diplomacy, and my outlook on the history of war and religion is predicated on my understanding of conflicts, inclusive of their causes, their manifestations, and their consequences. Thus, I perceive religious war, not as a distortion of religion or religious values, but as a particular manifestation of warfare, albeit with its root causes in spiritual experiences, religious institutions, and interaction with politics.

Thus we arrive at the central idea that serves as the guiding thread to this historical narrative, which is that religion, between the fourth and the late seventeenth centuries, was an inescapable factor in the wars that took place along the fault lines where the great monotheistic universalistic religions repeatedly and durably clashed. As a corollary, I argue that religion, during that period and in that part of the world, not only caused and shaped a great number of conflicts but essentially determined how these conflicts were fought. As such, religion defined the art of war, or arts of war, for a millennium, and by doing so, it exerted great influence in molding the societies that took part in these conflicts or were affected by them. In essence, religion was, during this period, the major driver of the wars that took place in Europe and in the greater Middle East. Although religion had an impact on war before and after that time, and, although religious wars also occurred outside that geographic area, religion and war were powerfully intertwined during this historical period.

CHAPTER I

The Rise of the Monotheistic Religions

It is the world religions which provoke the greatest historical crises. They know from the outset that they are world religions, and intend to be world religions.

—Jacob Burckhardt, *Reflections on History*

War and religion clearly predate the emergence of the Abrahamic faiths,[1] but the history of wars in the name of religion only really started to take shape progressively during the first centuries of the first millennium, reaching a threshold in the seventh century with a clash of religions that lasted several hundred years. And while religious-political violence in the Middle East and the greater Mediterranean region involved four religions, Judaism, Zoroastrianism, Christianity, and Islam, the main enduring religious conflicts involved the latter two. Judaism, which lacked the universalistic message that characterized the other monotheistic religions and concerned a minority with little political power, was itself a marginal player in this game, even though Jewish minorities, particularly in the Christian West, became a recurrent target of religiously motivated political violence. Zoroastrianism, the state religion of Persia until the seventh century, was all but obliterated as a political force when the Sassanian monarchy was overrun by the Arab armies in 636–42 CE. At the center of it all, the Roman Empire, after quashing Jewish resistance in Judea in the first century, reinvented itself in the third century by adopting Christianity as its state religion. Later, in the sixth and seventh centuries, the long, exhausting struggle between the Christian Byzantines, heirs of the Romans, and the Zoroastrian Sassanians paved the way for the Muslim Arab armies of Muhammad, which crushed the former and obliterated the latter. Unlike the Sassanians, the Byzantines survived the Arab onslaught, however, and by doing so, provided western Europe with a protection that enabled it to rise from the ashes. Like the Byzantines before them, western Europeans reinvented themselves by creating a foundational myth based on the Christian faith and the legacy of the Roman Empire, a combination that gave rise to the notion of Christendom. By the end of the millennium, the stage was set for the clash of civilizations that would ensue in the first century of the second millennium.

THE JEWISH-ROMAN WARS

For three essential reasons, Judaism holds a special place in the history of religion and violence. The first is theological: as a centerpiece of the Christian canon, the Old Testament, based on the Tanakh, or Hebrew Bible, places the plight of the Jewish people at the core of Christian teachings. The second reason, related to the first, centers on the ambiguous relationship between Christians and Jews, who form an integral part of the Christian religion despite having been the first to reject it, a position that for two thousand years now has generated some positive sentiments from Christians, as well as very negative ones. The third reason pertains to the peculiar makeup of Judaism, which ties a religion to a people, which has confined Jews to a precarious existence in what has, for the most part, been a very hostile environment. By dispossessing the Jews of their land, the Romans not only deprived them of part of their identity, but they also took away their geographical and political territory, reducing them, until 1948, to a scattered minority with few or no political and legal rights, except those obtained after 1789 as a consequence of the French Revolution (1790 for French Sephardic Jews; 1791 for all French Jews). This position placed the Jews on the receiving end of political violence, often as scapegoats, with little power to weigh on events, either great or small, other than through indirect channels. Still, against all these odds, individual Jews were often perceived as instigating wars, most notably when these wars involved both Christians and Muslims.

The event that determined for centuries to come the fate of the Jewish people was the war that pitted Rome against the Jews in Judea (which, as a Roman province, was much larger than the eponymous region and was subsequently reconfigured as Syria Palaestina by Emperor Hadrian in the second century). The Jewish Wars, as they were termed by the Jewish Roman historian Flavius Josephus, were, from the Roman perspective, a political conflict and, from the perspective of the Jews, a struggle to defend their land and their faith. The war was motivated by the logic of imperial hegemony, but, for the Jews, inasmuch as their homeland was considered a part of their religious identity, the defense of their people and their territory took on the character of a defensive holy war. As noted by Adrian Goldsworthy: "The Jews had a sense of identity which long predated the arrival of Alexander the Great, let alone the Roman Empire. Their faith bonded them and reinforced their sense of nationhood, while providing examples of miraculous victories over stronger enemies and escape from slavery. Jewish ritual made it harder for them to be absorbed into the Roman system."[2]

The so-called Sicarii, who constituted themselves as the avant-garde of the liberation movement that logically developed with the escalating tensions, effectively became the first known movement to practice terrorism on a grand scale, introducing techniques that would become the staple of many a rebel group throughout history.

The history of the Jewish people is the story of a community seeking to survive successive waves of imperial domination while creating a unique identity that enabled it to uphold the principles it sought to establish for itself under extreme duress. In this sense, the Hebrew Scriptures constitute, among other things, an inquiry into political philosophy that raises the same questions later grappled with by many thinkers, including Plato and Aristotle, the ancient Indian political strategist Kautilya (d. 283 BCE), Augustine and Thomas Aquinas, Machiavelli, Locke, Hobbes, and Rousseau. In essence, the quest of the Jewish people is similar to that of the political philosophers of the Enlightenment: the establishment of a social contract that upholds and guarantees the power of a legitimate authority whose purpose it is to ensure that each member of the group is equal before God or society. The glue that sealed this contract was the central idea that this people had a unique destiny mandated by God, and that this destiny was tied to a territory, the Promised Land.

The history of the Jews in the Alexandrian and Roman centuries is scarred by oppression, revolt, and suppression. There are striking similarities with the liberation movements that sprang up in the twentieth century during the period of decolonization, most of which combined a strong national identity with an equally robust ideological—usually Marxist-Leninist/Maoist— agenda. The reaction of the forces of occupation and the political techniques used to suppress the revolts at the time were analogous to those employed by the modern colonial powers, though these did not on the whole match the brutality of the Romans, who engaged in mass crucifixion. Despite the similarities, the confrontation between the Jews and their oppressors yielded opposite results, most probably because neither the Hellenistic monarchs nor Rome had to concede to a reluctant public opinion that might have had both the inclination and the power to question the brutality of the methods employed and thus restrain their use and effect. Be that as it may, the Jewish revolutionaries of the first century established strategies and tactics that prefigured those adopted by liberation movements throughout history. These strategies focused on gaining popular support, and they favored an indirect approach that combined guerrilla tactics in rural areas and terrorism in urban zones. Those who were at the receiving end, starting with the Roman authorities, did what governments have always done when faced with an insurgency: characterize the opponent as politically illegitimate, to be treated as a criminal rather than a military adversary. Then as now, the confrontation between rebel and oppressor was essentially a psychological conflict, each side pointing to the illegitimacy of the enemy's standing, objectives and actions.

The Jews initiated four significant revolts between the second century BCE and the second century CE, the last three against the Romans. The first rebellion, the Hasmonean Revolt against the Greek Seleucids, occurred in 167–60 BCE. The aptly named Great Revolt (66 CE–73 CE) was the most dramatic. It was to be followed several decades later by the Rebellion of the Diaspora, or Kitos War (115–77 CE), and the Bar Kokhba Revolt (132–36 CE). During this period of extraordinary turmoil, through the influence of the Pharisees, the orthodoxy that was to stamp Judaism for centuries emerged and the radical movement that was to become Christianity surfaced. Caught between the two responses, various movements and groups coexisted, including radical ones such as the Zealots and Sicarii.[3] Both (early) Christianity and Judaic orthodoxy turned away from the violence advocated by radical groups such as the Zealots and the Sicarii (the term "Zealots" may in fact refer to two different movements—the Sicarii and an altogether separate group, perhaps based in the countryside, rather than being urban, that formed late in the war).[4] Whatever the link, the Zealots/Sicarii made their mark early as urban guerrillas who made extensive usage of terror tactics, mostly in Jerusalem. Much like modern and contemporary terrorist groups, their strategy and tactics drew much criticism from other resistance movements. The Zealots/ Sicarii and similar contemporary groups constitute the first known movements to have practiced bottom-up terror tactics on a grand scale.[5]

The history of Jewish resistance to Rome is well known, owing to Flavius Josephus's detailed account of the clash, although the scarcity of other sources poses problems. Josephus himself was a Jew who sided with the Romans after fruitlessly leading a resistance movement.[6] In his preface to the French edition of *The Jewish War*, the historian Pierre Vidal-Naquet wrote a poignant and penetrating analysis of Josephus's choices and his legacy: Vidal-Naquet's explicit title, "Of the Good Use of Treason," underscores Josephus's role as a player in the history he was writing.[7] In a question going to the very root of the subject of the present book, Vidal-Naquet asks, "Was the Jewish War a religious conflict?"

There is no denying that the Zealot/Sicarii movement was religious through and through. Its ideology, as formulated by Judas of Galilee (who came to be known with the Roman census around 6 CE) stated that Judea had but one ruler, God, and that He would only side with those willing to seize their own freedom. Purification of the faith was high among the Zealots' priorities, as with all such radical fundamentalist movements. God was portrayed as intrinsically bellicose, as the "man of war" described by Exodus (15: 3). During the six decades separating the census from the Revolt of 66, the Zealots restricted themselves to guerrilla, including urban guerrilla, warfare, which they organized from their base in Galilee.

The Jewish Revolt, or Great Revolt, started in the spring of 66 CE in the coastal town of Caesarea, a Greek city with a large Jewish population ruled by the Romans. As Josephus tells it, the rebellion was triggered by a small incident involving the Greek owner of a parcel adjacent to a synagogue who decided, to spite his neighbors, to construct a large unsightly building right next to the temple. The Roman governor, after accepting a large sum of money (eight talents) from the congregation in exchange for the promise to stop construction of the contentious building, left the city, taking the money with him, without ever fulfilling his contractual obligation. The very next day, to add insult to injury, a local man decided to sacrifice birds in front of the synagogue on the day of Shabbat. Angered by the repeated affronts and sacrilegious taunting, the Jewish community responded violently.[8] Thus began the Great Revolt. And as Vidal-Naquet says, "There, in Caesarea, also began the Diaspora."[9]

Decades of resentments dating back to Herod the Great fueled the outrage and its tremendous explosive charge. Herod the Great, whose name has survived through his portrayal in the New Testament as the perpetrator of the

Massacre of the Innocents (Matthew 2: 16–18), was a key player in Middle Eastern politics during a period of great upheaval for the Roman Republic. Herod was a practicing Jew. His father, Antipater, himself of powerful figure, had laid the ground work for an amicable relationship with Rome when he gave his support to Pompey when he invaded Judea. This earned Antipater Roman citizenship, which he transmitted to Herod. When Antipater was named procurator of Judea (47 BCE), he gave the governorship of Galilee to his son who, after being forced to flee the area, came back in full force with the backing Mark Antony and Julius Caesar, to become the uncontested king of Judea (37 BCE). The struggle for power from which Herod had emerged victorious had been a brutal affair for everyone, starting with the Judean populations caught in the midst of it.

Herod's main rival, Antigonus the Hasmonean, had garnered the support of the Parthians, Rome's major adversary, in the struggle for supremacy around the Mediterranean. That region, now called the Near East, was of premiere geopolitical importance in the context of the superpower rivalry that opposed an emerging Roman empire and a reemerging Persian empire, the Parthians having disposed of what was left of the Greek Seleucid Empire. This rivalry was the dominant political and military fact of Mediterranean international relations for centuries. The history of Jewish–Roman relations can only be understood in light of it, and Herod was instrumental in setting that relationship on a new course.

Herod would rule his kingdom with an iron fist for thirty-two years, thus providing a much needed source of stability in a time of turmoil, but all the while nourishing the deep popular resentment that would fuel the revolt against the Romans after his death. After divorcing his wife, he married a Hasmonean princess, Mariamne, thereby affirming his ties with the Jewish community. Much like Josephus, the historian who would tell his tale, Herod was a Jew who played into the enemy's hand. The Gospel of Matthew's account of his killing of children in Bethlehem because, as potential rivals to his throne, they threatened his legitimacy, suggests that his legitimacy as a Jewish king may have been questioned, though the episode has not been corroborated elsewhere.

From Herod on, the accumulation of resentments that eventually provoked the outrage over the Caesarea incident coalesced into a positive effort to regain freedom and dignity for the Jewish people, who formed a united front against the Romans until it was quashed by the brutal Roman counteroffensive under

Nero's general Vespasian. Initially, the battle-hardened Zealots/Sicarii managed to take control of the Temple Mount and the citadel of Masada, and they successfully ambushed a Roman army at Beth-Horon, killing its commander, Gallusin. When the Romans, under the command of Vespasian's son, Titus (Vespasian had been proclaimed emperor in 69 CE), laid siege to Jerusalem, after having ravaged Galilee, dissensions occurred between radical and moderate factions in the city, which are the central issue of Josephus's history. After the seven-month stand at Masada that ended in 73 CE, the Romans obliterated what remained of the Zealot/Sicarii movement, tracking down all those who might claim direct filiation to King David, the Zealot's model king, or to Hezekiah, the Pharisee leader, executed in 47 BCE, who had started the dissident movement. One important consequence of the defeat was the redirecting of the religious nucleus of Judaism away from the high priest and the (destroyed) Temple and toward the decentralized regime revolving around rabbis, synagogues, and the Torah that became rabbinic Judaism. This radical shift was not unlike that of the Protestant Reformation, which would likewise steer away from Rome and the pope in favor of local ministers, congregational churches, and Bible study.

As described by Josephus, the Sicarii were the first religious group of note to accept violence, even extreme violence, as a means to achieve their ends, in their case to repel Roman imperialism. Others would follow: the redoubtable Hashashins, or Assassins (also known as the Nizarites), an offshoot of the Ismailis, the Indian Thugs or Thuggees (whose political objectives, if they had any, are unclear), and, in the Christian world, the combatant religious orders of the Knights Templar, Teutonic Knights, Hospitallers, and Knights of the Order of Saint James of the Sword (Order of Santiago), which benefited from the religious and political legitimacy granted them by the pope.

Starting with the Sicarii, and with the exception of the Christian warrior-monks, combatant religious groups typically operated with a serious deficit of political legitimacy, which, altogether, few managed to overcome. This is evidenced by the fact that in the English language, "zealot," "assassin," and "thugs" are common nouns with very negative meanings that correspond to the traits we commonly associate with these types of movements. In the case of the Zealots/Sicarii, their historical significance and reputation owed largely to the description of them by Josephus, who had tried to resist the Roman occupation and blamed his failure on the intransigence of the radical groups, which, in his eyes, played into the hands of the colonial power.

Though there were several Jewish revolts before and after the Great Jewish War, this particular conflict was the one that, in effect, ended all wars between the Jews and Romans with the dramatic stand-off at the fortress of Masada, an event that steered the history of the Jewish people in a new direction that has reverberated to this day, especially given the situation Israel has found itself in since 1948.

Although the Jews had been oppressed before by the Egyptians, Persians, and Greeks, Rome was a different beast altogether. In the Punic wars, the Romans had not only defeated their archrivals, the Carthaginians, but also proceeded to completely annihilate them as a people and a civilization, burning Carthage itself to the ground at the conclusion of the Third Punic War. This conflict had lasted several decades and ended in a fashion that foreshadowed the Great Jewish War with a dramatic stand at Carthage's citadel of Bysra, where nine hundred die-hards resisted to the last (146 BCE).[10] If we are to believe the historian Polybius, an eyewitness, the Roman commander Scipio Aemilianus Africanus wept "at the sight of the city perishing amidst the flames . . . and stood long reflecting on the inevitable change which awaits cities, nations, and dynasties, one and all, as it does every one of us men. This, he thought, had befallen Ilium, once a powerful city, and the once mighty empires of the Assyrians, Medes, Persians, and that of Macedonia lately so splendid."[11]

Whereas the Persian Achaemenids had practiced a global policy of toleration, and Alexander the Great had basically "gone native" when he conquered the Achaemenid empire, the Romans sought to impose their yoke on the world in a manner hitherto unknown, at least on this scale and in this part of the world. The Romans regarded all those who were not on their side as enemies to be suppressed.[12] And so it was with the Jews, who not only occupied a territory that Rome wished to subjugate completely but also defied the Roman policy of total assimilation by continuing to cling to their religious beliefs and ethnic identity. It is indicative of this totalitarian outlook that when Rome was later unable to resist and contain Christianity, it embraced it almost wholeheartedly. In any case, the Romans knew that religion was their main target, and their first order of things was to go after their religious symbols, as described by Josephus:

> And now did many of the priests, even when they saw their enemies assailing them with swords in their hands, without any disturbance, go on with their divine worship, and were killed while offering their drink-offerings [. . .] But there was noth-

ing that affected the nation so much, in the calamities they were then under, as that their holy place, which had as yet seen by none, should be laid open to strangers; for Pompey, and those that were about him, went into the temple itself where it was not lawful for any to enter but the high priest.[13]

As the war proceeded to its logical conclusion, the Roman army did what it always did and burned the Temple to the ground.

The clash between the Roman authorities and the Jewish people was inevitable, inasmuch as the former had the power to prevail. while the latter had the will and spirit to resist against all odds. Calling the Sicarii's uncompromising resistance at Masada, where nine hundred and sixty people committed suicide rather than surrender, "madness" and a "disease," Josephus writes: "So these people died with this intention, that they would not leave so much as one soul among them all alive to be subject to the Romans."[14]

But both the Jews and Judaism survived at the cost of losing the very fabric that defined what it is to be a Jew; from then on, the Jewish people, whose religious identity was attached to a particular piece of land, were largely confined to a semi-nomadic existence. The fledgling Christian community was then in its initial pacifist phase, but its successors would (much) later take up arms to recover the sacred territory from another religious group that also claimed the Hebrew Bible as its point of departure.

THE VARIETIES OF RELIGIOUS-POLITICAL EXPERIENCES

Before focusing on the religions that would in essence actively participate in the imperialistic designs of Persia, Byzantium, and the Islamic caliphates, let us briefly examine those experiences that took place during the first centuries of the first millennium that testify to a general movement toward the emergence of religion as an integral part of the political process. This movement, which logically manifested itself in the outer fringes of the Fertile Crescent, also gained momentum in the Indian subcontinent.

After the events of the first and second century (the revolts of 66–74 and 132–36), Judaism had entered into a period of "defensive consolidation" and was adverse to any kind of aggressive proselytizing or political maneuvering.[15] In consequence, the Hellenizing trend toward greater openness was brushed aside by a return to the old Hebrew and Aramaic tradition, which became the basis for the legal writings subsequently produced by rabbis starting in the third century. Still, the geographical spread of Jews in the Roman and Persian empires gave Judaism a physical universalism that might have translated into a universalistic outlook in a more favorable intellectual environment. In the end, though, it resulted in a defensive consolidation. This defensive attitude gave new impulse to the formation of a Jewish identity that looked to the Bible as a legal and historical source and developed a system of law; a national language, Hebrew; and a system of social norms and regulations that touched upon domains such as marriage, education, and worship.[16]

This attitude may be interpreted in many different ways. From a political standpoint, it was based on a realistic assessment of the balance of powers that warranted a strategic withdrawal. In other words, it hinged on the idea that if you cannot beat them and do not desire to join them, you had better set up a social structure so strong that it will allow you to survive in what is altogether a very inimical environment. From then on, Judaism definitively turned its back to any sort of proselytizing activity, and Jews essentially tried to remain on the sidelines of the religious wars that were to erupt in the Middle East and Europe, which in many ways shaped the destiny of the various Jewish communities that found themselves at the heart of the violence, and sometimes at its receiving end. The fate of Judaism illustrates an important point, that "monotheism does not of itself suffice to generate a proselytizing, actively rather than merely potentially universalist religion,"[17] thus underscoring the difference between an ethnic monotheistic religion and a universalist proselytizing monotheism.

Although the history of war and religion has essentially revolved around the clash between Islam and Christianity, the two principal religions that combined a universal message with political power, these were not the first religions to link these two elements. That privilege belongs to Manichaeism and, to a certain extent, Zoroastrianism, two religions born in Persia that both sought to gain political traction among governing elites. Zoroastrianism, the older of the two, began as a particularistic rather than a universalistic religion. But its challenge by Manichaeism, a religion that was universalistic from the start, seems to have given Zoroastrianism a universalistic impulse at a time when Zoroastrian Persia was pitted against Christian Byzantium. When the two clashed with emerging Islam in the seventh century, the Zoroastrians were permanently wiped off the map as a political force, thus leaving only two of the three universalistic protagonists standing. Though Manichaeism and Zoroastrianism might each have played a durable role in the clash of religions that took place around the Mediterranean from the seventh century on, they were both eliminated, politically and militarily, by stronger foes, who made sure that they had little chance to recover from their minority status. In point of fact, neither ever reemerged, and when Persia reaffirmed its national identity in the sixteenth and seventeenth centuries, it adopted the Shiite form of Islam as its state religion.

The Persian and Abrahamic faiths veered in different directions in terms of their social attitudes. The Persian religions seem to have been less prone to equality, which one might attribute, as does Marshall Hodgson, to the agricultural/rural nature of the Persian Empire, whereas Judaism and Christianity thrived initially in commercial/urban environments more conducive to a meritocracy-based outlook generated by that great equalizer, money.[18] It is true that at the time of Darius the Great (522–486 BCE), the acme of the Achaemenid Empire, Zoroastrianism was the religion of the elites and, as such, a legitimizing element of the Achaemenids' hold on power. No effort was made to impose the state religion on the whole of the empire, and other religious beliefs were tolerated in an immense territory comprising many different peoples and communities

What is important here is that, while the Semitic religions spread within a Roman Empire that retained its integrity, Zoroastrianism took root for the second time in the Parthian Empire, which was, at the time, fragmented, and where confessional communities took precedence over territorial communities. In reaction to the loose Parthian political order, the Sassanians who replaced them favored centralized absolutist government, with a strong aristocracy, attached to the official religion of the state. The attempt by the Manicheans to push Zoroastrianism aside would prove futile, illustrating the fact that the regime was irrevocably tied to the religion of the aristocracy. After the Manicheans, a Zoroastrian priest and prophet named Mazdak tried to launch a political revolution with egalitarian overtones. Even though he managed to persuade the monarch to adopt his cause, the backlash of the aristocracy and the clergy came in full force, and Mazdak's ideal of an ascetic spiritual fraternity was crushed, and he and his followers were massacred.

The victory of the Zoroastrian aristocracy led to the zenith of Sassanian civilization, the reign of Khosrow I Anushiruwân ("Immortal Soul") (r. 531–579). With renewed clout, wealth, power, and influence, the Sassanian Empire under Anushiruwân proved a worthy adversary of the Byzantine

Empire. These two huge territorial entities, each boasting of its high culture, motivated by a universalistic message, preached by a powerful, active clergy, and marshaling elaborate bureaucracies and formidable armies, were destined to come into collision, and they did. This heightened situation of overt hostility, which also played on internal political struggles, palace intrigues, and treachery, came about at the time when Muhammad was born.

ZOROATRIANISM AND MANICHAEISM

The state religion of the Sassanians, Zoroastrianism, sometimes called Zoroastrian Mazdeism or, simply, Mazdeism, takes its name from the founder of the religion, Zoroaster or Zarathustra, who lived in the seventh and sixth centuries BCE. Numerically speaking, Zoroastrianism is no longer one of the great religions, but it is one of the oldest religions to have survived to this day (Zoroastrians, who number perhaps 200,000, live chiefly in Persia and India). Zoroastrianism is characterized by its monotheistic character, its universalism, and its dualism. This dualism is found on various levels: corporeal/spiritual world; order/chaos; good/evil. Zoroastrians are thus engaged in a universal battle, both on spiritual and corporeal planes, against evil forces that inflict chaos and confusion upon the world. Evil must thus be fought with the greatest vigor and eradicated, thus allowing for absolute order to supplant chaos. Zoroastrians refer to themselves as worshipers of Ahura Mazda, the universal God and creator of the world. Facing God is the evil spirit Angra Mainyu. The formidable nature of the task, which translates as a duty for each devotee, warrants the use of force and the resulting violence. Those who systematically engage in the fight against chaos, confusion, and evil will be rewarded in the afterlife, and those who fail to do this will be punished. Apocalyptic eschatological concepts of the end of the world and ultimate destiny of humankind pervade Zoroastrian beliefs and theology. Portents that the end of the world is approaching include a recrudescence of violence, conflicts, chaos, suffering, and war. The dualism of life and the necessity that it brings upon people to fight the enemies of what is right and what is good became so ingrained in Persian society that it survived the fall of the Sassanid empire and became a central theme of the Persian national epic, thus forming an integral part of its identity, a fact that current observers of Persian politics might do well to explore and understand.

Though Zoroastrianism did not completely do away with the polytheism of earlier Persian religions, it did place its god, Ahura Mazda, above and beyond all others as the supreme divinity. As such, Zoroastrianism can be regarded as the first significant attempt to move away from polytheism and toward monotheism. The dualistic nature of Zoroastrianism, with the opposition of good and evil, is another characteristic shared with Judaism and Christianity. The extent of Zoroastrianism's influence on these religions has divided scholars, though no one denies this influence altogether. The religion itself evolved through the centuries and its formulation under the Sassanians differed somewhat from the original teachings of Zoroaster, though the extent of this departure from the teaching of the Prophet is difficult to measure. In any case, what concerns us here is how this religion played a role in the policies of the various Persian imperial incarnations, particularly the Sassanian, and how these played out *vis-à-vis* the other regional powers.

Whereas Zoroastrianism was the official religion of the Achaemenids (550–330 BCE), it truly became an integral part of the state with the rise of the Sassanians in 224 AD. The Sassanians—named after Sasan, an ancestor of Ardachir, the founder of the dynasty—were a priestly family that came to govern an empire. Whether by design or because of internal political pressure from his entourage, Ardachir did not claim to control both political and religious authority, and the latter was handed to a priest, Tosar, who proceeded to establish the canon by choosing the texts he saw fit, and leaving aside those that might potentially come to interfere with the governing of the state.[19] Generally, the universalistic pretensions of the Sassanian state went beyond those of the Zoroastrian clergy, which retained a particularistic outlook, thus creating a rift between the two attitudes, and a constant tension one did not find, at least to such a degree, in Constantinian Rome/Byzantium or the Islamic caliphates.

Between the fall of the Achaemenids and the advent of the Sassanians, Persia had been briefly under the control of the Macedonian Greek Seleucids, who inherited the territory after the division of Alexander the Great's empire, and then fell into the loose hands of the Arsacid Parthians. When the Arsacids were brushed aside by Ardachir, a young Arsacid priest named Mani attempted to counter the new rulers of the land by inventing a new religion, which came to be called Manichaeism, intended to challenge their newfound authority and legitimacy.

Manichaeism, unlike Zoroastrianism, was unequivocally universalistic and monotheistic. Mani saw himself as a prophet building upon the teachings of other prophets of various traditions, including Abraham, Buddha, and Jesus. Much like Zoroastrianism, but even more so, Manichaeism stressed the dual nature of humankind. Had it supplanted Mazdeism and become the state religion of Persia, as seemed likely at one point, history might have veered in an entirely different direction. As an adjective "Manichaean" has, however, come to signify a dualistic, good-and-evil view of things, a negative connotation comparable to the one irreversibly attached to the Philistines.

Born less than a decade before the fall of the Arsacids, Mani was educated primarily in the Christian, not the Zoroastrian, tradition, which is the chief reason that Manicheism has at times been considered a Christian heresy (though its departure from Christianity is profound enough that it should be regarded as a religion in its own right, as it is today by most scholars). Mani having come into contact with Hindu and Graeco-Buddhist communities while traveling to Afghanistan, in addition to the Christian tradition, Manichaeism also incorporated elements of Hinduism and perhaps also of the Graeco-Buddhist syncretism that was emerging at the time in Bactria. For reasons that remain unclear, Mani seems to have rejected Judaism. What is clear is that he sought to oppose his religion to Zoroastrianism, an attitude that was certainly guided by political motives more than theological ones. His attempt to approach the king indicates that, at that point, Zoroastrianism may not have been as solidly ingrained in the fiber of the state as it would be a little later. The repositioning of Zoroastrianism was most probably thanks, in part, to the menace Mani began to represent for the Zoroastrian clergy, provoking a violent backlash.

The early days were difficult and Mani initially only managed to persuade three followers to join him on his spiritual and peripatetic journey, one of these being his father. As Mani began his modest proselytizing travels in the provinces, the regime did not initially react unfavorably. In 242, upon his return from Afghanistan, Mani asked to meet with the King of Kings, Shapur I, who seemed to show a genuine interest in Mani's teachings. An audience was arranged, which resulted in Mani being granted permission to preach his doctrine. The honeymoon, however, was short lived. With Shapur's untimely death, and the short reign of his immediate successor, the course of events proved unfavorable to Mani. The rise of an increasingly intolerant regime that gave the Zoroastrian clergy greater power. Bent on exercising full control over religious matters, the Zoroastrian priests easily persuaded the political authorities to put an end to the expansion of Manichaeism. At this juncture, Mani's mission was drawing greater and greater support and the threat posed to the authorities by the emergence of the new religion, combined with Mani's ties to the Arsacids, was too great. The self-proclaimed *Apostle of Light* was unceremoniously thrown into prison, where he died shortly after being incarcerated.

By this time, the genie was already out of the bottle, however, and Mani's death had the reverse effect to the one sought by his executioners. Through a constellation of resilient minority communities that refused to yield to the threats from authority, Manichaeism took hold across the empire. As a consequence, the political regime and religious authorities grew increasingly menacing, and all religious minorities were in the political line of fire, including Christians and Jews. Manichaeism had begun on the frontiers of the empire, to which it was subsequently relegated. Multicultural and universalistic, it posed a threat to the particularistic, elitist Zoroastrian authorities, who, from that point on, sought to assert the Persian identity of their religion. Manichaeism would later take hold in Central Asia among the Uighur Turks, where it became the state religion before Genghis Khan and then Tamerlane turned the whole region upside down. "Manichaeism," says Garth Fowden, "was all too obviously and threateningly a religion of the cities and merchants for the taste of the traditional Iranian elites. In the world of Iran and Rome into which it was born, Manichaeism fell politically between two stools."[20]

The harassment of Christian communities in Persia was to weigh heavily on the politics of the region for centuries to come. With the split, informal at first and then definitive, between the Western and Eastern Roman Empires, the region would eventually oppose two rival superpowers defined by their religious ideologies. This clash between a Christian Byzantine Empire and a Zoroastrian Persian Empire was in many ways similar to the superpower rivalry that generated the Cold War in the twentieth century, though the wars between the Byzantines and Persians were far from cold. In those days, one did not fight by proxy alone (though proxies did exist), and the lesser powers had to pick sides. The ideological clash between the two empires was all too real, and it proved a rehearsal of sorts for the massive conflict that was to pit the West and the Muslim world for centuries to come after the fall of the Sassanians and the marginalization of Zoroastrianism that ensued. The intermingling of religion and politics in Persia, dating back to the sixth century

BCE, was to have a lasting impact on the country itself and on its relations with its neighbors: the reclaiming of Persia in the sixteenth century by the Safavids was marked by the will of the new rulers to break with the Sunni invaders (chiefly Arabs and Turks) who had imposed their yoke on the Persians for almost nine hundred years, starting with the Umayyad caliphate in the seventh century.[21]

CHAPTER 2

Christianity Becomes a State Religion

Religion has so much power over governments that, without it, all other
foundations of the state flounder

—Giovanni Botero, *The Reason of State* (1589), 2.16

The evolution of Christianity during the initial centuries of the first millennium was extraordinary, as was its metamorphosis from a feeble minority
religion of peace to a sword-wielding global powerbroker. As a history-
changing phenomenon of global proportions, only Islam can rival it, and Islam
did so in a much shorter span of time; a few years as opposed to a few centuries. Be that as it may, by the time Islam came to the fore, Christianity was
well grounded politically, both in the Eastern Roman empire and in the
polities that emerged from the rubble of the defunct Western Empire.
Although Emperor Heraclius's Christian troops were defeated by the Muslim
army of Khālid ibn al-Walīd at the battle of Yarmouk in Syria (CE 636), the
beleaguered Byzantine Empire was able, not only to survive the Arab onslaught,
but to recover, and it subsisted for another eight centuries.

How different would have been the outcome had the Eastern Roman Empire
not adopted Christianity as its state religion in the fourth century? All the elements in our possession point to a very different scenario. But the fact is we'll
never know what might have been had Constantine turned his back on the church,
or had Julian the Apostate, his successor but one, successfully restored paganism.

THE TRANSFORMATION OF CHRISTIANITY:
TURNING PLOWSHARES INTO SWORDS

In the medieval evolution of Christianity, the emperor Constantine I (d. 337
CE) and the Frankish king Clovis I (d. 511 CE) are highly significant figures,

for by publicly converting to Christianity, both contributed to transforming it from a religion of the oppressed into a tool of the powerful. The fact that one was an Easterner and the other a Westerner, in an age when East and West were drifting apart, would shape the whole history, not only of Christianity, but of Europe, the greater Mediterranean region, and the world beyond these. In Constantine, the medievalist Philippe Contamine perceives a transformation of the soldier's function that shaped the structure of Christendom:

> Beginning with Constantine, the Christianization of the warrior's function, in which it is possible to see an almost inevitable corollary to the christianization of governing powers and the alliance of the two swords, spiritual and temporal, resulted in a way in the sacralization of war, a reinforcement of the prestige of soldiers and the profession of arms. A battle between men was felt to be a fully praiseworthy action and *valliance* was a virtue that was a something a little more than human.[1]

In the Eurasian world of the fourth to sixth centuries, James Laine writes, we see "literate, cosmopolitan institutions—Christian, Zoroastrian, Buddhist, and Manichean—all seeking some advantageous relationship to imperial power. Minority religions like Judaism or Nestorian Christianity sought no more than a place to survive in a world where the majority community might, at best, tolerate them while reserving the right to really call the shots. [. . .] Perhaps of all of these, Christianity came closest to fusing religion and politics into a single culture, a project entitled Constantinianism, after the emperor who established Christianity as the religion of the Roman Empire."[2]

Our devotion to secular values and secular society has somewhat contributed to our understanding of religion and politics as being either fully integrated or totally separated. As is often the case in matters such as these, the reality is rarely so clear-cut and, in essence, the religions that emerged in antiquity, be they polytheistic or monotheistic, were in some way or another defined by the politics of their day. Christianity is, in this sense, no exception. Jesus himself was born in a time of great turmoil so that, in his mission, religion, and politics were inextricably tied together.[3] Jesus's response when asked if one should continue to pay Roman taxes was: "Give back to Caesar what belongs to Caesar and to God what belongs to God." Rather than contest Roman imperial rule through civil disobedience, insubordination, or insurrection, all prone to generate some kind of violence or a violent backlash, Jesus sought to create a parallel world, the Kingdom of God, accessible to all. The establishment of the Kingdom of God was immediate and it would ultimately, in the eyes of Jesus and his followers, supersede imperial rule, since God's power would change the human condition from the bottom to the top.

This is essentially what came to be three centuries or so after Jesus's mission when the Roman emperor Constantine converted and established Christianity as the official religion of the empire. During this span of three hundred years, the Christian community had gradually spread out through the whole of the Roman world and beyond and never relinquished Jesus's commitment to nonviolence. It seems, however, even before the Constantine revolution, that the involvement of Christian individuals in military service, and thus war, increased somewhat over time. Facts supporting Christian involvement in warlike activity are scant, but authors such as Tertullian point to it, and military participation may have been more common in the Eastern empire.[4] Tertullian also noted how many converts would in effect renounce their military career or involvement, which means that for many, indeed, probably for the majority, sanctioned violence was still incompatible with Christian principles. Essentially, then, if not absolutely, Christians adhered for the most part to a nonviolent stance until Constantine proclaimed Christianity to be the Roman Empire's official religion.

THE EVOLUTION OF CHRISTIAN ATTITUDES TO WAR AND PEACE

It is no coincidence that the chronological development of Christian attitudes to war and peace closely follows the interaction between Christianity and politics. As long as Christianity remained outside of politics, Christians held fast to Jesus's pacifist message, but once adopted by Constantine, Christianity began to grapple with the harsh realities of governance and, with it, war. Finally, after the church gained sufficient leverage to play a leading role in European politics in the eleventh century, the crusade—war launched and fought in God's name—supplanted the just war.[5] In this sense, we come full circle, the crusade being a revival of the holy war of the Old Testament. The inherent contradictions we encounter on the topic of war and peace are directly related to the different strands that make up Christian thought. The Old and New Testaments offer two very different narratives, while writings like those of Saint Augustine draw on other sources, chiefly Greek and Roman. One can find in Christian texts, starting with the Bible, all the arguments to exalt, justify or condemn war. To a certain degree, this is true of other religions as well, but none more so perhaps than Christianity. Given the difficulty of interpreting even the most pedestrian passages of the Bible (symbolic? metaphoric? literal?), let alone the more obscure passages, an objective analysis of the Christian teachings on war and peace is not easily arrived at. Critics bent on proving that Christianity is inherently violent, and that the seeds of this violence are sown in scripture, have plenty of ammunition, so to speak, to work with, but so do those seeking to prove the contrary. The evolution of Christianity as a religion is in any case, however, directly linked to Christians' attitudes to war and peace.

The first two attitudes we find in Christianity, pacifism and the justification of war, developed at approximately the same time and in the same geopolitical realm, and for a time, they ran parallel to each other. Pacifism was, until Constantine, Christians' main attitude to war, and they refused to perform military service, indeed, to carry arms. However, Roman philosophers and jurists had developed, for the first time in the West, a doctrine justifying the use of force. Cicero, principally in *De Officiis* (*On Duties*), expounded the basic tenets of what would ultimately form the basis of the Christian just war doctrine.

Christian attitudes to war were no doubt influenced by Christian scripture. These attitudes, however, went far beyond a mere exercise of exegesis for, generally, the authorities who defined and legitimized them went to great lengths to accommodate, sometimes circumvent, the pacifism of the New Testament. In this regard, this process was very different from what we find in Islam, where the development of Muslim attitudes to war—which in some ways mirrored the development of Christian attitudes—was essentially based on interpretations and reinterpretations of Quranic prophecies. This difference was made all the more possible in that the Quran, unlike the New Testament, does not shy away from the topic of war.

Anyone familiar with the Hebrew Bible will be hard-pressed to disagree with the fact that war is a recurrent topic of the Old Testament. War is, by a long shot, much more present in the Old Testament than in either the New Testament or the Quran. Given the tenuous and complex relationship between scripture and action, a full treatment of this altogether fascinating topic would, however, take us far beyond the scope of this volume, so let us limit ourselves to a couple of relevant passages from the Old Testament (and from the Dead Sea Scrolls). Deuteronomy 20 is an exhortation by Moses to his people that sets down the rules of engagement in battle. Note the pragmatic, even strategic, dimension of this text, which clearly identifies the limits of the violence as it relates to the ultimate goals of the war:

> When you go out to battle against your enemies, and see horses and chariots and people more numerous than you, do not be afraid of them; for the Lord your God is with you, who brought you up from the land of Egypt. So it shall be, when you are on the verge of battle, that the priest shall approach and speak to the people. And he shall say to them, "Hear, O Israel: Today you are on the verge of battle with your enemies. Do not let your heart faint, do not tremble or be terrified because of them; for the Lord your God is He who goes with you, to fight for you against your enemies, to save you." [. . .] And so it shall be, when the officers have finished speaking to the people, that they shall make captains of the armies to lead the people. When you go near a city to fight against it, then proclaim an offer of peace to it. And it shall be that if they accept your offer of peace, and open to you, then all the people who are found in it shall be placed under tribute to you, and serve you. Now if the city will not make peace with you, but war against you, then you shall besiege it. And when the Lord your God delivers it into your hands, you shall strike every male in it with the edge of the sword. But the women, the little ones, the livestock, and all that is in the city, all its spoils, you shall plunder for yourself; and you shall eat the enemies' plunder which the Lord your God gives you. Thus you shall do to all the cities which are very far from you, which are not the cities of these nations. But of the cities of these peoples which the Lord your God gives you as an inheritance, you shall let nothing that breathes remain alive, but you shall destroy them: the Hittite and the Amorite and the Cannanite and the Perizzite and the Hivite and the Jebusite, just as the Lord your God has commanded you, lest they teach you to do according to all their abominations which they have done for their gods, and you sin against the Lord your God. When you besiege a city for a long time, while making war against it to take it, you shall not destroy its trees by wielding an ax against them; if you can eat of them, do not cut them down to use in the siege, for the tree of the field is man's food. Only the trees which you know are not trees for food you may destroy and cut down, to build siegeworks against the city that makes war with you, until it is subdued.[6]

A similar exhortation is also found in Numbers 31, accompanied by a ruthless command to annihilate the enemy, save for a few innocent souls. This passage illustrates the moral dilemma of war, of killing another human as part of a legitimate collective act sanctified by God. It commands the killing of civilians, asks that untainted virgins be spared and that those who have killed purify themselves, as well as their personal possessions. This is an interesting and important element, for the issue of purity is central to all universalistic ideologies, be they religious or secular, including, of course, modern totalitarian ideologies. Indeed, purity may be the one element that all such ideologies, regardless of the historical and spatial context in which they emerged, have in common:

> So Moses spoke to the people, saying: "Arm some of yourselves for war and let them go against the Midianites to take vengeance for the Lord on Midian. A thousand from each tribe of all the tribes of Israel you shall send to war." [. . .]
>
> And they warred against the Midianites, just as the Lord commanded Moses, and they killed all the males. They killed the kings of Midian with the rest of those who were killed.[. . .]
>
> And the children of Israel took the women of Midian captive, with their little ones, and took as spoil all their cattle, all their flocks, and all their goods. They also burned with fire all the cities where they dwelt, and all their forts. And they too all the spoil and all the booty—of man and beast. [. . .]
>
> And Moses said to them: [. . .] "Now therefore, kill every male among the little ones, and kill every woman who has known man intimately. But keep alive for yourselves all the young girls who have not known a man intimately. And as for you, remain outside the camp seven days; whoever has killed any person, and whoever has touched any slain, purify yourselves and your captives on the third day and on the seventh day. Purify every garment, everything woven of goat's hair, and everything made of wood."[7]

Not all allusions to war are this graphic and the references to violence often take on a poetic form that extols the emotions that inevitably accompany collective engagements against an enemy, as in the Song of Deborah (Judges 5) or Psalm 68:

> Let God arise
> Let His enemies be scattered
> Let those also who hate Him flee before Him
> As smoke is driven away,
> So drive them away;
> As wax melts before the fire,
> So let the wicked perish at the presence of God.
> But let the righteous be glad;
> Let them rejoice before God;
> Yes, let them rejoice exceedingly.[8]

While the song of Deborah may be characterized as a primitive call for holy war,[9] the rules of war as expressed in Deuteronomy go a step further, with war envisaged as undertaken not just with God's assistance but on His behalf.

The topic of war in the Hebrew Bible essentially addresses the question of how to make sense of violence and killing and how this reality, indeed at times necessity, relates to an ethic that otherwise forbids killing other human beings. The problem is at the root of war, and all cultures and religions have grappled with it and continue to do so. Another underlying theme is the relationship among God, humans, and war. In other words, is God assisting the Israelites in the fighting or is he assuming the entire burden of Israel's protection? For a majority of scholars, the answer is both, with a historical evolution from the one to the other.[10] Another interpretation invokes the evolution from a "Joshua paradigm" to an "Abrahamic paradigm," the former recalling a heroic past when God provided Israel with a military victory, the latter expressing the exilic and post-exilic longing for a return to the land.[11]

In her penetrating analysis, Susan Niditch finds that the war tradition in the Hebrew Bible takes on several forms or trajectories. These include several attitudes based on the "ban," or *hērem*, whereby all of the vanquished are "devoted to destruction."[12] Prominent among these is the *ideology of expediency*, a *realpolitik* of sorts that condones the use of force, with God's blessing, as it relates to objectives. An example of this attitude can be found in David's war against the Philistines in 2 Samuel 5, but Judges 9: 56–57 warns about the pitfalls of expediency when those who practice it do so illegitimately: "Thus God repaid the wickedness of Abimelech, which he had done to his father by killing his seventy brothers. And all the evil of the men of Shechem God returned on their own heads, and on them came the curse of Jotham the son of Jerubaal."[13] The book of Esther is perhaps the more realistically brutal when it comes to inflicting pain on one's enemy. Esther 9 is unequivocally expedient in a manner reminiscent of the Melian Dialogue in Thucydides' *History of the Peloponnesian War*:

> Now in the twelfth month, that is, the month of Adar, on the thirteenth day, the time came for the king's command and his decree to be executed. On the day that the enemies of the Jews had hoped to overpower them, the opposite occurred, in that the Jews themselves overpowered those who hated them. The Jews gathered in their cities throughout all the provinces of King Ahasuerus to lay hands on those who sought their harm. And no one could withstand them, because fear of them fell upon all people. [. . .] Thus the Jews defeated all their enemies with the stroke of the sword, with slaughter and destruction, and did what they pleased with those who hated them.
> And in Sushan the citadel the Jews killed and destroyed five hundred men.[14]

The diverse examples of war in the Hebrew Bible testify to a greater understanding of the phenomenon than is found in either the Quran, with its vague and often contradictory passages on war and jihad, or the New Testament, with its unequivocal rejection of violence. The attitudes and ideologies found in the Hebrew Bible not only involve "multiplicity, overlap, and self-contradiction"[15] but provide insight into the ethics and dialectics of war and peace.

Another interesting text directly related to the relationship between the clergy and war is the "war rule" found in the Dead Sea Scrolls, discovered in 1947 at Qumran near the Dead Sea, which probably date back to the beginning of Roman rule in Judea/Palestine. This text belongs to the "expediency" repertoire; clearly delineating the role of priests in guiding soldiers to battle, all the while refraining from participation in the direct hand-to-hand combat, lest contact with the blood of the enemy jeopardize the sanctity of their priestly condition:

> Then the Priests shall sound the trumpets of Summons and three divisions of foot-soldiers shall advance from the gates and shall station themselves between the formations; the horsemen shall be on their flanks, to right and to left. The Priests shall sound a sustained blast of the trumpets for battle array, and the columns shall move to their [battle] array, each man to his place. And when they have taken up their stand in three arrays, the Priests shall sound a second signal, soft and sustained, for them to advance until they are close to the enemy formation. They shall seize their weapons, and the Priests shall then blow a shrill staccato blast on the six trumpets of massacre to direct the battle, and the Levites and all the blowers of rams' horns shall sound a mighty alarm to terrify the heart of the enemy, and therewith the javelins shall fly out to bring down the slain.

The text goes on, revealing the contours of this strategy of annihilation, not unlike that used by the Romans against their enemies, starting with the Carthaginians. This strategy (a staple, incidentally, of Napoleonic warfare), encourages the relentless pursuit of the enemy after his defeat and his absolute annihilation. In this case, the destruction seems to be directly linked to the godly nature of the conflict. The priests, even if they are physically behind the lines, are nevertheless major participants, who conduct the battle from beginning to end and even give the order to pursue and destroy the fleeing troops:

> All the people shall cease their clamour but the Priests shall continue to blow the trumpets of massacre to direct the battle until the enemy is smitten and put to flight; and the Priests shall blow to direct the battle.[. . .]
>
> All these [the soldiers] shall pursue the enemy to destroy him in an everlasting destruction in the battle of God. The Priests shall sound for them the trumpets of Pursuit, and they shall deploy against all the enemy in a pursuit to destruction; and the horsemen shall thrust them back on the flanks of the battle until they are utterly destroyed.

And as the slain men fall, the Priests shall trumpet from afar; they shall not approach the slain lest they be defiled with unclean blood. For they are holy, and they shall not profane the anointing of their priesthood with the blood of nations of vanity.[16]

This text was probably written by a rebellious group that retired to Qumran and opposed Roman rule. It is possible that Jesus Christ may have been associated in some form or another with this community or others like it. In any case, any such association with radical groups intent on violent action, if it ever happened, was clearly erased by those who promoted the idea of a pacifistic Christ in the New Testament.[17] Although condemning of any form of violent activity, the New Testament nonetheless contains a couple of ambiguous passages that seem to contradict the general message of Jesus Christ. In Matthew we read: "Do not think that I came to bring peace on earth. I did not come to bring peace but a sword."[18] Likewise in Luke: "And he who has no sword, let him sell his garment and buy one."[19] But altogether, the message is resolutely one of peace, and love. The line of thought that emerges from the War Scroll, and which is echoed by the Apocalypse of John, is the combination of two elements that have for two thousand years characterized certain Western attitudes to war and peace, right down until today with Christian radical groups: the will by ascetic groups to withdraw from society and constitute an avant-garde of sorts; the utopian vision of a complete and violent purification of the world taking place against an eschatological backdrop.[20]

THE CONSTANTINIAN REVOLUTION

Big revolutions are often foreshadowed by smaller ones. The takeover of the Bastille in 1789 in Paris, which symbolizes the beginning of the French Revolution, was in fact preceded by events that took place a year before in the Alpine towns of Vizille and Grenoble. And so it was with the Constantinian revolution. In 202, the king of Edessa (modern Urfa in southeastern Turkey), Abgar VIII, the Great, converted to Christianity and made his religion the official one of his kingdom. At least this is what we can surmise from the fragmentary information at our disposal regarding this episode, though there is evidence that the rulers of Edessa had shown a keen interest in Christianity for some time. According to Eusebius, bishop of Caesarea (a town in Israel north of modern Tel Aviv), an earlier king, also named Abgar, had an epistolary exchange with Jesus himself that opened the doors to Christian teaching in Edessa,

FIGURE 1. Colossus of Constantine
(ca. 315), Palazzo dei Conservatori,
Capitoline Museum, Rome. Photo by
Tim Adams. 2.0 Generic (CC BY 2.0).

which at that time had a political rapprochement with Rome and drifted away from Parthian Persia.[21] In any case, this event, barely a footnote in the history of Christianity, shows that the marriage between power and Christianity was already in the making. But, as is the case with many important events and discoveries, it is the second person that comes along who makes an impact rather than the first.

This person was Constantine, who had a lot more power to influence people than the king of a tiny city-state. "Politics begin where the millions of men and women are; where there are not thousands, but millions, that is were serious politics begin," Lenin observes.[22]

The emergence of a Constantine would have been unlikely a century or two before his time, and the fate of Rome and of Christianity would have taken a different course had another man become emperor at that point. Constantine's successor but one, the emperor Julian "the Apostate" (r. 361–63), in fact sought to revert to a Neoplatonic form of paganism, but died in battle against the Persians before he could effectively implement his anti-Christian policy.

Constantine made not one but two momentous decisions that altered the course of history: he declared to be Christianity to be the religion of the Roman Empire *and* he transferred the empire's capital—and center of gravity—from Rome to Constantinople. This geographical transfer would lead to the division of the empire into two entities, followed by the crumbling and disappearance of one of them.

Constantine was born perhaps in 273 and he died in 337. The third and fourth centuries in which he lived coincided, as we have seen, with the increasing interaction between religion and imperial power, a phenomenon witnessed not only in the West but also in Persia, China, and India, in other words, all the poles of civilization around which the geopolitics of Eurasia would revolve for centuries. In India, Hinduism had empowered itself to the point where it would be able to survive the invasions that brought Muslim rulers to the subcontinent. In China, Buddhism spread like wildfire but, though fully integrated as part of a pluralistic culture, never achieved the status of state religion in a country that always rejected such a notion and had the means to do so. In Persia, Manichaeism, which, like Christianity (and, later, Islam), was a monotheistic, universalistic proselytizing religion, never managed to take the place of the official state religion, Zoroastrianism. Thus, Manicheism was permanently downgraded to marginal status, much like Judaism and Christian Nestorianism, none of which would ever be directly associated with imperial power. Later, the legend of Prester John would excite the Western mind to the point that Europeans became convinced that Yuan China, thanks to the inroads made by Nestorians, might be ready to convert to Christianity. This, of course, was wishful thinking and the various embassies sent to meet the Great Khan, and later, also, to the court of Tamerlane, from the twelfth to the fifteenth century, all came up empty handed. Judaism did, probably, become the state religion of the Khazars, but the episode was brief and in any case, the empire built by the Khazars (eighth–tenth centuries) was, like most such empires of the steppe, devoid of any kind of political and bureaucratic foothold capable of sustaining it for a long period of time. Still, this episode, if true, showed that under the right conditions, Judaism might have had a successful encounter with imperial power.

Altogether, though, it was Christianity that substantially married politics and religion, thereby opening the gates of religiously motivated or justified violence. In one form or another, this violence, which often took the form of war, accompanied the history of Europeans for centuries to come. Hence, a religious community that had endured three centuries of persecution, most of which was instigated and effected by the higher authorities of the Roman empire, now became an integral part of Rome's political, social, and military makeup. This radical change in the relationship amongst the Christian community, the church, and imperial power was the work of one man, Constantine, but he did not, however, operate in a vacuum. Had Christians' proselytizing not been as effective as it had been during the decades that preceded Constantine's epiphany, Constantine might have had another spiritual awakening or no awakening at all.

The dramatic turn of events that took place at the turn of the fourth century did so during a war of succession involving four men vying for the imperial throne, left vacant after the death of Galerius in April 311. At the time, the Roman Empire was ruled under a complicated arrangement made by Diocletian in 293 that resulted in the splitting of imperial power into four units. The tetrarchy, as it was called, was loosely tied together through the authority of a senior emperor, Galerius at the time. His death ensured that three men now had an equal share in the power, Licinius, Maximin II, and Constantine. However, a fourth man entered the fray, Maxentius, who was Galerius's son-in-law—Maximin II being Galerius's nephew—but also the son of a former emperor, Maximian. Licinius and Constantine came to an agreement to eliminate the other two pretenders, with Licinius taking care of Maximin in the East and Constantine doing his part against Maxentius in the West. For Constantine, the decisive battle came to a head on the outskirts of Rome on October 28, 312. Decisive it was, for not only did Constantine defeat his adversary, but it was here, on the Milvian Bridge, that the future ruler of Rome had his great spiritual moment. Or, at least, it is here that the founding myth of Christian Rome originated. Whether or not Constantine's awakening happened on the spot or a posteriori is a chronological detail that will forever be shrouded in mystery. The legend of the Milvian Bridge was preserved for posterity by Eusebius, some twenty years after the fact in his biography of Constantine: "A most marvelous sign appeared to him from heaven [. . .] he said that at about midday, when the sun was beginning to decline, he saw with his own eyes the trophy of a cross of light in the heavens, above the sun, and bearing the inscription *Conquer by this*. At this sight, he himself was struck with amazement and his whole army also, which followed him on this expedition, and witnessed the miracle."[23]

Lactantius, who was tutor to Constantine's son Crispus, the other source for the Milvian vision, describes it thus: "Constantine was directed in a dream to cause the heavenly sign to be delineated on the shields of his soldiers, and so to proceed to battle. He did as he had been commanded, and he marked on the shields the letter X, with a perpendicular line drawn through it and turned round at the top, thus [the sign], being the cipher of Christ [X (chi) and P (rho) being the first two Greek letters of the name Christ]."[24] This sign, known as the *labarum*, a term whose meaning and origin is unclear, came to represent the reign of Constantine.

In any event, the victory of the Milvian Bridge allowed Constantine to enter the city of Rome as the victor and the uncontested leader of the Western Empire. After sharing the imperial power with Licinius for several years, Constantine finally got rid of him in 325, thereby becoming the sole ruler of a unified empire until his death twelve years later. This act was probably motivated in part by religion. Licinius was a pagan, and Constantine's growing commitment to his faith generated an increasing amount of suspicious sentiments between the two rulers. When the Armenians also converted to Christianity, Constantine found a natural ally who was strategically placed on the eastern frontier of the empire. Licinius, though he had agreed to tolerate the practice of the Christian faith in the area under his control, was increasingly perceived as an obstacle. When he undertook measures that seemed to go against the Christian communities living near the Armenian border, Constantine used this as a pretext to attack with the help of Armenian troops in what may have been the very first Christian crusade. It seemed like a small-scale affair, but the consequence was that the Roman Empire was reunified, with its center of gravity now poised to shift eastward.

For Christian apologists such as Eusebius, Constantine's conversion and subsequent control of the *imperium* was read as testimony to the victory of Christianity, inasmuch as Constantine's rule on earth mirrored that of Christ in heaven. That Constantine underwent the ritual of baptism only ten days before his death never really detracted from the official Christian narrative that reported his spiritual conversion as taking place during the height of a decisive battle on a bridge that, for all intents and purposes, was both a symbolic and a physical passage from one world and one era to another. More important, this founding myth of Roman Christianity was predicated on an event that was both bellicose and intensely political to the core. Indeed, Constantine had in one fell swoop eliminated a political foe through sheer brutal force, ensured power over a vast empire, and made Christianity a full partner in this ambitious enterprise. The writing was on the wall: "When Constantine became a Christian he created a golden opportunity to unite a wholeheartedly universalist religion and its abundance of scriptural authority and missionary impetus with an empire's forces of political, military, and economic expansion in order to create a genuine world empire."[25]

Traditionally, the Roman ruler derived his legitimacy from the cult of the emperor, but this had weakened over the centuries. In consequence, as witnessed with Aurelian and Diocletian, over the years, greater emphasis had been placed on the relationship between the emperor and divinity. However, the very nature of Greco-Roman polytheism limited the power that such an association could contribute. Moreover, the rapid growth of the empire's Christian population, especially in the late third and early fourth centuries, meant that the emperor's legitimacy now rested in part upon its popular support.[26]

Christianity had made huge social inroads during the third century, though the reasons for this dramatic success remain unclear. Possibly, it was due to its social activism and charitable work, notably in urban centers, where Christians organized soup kitchens to feed the poor (up to fifteen hundred people a day in Rome)[27] and established health care services during epidemics, work that perhaps foreshadowed the creation of famous orders of the Crusades like the Knights Hospitaller.

Christianity had thus attained a "critical mass," both in terms of its influence and in raw demographic numbers. Far gone were the days when, as the second-century theologian Tertullian lamented, "If the Tiber rises to the walls, if the Nile fails to rise and flood the fields, if the sky withholds its rain, if there is earthquake or famine or plague, straightaway the cry arises: 'The Christians to the lions!'"[28]

Although Nero, seeking scapegoats, had made Christianity illegal after the great fire of 64 CE, the threat allegedly posed by Christians to the integrity of the Empire was subsequently deemed insignificant, probably because their numbers remained small for a long time and their activities were of little concern to the authorities.[29]

The spread of the Christian faith around the Mediterranean was gradual and often irregular, but in the end its presence was felt everywhere in the region. Paul is the most famous of the traveling preachers, but he was not alone. Christian proselytizing simultaneously proceeded in various regions around the Mediterranean. The first Christians of the Roman Empire tended to be foreigners who had immigrated to cities, like the Lyon (France) martyrs of 177, who spoke Greek.[30] Conversion of rural folk tended to be slower and more difficult than that of urban populations, but in Phrygia, Egypt, and North Africa, for example, the countryside quickly proved receptive. The missionary work was arduous and required patience and determination. In Gaul, for example, the evangelization undertaken by Irenaeus of Lyon in the second century was not yet completed by the time Martin of Tours energetically decided to finish the job in the fourth. Invasions by pagans not yet converted to Christianity often meant that some of the work was erased and had to be undertaken a second or a third time. Generally, though, Christian proselytizing greatly benefited from the Pax Romana. The stability of the Roman Empire, the absence of frontiers over vast areas, and the facility with which one could move about were instrumental in allowing the religion to spread.[31]

Amazingly, this massive conversion was accomplished from the bottom up and essentially without violence. As early as 112, Pliny the Younger was astonished to discover that the region where he was appointed governor, Bithynia, had a significant number of Christian converts. Half a century later, the Greek philosopher Celsus described the religion, disparagingly, as seducing "artisans and women." Although the details surrounding the spread of Christianity in these early days are somewhat sketchy, it seems that most converts, though not all, were of modest social origin, and that women were quite active in the movement. Jews were chronologically the first group to be in contact with Christians. The fact that they were present throughout the empire prob-ably facilitated or accelerated the spread of Christianity.

All told, however, the proportion of Christians within the Roman Empire remained small at least until the fourth century. Thus, the growing influence of Christianity during the first centuries of the Common Era area are attrib-utable not to the sheer number of conversions, which, though they grew with time, remained modest, but to the prominence of the Christian church as an institution whose social and political weight was proportionally far greater than the demographic mass of its adherents. The church achieved this influ-ence by harnessing forces that had yet to be brought together, as Peter Brown points out:

> A polytheist society had been made up of innumerable small cells. Though sup-ported by immemorial custom, it was as delicate and as brittle as a honeycomb. The Christian Church, by contrast, brought together activities that had been kept separate under the old system of *religio*, in such a way as to form a compact, even massive, constellation of commitments. Morality, philosophy and ritual were treated as being intimately connected: all were part of "religion;" all were to be found in their only true form in the Church. In the polytheist world, by contrast, these were separate spheres of activity.[32]

Constantine may have been aware of this complex evolution and have exploited his knowledge and comprehension of the situation to further his own ambitions. What is evident, especially with the benefit of hindsight, is that the revolution instigated by Constantine gave a new lease on life to the Roman Empire, to the figure of the emperor, and to the Christian church. Now, Rome was united under one emperor and one God. From there on, the Christian attitude to war and the use of force would change dramatically. As a major stakeholder in the imperial power structure, the Christian church now had responsibilities that included, not only the defense and propagation of its faith and the protection of its followers, but also support of the empire and its citizens. These responsibilities included the physical protection of the state, in other words, its security, and the enhancement of what we might anachronistically refer to as its "national interest."

An important effect of the Constantinian revolution was to tighten the authority of the state, and of the church. Not only did Constantine consolidate the power of the emperor, but he managed to effectively reunify the empire under a single political roof. Likewise, he pushed for a centralization of church authority, which, until then, had been diffused through the various bishoprics scattered throughout the land, which essentially operated autonomously. Constantine pushed for greater integration by calling regular councils (over which he would often preside), a move that logically consolidated the power of the church into a centralized and sprawling organization. It became both more potent and more easily visible, and controllable, by the emperor. Thus, effectively, began the long relationship between church and state power that to this day has defined and redefined in countless ways the political organization and identity of Western societies.

Almost immediately, the newfound power and responsibilities of the church trickled down to Christian individuals and communities. From a practical perspective, this meant that Christians could now take an active part in military service, whereas, before, such participation was marginal. As early as 314, two years after the battle of the Milvian Bridge, the Council of Arles in southern France, presided over by Constantine, stipulated that "those who throw down their arms in time of peace are to be separated from the community" (Canon 13) which, though the wording is a bit confusing when taken out of historical context, basically meant that Christians, who were no longer under threat of persecution, were now attached to the service of the empire.[33] Coming from a position of inherent and unbinding weakness, Christians were now the purveyors of political and with it military power. For the church, this radical change made for an acrobatic and at times uncomfortable theological about-turn. Church authorities now needed to take an ethic of conduct tailored to a persecuted pacifistic minority and rework it for a community that was suddenly thrust into the role of principal partner in a universalistic *imperium*. In many ways, the church embarked on a centuries-long inner struggle to reconcile its ethics of peace and nonviolence founded on the teachings of Jesus Christ with the expediency of political action.

Constantine's overarching goal was no different than the one entertained by Cyrus the Great, Philip of Macedon, or Alexander the Great: the establishment of an empire that would span the Mediterranean and reach the outer frontiers of Persia and beyond. Cyrus and the Persian conquerors saw their empire as a mosaic of various peoples governed by a Persian elite devoted to a monotheistic religion; Philip was a pan-Hellenist who sought to unify the Greek world and rescue the Greek minorities of Asia from the Persian yoke; Alexander built on his father's vision to create a universal empire at the expense of Persia, but by doing so, unshackled himself from Philip's pan-Hellenism.

Constantine, in many ways, built on these three visions while creating his own. Like Alexander, his imperial ambitions were unbound by any kind of territorial limit; like Cyrus and the Achaemenids, he established a monotheistic religion as the foundation of his empire's identity; in the manner of Philip, he sought to protect and uphold the interests of all Christians, including those who lived outside the empire. His still-born campaign of 337 against Persia, officially established to rescue Christian minorities, was strangely reminiscent of Philip's own plans (foiled, like Constantine's, by his sudden death) to invade Asia Minor, then part of the Achaemenid empire, to rescue the Greek populations of that region.

Constantine could not have achieved his widespread power had he adopted a cynical view of religion either as a mere instrument of power or as an ideological tool to assert his legitimacy. Though politically extremely astute, he was also, at least partially, sincere. "But if his conversion should not be interpreted as an inward experience of grace, neither was it a cynical act of Machiavellian cunning," says Henry Chadwick. "It was a military matter. His comprehension of Christian doctrine was never very clear, but he was sure that victory in battle lay in the gift of God of the Christians."[34] Although one can easily get the impression that the fate of Constantine, of Rome, and of Christianity was settled at the Milvian Bridge, one must remember that the struggle, often decided through the use of force, lasted nearly two decades.

During that time, Constantine not only had to deal with political rivals but had to win over the pagan population, a portion of which was very hostile to Christians. In addition, Christians were far from being tightly bound, and the authority of the church itself revolved around regional poles with varying degrees of power. Local divisions could potentially spread rapidly to other regions, thereby threatening the entire edifice.

Fortunately for Constantine and for the fate of Christianity, the Roman Empire was not at the time under any external "existential" threat. In other words, it was still the dominant power of the region and neither the Huns nor the many other tribes that the latter pushed westward against the frontiers of the empire were as yet the menace that they would become in the latter part of the fourth century with the arrival of the Visigoths (battle of Adrianople, August 9, 378; sack of Rome, August 24, 410) and in the fifth century with the rise of Attila. Likewise, Persia, now under the yoke of the powerful Sassanian kings, was not the superpower that would rival Byzantium as the regional hegemon centuries later. Rome had enjoyed its hegemonic status since the fall of Carthage, and if there were signs that things were about to change, these were submerged in the general belief that the empire was immortal.

Constantine's understanding of international relations, at a time when the global balance of power was shifting from the West to the East, is what prompted him to move the center of power of the empire to the new, aptly named (after himself) city of Constantinople, the "New Rome," built on the foundations of a small provincial city called Byzantium. The reunification of the Roman Empire, however, did not last very long. In 395, a mere fifty-eight years after Constantine's death, the emperor Theodosius divided the empire along the same lines drawn by Diocletian, so that his two sons could share the power. This administrative division soon became a political one, and two separate entities eventually emerged. Though the Eastern Empire seemed under greater duress than the Western one, it benefited from the impulse given it by Constantine. While the more established portion floundered and soon withered—to the point where the fall, on September 4, 476, of its last emperor, Romulus Augustulus, was a nonevent—the "other" Roman empire that we now refer to as the Byzantine Empire prospered and survived until its demise in 1453 at the hands of the Ottoman Turks.

This political/geopolitical event of massive proportion had huge ramifications for Christianity. For not only did the Byzantine Empire ensure the survival of Christianity as a state religion, but the fragmentation of the Roman world between East and West allowed for the emergence of two separate Christian faiths that, in due time, would spread to the confines of Russia, to the Americas, and to parts of Africa and Asia. Also, and just as crucial, at a time when western Europe was kept busy with its deconstruction and slow reconstruction, Byzantium acted as the main stronghold against Arabic and Turkic invasions, in effect, against Islam. Alas, in one of the most ungrateful acts known to history, the Byzantine Empire was ravaged in 1204 by an army of marauding Crusaders supposedly acting in the interest of Christianity.

That said, the political unification of the Roman Empire by Constantine did little to quell the grave dissentions that were threatening the unity of the Christian church. This was true particularly in the eastern part of the empire, where Arius had challenged the orthodoxy of Alexander, bishop of Alexandria, on a point of doctrine—the relationship between God the Father and the Son—that provoked a formidable reaction among the clergy in all parts of the Empire, as far away as Britain. The controversy had a very local origin, and the speed at which it spread testifies to the quality of communications in the Roman Empire, something that no doubt contributed significantly to the inroads made by Christians in a short span of time. Arius, who was Bishop Alexander's presbyter at the time, gained the support of a rapidly increasing number of bishops, including Eusebius of Caesarea, and Constantine energetically sought to resolve the issue before it was too late.

The result was the organization in May 325 of the Council of Nicaea (Iznik, Turkey), which ended in an overwhelming vote, all but two of the more than two hundred and twenty bishops present having cast their ballot against Arius.[35] This, however, was not the end of the Arian controversy. After Constantine's death, the Arian faction, still powerful and influential among the clergy, despite the vote that seemed to show otherwise, launched an all-out attack on the rival party, whose partisans adhered to the Nicene Creed produced by the Council of Nicaea. Ultimately, after two decades of intense infighting, the Nicene faction won, and Arianism was all but wiped out, barely surviving for a while as the faith chosen by the Goths, who had been converted by the translator of the Gothic Bible, Ulfila.

Although Constantine's victories had been ensured by his military superiority over his rivals, his success was interpreted as a double victory for peace. This was the fusion between the Christian Peace and the Roman Peace, Pax Christiana and Pax Romana.[36] "Triumph on triumph gave to Rome the earth, and laid the road on which the Lord should tread. [. . .] And now, O Christ, a world prepared takes Thee, linked by the common bond of Rome and Peace," the Latin poet Prudentius wrote.[37] In essence, nothing seemed to divert Christianity from its historic commitment to pacifism.

In practice, however, things were evolving quickly. Christians, who, before, had systematically refused military service now formed the backbone of the Roman armies. Theodosius II, "the Younger"(r. 402–8), went so far as to exclude from military service all those who did not adhere to the Christian faith or who were suspected of practicing pagan rites. The clergy was now in a difficult position. As partakers in the governance of the Empire, they could not shy away from ensuring the security of the state. Some, like the bishop of Nibisis, encouraged the use of force, while others, most famously Martin of Tours, accepted the role of accompanying campaigning armies, but refused to participate in actual combat, arguing that "as a soldier of Christ, I cannot fight." Monks refused military service outright, preferring to retire from life and political responsibility, thereby foregoing family duties. Monastery life, throughout the history of Christianity, would channel the energies of those who were dissatisfied in one way or another with the orthodoxy of the church. Later, European monastic orders would wield immense influence and power, and they would be instrumental in imbedding the idea of holy war in church orthodoxy.

For now, though, monks remained faithful to Jesus's pacifist message. The emperor Valens, whose claim to fame is forever attached to his inglorious defeat and death at the hands of the Goths at Adrianople, would have none of this, and he sent soldiers into the desert to track down monks and force them to take part in combat. Generally, though, this attitude on the part of the monastic orders was deemed noble. For St. John Chrysostom, the duty to fight evil took on different forms and while the kings merely dueled against barbarians, monks had the more difficult task of fighting demons. In the end, "inasmuch as demons are more fearful than barbarians, the victory of the monks is more glorious."[38]

In essence, the situation demanded a revised ethical code for Christians that would adapt to their newfound relationship with war. Several questions had to be addressed: First, the attitude of Christians as opposed to the attitude of the clergy; then, the type of war that might justify the use of violence; finally, the attitudes that might be acceptable, or not, during combat. Ultimately, these questions would be formulated in greater detail under the two main categories of the just war theory, the *jus ad bellum* and *jus in bello*, both of which, many centuries later, would form the backbone of international law as we know it today.

But the first order of things was to move away from the pacifism of the early Christians. Ambrose of Milan (Saint Ambrose, 339–97) took to the task, being the first to formulate a nonpacifist Christian doctrine, from which Augustine of Hippo would develop his own ideas on the matter. War in the fourth-century Roman world was essentially a war against Gothic "barbarians" who practiced a heretical faith, Arianism, and it was easy to justify going to war against a people who threatened, not only one's territory, but, more seriously, one's faith, beliefs, and core identity. For the Christian clerical authorities, and for many centuries to come, the war against heresy would constitute one of the three bellicose activities justifying violence, along with the fight against pagans and the struggle against "nonbelievers"(i.e., Muslims). In his quest, Ambrose borrowed from multiple sources, establishing the first Christian just war doctrine, which others after him would build upon. His two main sources were Stoic philosophy and Old Testament theology.

Ambrose, Augustine of Hippo, and later Saint Thomas Aquinas are the three classic exponents of Christian just war doctrine, *bellum iustum*, which has nourished an ongoing debate on the ethics of war that goes on to this day. It evolved with Christian thought, with the practice of war, and acts, in some way, as a bridge between ethicists and soldiers. Ambrose, Augustine, and Aquinas were, not coincidently, Westerners (two came from Italy, one from Tunisia); for in the East, in what was to become the Byzantine/Orthodox world, war was, from the start, considered to be a necessary evil from which one could not escape.

In contrast to the geographically challenged Byzantine Empire, western Europe (and the parts of Africa that at one point or another were politically and culturally part of Europe), though prone to conflict and facing its share of invading armies, benefited nonetheless from natural protections. The Byzantines were not only exposed, like Westerners, to invaders from the north, but, also, to the constant menace of the Persians, the Bulgars, the Avars, the Turks, the Mongols, and the Arabs, not to mention lesser lights such as the Koktürks and the Alani. In point of fact, the Eastern Roman Empire was always injected with a high dose of realism that might not always be easily accommodated with the niceties of just war doctrine. Probably, the absence of a moral blueprint for political conduct allowed the Byzantine emperors a margin of maneuver that resulted in what came to be known as "Byzantine politics," and eventually symbolized amoral and immoral statecraft. The absence of a just war tradition in Byzantium also accounts for the fact that the crusading spirit that pervaded the West for centuries was largely absent, or, at least, much toned down, in the Byzantine Empire. A couple of rare instances that are significant exceptions to the absence of just war occurred when Heraclius launched a holy war to try to repulse the Avar, Persian, and Muslim armies in the seventh century and, later, during the wars against the increasingly menacing Ottoman Turks.[39] Perhaps, as John Haldon suggests, "it is precisely because the Byzantines fought under the symbol of the Cross, and because they saw themselves as soldiers of Christ fighting to preserve God's Kingdom on earth, that no theory or doctrine of 'holy war' evolved. Warfare was almost by definition of a religious character, since the East Roman empire was the sole orthodox polity fighting to preserve and extend the Christian faith."[40]

THE GENESIS OF THE CHRISTIAN JUST WAR THEORY:
AMBROSE AND AUGUSTINE

The just war doctrine, or just war theory, as it is often designated, implicitly posits that violence may be legitimate if it takes the form of a collective undertaking guided by a legitimate authority. In practical terms, this means that violence might be justified under certain circumstances when it meets a set of ethical criteria and when the decision to use force is undertaken by a governmental body, usually a state. Beyond the decision to go to war, or what came to be known as the *jus ad bellum*, comes the whole question of how the war is conducted, the *jus in bello*. Still today, when discussing such topics as nuclear proliferation or terrorism, proponents of just war theory use these two categories to assess the issue. Now, much like in the fourth century, just war theory marks a radical departure from pacifism, which categorically refuses violence under any circumstance.

Developed shortly after the Constantinian revolution, Christian just war theory constituted the first attempt at developing a Christian ethic of war and peace adapted to the new social and political environment. While the Eastern Roman Empire abandoned the pacifism of the early church and essentially never tried to replace it with a new system of norms, such was not the case in the West. While one may attempt to explain this dichotomy in various ways, the simplest explanation is probably that two particular men energetically tried to establish new norms, and that these two individuals, Ambrose and Augustine, lived in the Western Empire at a time when the two sides started to drift apart in opposite directions.

Ambrose and Augustine are inseparable. Augustine was a protégé and student of Ambrose. Without Ambrose, he might never have developed interest in the issue, and without Augustine's genius, Ambrose's thoughts on the matter might have had little impact on subsequent generations of Christian thinkers. Just war theory is often thought to have originated with Augustine, a towering figure of Christianity, whereas Ambrose is but a secondary one. Nevertheless, Augustine expounded on a theory whose major tenets were already laid down by his mentor, who himself drew heavily on another well-known thinker, Marcus Tullius Cicero, whose influence on the development of a Christian just war theory through Ambrose and Augustine was only truly reassessed in the late twentieth century.[41]

As a political representative of the Roman state—in essence, a high-ranking civil servant —before becoming the bishop of Milan, Ambrose was in a unique position to understand both the political and theological dimensions of Christians' attitudes to war. Recognizing that these attitudes were contradictory, he concluded that one needed to move beyond the pacifism of the early Christians. This he did without restraint nor, it seems, regret. "We may see in him [. . .] conflicting ideals of patriotism and religious integrity as well as some incipient efforts at resolving the dilemma which violence created for the Christian conscience," Louis Swift observes.[42] Whereas writers such as Tertullian or Origen had sought to reenergize Christian pacifism, Ambrose planted the seeds of holy war, though it would take another seven hundred years for this to reach fruition in the Crusades.

Ambrose grasped that Christians could not enjoy their newfound privileges without accepting the responsibilities that went with them. He did not try to diminish Jesus's message of peace and nonviolence. He merely set it aside and added another narrative. For this, he did not seek to create a new ethic but to adapt one that already existed, and, indeed, already formed an integral part of Roman culture: Stoicism.

Stoicism, or Stoic philosophy, originated in Greece where it was often opposed to Epicureanism, though both schools had much more in common than is often believed (a result of the fact that the bulk of Epicurean philosophy that has come down to us consists of critical texts by Stoic philosophers). Stoicism reached its peak in Rome in philosophers such as Plutarch, Cicero, Seneca, Epictetus, and the Roman emperor Marcus Aurelius. Though it may have affected only a narrow elite, its influence was deep and durable. Stoics believed that although destiny controls our thoughts and actions, it does so without hampering the autonomy of our decisions, the liberty of our thoughts, or our responsibility for our actions. In this regard, Stoic philosophy and Christianity were highly compatible, and Stoicism exerted a profound influence on the development of Christian thought as well as Christian morals. It was logical, then, that someone like Ambrose might seek guidance from a classic Stoic philosopher such as Cicero, who, with Seneca, was the most prominent and popular exponent of Stoic thought, and one who had devoted much thinking to the ethics of war. Cicero's discourse on war in his treatise *De Officiis* came to be the initial blueprint for a Christian theory of just war.

Cicero's ethics of war posed the major moral questions that ethicists normally grapple with when dealing with violence, and it provided answers. In many ways, these questions are similar to those that confront us today, dealing with the discrepancy between the morals of the individual and those of a collectivity and determining how each entity might respond to violence. Reinhold Niebuhr and Michael Walzer raise the same questions as Cicero, Ambrose, and Augustine did centuries ago. The reason for this historical coherence can be explained by the fact that in the West, the duties of the individual in matters related to war are invariably filtered through the authority of the state. This relationship, which appears obvious to most of us, is not universal. In the Muslim world, jihad is a moral duty that conditions both the individual and the community and does not necessitate the formal approval of the state or some other authority, governmental or religious.

The strength of the relationship between individual and state in the Western ethics of war is well illustrated by Michael Walzer's exposition of the problem: "The moral reality of war is divided into two parts. War is always judged twice, first with reference to the reasons states have for fighting, secondly with reference to the means they adopt. The first kind of judgment is adjectival in character: we say that a particular war is unjust. The second is adverbial: we say that the war is fought justly or unjustly."[43]

Cicero's discussion of the ethics of war is an integral part of his analysis of the duties of the citizen to the state. In it, Cicero makes a clear distinction between the private individual and the public citizen, between those qualities that characterize the good person and those that characterize the good citizen. In the chapter on friendship—considered since Aristotle as the principal bond of societies—Cicero establishes that the strongest social bond is the one that ties the individual to the state (in his words, the Republic). In short, "one must in all matters have one goal: condition one's self-interest to the general interest." Considering the enormous influence that Cicero exerted on Christian attitudes towards war and peace, the couple of paragraphs he actually devotes to this topic in book 1, "The Conditions for a Just War and a Just Peace," appear very meager. Though he does not go into great detail, however, Cicero does establish the principles that would serve as the building blocks of Augustinian just war theory.

War, first of all, should be seen as a last resort, to be undertaken only when all hope for finding a negotiated solution to a conflict has been extinguished. Secondly, the only motive for going to war is "the desire to live in peace without injustice." Thirdly, one needs to respect the enemies, at least those who have not shown "cruelty or ferocity in war." Fourthly, a war is considered just if it is undertaken by the proper authorities and with a formal declaration, to be delivered before any kind of significant military activity is embarked on. Cicero also seems to suggest that only soldiers may take part in a just war, though this portion is very vague. He also distinguishes between wars of choice and wars of necessity, the former demanding much greater restraint than the latter, and concludes by saying that one should respect "inferiors" (i.e., slaves) and treat them as one would treat any citizen. Just war, in this view, will ultimately ensure lasting peace and bring people together in a growing universal society of like-minded individuals committed to peace, justice, and friendship. In astonishing ways, this vision anticipates Immanuel Kant's essay "Perpetual Peace" (1795), which exerted a formidable influence on nineteenth- and twentieth-century thought and practice.

Ambrose embraced Cicero's principles outright. Furthermore, he endorsed the use of force, albeit with reservations, extolling the virtues of the individual willing to die for his country. While Ambrose's vision of the world is imbued with the universalism of the Christian church, he is adamant in his condemnation of the barbarians, against whom the waging of war would be legitimized by just cause. As enemies of the Empire, barbarians—more specifically, Arian Goths—were enemies of Christian orthodoxy, and it was thus the duty of the Christian to serve the state in its defense against these heretics. In this sense, the emperor was himself understood to be at the service of God.[44]

Thus, for Ambrose, the casuistry of war and peace was a very practical exercise and he proved uncompromising when Christian faith was challenged in any way. When a synagogue was burned to the ground by a group of Christian zealots in Callinicum (388), the emperor Theodosius reacted by demanding that the perpetrators be punished and that the synagogue be rebuilt using funds taken from the local bishopric. Hearing this, Ambrose wrote a letter to Theodosius, denouncing the reconstruction of "an abode of disbelief, a house of impiety, a shelter of madness under the damnation of God himself," adding that "the maintenance of civil law should be secondary to religion."[45] Although this emotional response may have been written in the heat of the moment, it reveals Ambrose's deep conviction that the defense of the faith warranted extreme measures. In this regard, his attitude departed significantly from Cicero's and hinted at things to come.

Regarding private conduct, Ambrose condoned the use of force in helping another in need, but condemned it all the same in the case of self-defense, the argument being that in the latter scenario, the recourse to violence was an attack on *pietas* (*caritas*), itself the foundational block of virtue. In other words, the recourse to violence as an act of individual self-defense amounted to choosing man over God. Similarly, Ambrose thought that the clergy should not physically partake in any kind of violent activity, saying: "it is not our business to look to arms, but rather to the forces of peace."[46] In short, while adopting Cicero's general approach as to what constitutes a just war, Ambrose managed to retain some of the fundamental elements of Christian pacifism, although his carefully laid out moral doctrine did not prevent him from moving the boundaries of what was deemed acceptable.

These contradictions, in effect, were those that would affect Christian attitudes to violence and war for centuries to come. It did not take long for others to tackle these complex issues, and Augustine quickly joined the fray. It was he who established the long-standing Christian just war theory. This dual doctrine, with the *jus ad bellum* and the *jus in bello*, would provide a justification for many forms of violent actions in the name of God while also supplying a framework through which to restrain violence when violence there was. The *jus ad bellum* would inevitably lead to holy war; the *jus in bello* would ultimately provide the blueprint for international law. The pacifistic strand of Christian ethics would live on, leading almost a parallel life, with its ups and downs, to be resurrected in a secular form at the turn of the twentieth century. But neither the *jus ad bellum* nor the *jus in bello* would provide much room for what had been, for centuries, the very foundation of Christian ethics.

Like many of the great political philosophers—Plato, Machiavelli, Hobbes come to mind—Augustine lived in a time of turmoil, and both his philosophy of history and his attitude to war and peace were influenced by the events that led to the disappearance of the world he once knew. "St. Augustine is the first author to deal more or less comprehensively with the subject of civil society in the light of the new situation created by the emergence of revealed religion and its encounter with philosophy in the Greco-Roman world," Ernest Fortin observes. "As a Roman, he inherited and restated for his own time the political philosophy inaugurated by Plato and adapted to the Latin world by Cicero, and as a Christian he modified that philosophy to suit the requirements of the faith."[47]

North Africa, from whence Augustine hailed, was to be overrun by the Vandals, while Rome was under threat from the Goths. These dramatic circumstances called for a theological explanation and reaction. The theological explanation is a foundational linear philosophy of history whereby

Christianity moves forward through exaltation and adversity, ultimately reaching a point of redemption, followed by the end of history. According to Augustine, the march of history is ordained by God, who alone has a full grasp of the overall plan; a plan that conforms to His own reason, one that escapes man's understanding and that cannot be explained by individual events. Though history is linear, it does not follow a linear progression: "Christianity, as Augustine understands it, does indeed provide a solution to the problem of human society, but the solution is not one that is attained or attainable in and through human society."[48]

This, of course, is a crude summary of a much more complex development. But this philosophy of history would go a long way, impacting such philosophers as Kant, Hegel, and Marx, and, closer to us, Francis Fukuyama, who revived the notion of the "end of history" in the late 1980s, at a time when the collapse of the USSR, the West's twentieth-century "barbarian" foe, seemed to signal the final victory of the West, a secularized West, indeed, but still defined by its core Christian values.[49]

In short, then, Augustine's philosophy of history, based as it was on his interpretation of the events that were befalling Rome during his lifetime, came to embody the West's vision of its destiny and its mission. It gave us, among other things, the American idea of manifest destiny, as well as the deep belief in progress that still marks the Western mind today. This interpretation of the march of history came, at different times, to justify war, invasion, and colonization, whether in the name of God, of a "civilizing mission," or, simply, of progress and freedom. This linear vision of history is to be contrasted to the cyclical one most notably exposed a thousand years after Augustine by another philosopher hailing from the shores of what is now Tunisia, Ibn Khaldūn, who would define his own attitude to history through his interpretation of the organic process of development and decay that he saw as the basis of Muslim states.

Augustine retained the idea of humans as social animals who achieve fulfillment through association with other human beings in a community of like-minded individuals. The foundation of this community is virtue; the cornerstone of a virtuous community is justice; and justice is governed by reason, which is governed by God. In this scheme, salvation is not to be found in philosophy, as the Greco-Roman philosophers saw it, but in God.[50] For Augustine, the only true virtue is Christian virtue, and those who display true virtue inhabit what he calls the City of God (the title of his *magnum opus*) or the heavenly city. In contrast to the heavenly city, the City of Man, or earthly city, displays man's propensity to disobey God, as symbolized by Adam's first refusal to acquiesce to God's command. The City of God is the city of the virtuous, and it is only there that one may attain true happiness and peace. But the world being what it is, civil society is indispensable as a supplement to the heavenly city. These two parallel worlds enable the Christian to live his or her life within different types of political societies where laws and customs do not need to conform to the laws that govern the heavenly city. The only requirement, then, is that the individual not engage in immoral actions. By acting virtuously, he or she benefits the commonwealth.

Here, Augustine was especially careful, as the fall of Rome was publicly characterized as a result of the social decay brought upon by Christianity, which, according to this view, had deflated the notion of patriotism and thus stressed the social fabric of Roman society to the point of being incapable of responding to foreign attacks. To this, Augustine had a forceful response, arguing that not only was Christianity compatible with patriotism, but qualifying it as a religious duty reinforced it.[51] Christians' attitudes to war and peace were to be understood in light of their responsibility to their kin and their commitment to the welfare of the commonwealth. A war can be just if fought for the right reasons by a legitimate ruler, and where it is necessary for the good of the commonwealth, it is one's duty to participate in it actively. However, although war is not irrevocably bad, in and of itself, the evils associated with it are, among them gratuitous violence, cruelty, and lust for power or money. Much like that of Ambrose, Augustine's just war theory is based on a Ciceronian view of justice, understood as a civic duty to "keep one man from doing harm to another, unless provoked by wrong."[52] This means that wars that avenge injuries can be considered just. Augustine adds a Christian twist to Cicero's definition of justice by positing that having lost their ability to create justice as a result of Original Sin, humans must therefore receive it from God; in practical terms, the justice he describes as the foundation of his ethics of war is essentially equated with civic virtue. Put differently, this means that justice, whether emanating from reason or from God, is a virtue that has to do with the manner in which an individual or a community treats other individuals and communities. Justice expresses itself as one's duty to right a wrong done to others or to the commonwealth of Christians. This wrong to be righted can originate from within the commonwealth or from outside. Augustine's doctrine implied that a just war could be undertaken against foreign enemies, against heretics, or even against rulers guilty of acting against the interest of the commonwealth—a notion that would generate a moral doctrine of its own around the concept of tyrannicide, a form of just war targeted at an individual (in the nineteenth century, the first generation of terrorists would adopt this doctrine as their point of departure, before evolving modern terror tactics).

Augustine's theory of just war was not just a moral or theological exercise. Confronted with foreign invasions and with a serious internal threat to the unity of Christianity, Augustine reacted in a fashion that conformed to his teachings. In a letter to General Boniface, the man in charge of repulsing the Vandals in North Africa, who at one point, after losing his wife, looked to throw in the towel and become a monk, Augustine had this response: "Not now! The monks indeed occupy a higher place before God, but you should not aspire to their blessedness before the proper time. You must first be exercised in patience of your calling. The monks will pray for you against your invisible enemies. You must fight for them against the Barbarians, their visible foes."[53]

Although the enemy had to be driven back with vigor, Augustine remained adamant that peace should be the overarching objective of (just) war. Again through his epistolary exchanges with Boniface, Augustine reiterated his doctrine:

> Peace should be the object of your desire. War should be waged only as a necessity and waged only that through it God may deliver men from that necessity and preserve them in peace. For peace is not to be sought in order to kindle war, but war is to be waged in order to obtain peace. Therefore even in the course of war you should cherish the spirit of a peace maker.[54]

To the twenty-first century reader, this advice might seem like common sense. But this is because Augustine's radical expression of the purpose of war has permeated Western society to the point where we have forgotten how attitudes to war, and peace were at other times very different. To Augustine, peace is indeed the normal state of affairs, while war is to be considered a temporary recourse to restore normalcy, an approach social scientists now describe as "positive peace." But in antiquity, the Middle Ages and the early modern era, right up to the eighteenth century, war was either considered to be a desirable thing, the boldest expression of human virtues such as courage and abnegation, or as a normal instrument of statecraft, a counterpart to diplomacy. Both the heroic vision and the realist approach envisaged peace as a momentary period between two conflicts; wars being, in this case, either desirable or inevitable.

Augustine, of course, lived in an empire, albeit a crumbling one, which, like most mature empires, sought to secure and consolidate its borders. What Augustine desired was the Pax Romana, now quickly evaporating before his eyes. Foreseeing the end of Roman perpetual peace, he entertained the hope that another, purer, more durable form of peace might emerge once the war was over. This reality must have comforted Augustine in the idea that the Romans were being punished for their sins, while the Christians, who were taking over, would ultimately establish a peaceful Christian commonwealth on Roman ashes. This vision influenced Marsilius of Padua, Thomas Aquinas, and Dante, among others. In the early eighteenth century, making the leap from Augustinian Christian peace to a secular vision of it, the diplomat and *académicien français* abbé Charles de Saint-Pierre published a *Projet pour rendre la paix perpétuelle en Europe* (Project for Perpetual Peace in Europe),[55] influencing among others Jean-Jacques Rousseau, whose writings on the subject would in turn inspire Kant to write his famous essay "Perpetual Peace."

What Augustine was trying to envision was a new peaceful order that would eliminate internal strife and religious conflicts, guarantee peace and stability within the limits of its territory, and be strong enough to fend off outside attacks. For Augustine, the goal of peace was not the only criterion to determine whether or not a war is just. The decision had to be guided by virtue:

> Moses in putting to death sinners was moved not by cruelty but by love. So also was Paul when he committed the offender to Satan for the destruction of his flesh. Love does not preclude a certain severity, nor that correction which compassion itself dictates. No one indeed is fit to inflict punishment save the one who has first overcome hate in his heart. The love of enemies admits no dispensation, but love does not exclude wars of mercy waged by the good.[56]

Augustine's attempt at defining an ethics of war that combined Stoic principles with Christian theology was a worthy one. His just war theory not only provided the clergy with a moral compass that enabled it to limit the effects of war but also served as a foundation for the development of a corpus of international law, and it continues to this day to inform Christian attitudes to war, peace, and current policy. It is a testament to Saint Augustine's penetrating understanding of the dialectics of war and peace that the theory has endured for more than fifteen hundred years.[57]

But Augustine's theory is resolutely vague when one seeks to answer the fundamental questions for which it seeks to provide a coherent response: "What makes a war just?" and "When is the use of force acceptable?"[58] Augustine himself wrestled with the problem when faced with the threats posed, not only by barbarian invaders, but also by internal strife, with the conflict between orthodox Roman Catholics and Donatists who espoused a more rigorous form of Christianity, notably as concerned the clergy, which, in effect, had created a schism within African churches (the Donatists, whose name is derived from their leader, Donatus, effectively broke away from the Roman Catholics in 312 over the election of the Bishop of Carthage). Although Augustine wrapped his attitude in theological justifications, in both cases his approach was pragmatic. In his eyes, the ends justified some of the means, even when these included coercion. Augustine regarded insincere conversions as a non-issue—conversions of all sorts, sincere or not, helping the causes of both Christianity and the empire.

For all intents and purposes, the Donatists were swiftly dealt with at the Carthage Conference of 411 where, in theory, they were allowed to present their case before the authorities. But being as they were the weaker of the two parties, their fate was a forgone conclusion. Shortly after the conference, Emperor Honorius gleefully signed an edict (January 412) proscribing Donatism. Donatists who refused to convert to Catholicism were marginalized, and Donatism eventually withered away. The demise of the Donatists is indicative of most dissenting or minority Christian movements that did not have the backing of a state such as was enjoyed over time by the Eastern Orthodox, Roman Catholic, or Armenian churches.

As with most things, Augustine struggled internally with the issue, but he managed to find a theological justification to a difficult deontological problem. By doing so, he paved the way for generations of like-minded individuals, both clergymen and statesmen, who would be faced with the inevitable decision of whether to use force in order to defend the faith or the state and who grappled with the restraints imposed on their action by a set of moral norms that political expediency often encouraged them to interpret in the broadest manner.

No sooner were the Donatists brushed aside than another theological dispute erupted once again in North Africa: the Pelagian controversy, so named after the doctrine of a British (perhaps Irish) scholar and theologian, Pelagius. Sensing that Pope Zosimus himself—having been energetically lobbied by Pelagius's staunchest follower, Caelestius—was being seduced by

Pelagianism, Augustine adroitly persuaded Emperor Honorius to take swift action, which he did by producing an edict in 418 banning Pelagians from Rome, officially for reasons of imperial security (or, in the terminology of the time, "peace").[59] Augustine's successful maneuvering—about which we know very little—shows that church and state could interact efficiently in an informal, but potent, system of checks and balances.

CHRISTIANITY AND THE INVENTION OF MEDIEVAL WARFARE

The fourth century was a momentous one; it saw Christianity move from a position of political destitution and weakness to one of participation, influence, and dominance. Church and state learned to cooperate with each other. The state took on new configurations in an unstable, fragmented geopolitical landscape, in which the Catholic Church was a pillar of institutional stability. Just war theory provided a moral compass in a very bellicose environment, where war was not only an instrument of power, but a way of life and the main engine of social reconstruction.

War in the West would be redefined by the Germanic culture of the ruling peoples of Europe and by the Christian makeup of the society that was to emerge from the ruins of the great Roman Empire. Ironically, for a religion that was condemned for so long by the Romans, Christianity provided the main link between the glorious past and the not so glorious present. While one may, like Victor Davis Hanson, perceive a continuity in the Western ways of war running from antiquity right through today,[60] the medieval period seems in many ways to present a clear break with the Greco-Roman tradition, which, in matters of war, seemed all but eclipsed until it was revived in the fifteenth century through a renewal in strategic thinking and practices. "With the invasion of Germanic peoples between the fourth and sixth centuries, followed by the foundation of Barbarian kingdoms, new forms of political power and institutions were created, society was organized in a new way and new values were recognized and experienced. These changes were necessarily accompanied by a transformation in ideas concerning war itself, as well as by changes in how warfare was practised," Philippe Contamine observes.[61]

The evolution of medieval warfare was a long process, which extended through several centuries before reaching maturity in the twelfth–thirteenth centuries. Starting with armies of Germanic soldier-peasants wielding their infamous battle-ax, the *Franscisca*, medieval warfare developed into the aristocratic model of the horse-mounted knight before reverting back to the peasant infantry, this time armed with long bows, crossbows, and pikes, and later with muskets and bayonets. For the entirety of the Middle Ages—just about one thousand years, though this depends on when one starts and ends the chronology (obviously, historians have differing views on this)—the church had a profound impact on how wars were fought, why they were fought, where and when they were fought, and with and against whom.

The influence of the church on the new culture of war was not independent of factors such as the evolution of the Western state, the development of new technologies, the geopolitical dynamics of Europe, and, most important perhaps, the threat posed by the rise of Islam. But the manner by which the church reacted and sometimes contributed to these events and development impacted Western attitudes to institutionalized violence and the conduct of warfare in no small measure. Although the church never relinquished its core message of universal peace inherited from the early Christians, it also fashioned a certain mode of warfare which, in the end, pitted small armies of eager aristocrats to fight one another at close quarters, with little effect on the local populations—other than the economic strain placed on demographically weak rural societies asked to fund perpetual campaigns, more often than not with little political impact. This approach conformed to the Germanic tradition of the Frankish people who ruled western Europe after the disintegration of the Roman Empire, in which war was considered a *judicium belli*, a judicial process,[62] with the outcome determined by divine will. Gregory of Tours, for example, tells of a typical episode where one of the protagonists, Gundovald the Pretender, explicitly states, "When we meet on the battlefield, God will make it clear whether or not I am King Lothar's son."[63]

Hence, the paradox of Western medieval warfare, whereby, on the one hand, war pervaded medieval culture and social life, but, on the other, it played out essentially as a social activity of a tiny elite. This development was made possible because medieval western Europe was for the most part culturally and politically homogeneous (though compartmentalized), geopolitically isolated, and comparatively marginal economically, thus soliciting little interest from the great powers of the age. War, then, was an essential part of medieval society, but it lacked real political purpose and, being an end rather than a means, threatened to disrupt the social order. In light of this, one of the main drivers of the Crusades was the need, clearly felt by the papacy, to channel all this bellicose energy outward in order to avoid potential chaos on the inside. Evidently, the situation at the marches of Europe, exposed as these regions were to attacks from armies with differing aims, means, and strategies, was altogether different than in the protected—by natural geography and space—areas to the west and the north. In consequence, although the Middle Ages inevitably evoke images of knights in their shining armor, and although wars were indeed frequent and much talked about, the age was, by comparison, much less violent than in the modern era and considerably less so than in the century and a half of total warfare that began with the French Revolution and ended with World War II. By and large, medieval western Europe was a far less violent and unstable place than most of the contemporary Eurasian continent. Feudal society, as Franco Cardini points out, "is a demilitarized society conceived—as paradoxical as this may appear to the modern mind—for war: a society of people without arms who are governed by warriors."[64] How it got to this point and why, and how the church played an essential part in this process, are the central themes of this story as it unfolded over the next centuries.[65]

THE CHURCH FILLS A VACUUM

We have seen how the Roman Empire, under the impulse of Constantine, reinvented itself as a Christian commonwealth with its eyes fixated on the East. Thus was initiated the break between East and West, formalized politically by the emperor Theodosius in 395, that would be formally consummated with the Great Schism of 1054. In the meantime, as the Byzantine Empire formulated the efficient grand strategy that would enable it to thrive and then survive for many centuries, the West was undergoing its own metamorphosis. In Clovis, king of the Franks (466–511), it would have a Constantine of its own.

For complex reasons that go beyond the scope of this discussion, the western part of the Roman Empire had been unable to resist the unrelenting waves of barbarian invasions. The Germanic people who invaded western Europe were pushed by the Huns, who were themselves pushed by other Turkic peoples out of Central Asia, thereby instigating a geopolitical domino effect for which the declining empire had little response, it being at the tail end of the whole movement. This process was brought to a dramatic and abrupt end when the armies of Attila were repulsed in 451 by a coalition of Roman, Gallic, and Gothic troops at the so-called Battle of Châlons (which probably took place near another city, Troyes),[66] where the armies were led by a man, Aetius, fittingly referred to in history books as "The last of the Romans." The decisive outcome of this indecisive battle, upon which Attila retreated eastward, was that the heart of Europe was effectively now under Germanic control. Incidentally, this would be the last time that the redoubtable Central Asian armies would threaten the West, notwithstanding the brutal but stillborn campaign orchestrated by Genghis Khan's greatest general, Sobodeï, against Poland and Hungary (which were both crushed but saved by the death of the Great Khan) in the thirteenth century. Attila himself died, probably from a bout of binge drinking, before he could launch a new campaign.

The decades that followed Châlons saw various Germanic tribes battling it out for territory, with the Vandals occupying North Africa, the Visigoths and Suebi settling down in the Iberian peninsula, the Ostrogoths overrunning what was left of the empire in Italy, and the Franks taking control of what are now France, Belgium, and Germany, while Britain sought to fend off the Angles and Saxons. For the most part, these newcomers, while retaining pagan beliefs and practices, had largely adhered to the Arian strand of Christianity. Western Europe was perpetually at war, divided, insecure, and fraught with chronic instability. The Catholic Church, through its bishoprics, was the only institution able to instill some sense of order and continuity into this chaos. In many ways, it gained great prominence and power from the anarchy brought about by the barbarians and the quick erosion of the Roman structures of the state that resulted.

In short, the church filled a vacuum of power by exploiting the legitimacy it enjoyed within a vast region whose population was by largely Christian. Through its local bishoprics, the church offered protection, especially in urban areas, as well as an administrative structure through which society could continue to function. For Catholicism, therefore, the great enemy was not paganism but the Arianism that the conquering barbarians were forcibly introducing in the conquered territories. Thus, although Arianism primarily only concerned a small elite group as compared to the majority of Christians who adhered to Roman orthodoxy, it posed an existential threat to the Catholic Church, which was in dire need of allies capable of wielding battle-axes and swords.

For this reason, the church would work hard to find a savior capable of fighting for its cause, and a winning one at that. The hard work would finally pay off thanks largely to Clovis's wife, the Burgundian princess Clotilda

(Chrotechildis, canonized as Saint Clotilde), who persuaded her pagan spouse to convert to her Catholic faith.[67] Without what might have seemed like divine intervention, the Catholic Church might well have been supplanted by Arianism, with consequences too formidable to assess. Instead, as Arianism looked poised to overtake all of western Europe, this moment signaled the beginning of the end of the Arians (the last of the Arian kings, the Lombard Garibald, was deposed—after a short reign of a few weeks—in 671). For this reason, the barbarian wars of the fifth and sixth century were not only political struggles between rival tribes, but highly contentious religious conflicts that were fought for the highest stake of all: the hearts, minds, and soul of the people.

The clergy was well aware that history was at a crossroads and clerics were active and, at times, influential participants, even in the thick of battle, as illustrated in vivid manner by the heroic deeds of Saint Lupus, Saint Aignan, and Saint Geneviève at Troyes, Orléans, and Paris, respectively, during the Hunnic campaign. This state of affairs was to change dramatically at the turn of the century when the energetic Frankish leader, Clovis would, through a combination of clever politics and successful military campaigns, unify the Frankish tribes and effectively create a nation and a state in what is roughly now France and part of Germany.[68] At the same time, though he was for a long time reluctant to cross the bridge, Clovis converted with great pomp to Catholicism, being baptized by the bishop of Reims, Remigius, along with three thousand of his soldiers on Christmas Day, December 25, 499 (or, perhaps, 508, depending on how one interprets the fragmentary sources). By doing so, Clovis improbably broke the momentum enjoyed until then by Arianism, thus dramatically reversing a trend that seemed irreversible, and effectively placing the Roman Catholic Church back in the saddle. Though it took a lot of convincing, his conversion was finally effected by the relentless lobbying on the part of Clotilda and her influential friend Remigius, and the decision was unequivocal. Thus, much as with Constantine, the individual who laid the foundations of the state also officially adopted a religion. This dual purpose was made clear when, shortly before his death in Paris at forty-five, Clovis called a church council in Orléans, drawing thirty-two bishops, with himself actively participating in the debates, and promulgated the Lex Salica, the Salian Law of the Franks, to regulate the life of the Frankish people.[69]

The support given by the church to the Frankish state, and the support it received in return, allowed the Frankish kingdom to thrive and the Catholic Church to overwhelm Arianism. This association would be far-reaching and in many ways defined medieval society in western Europe, with Clovis's Merovingian revolution followed three centuries later by Charlemagne's Carolingian revolution. Shortly after Charlemagne's long reign, the quick disintegration of the Carolingian order paved the way for the feudal order, around which a new Europe emerged. This time, however, the result was a fragmented, inward-looking geopolitical regime, into which the Catholic Church relentlessly tried to instill a universal message and purpose. This it did with all the more determination when a powerful new force suddenly emerged in the seventh century to challenge Christian Europe, generating a monumental clash of civilizations: Islam.

The Emergence of Islam

You have become the best community ever raised up for mankind, enjoining the right and forbidding the wrong, and having faith in God.

—Quran 3:110

In the Muslim community, the holy war is a religious duty, because of the universalism of the Muslim mission and the obligation to convert everybody to Islam either by persuasion or by force. Therefore, caliphate and royal authority are united in Islam, so that the person in charge can devote the available strength to both of them at the same time.

—Ibn Khaldūn

The long conflict that had pitted Rome and Byzantium against Persia took a dramatic turn in the seventh century with the emergence of Islam.[1] Much like the push of the Huns two centuries prior, and, later, of the Mongols and Timurid Turks, the Arab conquests would, in a very short span of time, yield formidable results. Unlike the Central Asian nomads, however, the Bedouin of Arabia durably asserted their authority over the territories conquered, in great part, because their newfound religion provided the legitimacy that enabled the Muslim governments to endure. Political legitimacy, so complex in European society, proved a much simpler undertaking in the Muslim world whereby the caliph, as the de facto commander of the Muslim community, inherited his legitimacy by reason of being a direct descendent of the Prophet. The only chink in the armor of this otherwise bulletproof proposition came about early in Islamic history when two relatives of Muhammad each claimed to be his legitimate heir, thus causing Islam to split into two rival communities, the Sunnis and the Shiites, which, until today, have retained an adversarial relationship. Had this event never occurred, and had Islam been united under

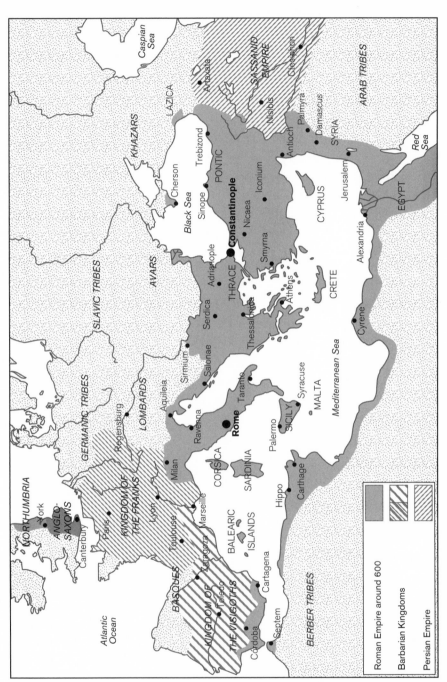

MAP 1. Europe and the Mediterranean before Muhammad

a single banner, its history would have been markedly different, since this deep division has caused many conflicts.

The sudden emergence of Islam shattered the geostrategic dynamics around the Mediterranean and beyond, which for centuries had revolved around the hegemonic struggle between the dominant Western power on the one hand—Greece (Athens, Thebes, Sparta), Macedonia, Rome (and Byzantium)—and Persia on the other. The West had consolidated its permanent hold on the Mediterranean—aptly named *mare nostrum*, "our sea," by the Romans—after the defeat of the Carthaginians in the first Punic War, when Rome had taken control of the seas from Carthage. Despite Hannibal's formidable offensive in Italy during the Second Punic War, Carthage was unable to regain the upper hand. After Scipio's defeat of Hannibal at Zama (in Tunisia) in 202 BC, Rome proceeded during the Third Punic War, essentially a punitive campaign against a vastly inferior foe, to erase Carthage from the face of the earth, acquiring full and uncontested hegemony over the Mediterranean from then on.

At the same time, Persia reclaimed its role as the central continental super-power of Eurasia. Despite the constant inroads made by eastern and northern "barbarian" armies—Germanic, Hunnic/Turkish, Iranian—on Rome and Persia, both had managed to survive and even thrive. Rome, after its fall as a city, nevertheless survived as an empire when the center of power moved eastward and finally settled in Constantinople in 327. The Roman Empire ultimately crumbled, and the pieces fell away one after the other, but the remainder united to form the new Byzantine empire, which, much like Rome, held on to its status as the dominant maritime power of the Mediterranean.

The wars of the emperor Justinian, most notably those conducted by his two able generals Belisarius and Narses, were designed to regain control of the Mediterranean by rolling back the Vandals from North Africa and Sicily (533–34 CE) and the Ostrogoths from Italy (535–54 CE) all the while resisting from the pressure exerted in the East by the Persians and the Avars. In 565, the year of Justinian's death, the Eastern Roman Empire effectively controlled the entire Mediterranean. The empires, kingdoms, and other entities that surrounded the Byzantines included, starting with Spain and moving clock-wise, the Visigoths, Franks, Bavarians, Lombards, Gepids, Avars, Alans, and Persians—the Avars and Persians being at the time the two most formidable actors on the stage, along with, further to the northeast, the Turkic Khaganate. The only bordering area that seemed innocuous at the time was the frontier with the Bedouin peoples of the Arabian Peninsula south of the Persian Empire. If one area seemed safe from invasion, this was it.

Much like Rome's fortunes, Byzantium's were tied to the intrinsic qualities of the ruler, which varied greatly with each individual. Wars of succession in the Byzantine Empire may not have been as dramatic as elsewhere, but commonly involved the maiming, mutilation, or blinding of an opponent so as to impede his capacity lead an army in the field. After Justinian's death, Byzantium entered tumultuous times, and when the emperor Maurice (Maurikios) was cruelly put to death along with his six sons by a usurping general named Phocas in 602, its power was already in retreat. John Mearsheimer ranks international regimes as bipolar or multipolar, and as stable and unstable, with the most dangerous configuration being unbalanced multipolarity, the most stable, balanced bipolarity. In these terms, the Middle Eastern world of the early seventh century, unsettled by the rivalry between Byzantium and Persia, was loosely bipolar and highly unstable, given the precarious balance of power.[2]

Although religion had played a part in this permanent conflict, especially in the years that followed the splitting of the Roman Empire into two entities, the main thrust of the conflict was political. When the Byzantine emperor Heraclius made a desperate attempt to counter the Persian threat by launching a crusade of sorts—which might conceivably be considered the very first crusade—his main motivation lay in his desire to rally the people around his cause. Heraclius had taken over control of the empire in 610 after the catastrophic years during which King of Kings Khosrow II Aparvēz ("The Victorious") of Persia, taking Maurice's murder as a pretext to invade, had sought to take advantage of the internal strife plaguing Byzantium and annihilate it.

Beyond the holy war rhetoric that marked his public discourse, Heraclius was really trying to prevent the imminent annihilation of the Byzantine Empire by an adversary who, at the time, seemed on the verge of imposing Persian hegemony over the greater Middle East. Still, that Heraclius chose to invoke God on that occasion illustrates the fact that religion was, at the time, an element important enough in the collective minds of the people to be called upon in such difficult times. In this respect, the Eastern Roman Empire had moved ahead of western Europeans who, being under less duress, had yet to make an about face on their whole approach to religion and the use of force. Although western Europe had been subjected to foreign invasions, these invasions did not involve people who were intent on imposing a new set of beliefs, and the pagan invaders from the east and the north adopted Christianity shortly after settling in their new territories. In this respect, Christianity proved a considerable factor in the West's ability to absorb foreign invaders.

As legend tells it, Khosrow II, who had married a Christian princess, had himself stormed Jerusalem and taken hold of the Holy Cross. Christian royal brides would play a significant geopolitical role for centuries to come in that part of the world. Much as Clotilda had persuaded Clovis to convert to Catholicism, their wives' advocacy of the Christian cause influenced various Turkic, Mongol, and, later, Ottoman leaders.

Persia, which, since the founding of the Sassanian dynasty, had adopted Zoroastrianism as its state religion, saw its priests wielding real power and influence in the governing apparatus. Unlike Byzantium, where religion had been a latecomer, Persia had for centuries witnessed the active presence of priests in the political process. Various religious minorities lived in the region, in areas controlled by the Byzantines, by the Persians, or by neither, and these minorities were regularly pushed around or abused by the dominant powers. Both the Byzantines and the Persians often displayed gross intolerance of their religious minorities, something that would soon change dramatically in the regions overtaken by the Arabs, as Muslims would quickly prove more tolerant than either Christians or Zoroastrians had been. At the time of the Arabic invasions, Constantinople had refused to make concessions or compromises with the Monophysite and Nestorian communities in Syria, or the Copts in Egypt, two regions that, incidentally, had briefly passed through Persian hands during Khosrow II's initial military successes, before being retaken by a resurgent Byzantium.

With rare exceptions, most nomadic people, be they Turkic, Iranian, or Bedouin, had until then remained faithful to their ancestral beliefs. To them, formal religion, especially Christianity, which was at that time still committed to its original pacifist message, was associated with the sedentary cultures that nomads loathed. Despite the inroads made by Saint Augustine on Christian teaching and the use of force, Christians had yet to make the 180° turn that would come about later, in part because of the threat posed by Islam to Europe. For Henri Pirenne, it was Muhammad who caused the Mediterranean world to split into two rival blocks, whose violent and protracted conflict shaped the evolution of Europe.

Reflecting the way many Europeans perceive their history, Pirenne saw Charlemagne as the dominant Western figure equivalent to Muhammad. By recreating the Roman Empire with a Christian stamp of approval—it was to

FIGURE 2. Equestrian statue of Charlemagne by Agostino Cornacchini (1725), St. Peter's Basilica, Vatican City, Rome. Photo by Myrabella. CC BY-SA 4.0 license.

be known for centuries as the *Holy* Roman Empire—Charlemagne declared Europe to be the formal territory of Christianity while clearly delineating the separation of the powers of the church and the state. Charlemagne's political legitimacy was in fact granted him by the pope, who designated him the successor of the Roman emperors, thereby denying that legacy to the Byzantine

Basileus, who, like his predecessors, considered himself the direct heir of the emperor Augustus and the long line of Caesars who came after him. By doing so, the pope also reasserted the idea that he, the pope, possessed spiritual legitimacy that gave him the authority to anoint the "political" emperor. By juxtaposing Charlemagne to Muhammad, Pirenne effectively identified religion as *the* defining factor that determined the rebirth of Europe, a bold claim indeed.

In fact, Charlemagne and Muhammad are separated by almost two centuries, which coincide with Islam's great thrust into the heart of Europe. Before that, although the proselytism of Nestorian priests had reached people as far as China, for example, Christianity, Judaism, and Zoroastrianism had not altered the geopolitical makeup of the East the way Islam would in the following decades and centuries, when Arabs and Turks, among others, would, one after the other, adopt Muhammad as their prophet. Islam's initial success was no doubt attributable to the formidable conquests of Muhammad's immediate successors, but its resilience rested on its unprecedented capacity to regenerate itself. "The first cycle of conquests," says Fernand Braudel, "the Arab cycle, created an Empire, a state, not yet a civilization."[3]

As Marshall Hodgson observes, this revolution was much more than a geopolitical one:

> Soon after the founding of the faith, Muslims succeeded in building a new form of society, which in time carried with it its own distinctive institutions, its art and literature, its science and scholarship, its political and social forms, as well as its cult and creed, all bearing an unmistakable Islamic impress. In the course of centuries, this new society spread over widely diverse climes, throughout most of the Old World. It came closer than any had ever come to uniting all humankind under its ideals.[4]

THE BIRTH OF A NATION, AND A RELIGION

Whereas Christendom grappled from the time of Constantine on with the tension between the ideal of universal peace and the reality of perpetual war, Islam never had such qualms. Although, as David Cook reminds us, "Islam did not begin with violence," but with a "peaceful proclamation of the absolute unity of God," violence was soon to come.[5] In contrast to Jesus, Muhammad was a warrior who fought weapon in hand for a cause he believed was just.[6] For Islam, war and violence may thus in certain instances be considered legitimate in the eyes of God.

The Islamic equivalent of just war is utterly different from what we find in the Christian tradition, though it is also based on dualistic opposition. In a nutshell, while the dualism of the Christian church is defined through the opposition between the world of God and the world of men, the dualism that also characterizes Islam revolves around the opposition between the *Dār al-Islam* (House of Islam) and the *Dār al-Harb* (House of War), in other words, between the inner space governed by Islam and the outer space governed by non-Muslims. This opposition, often construed in the West as a doctrine of permanent war against non-Muslims—and understood as such by modern fundamentalist groups—is soothed by injunctions to promote peace, including peace with non-Muslim entities. "If they keep away from you and cease their hostility and offer you peace, God bids you not to harm them," the Quran says (4:90). "Muster against them all [the unbelievers] the men and cavalry at your command, so that you may strike terror into the enemy of God and your enemy," the sura titled "The Spoils" admonishes (8:60), but "If they incline to peace, make peace with them" (8:61).[7] Much like the laws that govern nations are vastly different from those that *govern relations between nations*, those that govern Islam are different from those that dictate Muslim nations' attitudes to non-Muslim nations (and non-Muslims living or traveling in the Muslim world).

As Bernard Lewis underscores, religion was from the start the undisputed element that defined one in the Muslim world:

> For the Muslim, religion was at the core of identity, of his own and therefore of other men's. The civilized world consisted of the House of Islam, in which a Muslim government ruled, Muslim law prevailed, and non-Muslim communities might enjoy the tolerance of the Muslim state and community provided they accepted the conditions. The basic distinction between themselves and the outside world was the acceptance or rejection of the message of Islam. The conventional nomenclature of physical and even human geography was at best of secondary significance. [...] The real difference was religion. Those who professed Islam were called Muslims and were part of God's community, no matter in which country or under what sovereign they lived. Those who rejected Islam were infidels.[8]

According to the Muslim narrative, Muhammad, a traveling merchant, was already in his early forties when he received the first revelations from the angel Gabriel in the cavern of Mount Hira where he had retired to meditate. Encouraged by his wife Khadidja, he then embarked on a twenty-year mission to spread the word of Allah on the Arabian Peninsula. Ten years later, he and a handful of disciples were forced to move from Mecca to Medina, an event known as the Hegira, or "immigration," in 622, which became year 1 of the Muslim calendar. He subsequently returned triumphantly to Mecca with a growing army, but succumbed to illness in 632.[9] Muhammad's immediate successors, who had been his early companions, then embarked on the military campaigns that would quickly and decisively alter the geopolitical landscape of the greater part of the Eurasian continent. Thus, there are three distinct stages in the early history of Islam:

1. The pacific mission of the years 610/12–622
2. The increasingly bellicose character of Muhammad's mission (622–32)
3. The initial conquests of Islam, which, starting after Muhammad's death, lasted roughly a century and established the general contours of the Muslim world over three continents.

In certain ways, these stages mirror in a very condensed fashion the evolution of Christianity. The Quran, which includes the revelations as they came to Muhammad during the course of his life after 612, reflects this evolution, hence the contradictions in it on the topic of war, such as one also finds in Christian scripture between the Old and New Testaments. By the same token, while the Roman Empire had evolved over several centuries from an inclusive, largely pagan society into a full-fledged confessional empire with a state religion (in its Byzantine form), the emerging Muslim world, though not an empire to begin with, also evolved, with lightning speed, into an exclusive imperial monarchy, ruled by the caliph, under one God.

The surprising emergence of Islam, both as a religion and as the mightiest empire of the period, was undoubtedly circumstantial. It would not have been possible had other organized religions not altered the world to which Arabia belonged.[10] As Marshall Hodgson points out, in contrast to the earlier religions, these new traditions made personal demands, and neither tribal nor civic ones:

> They looked to *individual* personal adherence to ("confession" of) an explicit and often self-sufficient body of moral and cosmological *belief* (and sometimes adherence to the lay *community* formed of such believers); belief which was embodied in a corpus of sacred *scriptures*, claiming *universal* validity for all men and promising a comprehensive solution of human problems in terms which involved a *world beyond death*. [. . .] By the fourth and fifth centuries CE, these religious allegiances were not only generally prevalent; the stronger of them, in their several areas, were able to establish their representatives in some degree of political power.[11]

In other words, Muhammad's revelations did not come out of the vacuum of an isolated cavern, nor did they dispense with the political dimension of this spiritual awakening. In a world of competing exclusivist confessional empires, the establishment of a religion that sought to surpass all others was bound to provoke some kind of conflict. After Muhammad's death, his heirs would not wait for the inevitable war to come to them. Instead, they decided to pursue elsewhere a war that had previously been a local affair, choosing to attack their foes at an opportune moment, after they had exhausted their energies in a grueling conflict among themselves.

As stated in the Quran 2:129, Muhammad's mission was to revive Abraham's monotheistic faith. Islam, which integrates Judaic and Christian scripture, goes a step further in its monotheistic outlook by rejecting the Christian notion of the Trinity, which, by associating God with the Son and the Holy Spirit, had made unacceptable concessions to polytheism, according to Muhammad. Islam, born in a region that, at the time, saw many Arab communities espousing Christianity or Judaism, was thus significantly influenced by the two other religions of the Book, although radically moving away from them.

Muhammad's first objective was to create a critical mass of followers that, in time, would be powerful enough to fend off the attacks of his detractors and adversaries. In Mecca, where he started preaching, matters became increasingly tense, which led to his fleeing the city for calmer if not greener pastures. From then on, he engaged in what we might today call guerrilla activity, organizing raids, intercepting and looting caravans to fund his movement, and fighting his adversaries, sword in hand. These battles at times involved a significant number of troops: as early as 624, in the battle of Badr, three hundred Muslims confronted an army of one thousand Qurayshites, the Prophet's main adversaries at the time.

In many ways, like the Sicarii a few centuries before, Muhammad's actions resembled the strategy and tactics developed in the twentieth century by the various practitioners of revolutionary warfare such as Mao Zedong, Ho Chi Minh, and Ernesto "Che" Guevara, for whom resorting to arms and violence was sanctioned by the ideologies that fueled their movements, much the way religion legitimized the actions of these early Muslims in their own eyes. Gradually, the Muslims, thanks to their military victories, were able to convert former adversaries to their cause, thereby conclusively tilting the balance in their favor. Khālid ibn al-Walīd, the greatest general of the period and arguably one of the "great captains" of history, was an adversary of Muhammad's before he joined the Muslim armies.

The first few chapters of the Quran do not touch upon the topic of war against unbelievers, since Muhammad received his revelations at a time when the Muslims were incapable of mounting any kind of military operation against the powerful Quraysh tribe (into which Muhammad himself was born), but the topic of war is not altogether absent in these early passages.[12] At 2:249–51, the Quran alludes to the war between the Israelites and the Philistines, underlining the faith that may sustain the weak against a mightier opponent, something that related directly to the situation the Muslims faced against the Qurayshites:

> And when Saul had crossed the river with those who shared his faith, they said: "We have no power this day against Goliath and his warriors."
>
> But those of them who believed that they would meet God replied: "Many a small band has, by God's grace, vanquished a mighty army. God is with those who endure with fortitude."
>
> When they met Goliath and his warriors they cried: "Lord, fill our hearts with steadfastness. Make us firm of foot and help us against unbelievers."'
>
> By God's will, they routed them. David slew Goliath, and God bestowed on him the sovereignty and wisdom and taught him what He pleased. Had God not defeated some by the might of others, the earth would have been utterly corrupted. But God is bountiful to His creatures.[13]

This passage, especially the last verse, is interesting because, although the revelation came about at a time when Muhammad had no political or military leverage, it seems to open up the idea that God might use violence or war as a means to rid the world of evil. Also, the story portrays this particular struggle as one pitting believers against unbelievers. Muhammad's recourse to force—and, indeed, violence—came about later, when he had already fled for Medina, by which time he was able to muster what amounted to a traditional army, albeit a very small one. Quran 22:39–41, revealed shortly after the Hegira, is therefore more explicit in that regard:

> Give good news to the righteous. God will ward off evil from true believers. God does not love the treacherous and the thankless.
>
> Permission to take up arms is hereby given to those who are attacked, because they have been wronged. God has power to grant them victory: those who have been unjustly driven from their homes, only because they said: "Our Lord is God."

Had God not defended some men by the might of others, the monasteries and churches, the synagogues and mosques in which His praise is daily celebrated, would have been utterly destroyed. But whoever helps God shall be helped by Him. God is powerful and mighty: He will assuredly help those who, once made masters of the land, will attend to their prayers and render the alms levy, enjoin justice and forbid evil.[14]

This passage is important because it alludes to the idea of just war. From these verses we can infer that war can be waged to defend houses of worship, and the lands that house them. In other words, a war may be deemed just if it protects the physical structures that permit religious freedom, and by extension, religious freedom itself. The idea that *permission is given* seems to imply that the legitimate use of force must meet some criterion of authority, much as it does in the Christian just war doctrine, although the latter is more explicit in this area. Furthermore, the fact that war is conditioned by such factors to be permitted means that gratuitous acts of violence are proscribed. That one must have been "wronged" to wage a war, implies that one may fight oppression and persecution against one's beliefs, and it seems to vouch for a defensive attitude toward war. Another example of this attitude is found in 2: 190–93, although the initial defensive posture is offset by an implacable response:

Fight for the sake of God those that fight against you, but do not attack them first. God does not love the aggressors.

Slay them whenever you find them. Drive them out of the place from which they drove you. Idolatry is worse than carnage. But do not fight them within the precincts of the Holy Mosque unless they attack you there; if they attack you put them to the sword. Thus shall the unbelievers be rewarded: but if they mend their ways, know that God is forgiving and merciful.

Fight against them until idolatry is no more and God's religion reigns supreme. But if they mend their ways, fight none but the evil doers.

A sacred month for a sacred month: sacred things too are subject to retaliation. If anyone attacks you, attack him as he attacked you. Have fear of God, and know that God is with the righteous.[15]

That a just war must be tied to the principle of self-defense, however, is contradicted by other passages of the Quran that open up the possibility of more aggressive behavior. One of the earlier passages (9:5), for example, gives this advice: "When the sacred months are over slay the idolaters wherever you find them. Arrest them, besiege them, and lie in ambush wherever for them. If they repent and take to prayer and render the alms levy, allow them to go their way."[16]

This is corroborated by 9:28–29: "Believers, know that the idolaters are unclean. Let them not approach the Sacred Mosque after this year is ended. [. . .] Fight against such of those to whom the Scriptures were given as believe neither in God nor the Last Day, who do not forbid what God and His apostle have forbidden, and do not embrace the true Faith, until they pay tribute out of hand and are utterly subdued."

This passage, along with the *ahadiths*, or Prophetic sayings, formed the basis of jihad, understood here as the doctrine of permanent war. Other injunctions to fight in the name of God are found in this chapter, although what is meant by "fight" is open to interpretation. Again, these are to be understood in the context within which the revelations appeared, in this case early during Muhammad's mission (9:38–41):

> Believers, why is it that when it is said to you: "March in the cause of God," you linger slothfully in the land? Are you content with this life in preference to the life to come? Few indeed are the blessings of this life, compared to those of the life to come.
>
> If you do not fight, He will punish you sternly, and replace you by other men. You will in no way harm Him: for God has power over all things.
>
> . . . .
>
> Whether unarmed or well-equipped, march on and fight for the cause of God, with your wealth and with your persons.[17]

However one might interpret the various passages that refer to "fighting" in the Quran, the notion of jihad is indeed present in the text. As a doctrine of holy war, jihad was codified later on during the period when Islam projected itself beyond the frontiers of Arabia. As such, the doctrine served to justify Islamic imperialism, much as Christian holy war served to justify the Crusades and the Reconquista. Jihad is an ambivalent notion that has a larger meaning than holy war. In its original sense, it is a personal struggle and it can be used to mean various conditions, but, from the beginning and without any ambiguity, Jihad includes the notion of armed warfare.

Chronologically, the concept of jihad evolved through five distinct stages.[18] In the first stage, the time before the Hegira, references to war are indirect, while during the second stage, increasingly bellicose injunctions appear in the Quran. During the third stage (eighth and ninth centuries), which conforms to the imperial expansion of Islam, the interpretation of jihad as holy war gained traction. This is the offensive, bellicose concept of jihad favored by Muslim extremists today. If one were to compare it to Christianity, this would be the third stage (which followed pacifism and just war), the call for holy war.

The fourth period (ninth and tenth centuries), which corresponds to the stalling of Muslim expansion, opens the path to a defensive dimension of jihad aimed at fostering stability in the Muslim world and targeting potential disrupters of it, such as rebels and heretics. During this stage, however, the notion of jihad still retains its offensive character. Territorial conquest is regarded as being in abeyance until forces can be mustered to pursue it again. One could compare this stage to the second iteration of Christian attitudes to war, that of the just war doctrine developed by Ambrose and Augustine.

In the fifth stage (eleventh century), internal strife in the Muslim world led to a more personal, spiritual interpretation of jihad that encouraged an allegorical approach to the bellicose verses of the Quran, further developing the defensive aspect of jihad that had emerged during the previous period. Today, as an answer to fundamentalists, moderate Muslim intellectuals have revived this allegorical approach so as to offer an alternative that is more in tune with contemporary attitudes to violence. Although this interpretation of jihad could not qualify as pacifist, it comes closest to the attitude to war that prevailed during the first period of Christian thought on war and peace.

Mohammad b. Mansour Mubarakshah (1150–1224), an adviser to the sultan of Delhi, wrote a treatise on the *Rules of War and Bravery* in which he established a typology of wars according to their ethical values. At the top of the list, wars against infidels were deemed a religious duty. Wars of conquest pitting Muslims against one another were to be avoided or resolved through peaceful means or collective security, while wars against dissidents (Khadjarites), tax evaders, and bandits were all considered just. Unnecessary exactions were to be avoided during and after combat.[19]

In the fourteenth century, Ibn Khaldūn provided an interesting typology of wars, which he straightforwardly subdivided into two categories, just and unjust:

> Wars and different kinds of fighting have always occurred in the world since God created it. [. . .]The first (kind of war) usually occurs between neighboring tribes and competing families. The second (kind)—war caused by hostility—is usually found among savage nations living in the desert, such as the Arabs, the Turks, the Turkomans, the Kurds, and similar peoples. They earn their sustenance with their lances and their livelihood by depriving other people of their possessions. They declare war against those who defend their property against them. They have no further desire for rank and royal authority. Their minds and eyes are set only upon

depriving others of their possessions. The third is the (kind) the religious law calls "the holy war." The fourth(kind), finally, is dynastic war against seceders and those who refuse obedience. These are the four kind of wars. The first two are unjust and lawless, the other two are holy and just wars.[20]

Thus, we see that Islamic attitudes to war and peace underwent significant changes, which, much like those of Christianity, were dictated by political and geopolitical circumstances. Still, though one may disagree as to the comparative bellicosity of Christianity and Islam, the undeniable fact is that the strong pacifist impulse provided by Jesus Christ is largely absent in the Islamic tradition.

Eight verses in the Quran contain what we may describe as a "pacifist" message. Four of them were revealed before the Hegira, four when Muhammad was in Medina, where he had allied himself with Jewish communities whom he hoped to convert. In 6:106, the Prophet asks: "Do not revile the idols which they invoke besides God, lest in their ignorance they revile God with rancour."[21] And in 15:94–95: "Proclaim, then, what you are bidden and let the idolaters be. We will Ourselves sustain you against those that mock you and serve other deities besides God."[22]

Likewise, we find in verse 16:125–28 an exhortation that calls for restraint and proportionality:

Call men to the path of your Lord with wisdom and kindly exhortation. Reason with them in the most courteous manner. Your Lord best knows those who stray from His path and those who are rightly guided.

If you punish, let your punishment be commensurate with the wrong that has been done to you. But it shall be best for you to endure your wrongs with patience.

Be patient, then: God will grant you patience. Do not grieve for the unbelievers, nor distress yourself at their intrigues. God is with those who keep from evil and do good works.[23]

Regarding its attitude to war and peace, the Quran is closer in tone to the Hebrew Bible than it is to the idealism that pervades the New Testament. In consequence, Islam's attitude to politics and war is coherent and imbued with political realism. Religion and politics are intermeshed. This realism is also found in the Judaic tradition, but given the tormented history of the Jewish people, it has often taken the form there of fatalism. In contrast, Christian dualism has produced a social and political order balanced between an expedient realism and a pacifistic idealism.

The impact of the sacred texts on attitudes to war and peace was, however, molded by centuries of evolving attitudes and interpretations in social, political, and geopolitical contexts that themselves evolved significantly. The founding texts and the commentary that they produced are thus only significant for their usage at a given period and spatial context. Still, this "raw material" offers many insights as to what the general attitudes to war may have been for those who wrote these texts or who put into words the revelations they claimed to have received from supernatural sources. Many religious movements, communities, or groups have gone back to scripture to define their own attitudes to violence, war, and peace, or, sometimes, to justify their actions. Such groups have included the peaceful Quakers or Mennonites and, at the other end of the spectrum, Christian, Jewish, and Muslim extremists who have resorted to terrorism. Islam helped shape Christian Europe from the seventh century on and vice versa. David Levering Lewis underscores the crucial aspect of this "interaction," of what was and what might have been:

> At the beginning of the eighth century, the Arabs brought one of history's greatest revolutions in power, religion, culture, and wealth to Dark Ages Europe. The Arabs were to stay there until the end of the fifteenth century, and for much of that time—until roughly the beginning of the twelfth century—Islam in *al-andalus* (Muslim Spain) was generally religiously tolerant and, above all, economically robust. The Arab advance towards the Pyrenees petered out by the end of the first European century, but not, as in the lore and history of the West, because of military success. The *jihad* east of the Pyrenees eventually failed because of a revolution within the world of Islam.[24]

Lewis's is but one view of the issue, albeit the dominant one currently. But such is the importance of this topic today, when tensions between the West and the Muslim world have reached new levels, that it has generated a fierce debate among historians. When, in 2008, Sylvain Gouguenheim published a book demonstrating or claiming, depending on one's opinion on the matter, that Greek philosophy had found a direct path to European monasteries that owed nothing to Muslim transmission, this created a controversy of epic proportions among medieval scholars.[25] Some historians have also argued that the jihad tradition was all but dead until the Crusades forced Muslims to revive it under Saladin.[26]

The impact of the battle of Poitiers (732, also called the Battle of Tours and, in Arabic sources, the battle of the Palace of the Martyrs), which Lewis alludes to in the passage cited above, has itself been a long topic of debate since

FIGURE 3. *The Battle of Poitiers, 732*, oil on canvas by Carl von Steuben (1837), Musée du Château de Versailles.

Edward Gibbon, in his classic *Decline and Fall of the Roman Empire*, portrayed the victory of Charles Martel over the Saracens as a truly decisive battle and the founding myth of Christian Europe:

> A victorious line of march had been prolonged above a thousand miles from the rock of Gibraltar to the banks of the Loire; the repetition of an equal space would have carried the Saracens to the confines of Poland and the highlands of Scotland; the Rhine is not more impassable than the Nile or the Euphrates, and the Arabian fleet might have sailed without a naval combat into the mouth of the Thames. Perhaps the interpretation of the Koran would now be taught in the schools of Oxford, and her pulpits might demonstrate to a circumcised people the sanctity and truth of the Revelation of Mahomet. From such calamities was Christendom delivered by the genius and fortune of one man.[27]

This dramatic vision of Poitiers, enhanced by generations of schoolbooks, has maintained its status among the general public though academic scholarship has tended to diminish its importance.[28] In truth, too little is known about the details of this battle to arrive at a conclusive assessment of its consequences. Perceptions of its importance and impact have evolved with the changing moods of historiography, from Gibbon on, rather than because of new information on the matter.

THE MUSLIM CONQUESTS

After the conquest of Mecca, with the Arabian Peninsula now firmly under their control, the Prophet's successors turned to new conquests to the north, where, for centuries, two formidable empires had fought for supremacy in an unending cycle of wars. A brutal war between the Sassanian and Byzantine Empires had left both adversaries reeling. At the turn of the century, internal strife within the Persian Empire had pushed the legitimate heir to the throne closer to Constantinople and its able emperor, Mauritius. But after Mauritius was deposed and murdered by Phocas, the latter's weak hand led the Persian ruler Khosrow II to take his chances and attack Byzantium. Phocas was defeated and replaced by Heraclius, who had him quickly executed and proclaimed himself emperor. So as not to fight a two-pronged war against both the Persians and the Avars, who were also at the gate, Heraclius negotiated a peace with the latter, who, in exchange for a large tribute, promised to stay out of the conflict.

Under the able leadership of Heraclius, who showed great strategic savvy and formidable communication skills, the Byzantines eventually managed to save a situation that had looked all but catastrophic at the beginning of the conflict, when Persia seemed on the brink of eliminating its rival.[29]Heraclius's entry into Constantinople, witnessed by a huge crowd, was orchestrated in grand fashion, with the new emperor modestly dressed as a simple Christian doing penance. Portraying himself as the savior of Christianity, engaged in a holy war against the Zoroastrians, Heraclius went on to implement a vast structural reform of the empire, in the course of which he changed its official language from Latin to Greek.

The southern marches, where the threat would ultimately come from, had never proven to be in great danger. There, the Byzantines and Persians had traditionally maintained a status quo of sorts through their use of Arab client states, respectively the Ghassanids and the Lakhmids, which acted as strategic buffers against potential invaders from the Arabian Peninsula. In the years leading to the emergence of Islam, however, relations—on both ends—with these client states had deteriorated, and the southern frontier was not as solidly protected as it had been in the past. The Ghassanids, who had served the Byzantine Empire well and durably, had been brushed aside by Heraclius. Miffed by the fact that they had adopted Christian monophysism, a movement born out of a refusal to adopt the definition of Christ adopted at the Chalcedonian Council of 451, the emperor had decided to punish the Ghassanids by ending the payment of their annual tribute. This decision, based on ideological/religious differences rather than on a rational/strategic calculation, would come to haunt the Byzantines a few years later. Likewise, at the turn of the century, King of Kings Khosrow II had eliminated Nu'man III, the king of the Lakhmids, the Sassanians' client state (who had adopted Christian Nestorism as their religion of choice), after a dispute, thus leaving Persia's own southern frontier unprotected.

The war ended with the Sassanians in worse condition even than the Byzantines. Having looked forward to the crushing defeat of their ancestral adversary, the brutal and unexpected reversal of their expectations had been hard to swallow. The Persian Empire had not been annihilated, but its people were in a state of collective shock. Before anyone in Persia had even heard of the existence of Muhammad, the empire started to break apart at the seams.

A series of palace coups and premature deaths severely weakened the Sassanian leadership, and by the time the Muslim armies invaded Persia, the empire was in the unsteady hands of Khosrow II's grandson, Yazdegerd III. The great Persian poet of the tenth–/eleventh centuries, Ferdowsi, author of the classical epic *The Shahnameh*, famously described the sense of doom that may have hit the most perceptive souls of the day, in this case Rustam Farrokhzād, the general charged with repulsing the Muslim armies:

This house will lose all trace of sovereignty
Of royal glory, and of victory.
The sun looks down from its exalted sphere
And sees the day of our defeat draw near; [. . .]
Ahead of us lies war and endless strife,
Such that my failing heart despairs of life.
I see what has to be, and choose the way
Of silence since there is no more to say:
But for the Persians I will weep, and for
The House of Sasan ruined by this war:
Alas for their great crown and throne, for all
The royal splendor destined now to fall,

To be fragmented by the Arabs' might;
The stars decree for us defeat and flight.[30]

This realistic perception of things to come, as told by Ferdowsi centuries later, may have indeed been entertained by some keen observers of the time. But, for the most part, what we know of the events that led to the defeat of the Sassanian armies and the downfall of the Persian Empire seems to indicate that such an outcome looked improbable to most of those involved. After all, this was a centuries-old superpower that had been on the verge of subduing the formidable Byzantine Empire only a few years earlier. The idea that Persia could be decisively brought to its knees by an army of fanatical Bedouins from the desert would have been dismissed by most, if not all. And yet, in the span of a few short years, the Muslim armies did just that, defeating both the Byzantine armies of Heraclius at Yarmouk in August 636 and, shortly thereafter, those led by Rustam at Qadisiyya(636 or 637, in present-day Iraq).

It is hard to explain these surprising defeats of the two most powerful military apparatuses of the day by an army that had not even existed a few years earlier. For the most part, historians, including Pirenne, have attributed these victories to the galvanizing energy that characterized an army that fought in the name of God, combined with the weaknesses shown by opponents whose own energies had already been spent before the fighting had even begun. Both of these factors did indeed play their part, though it is difficult to assess how much relative weight they had. Most historians also tend to portray the outcomes of these confrontations as a foregone conclusion. In the West, these battles, which by any measure were as decisive as any in history, have largely fallen under the radar of military historians. Neither Yarmouk nor Qadisiyya figure in Sir Edward Creasy's immensely popular book *The Fifteen Decisive Battles of the World* (1851), nor do they appear in subsequent studies of decisive battles by General J. F. C. Fuller, B. H. Liddell Hart, or, closer to us, Victor Davis Hanson. By comparison, Poitiers/Tours, whose decisive character is more difficult to ascertain, is adequately discussed by most of these authors.

In the Muslim world, including Persia, the rendering of these events has chiefly taken the form of poetic or hagiographical recitals of one of the founding myths of Islam and the events and characters, real or fictionalized, that contributed to it. The main historical description of these early battles, by al-Ṭabarī, was written much later, at the turn of the tenth century, and served as the main source for generations of historians. These battles thus form part of the Muslim narrative that surrounds the life and mission of the Prophet and the actions of those who, after his death, inherited his mantle. The relative ease with which their armies had defeated the Byzantines and the Persians confirmed Muslims in the belief that Allah had kept his promise to Muhammad. The struggle in the name of Allah forms an integral part of the Muslim faith, which teaches that those who follow the correct religious path will meet with success in this world and heaven in the other.

EXPLAINING THE SUCCESS OF THE MUSLIM ARMIES

The moral, religious, and ideological components of war have been analyzed by strategic thinkers since the beginning of modern times. In his depiction of the French Wars of Religion, Blaise de Montluc alludes to these elements on various occasions. Raimondo Montecuccoli, the first real modern strategic thinker and himself a great general who fought the Turks, deems such intangible features to be an essential part of war, as do Antoine-Henri Jomini, Carl von Clausewitz, and Charles Ardant du Picq. The fourteenth-century Tunisian historian Ibn Khaldūn makes group cohesion a core element of his cyclical philosophy of history, itself based on the eight centuries or so of Muslim history that separated him from Muhammad. All point to the fact that there are vast differences in resulting behaviors between, on the one hand, the religious fanaticism that may push individuals to commit to a cause and, indeed, to want to give their lives for it, and, on the other hand, the morale that gives an army or a military unit the will to fight and the cohesion to do so effectively. It is well known, for instance, that mercenary armies for the most part lack this element, though citizen armies often possess it. Thus, while religious fanaticism or a strong religious attachment to one's faith or ideology may indeed boost the morale of an army, there are also other motivating elements. National, regional, or ethnic ties may, for example, produce the same results. In other words, the fanaticism or religious drive displayed by the Muslim armies is insufficient in and of itself to explain how these armies that came out of nowhere conquered half the known world in the span of a few decades.

Muslim armies were not always victorious. Alexandria, which was taken by the Arabs from the Byzantines in 641, for example, was retaken by the latter in 645. Before the first decisive victory against the Byzantines, the Muslims failed on several occasions to stop Heraclius's troops, though they themselves were never defeated outright in these confrontations. Also, when the internal divisions that would lead to the emergence of Sunnis, Shiites, and

Kharidjites started to undermine the nascent Muslim empire, it lost some of its momentum.

Much like the Mongol armies of the thirteenth century, the troops that formed the core of the Muslim armies were initially nomads well versed in war. Though the Bedouins came from the desert rather than the steppes, they shared many traits with their brethren from Central Asia: formidable riding skills (on horse *and* camel), endurance, capability to withstand hardship, exceptional hunting skills, great group cohesion, and unfettered loyalty to their group.

The Arabs possessed two characteristics that the Mongols never really enjoyed: a superior purpose founded on their religion and administrative/ organizational know-how derived from a society that also had an urban commercial tradition. The Prophet Muhammad himself was an effective preacher, general, military organizer, and political leader. The Bedouins, who until then had been divided into tribes fighting one another, could now direct their loyalties to one man and one group. Steered by able generals, strategists, and logisticians, this combined force coalesced around a common purpose and a common God. The only element missing was the experience of having fought together in much larger units against foes they might not yet have encountered. The Arab army was, however, growing steadily and incorporating more experienced elements, notably Ghassanid and Lakhmid troops, both of which embraced the opportunity to join the Muslims in fighting their former allies. Skirmishes against the Byzantine and Persian troops allowed the new army to familiarize itself before the decisive confrontations. The momentum initially generated by Muhammad kept growing, fueled by the size and quality of the Muslim forces and by the victories they won.

IBN KHALDŪN ON THE SUPERIORITY OF THE MUSLIM ARMIES

Outside of China, Ibn Khaldūn was probably the keenest observer of history to emerge since antiquity. One of the fundamental questions he sought to answer related to the formidable, and improbable, success enjoyed by the early Muslim armies. Ibn Khaldūn was not a theologian, nor was he encumbered by theological explanations. In fact, one could consider him to be the very first social scientist in the modern sense of the term. His intellectual method and his analyses thus have a particular resonance that speaks to our modern minds. He attributed the Muslim armies' success to a combination of two factors, one social, the other spiritual, both tied to the idea of sovereignty and power (al-Mulk).

In a nut shell, Ibn Khaldūn posits power as the main currency of politics and political relations. Power is the basis of sovereignty, which itself lies on the concept of 'asabiyya, a term that is difficult to translate in English but whose closest approximation might be "group feeling." The 'asabiyya thus presupposes a society that is based, not on isolated individuals, but on blood communities that define themselves in relation to others in an us versus them vision of intersocial relationships. With the appearance of religion, the 'asabiyya enters a new dimension, with the development of a religious union, al-ijtimā 'al-dīnī, which gives superior purpose to the us versus them proposition. With religion, the nascent communities of purpose now cooperate and fight together for "true" objectives that transcend the narrow vision that was theirs before they adhered to Islam. Now enlightened, the religious communities can come together and fight in unison for superior ("true") objectives for which they are ready to sacrifice their lives. But in order for this to happen, the religious communities must rely in the beginning on the blood ties that bound the original communities together. It is only later that they may dispose of these. In short, then, the success of Islam, historically, is predicated on the 'asabiyya displayed by the original Muslim communities.[31]

A pragmatist, Ibn Khaldūn also attributed the early successes of the Muslim armies to what he called "hidden factors," such as trickery, propaganda, and disinformation, which, in his view, played a greater role than the "external factors," such as the size of the armies, the troop formations, or the quality of the weapons. These hidden factors then "affect people psychologically, and thus generate fear in them," which causes "confusion in the centers of armies," leading to routs, which "very often are the result of hidden causes, because both parties make much use of (the opportunities offered by) them in their desire for victory." In conclusion,

> It is thus clear that superiority in war is, as a rule, the result of hidden causes, not of external ones. The occurrence of opportunities as the result of hidden causes is what is meant by the word "luck". This explains Muhammad's victory with small numbers over the polytheists during his lifetime, and the victories of the Muslims during the Muslim conquests after Muhammad's death. Terror in the hearts of their enemies was why there were so many routs during the Muslim conquests, but it was a factor concealed from men's eyes.[32]

By the time Ibn Khaldūn was sharing his thoughts on these events, the Muslim world had established a strong tradition in matters of strategic and tactical deception or "trickery." The thirteenth-century anonymous treatise on ruses, the voluminous and extensive *Raqā'iq al-hilal fi Daqāiq al-hiyal*,[33] bears testimony to this practice, one that was frowned upon by Westerners attached, at least in theory, to a direct approach to war. In the seventh century, however, both the Byzantines and the Persians practiced indirect tactics, especially the latter, whose experience in these matters greatly influenced the Muslim techniques that Ibn Khaldūn believed had given them the initial advantage. His thoughts on the effect religion can have on a nascent society, however, seem more in tune with what we know of the early Muslim conquests:

> Religious propaganda gives a dynasty at its beginning another power in addition to that of the group feeling it possessed as the result of the number of its supporters. As we have mentioned before, the reason for this is that religious colouring does away with mutual jealousy and envy among people who share in a group feeling, and causes concentration upon the truth. When people come to have the (right) insight into their affairs, nothing can withstand them, because their outlook is one and their object one of common accord. They are willing to die for (their objectives).[34]

The adversary, inasmuch as he is not guided by such higher purposes, is not as motivated and his troops might be afraid of death. In consequence, such adversaries

> do not offer resistance to (the people with a religious coloring), even if they them-selves are more numerous. They are overpowered by them and quickly wiped out, as a result of the luxury and humbleness existing among them. [. . .] This happened to the Arabs at the beginning of Islam during the Muslim conquests. The armies of the Muslims at al-Qādisīyah and at the Yarmūk numbered some 30,000 in each case, while the Persian troops at al-Qādisīyah numbered 120,000, and the troops of Heraclius, according to al-Wāqidī, 400,000. Neither of the two parties was able to withstand the Arabs, who routed them and seized what they possessed.[35]

Although love of luxury and coyness are not attributes that come to mind when describing Heraclius, one point that Ibn Khaldūn alludes to is well taken: the greater cohesiveness of the Arab troops. The Byzantines and the Persians both had to make do with heterogeneous imperial armies. Such was the social and ethnic structure of their empires that they could not levy armies of committed citizen soldiers the way the Romans had done. Still, even though these armies suffered from the same problems that invariably affect these types of military outfits, they still managed to hold their own against a variety of adversaries, including the redoubtable armies of nomadic archer-horsemen. These formidable armies from Central Asia and the Iranian plateau did not venture west for a particular purpose, however, other than being forced to emigrate by other nomadic armies. Under these circumstances, having their backs to the wall, they were more inclined to negotiate some kind of territorial deal with the established powers. These agreements often involved some sort of participation in the wars that opposed the Byzantines and the Persians, or as allies against other menaces from the Central Asian steppes. More important, they could be bought, and more often than not, they were. Tributes were part of the diplomatic arsenal of the two superpowers and were an effective instrument, at least as long as the imperial treasury was equal to the task. During times of war, the financial strain was great.

The Muslim armies, on the other hand, had a higher purpose and, therefore, could not be bought. Their objective was to conquer, and they were uncompromising. The only way to stop them was to defeat them, the only way to stop them permanently was to annihilate them. Thus, while they displayed the same qualities as other nomadic armies, they did not have the same diplomatic flexibility. In the long history of nomadic armies, only the Mongols attained a motivation similar to that of the first Muslim armies with Genghis Khan's grand design of creating a universal empire. But this grand design was irrevocably attached to one individual, and, upon his death, the purpose was lost. After a couple of generations, the Mongol Empire disintegrated, and it was all but gone within a century. By contrast, Muhammad tied his grand design not to an individual but to God, His Prophet, and a religion, thus ensuring a perennial energy to the enterprise, something the Mongolians were never able to generate.

At base, the desert Bedouins displayed very similar qualities to the steppe warriors, which compared favorably to those, or the lack thereof, of sedentary people: "They have no walls or gates. Therefore, they provide their own defence and do not entrust to, or rely upon others for it. [. . .] They go alone in the desert, guided by their fortitude, putting their trust in themselves. Fortitude has become a character quality of theirs, and courage their nature."[36] These qualities however, have a downside in that they rarely predispose those who display them to seek unification, cooperation, or subordination. So how may one harness this fantastic disposition? For Ibn Khaldūn, there was only one answer:

> Because of their savagery, the Bedouins are the least willing of nations to subordinate themselves to each other, as they are rude, proud, ambitious, and eager to be the leaders. Their individual aspirations rarely coincide. But when there is

religion (among them), through prophethood or sainthood, then they have some restraining influence on themselves. The qualities of haughtiness and jealousy leave them. It is, then, easy for them to subordinate themselves and to unite (as a social organization). This is achieved by the common religion they now have [Islam]. It causes rudeness and pride to disappear and exercises a restraining influence on their mutual envy and jealousy. When there is a prophet or saint among them, who calls upon them to fulfill the commands of God, rids them of blameworthy qualities, and causes them to adopt praiseworthy ones, and who prompts them to concentrate all their strength in order to make the truth prevail, they become fully united and acquire superiority and royal authority.[37]

THE BATTLES OF YARMOUK AND QADISIYYA

The modalities of Muhammad's political succession had not been firmly established by the Prophet, but it went fairly smoothly. It was only a few years later that one of the pretenders to the throne, his son-in-law Ali, launched an all-out attack to claim his due. For the time being, at a crucial point when the Bedouin alliance was threatening to break up after the disappearance of the Prophet, the smooth succession would provide the needed political stability. This would be ensured by the two men who became the first caliphs, Abu Bakr and Omar, both of them in-laws of the prophet and both laying claim to be among his earliest companions. Their strategy was in line with Muhammad's: consolidate the Muslims' hold on the Arabian Peninsula and launch raids against the Byzantines and the Sassanians.

Muhammad himself had organized an ambitious expedition against the Byzantines in 630, but it had only got as far as the outskirts of Arabia. At that point, such raids only formed a small part of Muslim strategy and were originally motivated by the desire to maintain religious unity and propagate the faith. At this stage, there was no great geostrategic grand design, or at least no formal one. The first caliphs seem to have been improvising their course of action without a predetermined plan, following the wave of events that they themselves were provoking without always anticipating the consequences. In any case, the string of improbable Muslim successes further convinced them all that God was on their side.

After successful raids into Mesopotamia (Iraq), Abu Bakr had entrusted Khālid ibn al-Walīd with making war on Heraclius, whose health had been impaired by the long war against the Sassanians. From Homs, Heraclius had entrusted his brother Theodore with leading the Byzantine forces. The Arabs had sent an army directly from Medina, which Khālid was to join with his own troops coming from Mesopotamia. On both sides, changes were made at the top, the Byzantine army finally being led in the field by an Armenian general, Vahan, while Khālid, who at one point had been relieved of his command by the new caliph, Omar, was reinstated.

For months, both armies delayed the engagement in order to levy as many troops as possible. Through Vahan, Heraclius attempted to buy peace from the Arabs, but to no avail. As the Muslim armies were advancing, many of the non-Orthodox Christian communities that felt the strain of Byzantine rule decided to join forces with the Arabs, some opting to convert to Islam. "The inexorable driving force, therefore, behind the Islamic conquests of Syria, Anatolia, North Africa and Spain, could be said to have been conversion," Franco Cardini suggests.[38] Indeed, after retaking Jerusalem from the Persians in 629, Heraclius had decreed that Jews and Samaritans be forced to convert to Christianity. Islam, contrary to Christianity, did not place anyone under such an obligation. The West, familiar as it is with the forced conversions that characterized many episodes of its history, has often overlooked the fact that Islam has gained converts by attraction or persuasion rather than by coercion.

The inevitable confrontation took place in mid-August of the year 636. Facing 15,000 to 30,000 Muslim troops, Vahan possibly had 50,000 soldiers at his disposal but probably not more than that. As with most battles, the exact numbers are unknown and difficult to determine. With superior numbers, Vahan had the confidence to project the mass of his infantry against the Arab center. Khālid ibn al-Walīd hoped to wear down the adversary to the point where he might be able to launch a decisive counteroffensive. Considering his numerical inferiority, the Arab general knew that he might not have more than one opportunity to counterattack. Before the battle, according to al-Tabarī, Khālid ibn al-Walīd had someone read verses from the Quran and requested that those who had been companions of the Prophet break rank for all others to identify them and be inspired. Addressing Allah, Khālid then pointed to these men who "had helped establish the religion in his name," implying that all those present would do the same by defeating the enemy.

Unlike most pitched battles of the day, this one would last more than a few hours; it was an agonizing confrontation that would prolong itself for several days, probably six altogether. The first couple of days saw skirmishes. On the third day, Vahan decided that he had waited long enough, and that a massive attack was in order. The Arab army took the blow, but at one point it seemed on the verge of breaking apart. From there on, we have several versions of the battle. According to a firmly established belief, the Muslim women castigated their fleeing sons and husbands, now ready to accept defeat, and forced them back into the fighting. One rendering of the event holds that a propitious desert storm favorable to the Arabs blinded the Byzantines and paved the way to victory. More realistically, Khālid intelligently bided his time and waited for the right moment to organize his counteroffensive, which may have been set in motion on the fourth or on the sixth day. In any case, Vahan launched a second offensive on the fourth day, committing all his troops in the process. Still, victory eluded him. It is possible that on the fifth day, Vahan unsuccessfully tried to negotiate with Khālid, and that he made a last ditch effort to overrun the Muslims on the sixth day. Whatever the case may be, his forces were spent. At one point, Khālid noticed that the Byzantine cavalry (which included Arab mercenary troops) had detached itself from the main corps. This was the moment he had been waiting for. With lightning speed, he attacked the exposed left flank of the enemy. With its lines of communication cut, the Byzantine army collapsed, unable to resist the onslaught, and disintegrated. Various legends surround the events, few of them substantiated by hard evidence. In the West, for example, it was fashionable to attribute the defeat to the idea that the Arab troops fighting with the Byzantines had been persuaded by Khālid to change sides during the battle. In the Muslim world, the victory has long been attributed to divine meteorological intervention.

From what we can gather from the few details at hand, however, it is more probable that the battle was decided by the superior leadership of Khālid ibn al-Walīd, who strategically and tactically outwitted his adversary. The strength and resolve of his troops enabled him to achieve this while overcoming the handicap of having inferior numbers at his disposal. From this point on, intelligence in battle would constitute the core element of the emerging Muslim culture of war, in contrast to the Christian ideals of chivalry and bravery. In time, Muslim armies would develop military strategies based using any available means to defeat the enemy regardless of moral restraints, no holds being barred in a war undertaken in the name of God. The heavy emphasis on cunning rather than brute force meant that Muslim strategic culture tended to produce conflicts that resembled a large-scale game of chess.[39]

In contrast, the strategic culture of the West, based as it was on the Germanic Christian ethos, has consistently—to this day—followed the model of the duel that determined which of the two adversaries was the most worthy in the sight of God. Hence, it tended to produce a strategy based on direct confrontations where force, technique, courage, and endurance played a bigger part than intelligence, and where the ritual of battle was often as important as military expediency. Over centuries, this emphasis on brute force produced an almost fetishistic attitude that favored the constant development of new, more sophisticated and destructive weapons. Ibn Khaldūn had noticed a fundamental dichotomy between what he described as Arabic and non-Arabic approaches to war: "Since the beginning of men's existence, war has been waged in the world in two ways. One is by advance in closed formation. The other is the technique of attack and withdrawal. The advance in closed formation has been the technique of all non-Arabs throughout their existence. The technique of attack and withdrawal has been that of the Arabs and the Berbers of the Maghrib."[40]

The Byzantines could not prevent the Arab armies from profiting from the momentum they had generated with this formidable victory. From then on, the Muslims were able to make inroads into the regions around the Mediterranean. After taking Egypt, a major economic breadbasket, the road was open for the conquest of North Africa and, from there, the Iberian Peninsula. On the Western front, the Muslims would march beyond the Pyrenees toward southern France, where they were able to take hold for a time, and then, toward Poitiers, where they were stopped by Charles Martel. After being definitively pushed back behind the Pyrenees a few years later (Pepin's victory at Narbonne in 759 dealt the final blow), they would settle durably in Spain and Portugal before gradually losing ground over several centuries, until their final expulsion from the Iberian Peninsula in 1492/97. Geopolitically, the takeover of a good portion of the Mediterranean coast constituted a formidable rupture with the past, and it completely transformed the geostrategic dynamic around the Mediterranean Sea. The consequences of these conquests have divided generations of historians, who disagree as to the depth of this separation of the region into two separate entities. Though the disagreements over the issue will never be settled definitively, no one will deny that the Muslim conquests in the west constituted a break with the past, when the Mediterranean world had functioned as a single entity.

For the Byzantine Empire, the defeat at Yarmouk was the dawn of a new era, marked essentially by a defensive strategy dictated by necessity, toward which it adapted remarkably well. The empire fully embraced its Christian identity, while its Roman heritage inevitably eroded. But rarely would the

Byzantines seek a true rapprochement with the other Christians in Europe, preferring instead to play on political alliances and rivalries in order to survive, regardless of the religious identity of the other players with whom they were forced to interact. Although the religious card would become an important factor in the international relations of the region (the Armenians, for instance, were also Christian and often allied themselves with the Orthodox Byzantines), it would never predominate over all the other elements at play. In fact, the Byzantines would suffer as much at the hands of other Christians as at those of the Muslims.

On a symbolic plane, the defeat at Yarmouk proved equally damaging to the spirit of the Byzantines. After losing Jerusalem to the Sassanians in 614, along with the True Cross, which had been carried away to Ctesiphon, the Persian capital, by King of Kings Khosrow II, Heraclius had triumphantly returned to the holy city fifteen years later, walking barefoot into Jerusalem carrying the Cross, which he had retrieved from his enemy. Now, less than ten years after this dramatic moment, in 638, Jerusalem was falling into the hands of Caliph Omar, who also staged his entry by penetrating into the city riding an old camel and dressed in a simple desert garb, giving assurances to the local religious authorities that the peoples of the Book would be respected and protected.

From then on, for Muslims, Jerusalem would become the third Holy City, after Mecca and Medina. For Christians, the reclaiming of the city and retrieval of the True Cross would, with time, become the focal point of the crusading movement that would take hold in the eleventh century. The defeat of the mighty Byzantine Empire at Yarmouk was, in and of itself, a remarkable event. More remarkable still was the fact that the Muslim armies were able, almost simultaneously, to claim another victory against Persia.

Like the Byzantines, and for the same reasons, the Persians had been weakened by years of war. But, unlike their rivals, who had remained under the steady leadership of Heraclius, the Persians were now nominally under the authority of a boy. What's more, all the political intrigues that had plagued the Persian leadership following Khosrow II's reign and downfall had not contributed in the least to strengthening the government and the military apparatus. Nonetheless, the depth of the Persian Empire had enabled it to reclaim the territories briefly acquired by the Muslim armies in Mesopotamia. Based on this alone, the Persians were confident that they could repulse the Arabs. They did not realize that the fate of the Sassanian dynasty was hanging in the balance.

Much as at Yarmouk, the Arabs were once again in a position of numerical inferiority. Although the numbers given by al-Ṭabarī, our main source for this battle, are probably not accurate (12,000 and 120,000 troops respectively), one can surmise that the Muslims may have gathered about 30,000 soldiers and the Persians perhaps two or three times that number.

We do not really know when the battle of Qadisiyya was fought, but it was probably in November 636, only a few weeks after Yarmouk; perhaps before that.[41] The Muslim army was in the able hands of Saʿd ibn Abī Waqqās, one of the earliest companions of the Prophet. Although the army included men who had fought at Yarmouk, this was a different outfit. On both sides, the infantry made up the bulk of the troops and included a good number of foot archers. While, as usual, the Arabs traveled with their camels, the Persians brought about thirty war elephants to the battle, a choice that indicated that the Sassanians were likely to employ shock tactics.

Overall, this battle proved more intense even than Yarmouk. The fighting spread once again over several days and, even at night, its intensity never seemed to abate. Consequently, this came to be a battle of attrition that saw many men perish each day. The presence of the elephants, the strong desert winds, and the untimely death of the muezzin all contributed to the legend of the battle. Much like the Byzantines, the Persians attempted to overrun the Arabs with a concentrated attack on their center. But, again, the Arab troops were formidably resilient, and they were able to withstand attack after attack. Dealing with the elephants proved difficult, and initially their presence made a huge impression, effectively paralyzing their adversary and scaring off the horses, which contributed to the Muslim infantry finding itself exposed. On the third day, the Persian commander, Rustam Farrokhzād, decided to launch a massive attack, and he placed all the elephants at the center of the Persian formation, a decision that proved counterproductive, since it disrupted the advance of his infantry. By that time, the Arabs had come up with a new technique to neutralize the beasts: archers would attempt to fire an arrow into one of the elephant's eyes while another soldier would try to get under its belly and puncture its stomach with a sword. The technique effectively worked on the first two elephants targeted, which had the effect of releasing the Muslim troops, who now fought with renewed confidence.

As darkness enveloped the theater, the battle continued unabated and by the next morning, the two armies had reached complete exhaustion. At this crucial point, Saʿd ibn Abī Waqqās managed to persuade his shattered troops to rise for one more go. This proved too much for the Persians and, with the death of Rustam during the attack, their entire force fell apart. A strong sandstorm, with winds favorable to their adversary, may have helped to seal their fate. Unlike Yarmuk, where superior command had decided the outcome of the battle, this day belonged to the Muslim soldiers, who had shown more spirit and resolve than the enemy. After Qadisiyya, the Muslim armies retook Mesopotamia, this time for good, and marched into Persia, which fell definitively after a final military confrontation, in 642, at Nahāvand.

From there on, the expansion of the Arabs was dazzling. Much like Alexander the Great they managed to grab vast regions that already benefited from efficient administrative and economic structures. Both the Byzantine and the Sassanian Empires comprised diverse ethnic, linguistic, and religious communities, which were, for the most part, not too bothered to see the authority change hands. The Quran said little about how the vanquished should be treated, and Muhammad's own example provided contradictory guidance. He had expelled (or worse) the Jews from Medina, but elsewhere had accorded protected (dhimmi) status to those belonging to religions of the Book (Jews and Christians), as well as to Zoroastrians, Mandaeans and Sabians.

The initial push of the Muslim armies lasted a full century, after which the contours of the Muslim world were more or less set. While the first generation of Muslims was almost exclusively Arab, the Muslim world soon embraced diversity even if, initially, the statute of non-Arab Muslims (mawālī) was itself a bit murky. In fact, the first converts often became clients of Arab aristocrats and thus made do with a secondary status not in line with the equality that theoretically characterized the Muslim community.

Shortly after the defeat of the Byzantines and Persians, the Muslim community plunged into civil war (656–61) over the succession of the caliphate, which would have a formidable impact on the future of the religion and the community. Since Muhammad had not given clear instructions relative to his succession, the issue was bound to erupt at some point or another, which it did in 656, by which time the Muslim troops had already marched through Libya, Armenia, and Azerbaijan, getting as far as Khorasan, northeast of Persia.

The brewing struggle came to a head not in Mecca or Medina but in Mesopotamia, where Muhammad's son-in-law Ali had established his capital at Koufa. After the assassination of Uthman ibn Affan, the third caliph, Ali had proclaimed himself caliph. but the events that had led to his accession to power had severely weakened his claim to be the legitimate leader of the whole community of the Muslims (*umma*). After moving to Koufa, he was challenged by his former allies, including Aisha bint Abu Bakr, one of Muhammad's widows, who came to Mesopotamia with an army ready to topple him. But Ali proved stronger, and he claimed victory in the so-called battle of the Camel at Bassora (Basra, Iraq). Still, this military success did not rally the community behind him. Egypt and Arabia stayed put while Mu'āwiyah ibn Abī Sufyān, the governor of Syria and a relative of Uthman, challenged his authority. After a protracted struggle, Ali finally won the day, on July 26, 656, and a truce was signed that called for a future arbitration. Nevertheless, Ali's position remained tenuous and a dissident group, the Kharidjites, decided to break away. The arbitration, rendered in 658, found Ali guilty of the murder of Uthman. This led to a backlash against the Kharidjites (659), which in turn pushed Mu'āwiyah to claim the title of caliph (660). Finally, in 661, Ali was murdered by a Kharidjite just as he was about to embark on a war against Mu'āwiyah.

In the span of half a decade, the Civil War had provoked the emergence of two major dissident groups, the Kharidjites and the Shiites, with the latter being formed, after Ali's death, by his partisans. Muhammad's vision of a united and indivisible *umma* was forever shattered. Now fragmented politically, spiritually, and theologically, the Muslim community would never again be reunited under the same banner, despite the efforts of such formidable individuals as Saladin, the twelfth-century sultan of Egypt and Syria; the Mamluk sultan of Egypt Baibars in the thirteenth century; and the eighteenth-century Persian ruler Nader Shah, who would attempt to federate the Muslims through the power generated by their military genius and by their conquests.

Once rid of Ali, Mu'āwiyah quickly took to the task of putting the pieces back together. He moved the government, this time to Damascus, and gave it renewed authority relative to the provinces, while consolidating his ties with the Arab nations. In order to infuse some stability to the edifice, he proclaimed a new dynasty, called the Umayyads, complete with a hereditary transfer of power. All these provisions, however, did not prevent a second civil war from erupting upon his death, before order was reestablished by Caliph Abd al-Malik, who reorganized the government and overhauled the tax collection system, allowing territorial conquests to resume. From there, at the turn of the eighth century, the Muslims pushed forward once again, this time all the way to Central Asia, taking Bukhara and Samarkand, and moving to

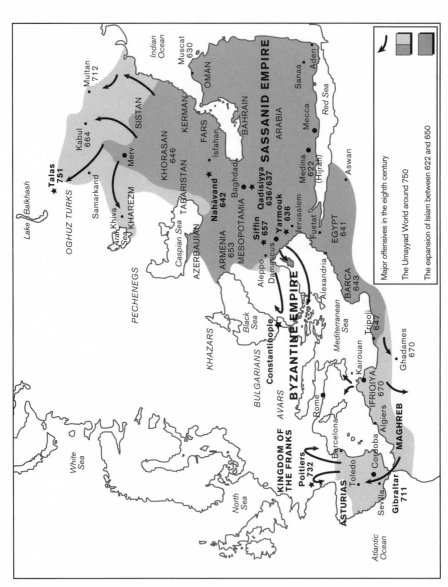

MAP 2. The expansion of Islam in the seventh and eighth centuries

Balochistan and the Indus region in 711 and to the Punjab in 713. By this time, they had managed to tame the redoubtable Berber tribes of North Africa and had passed through the straights of Gibraltar and moved into Spain. By 716, they also threatened Constantinople, establishing a siege that would last more than a year. The limits of their expansion were reached in the west with the Muslim defeat at Poitiers and twenty years later at Talas in Transoxiana (751), with an unexploited victory over a Chinese army. This period of expansion saw the building of a fleet, expanded commercial activity, the spread of Arabic as the official language of Islam, and substantial urbanization, which produced a flowering of the arts.

The Umayyad caliphate lasted less than a century, and in 750, it was supplanted by the Abbasids, who elected to rule from Baghdad. In this second phase of its history, Islam ceased to expand but, under the influence of a resurgent Persian culture, it entered its Golden Age, epitomized by the rule of Caliph Hārūn al-Rashīd (763–809) and the tales of the *Arabian Nights*. A Persian dynasty seized Baghdad in 945, and the Seljuk Turks would do so in 1055, but the Abbasid caliphs retained their religious authority there until the apocalyptic sack of the city in 1258 by the Mongols under Hulagu Khan. The Abbasid caliphate was subsequently reestablished in Egypt by the Mamluks, where it survived until the sixteenth century, although its political power was a thing of the past, and its function was largely ceremonial.

When another Muslim empire emerged in the eleventh century, the reunification of Islam was undertaken not by Arabs but by Turks from Central Asia. Tugril Bey (990–1063), a grandson of an Oghuz Turkic warlord named Seljuk, founded what became known as the Great Seljuk Empire, becoming the first of a long series of Turkic sultans and caliphs, many of whom displayed a bellicosity worthy of the Arab commanders of the seventh and eighth centuries.

Toward a Clash of Civilizations

The LORD is a man of war.

—Exodus 15:3

The history of Europe between the seventh century and the turn of the ninth witnessed the radical evolution of a continent that, since the fall of the Western Roman Empire, had moved away from deconstruction and toward reconstruction. The will to reunify the core of western Europe under Frankish rule was accompanied and, indeed, motivated by Clovis's understanding that religion would play an important part in this political renaissance and the forging of a new identity. This process predated the emergence and rise of Islam, at a point in time when western Europe and the Roman Empire of the East (Byzantium) were moving in separate, albeit in some ways parallel, directions. So, how did this new situation affect Europe?

To answer this question, or at least attempt to do so, we cannot avoid the Pirenne thesis alluded to earlier, which revolves around what Pirenne saw as the main driver of the evolution of Europe during the centuries leading up to the coronation of Charlemagne in 800.

Pirenne starts with one premise, upon which the second one is predicated. His first assertion is that the German invasions did not put an end to the Mediterranean unity that defined antiquity, which meant that after the fall of the last Roman emperor, European society retained the essential characteristics of the classical Graeco-Roman culture. Starting from there, Pirenne presented an argument that historians have had to grapple with ever since:

> The cause of the break with the traditions of antiquity was the rapid and unexpected advance of Islam. The result of this advance was the final separation of East from West, and the end of the Mediterranean unity. Countries like Africa and

Spain, which had always been part of the Western community, gravitated henceforth in the orbit of Baghdad. In these countries another religion made its appearance, and an entirely different culture. The Western Mediterranean, having become a Musulman lake, was no longer the thoroughfare of commerce and of thought which it had always been.

The West was blockaded and forced to live upon its own resources. For the first time in history the axis of life was shifted northwards from the Mediterranean. The decadence into which the Merovingian dynasty lapsed as a result of this change gave birth to a new dynasty, the Carolingian, whose original home was the Germanic North.

With this new dynasty the Pope allied himself, breaking with the Emperor, who, engrossed in his struggle against the Musulmans, could no longer protect him. And so the Church allied itself with the new order of things. In Rome, and in the Empire which it founded, it had no rival. And its power was all the greater inasmuch as the State, being incapable of maintaining its administration, allowed itself to be absorbed by the feudality, the inevitable sequel of the economic regression. [. . .] This development was completed in 800 by the constitution of the new Empire, which consecrated the break between the West and the East, inasmuch as it gave to the West a new Roman Empire—the manifest proof that it had broken with the old Empire, which continued to exist in Constantinople.[1]

There, according to Pirenne, is where the Middle Ages begin, following a century-long evolution, from 650 to 750, that coincides with the expansionary push of Islam. It is during this period that the "anarchy of the antique world is lost," and when the bedrock of a brave new world is firmly laid down.

Since its inception, the Pirenne thesis has been partially debunked, mainly because the facts provided by Pirenne to back his theory have proven somewhat tenuous. His idea that commercial ties were essentially severed, for example, has been shown to be exaggerated. Regarding the thesis itself, however, much points to the drifting of two worlds that evolved separately and then came back together to clash in a big way. By this time, their respective religious identities were clearly defined. That Pirenne's motives behind his thesis were founded upon a racial or even racist interpretation of European history is difficult to prove, though this is what he has been accused of by some contemporary historians.[2] There has appeared of late a countervision of a diverse, multicultural world, where private or public relationships between Europeans and Muslims were much richer than previously thought. This vision essentially caters to the spirit of the time (our time), much as Gibbon's or Pirenne's catered to theirs (Gibbon died in 1794, Pirenne in 1935). It reflects a liberal social and political outlook that emanates from the moral values upheld by democracy and humanism, which tend to condemn power politics and the use of force, while promoting the idea that rational human beings are, more often than not, likely to cooperate with one another. Viewed from this angle, there is no "supposed incompatibility of Christianity Judaism, and Islam, nor an allegedly 'timeless' struggle between East and West," that is, between "a protocolonial Europe" and an "introverted Islamic Middle East."[3] In consequence, the unity of the Mediterranean reappears, as does its historical continuity, and the vision of clash of civilization evaporates.

Evidently, the idea of a "clash of civilizations" now carries a heavy intellectual baggage since it was reformulated as a paradigm for the new world order that purportedly came about with the end of the Cold War in the early 1990s. Notwithstanding this controversial—and in my opinion, largely flawed, or at least grossly exaggerated—interpretation of contemporary history, can we characterize the Mediterranean world of the Middle Ages as a clash between two faith-driven civilizations?

The answer, in a nutshell, is yes . . . and no. Yes, because religion was the driving force that was to shape geopolitical relations around the Mediterranean for centuries, all the way to the sixteenth century. No, because neither the Christian nor the Muslim world ever acted, save for very short periods of time, as a unitary entity. The Muslim world was divided almost from the start by the deep divisions between Shiites and Sunnis (and the minority Kharidjites) and even within the Sunni community, it was often politically fragmented. Christians were also divided from the start between the Orthodox Roman Empire of the East and the emerging Catholic Europe that entertained the ideal of recreating a new Roman Empire under the banner of the Catholic Church. For all of these, the creation and development of a powerful empire was thus the ideal toward which they strove. The Byzantines sought to recuperate the power that had been theirs during the Golden Age of Justinian; the Frankish kings sought to revive the great Roman Empire; orthodox Muslims sought to uphold the Muhammadan ideal of a vast empire that would place the "community of the faithful" under one umbrella; and the Shiites sought to create a power base for themselves capable of challenging the Sunnis.

Established empires are peace seekers in that they strive for stability within their borders. Inversely, they are jealous of their territorial integrity and naturally aggressive against their neighbors. Often, to avoid potentially destabilizing internal unrest and violence, they externalize the natural propensity for aggression deriving from the military ethos of their initial conquests. With so many empires or imperial pretenders now occupying the space around the Mediterranean, it was only natural that they would come to clash with one another, just as the Cathaginians and the Romans, and the Greeks/Macedonians/Byzantines and the Persians, had done in the past. Only now, rather than on the ethnic or linguistic makeup of a ruling elite, the imperial quest was founded on a religious platform that made everyone a part of the imperial project. These societies were subdivided by rigid class hierarchies that invariably saw an aristocratic elite wield power over its people (Franks, Arabs, Turks). But under God, all were equals among equals. Religion thus became the single most potent element that drew peoples together, and the one for which all were willing to risk their lives. In Europe, the old regional ties that still bound people to their communities (Catalans, Basques, Bretons, and Scots) were gradually assimilated into greater national entities through their identification with a single religion.

In the Muslim world, following a reverse process, foreign invaders from Central Asia were quickly absorbed through their adherence to the Islamic faith, while their military skills were put to use against Muslim rivals and non-Muslim enemies. Confucian China used the same technique, absorbing Mongols and Manchus, who were overcome by the cultural attraction. While the Chinese example testifies to the fact that religion, at least "traditional" religion, is not indispensable to absorbing foreign invaders, it also shows that a strong system of values, an efficient bureaucracy, and social cohesiveness are probably necessary. By the same token, the invading peoples who were absorbed all lacked formal ties with another religion. The Mongols remained pagans to the last, while the various Turkic nations were either pagan or early converts to Islam (with the exception of the Jewish Khazars, whose conversion to Judaism remains shrouded in mystery).[4] But Persia is the most interesting case of all. That such a country with a strong religious makeup might have been absorbed so easily is perhaps accounted for by the fact that Zoroastrianism was ultimately a religion for the ruling elite, which did not trickle down to the masses that composed this vast empire, especially after this elite was obliterated.

In Europe, and more specifically in the Iberian Peninsula, in what is now Spain and Portugal, Catholicism became the rallying point of the resistance. The only other instance of such fierce opposition to the Muslim onslaught was found in North Africa among the Berber tribes that lived in the mountainous regions of the Maghreb. Mountain people everywhere are notorious for their capacity to resist invaders. Berbers were no exception, and they managed to retain a degree of autonomy that few other people enjoyed anywhere in the Muslim world though they did, in the end, convert, at times with fanatical zeal.

The clash of civilizations that broke out at the very end of the eleventh century was slow in coming. Aside from the Iberian Peninsula, where Christians, Muslims, and Jews were in direct contact with one another, mutual contacts between Muslims and Christians were sparse, at least from what we can gather from the texts written at the time. This, of course, did not include the Byzantines and the Armenians, and various sources emanating from them paint Islam and Muslims in a dim light. Some of these descriptions, like those of Sophronius, the patriarch of Jerusalem at the time of the Muslim conquests, reached the pope in Rome. In the eighth century, John of Damascus's depiction of Muhammad as a false prophet and a heretic surely made an impression,[5] as did others, like Maximus the Confessor's seventh-century diatribe, *A Discourse of Defamation against the Sorceries Invented by the Vile Dog Mohammed*. What little knowledge Europeans had of Muslims came chiefly from their encounters with the invaders of France in the eighth century.

For the most part, then, Muslims were perceived as another pagan people, akin to the various peoples that had ransacked Europe. The names used to describe them, the most common being "Saracen," were taken from the Old Testament and did not include any reference to Islam, as is evidenced by a passage in the Venerable Bede (673–735) that alludes to the Saracens as "a terrible calamity."[6] Elsewhere, the eruption of Muslim armies in Europe was interpreted as a punishment for Christians' sins. In short, the nature of Islam escaped the vast majority of Europeans. An anonymous text entitled *The Chronicle of 754* mentions the Arabs but does not say a single word about their faith. For a long time, Europeans were largely or completely ignorant of this new religion, and even those few who had contacts with Constantinople knew very little about it.

Though they had a good understanding of Christianity in general, Muslims were just about as ignorant about the "Franks." They saw northern Europe as of a vast, fertile but cold area inhabited by fierce people. Al-Mas'udī, a geographer, refers in the latter half of the tenth century to the Franks adherence to the Christian cult and allegiance to a church authority based in Rome.[7] "The inhabitants, Christians, obey a strong, valorous king, who relies on a formidable army," the tenth-century Andalusian traveler Ibrahim ibn Yaqub says of the land of the Franks.[8] Although commercial exchanges took place between Spain and France, we find little testimony as to whether these generated much interest in the other culture and religion.

Two events, however, were to shape the future of this relationship: the decision by Caliph Uthman to support a fleet and the gradual push of the Franks toward the Mediterranean. The first event effectively contributed to the fracturing of the Mediterranean region, the other to the progressive shift of northern Europe's geostrategic center of gravity towards the south. A third event, the Spanish Reconquista of the Iberian Peninsula provided the impetus for the crusading spirit that was to engulf the totality of Europe. At the turn of the ninth century, the creation of a powerful centralized empire by Charlemagne proved that Europe was capable of producing a superpower of its own. But Charlemagne's lack of naval capability doomed his efforts in Spain, where his armies essentially remained in the vicinity of the Pyrenees, incapable of making significant inroads much beyond the valleys on the other side of the mountains.

Charlemagne's push toward Spain did set a precedent, however, and it set the stage for things to come, as Christianity steadily took a hold on European society, while political and military authorities gradually coalesced against a common enemy. The papacy, always concerned by the intemperate nature of this emerging society, attempted to contain this violence by formulating effective codes of conduct designed to regulate, if not eliminate, armed conflicts. When the time was ripe, Rome ingenuously tried to redirect the negative energy toward the outside. Inspired by the Spanish resistance and the Reconquista, it came up with an idea that seemed destined to sprout up at some point or another: holy war.

THE MUSLIMS TAKE TO THE SEA

The history of Muslim seafaring in the Mediterranean has often been overlooked by historians who considered Arabs to be "sons of the desert" and Turks "sons of the steppe." Yet, from 649, when Muʿāwiyah, the future Umayyad caliph, sent an expeditionary force to the island of Cyprus, all the way to the early years of the nineteenth century, when Thomas Jefferson decided to rid the Mediterranean of the Barbary pirates, Muslim maritime activity in the Mediterranean remained an important element of the geostrategic makeup of both Europe and the Middle East.

Initially, under the first caliphs, Muslims had been reluctant to venture onto the open seas. Although the Arabs had some maritime experience, if only because of their commercial activities around the Arabian Peninsula, as soldiers, they were resolutely tuned to land warfare. Now that they had taken hold of a good portion of the Mediterranean, naval power was indispensable, especially considering that Byzantium initially enjoyed maritime supremacy. Thus, shortly after Cyprus, Rhodes, and Kos were first targeted (in 654), the Muslim fleet was fighting its first naval battle against the Byzantines.

Constans II had deployed a fleet of some 500 or 600 ships to roll back the Muslims in North Africa. Hearing this, Mu'āwiyah dispatched 'Abdallāh ibn Sa'd ibn Abī Sarh, the man in "charge of the sea,"[9] to oppose the Byzantines. The two fleets fought it out at what would be called the Battle of the Masts (655), where the Muslims proved superior, thus effectively establishing themselves as a force to be reckoned with on open water and terminating the maritime supremacy enjoyed until then by the Byzantines. Still, when a Muslim fleet attempted to take Constantinople in 674, the Byzantines were victorious. The Greek poet Theodosius Grammaticus wrote in celebration:

> Where now, O cursed one are your shining bright ranks of arrows?
> Where now the melodious chords of the bow strings?
> Where is the glitter of your swords and spears, your breast plates and head-
> borne helmets, scimitars and darkened shield?
> Where are the twin-decked, fire-throwing ships,
> And again, the single-decked ships, also swift in the battle step?
> What do you say, miserable and voracious Ishmael?
> Christ was mighty in the work of salvation and He rules as God and Lord.
> He gives strength and supports the battle.
> He shatters the bow and grinds down the human power.[10]

This defeat did not, however, deter the Muslims from pursuing an active naval strategy. Hence, their relentless push to gain a foothold in Sicily, with expeditions as early as 652, before the takeover of North Africa, and then in 720, 727, 728, 730, 732, 752, and 753. By 810, they had made inroads into Corsica and Sardinia, forcing Charlemagne to dispatch one of his sons to deal with the situation. The papacy came to associate these defensive measures with the idea of just war, and when Charlemagne was ready to launch his campaign against the Saracens in Spain in 778, Pope Hadrian I sent a message of support:

> Upon hearing the news [that the Saracens "want to enter France and devastate its territories"] we have been in a ceaseless state of agitation and affliction but the Lord our God never allows such events to take place, no more than the blessed Peter, prince of the Apostles. Regarding us, dear son and great king, we never cease

to implore clemency for you from our Lord God, along with all our priests, our religious monks, all our clergy and our entire people, so that he can submit these abominable Abarenes to your authority.[11]

Calling the Saracens "contrary to God," Hadrian characterized Charlemagne's campaign as a defensive war, and therefore implicitly a just war, though he did not use the term, against a pagan invader. As a just war against a people "with no God," the use of force thus was condoned by the papacy, and Charlemagne was blessed for his initiative. Also in a letter to Charlemagne, Pope Leo III described the Saracen menace in 813 as affecting "Christianity," saying: "Inasmuch as we have the capability, we will assign the task, to ourselves and to you, of crushing them and fighting them on the seas; and should we not, on our own, achieve this, then we will push them back beyond the frontiers of Christianity by acting ourselves on one end, and you on the other."[12]

With the creation of an arsenal in Tunis, the Muslim's North African fleet gained its autonomy, which made the threat even more potent. Creating a strong fleet is far more demanding than levying an army. Building and maintaining a fleet calls for superior administrative, organizational, economic, and strategic capabilities, as well as long-term planning. To illustrate the importance of the Muslim arsenals at that time, one need only point to the fact that the word "arsenal" is itself derived, via Italian, from the Arabic *dār-aṣ-ṣinā'a*, "house of manufacture."[13] Had Charlemagne developed such a naval capability, history might have been very different indeed. For the time being, though, the Franks, both before and after Charlemagne, proved no match on the sea, which may explain why they were never able to launch the ambitious southern offensive that Charlemagne dreamed of. After a hiatus caused by internal conflicts, new expeditions were mounted by the Muslims, starting in 827. By 831, they had taken Palermo from the Byzantines, then Messina in 843, and, finally, Syracuse in 878. Ibn Khaldūn understood Arab maritime strategy to be a fundamental element of Islam's hegemonic aspirations:

> The royal and governmental authority of the Arabs became firmly established and powerful at that time. The non-Arab nations became servants of the Arabs and were under their control. Every craftsman offered them his best services. They employed seagoing nations for their maritime needs. Their own experience of the sea and of navigation grew, and they turned out to be very expert. They wished to wage the holy war by sea. They constructed ships and galleys and loaded the fleet with men and weapons. They embarked the army and warriors to fight against unbelievers across the sea. [. . .]

During the time of the Muslim dynasty, the Muslims gained control over the whole Mediterranean. Their power and domination over it was vast. The Christian nations could do nothing against the Muslim fleets, anywhere in the Mediterranean. All the time, the Muslims rode its wave of conquest. There occurred then many well-known episodes of conquest and plunder.[14]

In the end, it would take another seafaring people, the Normans—Norsemen (Vikings) who had by then settled in France—to roll back the Muslims in the Mediterranean, at precisely the same time that the Crusades were launched. The Normans' success at sea was in no small measure instrumental in the Franks' successes in the Middle East.

In the meantime, however, the Franks had been utterly incapable of building a fleet capable of rivaling those of the Muslims or the Byzantines. For this reason, independent Muslim fleets from North Africa or Spain were able to launch regular raids on the Italian coast. In 812, Pope Leo III declared a state of emergency after a series of raids by a North African fleet on Italy's coastal islands. In light also of the resurgence of piracy, commercial exchanges on the Mediterranean were significantly reduced, if not completely stopped.

The constant threats Muslim raids posed, particularly in Italy, contributed to the identification of Muslims with danger. This danger, evidently, was all too real, and after the Muslims threatened Rome itself in 846, the pope created a league (849) of three cities, Amalfi, Gaeta, and Naples, and gave his benediction to the fleet as it departed to repulse the enemy. At the same time, a wall was erected to protect the Vatican. The raids persisted, however, even though they were often short-lived and there was no significant territorial penetration. These brutal incursions were often accompanied by systematic plundering of places of worship. In central Italy in 883, for example, the abbey of Monte Cassino was destroyed, and in 890–98, the abbey of Farfa long resisted a seven-year siege, illustrating the significance of this symbolic battle and the resolve of those who came to Farfa's defense, though in the end the monks were forced to flee. At times, the Italian and Byzantine fleets would cooperate to repel the "Saracens" but these alliances were circumstantial and, in the end, the Italians did little to help the Byzantines maintain their hold on Sicily. The papacy may have sought to instill a Christian feeling into this struggle, but it was never as solid as Rome wanted it to be. Still, by the time Rome instigated a holy war in the eleventh century, anti-Muslim feelings were running high. Although the First Crusade was initially construed as a pilgrimage to recover Jerusalem and the True Cross, it easily and logically shifted toward a full-fledged war against the Muslims. "The man of the Middle Ages by essence, by vocation, is a *pilgrim*, and, during the twelfth and thirteenth centuries, in the highest and most dangerous form of earthly pilgrimage, a *crusader*," Jacques Le Goff observes.[15]

Although Charlemagne's foray into Spain was unsuccessful, this was the first instance where the papacy showed signs of moving beyond just war. Pope Leo IV took the first step toward the idea of holy war in 847. At that point, Italy was under threat from Muslim raids, and Leo IV made the first promise of absolution from sin in exchange for military service:

> To the armies of the Franks,
>   Brushing away all fear and all sentiments of terror, apply yourselves to act valiantly against the enemies of the holy faith and the adversaries of the whole country. [. . .] for all who will loyally die during one of the battles of this war [. . .], the celestial kingdoms will not be refused. In fact, the Almighty is fully aware that should one among you come to die, he will have died for the truth of the faith, the salvation of his soul, and the defense of the Christian homeland. This is why, as a consequence, he will receive from him the aforementioned reward.[16]

THE PEACE AND TRUCE OF GOD

The eighth and ninth centuries were momentous in the Catholic Church's rapidly evolving attitude to violence and war, influenced by the growing menace of the Muslims, on the one hand, and by the rise and fall of the Carolingian empire, on the other. Stuck in the middle, so to speak, the church felt compressed and vulnerable. After being empowered by the imperial rule of the Carolingian dynasty, it was then put on the spot by the anarchy that resulted from its collapse, all while under attack by Muslim armies and raiders. Forced to react to all these events, Rome proceeded to move incrementally from rejecting violence to condoning it under certain circumstances, to encouraging it and even instigating it. While it may have effectively organized holy war on a grand scale by the end of the eleventh century, it also laid down norms and principles destined to control organized violence and established firm spaces for peace through the movement that would become known as the Peace and Truce of God.

Our own understanding of the Peace of God movement has evolved over the years.[17] Long thought to have been generated by the church in order to contain the feudal anarchy that seemed to overtake Europe after the fall of the Carolingian order, it is increasingly understood, at least at its inception in the mid tenth century, as a more restricted attempt by church authorities to protect their property from aggressive feudal lords ready to encroach on ecclesiastical territories. (The anarchy that was long believed to characterize Europe during that period has itself been downplayed by recent historiography.[18]) The purpose of the Peace of God was "to place under special ecclesiastical protection certain categories of persons such as monks, the clergy, the poor; and certain categories of material things."[19]

The oldest document relating to the Peace of God (*pactum pacis, constitutio pacis, restauratio pacis et justitiae, pax reformanda*), from the Auvergne region of central France, dates from 975. It states that "because we know that without peace nobody will see the Lord, we warn men in the name of the Lord that they should be sons of peace."[20] In this, the first known charter for a Peace of God, the bishop of Le Puy, Guy of Anjou, exhorted the lords of the area to respect the property of the church and restore "those things that have been taken, like faithful Christians." To ensure that everyone complied, the bishop raised a small army, thus persuading even the most reluctant to give back what they had taken. Shortly thereafter, a similar Peace was imposed in the town of Charroux (989).[21]

The Truce of God (*treuga dei*), an attempt by the church to restrict the days when private wars were permitted, complemented the Peace of God. The first known instance dates from 1027 in Catalonia with the Council of Toulonges, whose *pactum sive treuga* ruled that "no inhabitant of this county or this bishopric may attack an enemy between the ninth hour on Saturday and the first hour on Monday."[22] From this modest attempt, the movement would grow over the next centuries, giving the church an authoritative voice in the regulation of war.

Rare instances were known when the Peace/Truce of God was corrupted into violence in the name of peace, as happened in Bourges, in central France in 1038, when the bishop ordered all males over fifteen years of age to arm themselves and then employed them as marauders, but was stopped by a local lord.[23] This outcome seems to indicate that an informal system of checks and balances prevented even the church from abusing its powers in this manner. Local wars were understood to be limited, and this quickly came to apply to all of Christendom. The rules that increasingly came to govern war and peace for Christians did not, however, apply when facing a non-Christian enemy.

Whatever their motives or the context within which they appeared, the peace councils that began to be held at the end of the tenth century gave the church a renewed authority on matters related to peace and war. So much so that a century later, the church could forcefully persuade the European nobility and a significant portion of the peoples of Europe to leave everything and go fight a war on another continent.

Although the various, and apparently contradictory, attitudes to war discussed so far may have been parallel, they were all linked. One of the motivations behind the emerging idea of holy war was to ensure peace in the Christian world. The sanctification of war that appears in the middle of the ninth century paved the way for a return of the church as a purveyor of peace, order, and stability in a world that was torn by violence and conflict after the collapse of the Carolingian order. The cross, which would come to symbolize the fight against the Muslim crescent, appears on the battlefields of Europe during this period, both as a sign that Christian soldiers are protected by God against their pagan enemies, and as a symbol of the sanctity of their struggle. We see the cross used this way as early as 897, when Paris was besieged by the Normans, and, more prominently, during the wars of the Spanish Reconquista: in 1058, during his victorious battle against the Muslims, Ramon Berenguer I, count of Barcelona, carried the cross in front of his troops "in the manner of Constantine."[24]

CHARLEMAGNE AND THE "EMPIRE OF CHRISTIANITY"

With the church now at the forefront of the political and moral reengineering of European society, the clergy gained a degree of legitimacy that enabled it to shape and direct the course of events. In doing so, it further consolidated the Christian identity of the Frankish people around which Europe coalesced, redirecting their energies against two ideal foes: the Muslims and the pagans.

The rise of the Carolingians, whose orchestration of the removal of the Merovingian dynasty was officially approved and supported by the pope, further reinforced the ties between the Frankish kings, begun with Clovis, and Rome. As a token of his appreciation, Pepin the Short gave Ravenna back to the pope and reaffirmed papal authority in his kingdom, thus providing an aura of sanctity to the protection of the Holy See that assimilated the defense of the Carolingian Empire to the defense of Christianity.[25] These ties were further consolidated by Charlemagne, who invaded northern Italy to overthrow the king of the Lombards at the behest of the pope, a campaign (773) that served the interests of both the papacy and Charlemagne, who, in 799, restored the fleeing Pope Leo III, accused of adultery, to the Holy See.

In short, at a time when the two formal Christian authorities, Rome and Constantinople, proved incapable of protecting the Christian community and, for varying reasons, were somewhat discredited, (Byzantium was then under the authority of the controversial empress Irene, who had blinded her own son), Charlemagne appeared as the protector of Christendom.

It may be that Charlemagne himself felt invested by a divine mission to convert pagan peoples by force. Well-versed in the Old Testament, Charlemagne may have regarded himself as a new David. This, at least, is how one of his modern biographers, Alessandro Barbero, interprets Charlemagne's brutal campaigns against the pagans, especially the Saxons, 4,500 of whom he ordered decapitated at Verden an der Aller in Lower Saxony (though this fact is disputed by some who argue that the word *decollare*, meaning "decapitate," may have been confused with the word *decolare*, meaning "relocate"). In so doing, Charlemagne may have been inspired by David's treatment of the Moabites, an episode in the Old Testament that seems to have inspired him and from which "it is difficult not to discern a practical and cruelly coherent application of that model in the massacre of Verden," Barbero argues.[26] Whether or not this is true is difficult to say with any degree of certainty, but the official chronicle of the campaign in the *Annales Regni Francorum*, seems to corroborate Charlemagne's religious motivation, saying that his attitude was that either the Saxons were to be "defeated and subjugated to the Christian religion or completely swept away."[27] Furthermore, with his *Capitulare de partibus Saxonie* (785), Charlemagne made any act deemed offensive to Christianity and its representatives to be punishable by death.[28] Simultaneously, he adroitly negotiated with the Abbassid caliph Hārūn al-Rashīd, with whom he enjoyed excellent diplomatic relations, to guarantee the protection of Christians in the Holy Land. Given the keys to the Church of the Holy Sepulchre (and a live elephant), Charlemagne was thus symbolically approved by a Muslim caliph as the protector of all Christians, which, needless to say, drove Eastern and Western Christendom further apart.

Charlemagne sought to make the clergy an integral part of his military in waging what was held to be a just war to convert pagans. The clergy, then, was not only made responsible for recruiting soldiers within the limits of its bishoprics, but priests were also expected to lead their men into battle, sword in hand. This demand did not sit well with all ecclesiastical authorities, some of whom argued that everyone should stick to their respective duties, with laymen responsible for fighting visible enemies and clerics for combating invisible ones.[29] Later, during the Capetian restoration, King Louis VI endorsed this active participation of the clergy in fighting, as attested by a contemporary description:

> Because King Philip [Louis's father], worn out by age and sickness, had allowed his princely power to decline and the royal justice had become too lax to punish tyrants, Louis was at first obliged to ask for help from the bishops all over his kingdom to put an end to the oppressions of bandits and rebels. As a result, the bishops set up the communities of the people in France, so that the priests might accompany the king to battle or siege, carrying banners and leading all their parishioners.[30]

Notwithstanding these quarrels about lay and religious authority (which would take center stage starting in the eleventh century), the Christian character of the Carolingian Empire became its dominant feature and it was thus understood as the "Empire of Christianity." Charlemagne's son, the aptly named Louis the Pious (778–840), further consolidated the idea of a "Christian state" which would resonate long after the fragmentation of the empire following the peace of Verdun, when it was divided among Charlemagne's grandsons (843). Much the way the reunification of the Muslim *umma* constituted the ideal behind the jihad, a return to the Golden Age of Charlemagne would establish itself as the founding myth of a united Christian or secular Europe, even when that dream seemed unattainable. With Charlemagne, the emperor's authority in upholding the interests of the Christian community was understood to bestowed directly by God, without the intercession of the Church. In the centuries to come, however, Rome would reestablish the pope as God's principal messenger and go-between with humankind, which would ultimately provoke much friction between the temporal and spiritual authorities.

The collapse of the Carolingian Empire, long attributed by historians to pressures from outside, was probably caused by deep-seated internal dysfunctions. Still, the foreign invasions played their part and, as Jean Flori suggests, probably had "a considerable role in terms of ideology, the formation of attitudes and behaviors."[31] Monks, often at the receiving end of the attacks not only of Muslims but also of Norsemen, whose first foray took place in 799, and

Hungarians, who threatened Germany in the mid-900s, may have perpetrated a sentiment of terror and a general psychosis among the population. The image of the cruel pagan invader demonized these foes, sanctifying the wars launched against them. The passage from just to holy war was not yet complete, but already these wars had a strong ideological and moral character—an "us against them" line had been drawn between the adversaries, religion being the clear marker.

Until around the year 1000, the Western Christian world was principally engaged in defensive wars, but beginning with Charlemagne, its territorial consolidation was accompanied by missionary activities. In the tenth century, the Holy Roman Empire had assumed the role in providing Christendom's security that had once been Charlemagne's. When King Otto of Germany defeated the Hungarians at Lechfeld in 955, the sanctity of the battle was symbolized by his carrying the Holy Lance that had purportedly belonged to Longinus, the centurion who pierced Jesus's side. The fate of the Normans, the Hungarians, and the Poles, all pagans, followed the logic of history: absorption and then conversion. When, a few years later (in 1000 CE), Stephen was crowned king of Hungary, the Holy Roman Emperor sent as a gift the aforementioned Holy Lance, a symbolic gesture if there ever was one, conveying: "Now, you are one of us." A quarter of a century later, the Polish king Bolesław the Brave was similarly gifted with a replica of the Holy Lance.

There was little chance, however, that the Muslims would suffer the fate of the pagan Normans, Hungarians, and Poles. A clash of people was not to be equated with a clash of religions, and, as both Christians and Muslims would quickly learn, the deep religious divide between the two worlds would create an entirely different dynamic. Surely, the growing conflict between Christians and Muslims was fueled by elements that were more political than religious, but at a time when politics and religion were intermeshed, one could not really separate one from the other. The wars against all non-Christian peoples were now characterized as such, with the "pagans" having replaced the "barbarians" of yore, the non-Christian thus taking the place of the "non-civilized." This shift, however, implied, much as it did before, that the "pagan," like the "barbarian," could be "civilized," now meaning "converted."

This attitude, however, which had characterized the Graeco-Roman world for centuries, was not viable with other monotheistic religions. The Jews had been overrun by Rome and, as a religious minority, were more or less tolerated by Christians. But the Jewish communities scattered around Europe had always resisted conversion and refused to yield, an attitude that would lead to intensifying pressure, violence, isolation, humiliation, and, for some, expulsion. Against such a vast territory as the one controlled and inhabited by Muslims, absorption was thus out of the question. The "infidel," unlike the pagan, could be neither tamed nor converted. He had to be crushed.

As Europe chaotically but progressively regained its footing, it was only a matter of time before it launched what was considered to be a counteroffensive against Muslims who had infested the shores of the Mediterranean, which Europeans always considered to be theirs, most notably in attempting to recreate the Roman empire and reclaim its crown jewel, the *mare nostrum*. The new layer that was added to this heritage, Christianity, not only served to provide Europeans with a cementing identity, it also gave Christendom a mobilizing project around which it could now coalesce: the retrieval of that most sacred object, the True Cross, and of that most sacred city, Jerusalem.

THE TURNING OF THE TIDE: URBAN II
LAUNCHES THE CRUSADES

When, on a November day in 1095 at an ecclesiastical conference in the central French town of Clermont (Clermont-Ferrand), Pope Urban II quietly, but resolutely, launched his appeal to retake the Holy Land, few among those around him who heard the call could have suspected that these words were about to change the course of history. Indeed, few events in the history of humankind have had such a lasting impact on so many people. In point of fact, one could argue that Urban's appeal might have been one of the single greatest historical game-changers of all time; the first of the appeal's ramifications were quickly felt, and the consequences were as immense as they were intense and long-lasting. The First Crusade, as it would later be known, not only generated a series of military interventions in the Near East, but completely transformed the geostrategic dynamics around the Mediterranean, setting the tone for a conflict between Christians and Muslims that would last into the eighteenth century and even, one might argue, right down until today. It was "the conflict that set these two world religions on a course towards deep-seated animosity and enduring enmity," Thomas Asbridge observes.[32]

As a watershed moment in history, the First Crusade ranks alongside the battles of Gaugamela and Actium, which respectively saw the fall of the

Achaemenid Empire and the birth of the Roman one, and its impact can be compared to the combined defeat of Byzantium and Sassanian Persia by Muslim armies in 636 or, later, with Martin Luther's decision to post his ninety-five theses on the door of a church in Germany. In many ways, Urban's appeal was a consequence of the former events, and it certainly was one of the long-term causes of the latter.

Like many events of such magnitude, this one played on profound social, political, and economic transformations and evolutions, both in Europe and in the Middle East, without which the Crusades would not have been possible. But it was also directed by tangible elements such as timing, luck, and even ignorance. And, but for the intervention of one individual, it might never have happened at all.

But happen it did, and, although the Crusades to the Holy Land spanned only a few centuries, the crusading spirit survived until the eighteenth century and was even incorporated into some of the secular ideologies that emerged subsequently. Although the West generally likes to see itself as a direct product of Greece and Rome, and, essentially, as a secular civilization, this is very different from the image it long held of itself as a Christian community tied together not only by a common history, culture, and belief system, but also by the idea that it should eventually constitute itself into a Christian republic,[33] one that would be inherently peaceful within (once purified of its heretical elements) but morally justified in using violence when deemed necessary. This ideal of a Christian republic would later be expunged of its religious elements and, through the abbé de Saint-Pierre, Rousseau, and Kant, would lead to key concepts that few, today, would associate with the idea of a Christian Republic: the European Union, Wilsonian Collective Security (embodied by the League of Nations and now the United Nations), and the theory (or doctrine) of the Democratic Peace.[34] For the historian Jonathan Riley-Smith, the political ideal of a Christian Republic is a key to understanding the relationship between Christianity and violence:

> For most of the last two thousand years Christian Justifications of war have rested on two premises. The first was that violence [. . .] was not intrinsically evil. [. . .] The second premise was that Christ's wishes for mankind were associated with a political system or course of political events in this world. For the crusaders his intentions were embodied in a political conception, the Christian Republic, a single, universal, transcendental state ruled by him, whose agents on earth were popes, bishops, emperors and kings. A personal commitment to its defence was

believed to be a moral imperative for those qualified to fight. Propagandists gave this theory expression in terms the faithful could understand: within the earthly extension to Christ's universal empire the Holy Land was his domain or patrimony.[35]

The series of events we refer to as the Crusades both symbolize and epitomize the idea of war in the name of God. Indeed, any war that might be remotely tainted by religious or ideological overtones is deemed a "crusade" or a "holy war," two expressions that are implicitly negative and hark back to one of the darkest periods of the Dark Ages. Since Machiavelli, and all the more so since the Enlightenment, our vision of political relations generally rejects political actions that fall outside a realist or utilitarian (in the common usage of the word) framework. Politics and its principal means, diplomacy and military force, are meant first and foremost to enhance our power, our influence, and our wealth.

The Christian world in the year 1000 had a very different frame of mind, with faith at the center of people's concerns. Reeling as it had from several centuries of hardship, it had been on the defensive as long as people could remember. Coming on the heels of the Germanic and Hunnic invasions that had provoked or, at least accelerated, the fall of the Roman Empire, Europeans had had to fend off Muslim invasions in the south, Viking raids in the north, and the pressure of the Magyars (Hungarians) in the east. The Byzantine Empire had, however, long provided western Europeans with a buffer against threats from Asia, be they Turkic or Iranian and the battle of Poitiers/Tours, followed by Pepin's campaigns in southern France, confirmed the role of the Pyrenees as a defensive rampart (though, contrary to common belief, the Muslims were not prevented at the time from continuing their raids in southern France).

Like most peoples with little religious inclination, the Normans were quickly converted to the dominant belief system and they, too, would become champions of Christianity, much as the Turks and the Iranians had become champions of Islam. That various nomadic peoples had converted to one of the Abrahamic religions, including Judaism with the Khazars (their foes, the Bulgars, also briefly entertained the idea of converting to Judaism),[36] certainly injected an element of violence into the politico-religious conundrum. For warrior peoples who lived and died by the sword, religion was just another pretext for war.

In many parts of Europe, Asia, and the Middle East, alongside the more traditional struggles for power and territory, the defense of the faith had become an integral component of the conduct of international relations. The leap into the next millennium did bring about a significant change in attitudes, but Christianity, formerly a pacific spiritual undertaking, was at this point fully enmeshed in politics. By now, it had come to accept war, under certain conditions, as a necessary evil.

Given the change in perspective and attitude, were Islam and Christianity logically heading toward an inevitable collision? Or was this clash, in part at least, provoked by circumstances? The question has occupied scholars for generations, and answers have varied significantly. As recently as the 1980s, the consensus regarding the origins of the Crusades was that the eleventh century had witnessed a huge economic and demographic upturn of revolutionary proportions that created the conditions for ambitious foreign adventures beyond the shores of Europe. Looking back, it now seems obvious that this particular vision was influenced by the Marxist outlook that pervaded the major historical schools and currents in Europe between the 1930s and 1980s. The retreat of Marxism that coincided with the collapse of the Soviet Union allowed the emergence of a new generation of historians with new approaches, and, today, the idea of an eleventh-century revolution has been toned down somewhat, even if evidence suggests that Europe did indeed undergo significant demographic, economic, and social change at that time.

Similarly, the popular idea that the Crusades provided an outlet for landless knights or for Italian cities looking for new markets is based in part on a materialistic vision of history that might fit with our current sensibilities, but may not correspond to the economic and commercial realities of eleventh-century Western Europe. By the time the First Crusade was launched, Italian merchants were already present in the Middle East, with Amalfi and Genoa trading in Egypt, and Venice in the Byzantine Empire, for example. In 1082, Emperor Alexis I granted the Venetians an area in Constantinople where they could conduct their business, as well as complete exemption from customs duties throughout the empire. The Crusades would greatly favor Italian commerce, and, as early as 1098, the new Frankish prince of Antioch, Bohemond I granted Venetian merchants the same rights and privileges they enjoyed in the Byzantine Empire. But, initially at least, the maritime republics were dubious about a movement that, in their eyes, was more likely to wreck their newly opened markets than to expand them. Merchants naturally prefer the status quo to political turmoil. Once things settled down, this hesitancy would be replaced by a growing enthusiasm for the Crusades.[37]

Regarding the idea that the Crusades offered opportunities to landless aristocrats, at the time, Europe still had much land to be distributed or cleared; enough to accommodate the poorer scions of the aristocracy looking to exploit land. The idea that the younger, landless members of the aristocracy were the ones sent to the Near East is contradicted by the fact that older and higher-ranking members of the aristocracy saw participation in the Crusades as both the greatest of honors and a unique opportunity to seek glory and enhance their military prestige.

In feudal society, military prowess and faith ranked higher than anything else, and no endeavor was deemed more desirable than taking arms to defend one's God, something perceived not only as a personal investment but, more important, as a moral and spiritual obligation. The emergence of powerful religious-military orders during that period is testimony to this reality.

Alas, our growing interest, as a society, in grassroots, participatory politics has recently given traction to the idea of what are commonly referred to as "people's crusades," as opposed to "knights' crusades," a notion reinforced by the idea that the Crusades were in some ways an early instance of class war. For those not convinced by this argument, such as traditionalists like René Grousset, a people's crusade had all the unsavory characteristics of a mob. As increasing research surfaces concerning the social dimension of the Crusades, one can now have a more balanced view of the situation.[38] Undeniably, a grassroots movement paralleled the aristocratic crusade and, though the social motivations may have been different, a strong spiritual undercurrent drove both in the same direction.

The very idea of a holy war or a crusade developed over time. The latter term itself was not used until around 1250 in Europe, and much later in the Muslim World, where the word "crusade" only came into use in the nineteenth century, through translations of Western chronicles. In effect, the conflict we know as the Crusades was perceived by Muslim historians as part of a much longer conflict between Christianity and Islam that extended all the way to the twentieth-century wars between Europeans and Ottomans.[39] This major difference in how the conflict was perceived in the East and in the West has received much less attention than it deserves. This dichotomy certainly accounts for variation in how the East and the West may envision the current tensions of the twenty-first century: as a historical anomaly on the one hand, or, on the other, as the continuation of a centuries-old conflict that never really ceased.

Although Pope Urban II had focused his appeal on Jerusalem, Muslim observers at the time saw the invasion of Syria as but one element among others in a new grand strategy on the part of the West to expel Muslims. The twelfth-century Iraqi historian ʿIzz al-Dīn ibn al-Athīr describes the origin of the aggression as a succession of events originating in Spain: "The power of the Franks and their increased importance were first manifested by their invasions of the lands of Islam and their conquest of parts of them in the year 478 [1085–86], for [that was when] they took the city of Toledo and other parts of Spain. [. . .] Then, in the year 494 (1091–92), they attacked and conquered the island of Sicily. [. . .] When it was the year 490 [1096–97], they invaded Syria."

Ibn al-Athīr, a Sunni, also offers an alternative version of the events, which he admits he cannot prove, in which the Shiite Fatimids, "became fearful when they saw the strength and power of the Saljuq state, that it had gained control of Syrian lands as far as Gaza, leaving no buffer state between the Saljuqs and Egypt to protect them," so that they "therefore sent to the Franks to invite them to invade Syria, and conquer it and separate them from the [other] Muslims but God knows best."[40] This passage implicitly asserts that the Fatimids are not Muslims (the word "other" is absent in the original text and was added by the translator). This text, written shortly after the events unfolded reveals the extent of the rift in the Muslim world, and the fact that Muslims understood that the renewed confidence and strength of the Europeans now targeted Islam as a whole. As Muslims tended to view the world as divided between cultural/religious blocks naturally in conflict with one another, this is not surprising. Furthermore, Muslim observers never fell into the trap of envisioning "Christians" as one homogeneous block, and they clearly distinguished between the Eastern Orthodox Christians of the Byzantine Empire, referred to as the "Romans," or Rum, and the Western "Franks."

The permanent settlement of Westerners in the Near East would later give them more insight into the subtleties of Muslim politics—but these distinctions were not initially as clear-cut, and neither was the rift between Shiites and Sunnites. Muslims were generally viewed as a whole, whether they were described as "Saracens," "Turks," "infidels," or "Muhammadans." Since Islam accepts Christ as a Prophet, this may explain why Muslims chose not to refer to the enemy as Christians, but rather as an ethnic group undistinguished by any religious appellation. Since the notion of the *dar al Islam* can be interpreted as a territorial one, naming the adversary by its territorial roots thus conformed to the whole internal-external dichotomy that is an integral part of Islam.

"THE PILGRIMAGE"

As a general rule, those responsible for justifying an act of aggression that is not warranted by necessity often resort to some kind of pretext to rally the various stakeholders and gain public support. In the fourth century BCE, Philip of Macedon and Alexander the Great decided to invade Persia on the pretext of helping the Greek minorities of Asia Minor, and three centuries later, Julius Caesar managed to convince the Senate that the fragmented territory that was Gaul should be considered a direct threat to Roman security. Whatever the political environment or the historical context, inflated or invented pretexts for military aggression are an essential tool of the trade. Though never subtle and rarely original, they are, more often than not, redoubtably efficient. People, it seems, are easily swayed to let their governments use military force.

Thus, what came to be known as the First Crusade was first portrayed in the vaguest terms, both as an action to help the beleaguered Christian minorities living in the Near East, much as Alexander had done, and as a militarized pilgrimage to recover the Holy Land, whether by persuasion or sheer presence of numbers. A "war" it was not, nor even an act of aggression, at least officially. Thus, it came to be understood by contemporaries as, modestly, a "pilgrimage," a term with formidable resonance at the time.

For a Catholic Church, mindful of keeping up appearances as the principal guarantor of peace, this was a clever way of initiating an all-out war without declaring it. By focusing on getting back the True Cross and Jerusalem, this attitude was in line with the Peace of God movement, designed to recover things belonging to the church. The difference between this and the more modest endeavors of various bishoprics was a matter of scale, corresponding to the pope's newfound control of the church, previously governed by the decentralized authority of the bishops. Now, to claim return of the greatest property of all, this effort warranted the involvement of all of Christianity. As an integral part of the Peace of God movement, it was thus important to use the correct language and to avoid words that might indicate that this action was altogether a violent one.

This, of course, was a deliberate play with words, for, at least among the nobility, the intrinsic character of this "journey" was all too clear. The instigator of the Crusade, Urban II, was himself unequivocal about his intentions, even though, for propaganda purposes, he publicly refrained from characterizing the expedition as a holy war. In a private letter, dated October 7, 1096, to the Benedictine monks of the Vallumbrosan Order (named after the abbey of Vallombrosa in Tuscany), who had expressed their wish to join the "pilgrimage," he had this response:

> We have learned that several of you have expressed the desire to join the warriors [milites] who are heading to Jerusalem to liberate Christianity. The offer is just, but it is not its practical. Indeed, as far as we are concerned, it is the task of the warriors whom we have mobilized for this expedition so that with the help of their armaments, they may repress the ferocity of the Saracens and restore the lost freedom of the Christians. We do not wish for those who have [. . .] devoted themselves to the spiritual fight to take up arms, nor do we want them to undertake the voyage. More than that: we forbid them to do so![41]

Despite their blatantly brutal character, which completely refuted the idea that this was a peaceful pilgrimage, until the mid-thirteenth century, the Crusades were referred to in the West as "The Expedition," "The Journey to Jerusalem," "The Voyage to the Holy Land," or simply "The Pilgrimage," all terms devoid of any violent undertones.[42] Faith thus seems indeed to have been the chief motive behind them at the start. From the outset, then, the movement was governed by ideological considerations, whose impulse never seemed to lose momentum. The numerous deaths resulting from the Crusades must have bothered some people, as we might suppose from the French Dominican friar Humbert of Romans's specious justification of them in 1270: "The aim of Christianity is not to fill the earth, but to fill heaven. Why should one worry if the number of Christians is lessened in the world by deaths endured for God? By this kind of death, people make their way to heaven who perhaps would never reach it by another road."[43]

By then, the Church had moved well beyond its pacifist roots. Contamine suggests that not only did it have few qualms about the war, but that it understood full well how it might profit from it: "Whatever the reservations of the church in the face of war (reservations often masked by the use of an abstract scholarly vocabulary and formal analyses), it is clear that Christianity and war, the church and the military, far from being antithetical, on the whole got on well together. They existed in a state of constant symbiosis, each profiting from the other's support."[44]

The peculiar nature of crusading was that it was conducted as an individual act of penance and self-sanctification before it evolved into a call to arms to defend God, Christ, the church, and Christianity. For this reason, the first generations of Crusaders were perceived, and referred to, as "pilgrims," and they and their families enjoyed the status, privileges, and protection generally accorded pilgrims. Hence, the bellicose nature now associated with the crusading movement was initially diluted in the original appeal and message. In practical terms, though, the first to take part in the journey, be they referred to as Crusaders or pilgrims, embarked almost immediately on the path of violence: before they had even left the shores of Europe, they had victimized the various Jewish communities that had the misfortune to inhabit the towns that dotted the road to the Holy Land. For all intents and purposes, this journey was different from other pilgrimages, and whether they were seeking penance or fighting for Christianity, these men and women were clearly on the warpath.

However one may view the Crusades, few would dispute that the First Crusade was born of choice rather than of necessity. By qualifying it as a pilgrimage or a journey, one could thus circumvent the conditions needed for the endeavor to meet the general requirements of a "just war" as expounded by Saint Augustine, which, being offensive in character and far from a last resort, it was clearly not, even under the most liberal interpretation and definition of what a just war may be.

The terminology employed at the time, then, was neither coincidental nor innocent, since it underplayed the bellicose character of this peculiar pilgrimage, which in effect had all the characteristic of an offensive operation, indeed, a war. Nor did this action have limited scope, as attempting to recover the Holy Land would undoubtedly trigger a hostile response from those who currently controlled it. That the common soldier or pilgrim may not have understood all the implications is evident. However, those at the top must not only have been aware of this fact, but, most probably, must have anticipated and indeed relished the idea that the provocation would trigger a clash of sorts between two civilizations. Evidently, as violence tends to breed violence, especially when fanaticism is involved, this initial step had all the makings of a violent conflict that might extend indefinitely. Their initial enthusiasm probably convinced the crusaders that this adventure would only last a few weeks, as is often the case when popular wars are started. But wars of choice, though they may be conditioned by a variety of factors designed to facilitate the decision to use force against someone else, cannot materialize without the spark that initially ignites the conflict. What then, were the elements that made such a war possible or even desirable? And where did the spark originate?

WHY A CRUSADE?

The historian is confronted either with a surplus of details, whose comparative and absolute relevance can only be determined subjectively, or with an information deficiency that logically leads to all sorts of speculative theories. Often, one has to juggle the two problems simultaneously. In other words, so many facts need to be taken into consideration, weighed, and organized, and so much vital information is either absent or unreliable, that historical objectivity is an ideal that may be sought but rarely, if ever, attained.[45] Rather than presenting facts as though they were devoid of any kind of subjectivity, most self-respecting historians will transparently opt for a subjective position, which they will try their best to defend with facts and analysis. Other historians will disagree, and they, in turn, will present their own visions. This is how historiography progresses, usually fueled by new discoveries, new inputs, and the resulting debates.

My own interpretation of the Crusades is strongly predicated on three ideas. The first of these is that history is occasionally rocked by the convergence, in part purely coincidental, of various elements that, through some spark or another, will combine significantly to alter the course of history. The second idea is that at these points, which might only last a very short time, the intervention of a single individual, whether or not he or she is conscious of it (usually not), can determine which direction the course of history might take. Thirdly, I believe that the elements that coalesce to alter the course of history vary but that sudden geopolitical changes more often than not enter in the balance: I do not think, for instance, that economics or demographics or class struggles account for all the great movements of history even if they might play a role in many of them; I do, however, believe that changing geopolitical situations, in other words, the sudden transformation of the balance of power, account for a lot, and that these changes are often the result of interpersonal struggles and internal power politics. Contrary to social and economic change, which is generally slow, geopolitical transformations are unpredictable, and they can be very sudden, thus taking everyone by surprise. Over time, historiography has shifted from an emphasis on "great events," usually "decisive" battles, and "great leaders" to a history favoring long-term social and economic undercurrents, as best exemplified by the *Annales* school. The reality, in my opinion, is that history is moved by both. Striking a balance between those extremes is difficult, however, and one will inevitably fall on one side of the spectrum or the other. Personally, I tend to veer, albeit cautiously, to the side that is, for lack of a better term, called "traditionalist."

When it comes to the origins of the Crusades, I do believe that geopolitical factors played a significant role, and that had Eudes of Châtillon, the future Urban II, not been elected pope in 1088, they might never have taken place. That being said, Urban did not live in a vacuum; had his predecessor not paved the way, or had events not unfolded the way they did, he might not have made the call, or his call might have fallen on deaf ears. As it were, when he did make the appeal, the response was immediate, loud, and unequivocal: "God wills it," the crowds that first heard it chanted. And indeed, "God wills it," in other words, "We want it," would become the battle cry of the first "pilgrims"/ Crusaders.

What were the various events and undercurrents unfolding in the eleventh century that would collectively contribute to the launching, and ultimate success, of the First Crusade? I list them here in no particular order, and while some elements interacted with one another, others, at least initially, did not:

The fragmentation of Arab states in North Africa and southern Spain.

The transformation of the church and the papacy, which gained influence and authority, most notably under Pope Gregory VII (r. 1073–85).

The counterattack, starting in 1030, against the Arabs in Iberia.

Increasing tensions in the Muslim world between Shiites and Sunnis.

The great eastward push of the Turks, first by the Ghaznavids, and then, more formidably, by the Seljuks.

The sudden fall of the Fatimids, one of the greatest Arab dynasties.

The no less surprising contraction of the Byzantine Empire.

The emergence in southern Europe of new power brokers, the Normans.

The end of external threats from the Vikings, the Arabs, and the Magyars in Europe.

Europe experiencing an economic and cultural renaissance of sorts, while the Arab world imploded.

The growing rift between Eastern and Western Christianity, with Byzantine emperors clinging to the idea that they were the true defenders of the faith, while Rome looked to the moment when it might reverse this balance of power in its favor. The so-called schism of 1054, of little consequence at the time, illustrates the rift, although hope for reconciliation remained.

EUROPE AND THE MIDDLE EAST IN 1095

The Mediterranean, which had seemed an ocean of stability only a few decades earlier, was anything but that by the end of the eleventh century. Islam's classic age, which had reached its apogee with the Abbasids in the ninth and tenth centuries, was all but over. Perhaps, as Ibn Khaldūn later suggested, empires that cease to expand are inevitably condemned to perish, since *"By its very nature, royal authority claims all its glory for itself and goes in for luxury and prefers tranquility and peace."*[46] And, indeed, Arab expansion, notably in Europe, had all but ceased by the turn of the ninth century, and the Iberians would soon begin to nibble back their territory. The gradual repulsion of the "Moors" (who were mainly Berbers) from the Peninsula by a people bound by a purpose and a strong sense of religious identity was the source from which everything else unfolded.

In effect, the Iberian wars between Christians and Muslims were what set everything else in motion, and although the process was a slow one, it firmly planted the seeds of the crusading ideology that would sweep Europe in 1095–96. As such, these seeds took time to grow and expand but, when the time was ripe, they proved to be deeply rooted even in areas far removed from the Iberian Peninsula.

Subjugation of one people by another almost always breeds a strong sense of bitterness and resentment, which brews silently and, in time, leads to violent backlash.[47] Although the Arab culture of Andalusia is rightfully considered to be one of the most advanced of its time, and although tolerance and temperance were among its chief characteristics, such things have little bearing for people who are willing to risk death in order to regain their liberty and their independence. For, while Muslim monarchs may have tolerated minorities, ensured that they enjoyed economic freedom, and given them protection, non-Muslims were still second-class citizens bound by different rules.

As fellow Christians, Europeans as a whole would take this fight as their own, transforming what was essentially an anti-colonial struggle bound to a limited territory into a holy war of universal proportions and purpose. Had Europe been tightly divided into national entities, such a purpose might never have arisen; however, Europe was a fluctuating mosaic of rival provinces, often ruled as private hunting grounds by bellicose warlords whose tenuous political legitimacy lay in their ability to thrash their opponents. In many ways, the times present a picture resembling the one Thomas Hobbes would famously describe in his *Leviathan* of life as invariably "solitary, poore, nasty, brutish and short."[48] Conditions varied from region to region and between rural and urban areas, of course, but wars were frequent, and although the armies were comparatively small, civilians were all too often their victims. In this unstable and volatile environment, the church provided a moral and spiritual compass for populations who found in their religion a solace for their desperate condition and a sense of identity that bound individuals to a greater community of purpose.

Although merchants and traveling clerics would have brought news of what was going on in the East, the pope is unlikely to have had a clear grasp of all the geopolitical changes that had altered the geopolitical dynamics around the Mediterranean. Whether or not Urban II was aware of what lay behind his call to arms cannot be known, but he must have sensed that all the elements for a crusade were in place. And indeed they were, probably much more so even than he might have thought.

The politics of the region we might refer to as the Greater Middle East, then as before, were governed by traditional power struggles between existing entities; by the constant pressure from Central Asian nomadic tribes forced by others to move forward; by devastating internecine wars, in particular between Shiites and Sunnis. The Byzantine Empire was a key to the global stability of the region and, for Europeans, a protective bastion that shielded them from eastern menaces. The Persians, overtaken by the Arabs four centuries prior, were pressing to regain some autonomy. The Arabs themselves, divided and fragmented, were being increasingly challenged by Turkic steppe warriors who were militarily superior to the commercially minded urban populations of the region.

The Arab-Muslim expansionary movement that had begun with Muhammad's first conquests in the early part of the seventh century, had proceeded with fits and starts before it came under pressure from external menaces and had started to wane by the tenth century. But, if conquest had all but ceased, Arabic culture and language was continuing to expand both east and south into sub-Saharan Africa. At the same time, Persian culture was making a comeback of sorts, while the Turks were rapidly gaining a steady foothold among the elite of the Arab armies. In time, this Turkish military presence would soon prove indispensable, and it would logically translate into political power.

The apogee of the classical Arab-Muslim age was reached by the Abbasid dynasty under Caliph Hārūn al-Rashīd (r. 786–809). The capital of the

Abbasid Empire, Bagdad, was probably the most populous city in the world, perhaps the most sophisticated. However, new urban centers started to emerge elsewhere: Cordoba in Spain, Fez in Morocco, Kairouan in Tunisia, and Cairo in Egypt. The sheer size of the Muslim world, larger than the Roman Empire and roughly equivalent to the short-lived Alexandrian empire, would, over the long run, prove unsustainable as a single homogeneous entity. After Hārūn al-Rashīd, a long, steady decline began. Not only was the Abbasid caliphate challenged from within by the Shiite Fatimid dynasty, based in North Africa, but its frontiers began to crack open, with Shiites also challenging the Abbasid order in the Arabia and Persia. Shiite power manifested itself in Persia with the Buyyids (945–55), in the Arabia with the Qarmat movement, and in Egypt with the Fatimids (909–1171), who seemed poised to defeat the Abbasids when they occupied Bagdad in 1059–60.

As if things were not sufficiently complicated, the Sunni population was itself rocked by divisions with the emergence in the eighth century of several rival theological schools. As the Abbasids were facing this double-edged (or triple-edged) sword, Europeans had formalized the separation between church and state. Unlike Islam, Christianity in Europe knew few religious divisions, since the Roman Catholic Church had consolidated its authority in all matters religious, as was vividly illustrated by the brutal treatment meted out to the few who challenged its authority.

In practical terms, the Abbasids were unable successfully to confront all their adversaries simultaneously and they had to pick and choose their battles. Rather than face total annihilation, they let go some of their power in the territories at the periphery of the caliphate, a wise policy that enabled them to retain some clout until the thirteenth century. In effect, they would outlast the Fatimids by more than a century, who were rolled back and weakened by the Seljuk Turks, the new champions of Sunni orthodoxy, and then finally crushed by Saladin in 1158.

At the same time that it was fragmenting, however, the Muslim world experienced tremendous commercial and economic expansion, which triggered a formidable growth of urban culture. Paradoxically, this commercial activity greatly benefited the Italian city states, which would later be able to engage in increasingly bellicose naval activities against Muslim states. By the same token, the massive urbanization of Arab society weakened its military resolve and facilitated the takeover of power by Turkish elites. The slave trade, an important element of Muslim society, would fuel its armies for centuries to come with the efficient slave-soldier system that eventually came to form the basis for two of the most formidable armed forces of the Middle Ages and the Renaissance: the Mamluks in Egypt and the Ottoman janissaries.

But the great transformation of the eleventh century resulted from the sweeping arrival of eastern Turkic armies, first with the Ghaznavids at the eastern end of the caliphate, then with the Seljuks, who overran practically everyone and everything. In 1046, under Tugril Bey, the Seljuks first invaded Persia and then took Baghdad itself. Under the second Seljuk sultan, Alp Arslan, they subsequently took Aleppo and inflicted a crushing defeat to the Byzantines in Manzikert in 1071. Deprived of the taxes from lost provinces that had previously supported it, the Byzantine Empire now faced three separate threats, from the Seljuks, from the Pechenegs, another semi-nomadic Turkic people from the steppes of Inner Asia, and from the southern Normans, based in Sicily.

The emperor Alexios I Komnenos (r. 1081–1118), who saw himself as the defender of the Roman Empire and of the Christian faith thus looked to what must have seemed like the logical recourse: Europe, and more specifically Rome. In 1089, already facing intense pressure, he had asked for and received five hundred mercenaries from Robert of Flanders, and in 1095, he made another plea for assistance, this time to the pope. In Piacenza, the Byzantine delegation asked the church to arrange for the organization of a small expeditionary force to help fend off the danger. The idea, again, was for a few hundred mercenaries, certainly not the tens of thousands of armed "pilgrims" who would flock to Constantinople a year later! In hindsight, this plea, inasmuch as it had any kind of impact on Urban's decision to launch his crusade, would come to haunt the Byzantines for centuries to come, as it opened a Pandora's box out of which came some of the destructive elements that ultimately brought the Byzantine Empire to its knees.

As much as Alexios's demand would logically appear to have influenced Urban II, it is difficult to assess the exact impact this demand may have had on the pope's decision to call for a crusade. All we can assert is that it reinforced the idea that Christianity was under siege and, just as important, that the Byzantine Empire was losing ground. In the greater scheme of things, this was probably seen by the pope as a good thing. For one, it helped him sell to the public the idea that Christianity was under threat, and, secondly, it meant that, in the geostrategic power game, the West might now be in a position to gain the upper hand over its erstwhile rival in the East. Just as Urban was conveniently placing all Christianity under one banner, it was logical that the double danger posed by Turks on the one hand and the Saracens (Arabs/ Berbers) on the other should more easily be understood as a single menace posed by one religion, Islam, and driven by a sole purpose: to overrun Christians and Christianity.

In this respect, Manzikert was a boon for those like Popes Gregory and Urban, but not just them, who sought to exploit the danger, either real or perceived, to mount a massive military response against Islam. By all measures, Manzikert was a game-changing event of massive proportions. The decisive defeat of a Christian nation at the hands of a Muslim foe had an extraordinary psychological impact in all of Christendom at a time when Europeans felt empowered with newfound vigor and ambition. With the last bastion against Islam suddenly diminished, perhaps it was time for Christians in the West to assume the mantle. Already, in Spain and in Italy, Christian armies and navies were showing their mettle and rolling back the Muslims, not only in Iberia, but also in places like the Balearic Islands or Sicily.

Thus, from the Western perspective (not so, evidently, in Byzantium), it is not because Muslims were becoming a greater threat, which they were not, but because they were becoming less so that the First Crusade was made possible. The tables, it was becoming clear, were starting to turn in Europe's favor, especially if one lived in Italy or in Spain. Taking Jerusalem seemed possible for the first time in centuries. And, with Constantinople now seemingly Christendom's weakest link, the time seemed ripe to launch a counterattack against the Muslims.

If the Middle East was disintegrating, Europe was doing the reverse, with various pieces seemingly coming together. The foundation of the Holy Roman Empire by Otto the Great in 962 and the takeover of France by the Capetian dynasty in 987 both contributed to providing Europe with the political stability it had lacked since the meltdown resulting from the partition of the Carolingian Empire at Verdun. Along with this newfound geopolitical stabilization, Europeans now enjoyed the spiritual unity provided by the Catholic Church, with its common ecclesiastical and administrative language, Latin. Europe was also experiencing social harmonization around a feudal order, and with the economic boom and demographic growth that characterized the eleventh century added to the list, the continent was suddenly in much better shape than it had been in centuries.

THE POPE PLAYS POWER POLITICS

The simultaneous rise of the Catholic Church and of the great kingdoms also provided a backdrop for a protracted political struggle between the pope, on the one hand, and the Holy Roman Emperor and the king of France on the other. These growing tensions played their part in the launching of the First Crusade, which occurred less than two decades after the strained Investitures Controversy that opposed Pope Gregory VII to the Holy Roman Emperor, Henry IV. The controversy, which would erupt again almost on a regular basis, resulted from a power struggle between the Salian emperors and the pope that revolved around the right to appoint local bishops. The controversy itself was but the tip of a massive iceberg that was to profoundly alter the nature of medieval society.

Essentially, the Investiture quarrel centered on the extent of lay rulers' authority over local ecclesiastics. While Henry IV claimed territorial authority over everyone, including the clergy, Gregory claimed spiritual authority over the clergy, whatever its geographical situation. Although the notion of the indivisibility of sovereignty had yet to be developed by future generations of jurists and political theorists, this is what this struggle was all about. The issue would not be fully resolved until the seventeenth century, when, in the context of the religious conflicts that would ravage Europe, religion was effectively flushed out of European politics.

What are sometimes referred to as the Gregorian Reforms were a significant event without which the Crusades would probably not have occurred, at least not at the time that they did or in the form that they took. Although the Gregorian Reforms were the culmination of a movement that began before Gregory (and continued after him), it peaked during Gregory's tenure. At this point, the two rivals, who by now were adversaries, went to war, Gregory having secured important military alliances, including that of Robert Guiscard de Hauteville, the volatile Norman (French) conqueror of Sicily, who was also fighting the Byzantines.

The intrusion of Norman armies in the Mediterranean had further destabilized the whole area. A few decades earlier, the Normans had pushed the papacy to the brink. In 1053, Pope Leo IX, assisted by an expeditionary force sent by the Holy Roman Emperor, had led his troops in the Apulia region at the tip of the Italian boot to counter a Norman army. Defeated and captured at Civitate, Leo lauded the "soldiers of Saint Peter" who had died as martyrs. Leo's defeat and his characterization of his efforts struck a chord, and, upon his death, various authors used the episode to make the case for holy war. By the time Gregory ascended to the papal throne, the notion of holy war was well established, and Gregory himself at one point entertained the idea of launching a crusade.

In the spring of 1074, shortly before the Investiture Controversy erupted, Gregory had actively sought to mount an offensive against the Seljuk Turks. In his letters, Gregory did not go as far as condoning full-fledged violence, preferring to characterize his idea as a show of force designed to persuade the Turks to refrain from any violence of their own against Christian pilgrims. Shocked by the Byzantine defeat at Manzikert, and by the violence that ensued from the Seljuk conquests, Gregory sought to go to the aid of Christianity's "fallen brothers." In a series of letters to various lay rulers, including Henry IV, Gregory asked that he be entrusted with taking an army to Constantinople, saying in a letter dated December 16, 1074: "In the name of Saint Peter, we implore, we advise, we invite those of you who seek to defend the Christian faith and to serve the Celestial Lord to take up arms and join us."[49]

Although the demand never caught on and was ultimately derailed by the quarrel with the Holy Roman Emperor, it clearly showed that this type of intervention was in the air. Gregory's appeal was not for a "pilgrimage," nor did it concern Jerusalem. It was a straightforward call for a holy war to defend Christians—Orthodox Christians—against Muslims. As such, it was even more radical than Urban II's later call to take back Jerusalem.

Though unsuccessful in his plea, Pope Gregory understood that the church was now at a point in time when it could successfully engage in power politics with the most influential rulers of Europe. He also understood that should the church choose to out of politics or indirectly participate from the sidelines, it might risk being forever marginalized by the secular powers. In this light, Gregory sought to further expand the autonomy of the church vis-à-vis the Salian kings and emperors. He looked to further its authority by asserting the primacy of the bishop of Rome over all the Catholic bishops and, by doing so, that of the spiritual realm over the temporal one. In making these assertions and in backing them up with the proper means, Gregory effectively expanded the notion that wars fought to defend the Church were just wars, worthy of sanctification. And, in reaffirming the existence a territorial entity called Christendom, whose highest authority was the church, the pope placed himself above all the lay rulers, asserting that the spiritual authority is unequivocally above the temporal one.

The Crusades called for by his successor, Pope Urban, can thus be understood, or at least interpreted, as a way to translate this bold attitude into an effective policy. The fact that Gregory was ultimately defeated by Henry IV (who installed another pope, Clement III, in his place) probably served as an invaluable lesson for Urban, who more successfully engaged in this game of power politics.

JERUSALEM

The last piece of the puzzle concerns the focal point of the First Crusade: Jerusalem. Gregory's call to go to war for Byzantium had fallen on deaf ears. The appeal, it seems, lacked that essential element of all religiously motivated calls to violence: symbolism. As symbols go, none was as powerful as Jerusalem. "In 1095," Jay Rubenstein writes, "Jerusalem was the center of the earth, the site of Christ's death and resurrection, where God had trumped the devil and worked salvation for humanity. Men and women across Europe dreamed of visiting that city, of praying before the tomb of Christ, of catching, if only for a moment, a direct glimpse of heaven. Out of such dreams and desires the First Crusade was born."[50]

Pope Urban's famous sermon at Clermont, on November 27, 1095, came a day after he had officially closed the council that had dealt with the progress of the Gregorian reforms in Southern France. In other words, this had been business as usual. In attendance that day were the clergy that had participated in the proceedings of the council, plus lay onlookers, mainly from the local aristocracy, who had been invited to listen to Urban's speech. The priest Fulcher (Foucher) of Chartres was among them, and his record of the exhortation gives us an idea of some of the points that were made by the pope, specifically about the members of the knighthood and the need to channel their destructive thirst for violence:

> May they engage in the fight against the infidels—a war that is worthy of being fought and merits to end in victory—those who until now devoted themselves to private and abusive wars at the expense of the faithful! May they now become the knights of Christ, those who were only bandits! May they now engage in a righteous struggle against the Barbarians, who until now fought wearily against their brothers and their parents! It is the eternal reward that they will now seek, when before they became mercenaries to seek a few miserable pennies. They will work over there for a double honor, those who fought here at the expense of their body and soul. Here, they were sad and poor; over there they will be happy and rich. Here, they were the enemy of the Lord; over there, they will be His friends.[51]

We know from various accounts that the speech was a huge success and that Urban's eloquence and charisma had much to do with that. Jerusalem was the focal point of the speech, which allowed him to provide his appeal with a coherent and simple message as strong in its symbolism as it was easy to comprehend in its strategic application.[52] The objective was straightforward and seemingly attainable, while meeting all the expectations of a people infused to the core with religion and living in what was essentially a violent physical, psychological, and intellectual environment. His focus on Jerusalem does appear in a formal document, a written appeal sent to Flemish populations shortly after Clermont: "We believe, brothers, that you have already heard through the report of many different people about the savage barbarism that has devastated God's churches in the East with wretched destruction, including the holy city of Christ, made famous through his suffering and resurrection, now disgracefully reduced to slavery along with the rest of the churches, shameful to say!"[53]

Jerusalem had become the focus of the future Crusade and, indeed, of all the Middle Eastern Crusades. By the same token, Jerusalem would also become, a century later, the rallying point of Saladin in his effort to reunify the Muslim populations. Notwithstanding the historical heritage of a city that had been equally important to David and Solomon, Jesus Christ and Muhammad, it also was believed by Christians destined to become, in the future, the theater of the confrontation against the Anti-Christ whereby the terrestrial Jerusalem was to be replaced by the celestial Jerusalem that foreshadowed paradise.

Thus, for Christians, Jerusalem was the place of origin that had laid the foundations of their faith *and* the place that would witness the dramatic events marking the end of time. In the intellectual framework of medieval Europe, this was the overarching superstructure around which all thoughts revolved. As an apocalyptic consciousness seemed to spread all over Europe during the eleventh century, a general desire was deeply felt by many individuals from all social backgrounds to go to Jerusalem where, hopefully, they would witness the coming of Christ and his triumph over the forces of evil, thereby saving their own souls in the process. For this, people were ready to sacrifice everything: their families, their property, their lives. It is for this reason that, contrary to a long-held belief, the lords at the upper echelon of the social ladder were themselves the first to join the fray, not just their impoverished younger brothers who might have found in the adventure a way to gain wealth and glory.

The Muslims had taken control of Jerusalem in 638, but the city remained largely open to Christian pilgrims. In 865, a pilgrim known simply as "Bernard" noted the activity of a hostel for Christian sojourners, probably the same one that was opened with the bequest of Charlemagne and the consent of Caliph Hārūn al-Rashīd, whereby "all are greeted who come here for their faith and who speak the Roman language."[54] The fate of Jerusalem, however, was conditioned by the numerous power struggles that rocked the Muslim world, that between the Fatimids and the Abbasids, for example, and between the long-settled Arabs and the incoming Turks. As Jerusalem fell under the control of one or the other, violence was almost certain to erupt, often targeted at the various non-Muslim minorities that inhabited or passed through the city. One such example took place in 1009, when the Fatimid ruler of Egypt, Caliph al-Hākim bi-Amr Allāh, sacked the Church of the Holy Sepulchre and burned down other churches and synagogues. It is unclear what his direct motivation may have been, but, in Europe, the event did not go unnoticed, generating various conspiracy theories against Jews, considered to be deicidal (this was anti-Judaism, not anti-Semitism, which is a later phenomenon), who then became targets of Christian ire, most notably in France. "They became objects of universal hatred," said a contemporary observer, Rodolphe Glabet, "they were driven from their cities, some were put to the sword, others were drowned in rivers, and many found other deaths."[55] This was the first pogrom against European Jews caused by the events in Jerusalem.

After the disappearance of al-Hākim on an excursion one night in 1021 outside Cairo (neither he nor his body was ever found), the rebuilding of the Church of the Holy Sepulchre began in earnest, as did the Christian pilgrimages. So much so that when several thousand pilgrims from Germany ventured to the Holy City in 1064–65, they were caught unawares in the crossfire between the Seljuks and the Fatimids, only to be rescued by the latter from a sure death at the hands of the aggressive Turks, in what appeared to many of the victims as a miracle of sorts. Still, the incident drew massive concern in Europe, and was soon amplified by the Manzikert disaster of 1071.

The year 1033 had marked the one thousandth anniversary of the death and Resurrection of Christ, which had revived interest in the Holy City, while arousing new apocalyptic fears and sending scholars scurrying to make astronomical and scriptural calculations as to the imminent end of the world. They came up with the year 1065, when Holy Saturday and the Incarnation fell on the same day (March 25), which coincided with the date of the Creation. Hence the organization of the German pilgrimage that year to Jerusalem to witness the Day of Judgment, which indeed nearly marked the end for those who had undertaken it.

Thus, a sense of apocalyptic doom seemed to overtake Europeans during the greater course of the eleventh century and progressively, all eyes focused on Jerusalem. The fact that the Church of the Holy Sepulchre was under control of the "infidels," and that this control was faulty, made for a situation that, in the eyes of the general population, was increasingly intolerable. Though historians today are less convinced than previous generations about the actual instability and violence that may have been provoked by the irruption of the Turks around the Holy City, contemporary Western writers tended to portray the situation as dire and precarious for Christians. Other travelers, like the Andalusian scientist Abū Bakr ibn al-ʿArabī, who stayed in Jerusalem in the early 1090s, thought otherwise, highlighting in his case the vibrant intellectual atmosphere that he found in the city.

Whatever the real situation may have been, by the end of the century, Europeans were ready to act, and to act forcefully. All that was needed was to find the right formula and the right formulation, both of which Pope Urban managed to do with a high degree of mastery.

CHAPTER 5

The Middle Eastern Crusades

Religious wars are not caused by the fact that there is more than one religion, but by the spirit of intolerance [. . .] the spread of which can only be regarded as the total eclipse of human reason

—Montesquieu, *The Spirit of the Laws*

When roughly a hundred thousand "pilgrims" set out for Jerusalem from all corners of Europe during the first months of the year 1096, the Middle East was in the midst of a political crisis not unlike the one that had provoked the demise of the Carolingian Empire three hundred years before. The recently converted Seljuk Turks had all but taken over power from the Abbasids (who remained in place as the official heads of state to conform to Islamic law and practice, caliphs being descendants of the Prophet). When, on November 15, 1092, the Seljuk sultan, Malik-Shah, died, the region plunged into chaos.

Like many Turkic, and later Mongol, empires, this one did not escape the inveterate inability on the part of steppe rulers to ensure a peaceful transfer of power. Quickly, the Seljuk Empire was ripped apart by Malik-Shah's sons, nephews, and cousins. His sons, themselves divided, had retained Persia. His nephews, also adversaries, had taken Syria, with one ruling in Aleppo, the other in Damascus, while another entity had emerged in Asia Minor. At the same time, the Fatimids of Egypt were looking at the situation with an eye to seizing the opportunity to quash their Sunni rivals. All in all, these deep-seated religious and personal rivalries would prevail over any sense of Muslim unity, even as Christian armies started to appear in the horizon. A jihad there would be, but not until the emergence of the great Muslim unifiers, Nūr ad-Dīn and Saladin, more than half a century later. In the meantime, the first Crusaders would take advantage of the deep divisions that had brought the Middle East to the brink.

Around the same time that the Middle East came under pressure, the Muslim kingdoms of Spain and Portugal were themselves disintegrating into ever smaller, adversarial entities, each one falling prey to the menacing Christian armies that were fully engaged in their own Holy Wars to recover what they deemed theirs. Among those who had flocked in support of the Spanish *reconquistadores* were southern French counts, including the redoubtable Raymond of Saint-Gilles, better known as Raymond of Toulouse, who had participated, along with other luminaries such as Hugh VI of Lusignan, in the expedition that led to the siege of Tudela in 1087. These men, almost a decade before Urban II's appeal, were already in full holy war mode against the Muslims, and it was on them that the fate of the first Crusaders would ultimately rest.

Needless to say, help from the North African and Iberian Muslims was not to be counted on by the (soon to be) beleaguered Seljuks. "Reflecting on the First Crusade and its role within interfaith relations, the only conclusion is that it was a mess," Nicholas Morton observes.[1] To add to the mayhem, a new player emerged: the Ismaili sect of the Assassins.

TERROR IN THE MIDDLE EAST: THE ASSASSINS

The Ismaili sect originated in 765 with the death of the sixth (Shiite) imam, Jaʿfar al-Sadiq, which generated a struggle for power between his two sons, Ismāʿīl and Mūsá. The partisans of Mūsá, who were the majority, created the mainstream Shiite movement, while Ismāʿīl's partisans coalesced around a radical underground movement. Backed by the Fatimid regime, Ismāʿīl's followers lived on the margins of Muslim society in Persia. There, they developed a solid theological and philosophical foundation that would serve their cause as they proceeded to gain support amongst disgruntled local populations. With the crisis that befell the Abbasid Empire in the eleventh century, the sect felt the pressure and it broke into two further parts, the Mustaʿali and the Nizari, the latter being the more radical of the two. When the Seljuks took over from the Abbasids and defended the Sunni faith with the zeal of recent converts, the Nizari undertook to fight the new regime.

As a fringe movement the Nizari were both weak—the Fatimids, themselves weakened, could not ensure the same support as before—and determined, so that they resorted to the preferred technique of most weak and determined underground political movements: terror. Whether it is because they smoked hashish before undertaking a terrorist act or for some other unknown reason, they came to be known as the Hashashins, a word that came down to us as "assassins" and became synonymous with murderers. In many ways, the Assassins resembled the twenty-first-century terrorist movements that make daily headlines, and they used similar techniques. Entrenched in a fortress in northern Iran, the Alamut, which served as their sanctuary and headquarters, they profited from the instability brought upon by the fragmentation of the Abbasid caliphate and from the arrival of the Crusaders. Also active in Syria, they were responsible for several murders of eminent political and military figures, both Turkish (or affiliated) and Christian, as well as countless acts of terror. Although their assassination of Christian leaders such as Conrad of Montferrat received more attention in the West than their other deeds, their principal enemy and focus was the Sunni establishment. "Their murders were designed to frighten, to weaken, and ultimately to overthrow it," Bernard Lewis writes.[2]

Although they played their part in the unfolding of events that took place in the Middle East during the time that immediately preceded and then followed the First Crusade, they were never able to gain a solid political foothold in the region. In the end, they were completely routed when the Mongols, under the direction of Hulagu Khan, one of Genghis's grandsons, stormed their fortress in 1256.

What little remained of the sect in Syria had little impact on the global politics of the region, which, by then, was being stabilized by the rise of the Mamluks who, under Baibars, decided to annihilate the remnants of the movement, which, a few years before (in 1174 and 1176), had unsuccessfully tried to kill the founder of the Mamluk dynasty, Saladin. Though almost extinct, the movement somehow managed to survive, albeit on life support, and as late as the turn of the fifteenth century, the Assassins were thought to have plotted against Tamerlane. The Assassins pursued a three-pronged strategy that included terror, propaganda, and limited military actions.

By the time the first pilgrims or Crusaders had undertaken the voyage to Jerusalem, the Assassins had already committed several successful terrorist attacks. One of these, aimed at the most prominent political figure of the time in the Islamic world, Nizam al-Mulk, an exceptionally capable Persian statesman who steered the inexperienced Seljuks, had provoked a huge psychological impact that reverberated throughout the Muslim world. The year was 1092 and, two years later, the Assassins were gaining ground in Persia, taking various towns, including Shadiz near Esfahān (Ispahan). In Esfahān itself, they launched a campaign of terror aimed at the population, but, as in other places, it backfired. Still, the Seljuks were effectively weakened by the relentless campaign, and the internal pressure played its part when the first Crusaders marched into Anatolia. Ibn al-Athīr, Arab chronicler of the Crusades, attributed the initial successes of the Crusaders to these divisions: "When the Franks—may they be cursed by God—became the masters of the Muslim lands they had conquered, this coincided with the fact that the rulers and armies of Islam were busy fighting one another, thus resulting in discord and disunion among the Muslims and dispersion of their forces."[3]

THE WARLORDS TAKE OVER THE CRUSADES

Launched by the pope, the Crusades were quickly taken over by ruthless lay military leaders whose names, almost a thousand years after the fact, remain familiar: Godfrey of Bouillon, his brother Baldwin (Baudouin) of Boulogne, Bohemond of Taranto, and the aforementioned Raymond of Toulouse. Others included Hugh of Vermandois (also known as Hugh the Great), Stephen of Blois, and the two Roberts, one of Normandy, the other of Flanders, both cousins. Some, like Raymond and Godfrey, traveled by land, though they chose two different routes (one via Trieste and the Albanian port of Durrës (Durazzo), the other through Vienna and Bulgaria). Others, like Hugh, the two Roberts and Bohemond, chose to travel by the sea via Bari and Durazzo.

Some of these men, like Godfrey of Bouillon, seem to have been genuinely moved by the religious motivations originally behind the enterprise. Others, like Baldwin of Boulogne, seem to have been driven primarily by greed and the lust for power, seeking to acquire territories in the Near East that they never could have gained in Europe. Still, the thirst for riches and power that consistently, from the start, led the Crusaders astray was regularly redirected toward the religious objectives that formed the core element of the crusading movement. During the entire duration of the Middle Eastern Crusades, despite the multiple sideshows that kept distracting the actors, great and small, in this tragedy, Jerusalem always remained the central focus for Christians and Muslims alike. Ultimately, whoever controlled the Holy City had a substantial psychological advantage over the enemy. The Christian armies that stormed the Near East in 1099 won that advantage, only to lose it again a while later.

"For all those who will have undertaken the journey to Jerusalem looking to liberate the Church of God, inasmuch as this endeavor is guided by piety and not to gain honor or money, this journey will serve as his penance," stated the decree dispatched all over Europe that set the events in motion. Although the journey called for by Urban II was prepared with some sense of purpose around a handful of powerful warlords, the appeal itself soon escaped the control of the church, with dozens of self-appointed recruiters at work throughout both urban and remote rural areas of Europe.

One such emerged from the lot, Peter the Hermit, who traveled from town to town on a donkey rallying his unarmed troops, the *inermes*. Traditionally, historians have opposed the Crusade of the poor and anarchic, led by the likes of Peter the Hermit, to the Crusade of the powerful and better organized spearheaded by Pope Urban.[4] The appeal itself appears to have been, for the most part, genuine for the masses who sought neither riches nor glory. Most of those who came back did so with even less money than when they left. Men, women, and children joined the fray.

The Crusade was officially launched on August 15, 1096, eight months or so after Pope Urban's call for the taking back of the Holy Land at the Council of Clermont. The organization that received the most attention and the best preparation was the one headed by Raymond of Toulouse. A formidable army of mainly southern French soldiers, it was the last one to leave. The informal pilgrim armies, on the other hand, formed hastily and jumped the gun so to speak, leaving several weeks before the official date of departure announced by the church. Among these, Peter the Hermit's army of several thousand marched on straight to Constantinople.

With tens of thousands of people heading south and little by way of logistics, the affair was chaotic from the start. In Germany, the pilgrims savagely attacked Jewish communities, giving the first hint of things to come. In Mainz, according to a contemporary account, the "pilgrims" "killed the Jews, about seven hundred in number, who in vain resisted the force and attack of so many thousands. They killed the women, also, and with their swords, pierced tender children of whatever age and sex. [. . .] From this cruel slaughter of the Jews a few escaped; and a few because of fear, rather than because of love of the Christian faith, were baptized."[5] Other violent outbreaks took place in Cologne, Worms, and Speyer. These outbursts were not confined to Germany, moreover. They occurred in Rouen in Normandy and Prague too, among other places.[6] Peter the Hermit, for one, instigated such attacks. Such acts of violence seem to have been driven principally by religious motivation, since Jews were often given the choice of converting or being killed, even though the church officially banned forced conversions. That being said, when Godfrey confronted the Jewish populations of Mainz and Cologne, a large tribute offered to him by the authorities guaranteed their safety. In Godfrey's mind, this money would come in handy when confronting his primary enemy. The princely armies may not have been as erratically violent as the popular ones, but whatever restraint they may have shown toward the Jewish communities of Europe was most likely motivated by self-interest.

If Jerusalem was the target of the campaign, Constantinople was the first point on the horizon, and, from a practical point of view, reaching the New Rome was what kept the pilgrims moving. As part of the deal with the original Rome, the Byzantine emperor Alexios Komnenos had promised assistance and food to the Crusaders when they reached Constantinople. However, he expected a few hundred mercenary soldiers, not thousands of unruly peasants. As the first Crusader armies reached Constantinople, it rapidly became clear that the entente cordiale between Eastern and Western Christians was going to be a complicated affair. As the troops advanced into Anatolia, things started to unravel in a bad way. The events around Antioch, in particular, set a new direction for the Crusade that did not bode well for the creation of a united Christian front.

Antioch had been taken over by the Turks a few years before, and the loss of this commercial city had been one of the reasons the emperor Alexios had sought assistance from the West. As the princely armies of Bohemond, Godfrey, and Baldwin advanced into Anatolia, they defeated the hard-charging Turks at Nicaea (modern İznik) and Dorylaion, despite being thrown off by the tactics of the steppe warriors and the long-range arrows of the foot archers (who shot from the ground with a very high-poundage bow, using the strength of their legs to pull back the string). The Turks themselves were taken aback, since they faced a very different opponent than they normally associated with Christian armies. Feudal armies, with their tight formations of heavy cavalry, would prove to be a formidable adversary, and it would take the military genius and political savvy of a Saladin, as well as some luck, to eventually defeat them. Initially, the armored knights proved superior to the Turkish mounted archers, and their religious zeal, in contrast to the attitude of the pragmatic Byzantines, took the Turks by surprise.

After these initial successes, the Crusaders advanced on the Anatolian plateau with great logistical difficulty, heading toward Antioch, one of the jewels in the Seljuk crown. The fortress, then displaying a formidable defensive wall of four hundred towers, was under the control of a Turkish emir, a vassal of Fakhr al-Mulk Radwan, the Seljuk ruler of Aleppo, with whom he had strained relations. Had the Seljuks been united, or even momentarily willing to put their differences aside, they might have easily overpowered the suffering Christian army. But with help either denied, delayed, or poorly coordinated, Antioch was ultimately left on its own. The half-hearted expeditionary forces dispatched from Damascus and, a while later, from Aleppo were, one after the other, easily repulsed by the Crusaders. Notwithstanding these victories, the Christians were not doing well, but after narrowly escaping disaster on several occasions and enduring months of misery, including famine and epidemics, they succeeded—in what they interpreted as a miracle of sorts—in bribing one of the defenders to let them into the city, where they massacred Christians and Muslims alike, being unable to distinguish between them.

Although it had been agreed that lost territories would be returned to Byzantium, Bohemond was not about to relinquish Antioch to it, and Emperor Alexios felt completely betrayed. But Bohemond had, on a fake pretext, lured the Byzantines who had accompanied him on the journey to Antioch to go back home to the emperor and then used their retreat as an abandonment and a breach of the contract. Needless to say, this dishonest ruse from an ally did not impress the emperor. From then on, the Byzantine-Crusader alliance became at best a tenuous one, pushed on one side by common interests and a common adversary, pulled on another side by mistrust, hatred, and deepening resentments.

Like Bohemond, Baldwin entertained ambitions of his own, and he had his eyes on Edessa (modern Urfa in Turkey), which was governed by a Greek orthodox Armenian, Thoros. With no inheritance to speak of, Baldwin had married a wealthy, powerful woman, Godehilde of Tosny, who accompanied him on the Crusade but died during the journey through Anatolia. While his brother Godfrey and the others were advancing with difficulty toward Jerusalem by way of Antioch, Baldwin set on his own course in October 1097, reappearing in the chronicles several months later, having carved out for himself a significant amount of territory through wily dealings with local Armenian lords, including Thoros, who sought his help and, with no heir of

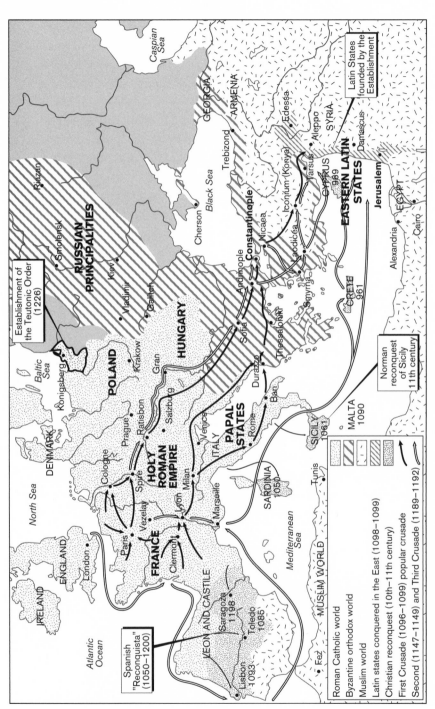

Caspian Sea

GEORGIA

ARMENIA

Latin States founded by the Establishment

Edessa

Aleppo

SYRIA

Damascus

TARSUS

CYPRUS 989

EASTERN LATIN STATES

Jerusalem

EGYPT

Cairo

Alexandria

Establishment of the Teutonic Order (1226)

Riazan

Smolensk

RUSSIAN PRINCIPALITIES

Kiev

Vladimir

Galitch

Cherson

Black Sea

Trebizond

Constantinople

Nicaea

Iconium (Konya)

Laodicea

Smyrna

Adrianople

CRETE 961

Baltic Sea

Königsberg

DENMARK

POLAND

Krakow

Gran

HUNGARY

Sofia

Thessaloniki

Durazzo

Bari

MALTA 1090

North Sea

Prague

Ratisbon

Salzburg

HOLY ROMAN EMPIRE

Cologne

Spire

Vezelay

Milan

Venice

PAPAL STATES

Rome

ITALY

SICILY 961

Norman reconquest of Sicily 11th century

Tunis

IRELAND

ENGLAND

London

FRANCE

Paris

Clermont

Lyon

Marseille

SARDINIA 1050

Mediterranean Sea

Atlantic Ocean

LEON AND CASTILE

Saragoza 1198

Toledo 1085

Lisbon 1093

Spanish "Reconquista" (1050–1200)

MUSLIM WORLD

Fez

Roman Catholic world

Byzantine orthodox world

Muslim world

Latin states conquered in the East (1098–1099)

Christian reconquest (10th–11th century)

First Crusade (1096–1099) popular crusade

Second (1147–1149) and Third Crusade (1189–1192)

MAP 3. The Reconquista and the Middle Eastern Crusades, tenth–twelfth centuries

his own, adopted him as his successor. Conveniently, Thoros was killed shortly thereafter, perhaps through the intervention of Baldwin, though the details are sketchy. In any case, Baldwin became the first of the Crusaders to win territory for himself in the region. His newfound power would significantly help the crusading effort by providing a base, a sanctuary, and a lifeline for the main Crusading army, which, at this point, the beginning of spring 1098, was not doing so well.

Much like their adversary, the princely Crusaders were now actively placing their own personal interests ahead of those of the community with whose fate they were entrusted. What little godly restraint they may have felt was disappearing fast, and the restless, fatigued, but all conquering soldiers were now committing the most horrendous crimes against humanity, mixing terror tactics with uncontrolled zealotry and gratuitous destruction. The usual crimes—rape, murder, theft—were committed, but the Crusaders went further still, engaging in mass decapitations; the "roasting" of spies—rotisserie style—presumably to send a message to other undiscovered spies; as well as acts of cannibalism. With the constant and mounting abuses, the Crusade was quickly losing steam and heavenly goals were being brushed aside by more earthly considerations. The crusading spirit seemed on the verge of being crushed by the lust for power and greed of a few individuals, but it rose from the ashes and put the Crusade back on course.

What is remarkable, then, is not that a few ambitious and powerful warlords fulfilled their own personal ambitions, but that the commoners who constituted its rank and file then managed to steer the Crusade back toward its original goal. This is all the more extraordinary in that the feudal order was as hierarchical a social system as there ever was, with the top echelon wielding all the power, and the masses enjoying none. It is thus a testimony to the strength of the crusading ideal and ideology that it gave the people the power to shift the Crusade back on course.

PETER BARTHOLOMEW'S VISIONS SET THE CRUSADE BACK ON COURSE

The Crusade was essentially reinvigorated by a wily, or saintly—depending on who interprets the events—individual by the name of Peter Bartholomew, sometimes described as a monk, who had joined the Crusade as the servant of a nobleman. One night during the siege, in late December 1097, shortly after the Franks had been routed at the gates of the city, a traumatizing event that had been followed by a series of earthquakes, Peter Bartholomew supposedly had a vision in which Saint Andrew (brother of Saint Peter, once bishop of Antioch) entrusted him (in his sleep) with a mission to find the Holy Lance, the Roman spear that pierced Jesus's side as he hung on the Cross. Keeping this to himself for the present, as advised by Saint Andrew in his dream, Bartholomew only informed his superiors of his vision a few months later, at the height of the battle. His revelations were well timed, because the soldiers were weary, and one Stephen of Valence had recently had a vision too, in which Jesus Christ, angry at the ungodly turn of events, had entrusted him with steering the Crusade back on course through an appeal to Bishop Adhemar, the highest-ranking cleric present, promising that the city would fall a few days later. An Italian cleric had moreover told soldiers that he had encountered a priest who asserted that he had met Saint Ambrose (d. 397 CE) on the road, who had told him that Christians who kept the faith and pursued the holy war would be rewarded by winning Jerusalem in three years time, which by that point was only a year away.

As if these visions and encounters were not enough, the night before the search for the Holy Lance was to be organized, a comet flew into the sky from the west and appeared to land in the enemy's midst. The next day, June 14, 1098, Bartholomew addressed the Frankish army, berated its leaders for losing sight of their mission, and then theatrically proceeded to uncover the Holy Lance in Saint Peter's Church, grandly carrying it out to show the Crusaders. Catholic authorities have treated this event as credible, but the Muslim chronicler al-Athīr debunks it:

> There was a monk there, of influence amongst them, who was a cunning man. He said to them, "The Messiah (blessings be upon Him) had a lance which was buried in the church at Antioch, which was a great building. If you find it, you will prevail, but if you do not find it, then destruction is assured." He had previously buried a lance in a place there and removed the traces [of his digging]. He commanded them to fast and repent, which they did for three days. On the fourth day he took them all into the place, accompanied by common people and workmen. They dug everywhere and found it as he had said. "Rejoice in your coming victory," he said to them.[7]

Right after the fall of Antioch to the Franks in 1097, a Turkish force led by the emir of Mosul in Mesopotamia, Kürboğa, arrived to relieve the besieged, and the Christians holding the city found themselves in the uncomfortable position of being encircled by it in what was effectively a blockade. Reinvigorated by the predictions if Bartholomew and the others, however, as well as by the finding of the Holy Lance, the Franks launched a successful sally against Kürboğa. During the fighting, several people declared that they had seen an army of saints in white armor, wielding white banners and mounted on white horses, fighting alongside the Crusaders—fallen pilgrims, these eyewitnesses surmised, who had come back from the dead to aid their brethren.

Bohemond kept Antioch, and the people got their crusade back. Now they could once again fix their attention on Jerusalem.

MARCHING TO JERUSALEM

Bohemond and his companions soon turned their backs on heavenly matters. These gestures from God had galvanized their men, and they had fought as one to repulse the Seljuks, but they were soon embroiled once again in petty rivalries. As a consequence, the Crusade stalled for several months until the popular sentiment once more prevailed over the self-interest of the leaders. Only this time, the anger felt by a majority of the soldier-pilgrims took a violent turn with the eruption of a major uprising in al-Maʿarra (Maʿarrat al-Nuʿmān in northwestern Syria), on January 5, 1099. Growing impatient, galvanized by Peter Bartholomew's theatrics, and weary of the feuds between their leaders, the rank and file had first expressed their frustrations by engaging in gruesome massacres of the adversary as well as acts of cannibalism. "I tremble to say it," reported Fulcher of Chartres," but many of our men, seized by the madness of hunger, cut pieces from the buttocks of the Saracens, who were dead at the time, which they cooked and ate, and even if they were barely warmed over they savagely filled their mouths and devoured them."[8] Finally, their frustrations boiled over, and Raymond of Toulouse was in danger of losing his grip on the army.

Shaken by the events, Raymond of Toulouse decided to steer the Crusade back on course by making a symbolic gesture. A week after the flare-up, on January 13, he marched out of the city barefoot, heading south toward Jerusalem. The other barons, Bohemond, Godfrey, Baldwin, and Robert of Flanders were occupied elsewhere but, as Raymond's army marched victoriously toward the Holy City, they rejoined the fray. By the beginning of summer, the army, now resupplied by Genoese ships anchored in Jaffa, was approaching the gates of Jerusalem, which they reached on June 7. The city, retaken by the

FIGURE 4. *The Taking of Jerusalem* (1099), oil on canvas by Émile Signol (1847), Musée du Château de Versailles.

Fatimids a few months earlier from the Turks, had been reinforced in view of the coming battle. On July 14, 1099, the Franks launched their attack.

The various leaders participating in the assault had divided their efforts, with individual armies responsible for attacking one corner of the city. After two days of intense fighting, the Franks moved in. Once in control of the city, they proceeded to slaughter all the Muslims and the Jews. That same night, July 15, they washed themselves, got rid of their blood-soaked clothes to change into clean ones and proceeded to the Church of the Holy Sepulchre. There they fell on the ground, arms spread out to form a cross.

Soon after the takeover of the Holy City, Godfrey was elected to head the newly formed kingdom of Jerusalem. A year later, upon his death, his brother Baldwin succeeded him. In the coming years, the Franks would consolidate their position in the Near East, from the coast to the interior. Four Latin states emerged out of the war: the kingdom of Jerusalem, the principality of Antioch, the county of Edessa, and the county of Tripoli, all of them organized under the authority of the king of Jerusalem. Only three and a half years after the call to arms at Clermont, Jerusalem was under Christian control. The Muslims, for the most part, did not understand what just hit them, many believing that they had been overrun by a mercenary army in the service of the Byzantines.

The creation of the Latin states of the Orient had many ramifications. It completely transformed the geostrategic dynamic around the Mediterranean, as well as the geopolitical landscape of the Near East; it legitimized the idea of a Christian holy war; it further marginalized the Byzantine Empire; it provoked a Muslim counteroffensive, ultimately resulting in the unification of Sunni Muslims around a jihad; it saw the emergence of military-religious orders, with the creation of the mysterious Knights Templars, the Hospitallers, also known as the Knights of Saint John (the name of their hospital in Jerusalem), and, of greater historical significance, the Teutonic Knights and the Mamluks.

The Israeli historian Joshua Prawer argues that the Frankish kingdom of Jerusalem was the mold in which all forms of Western colonization were subsequently cast, including a rejection of cultural diversity and the creation of a social system akin to apartheid. Published at a time when the critique of Western colonialism was at its most virulent, the more radical aspects of his thesis have been challenged by new studies showing greater cultural interaction between Christians and Muslims than previously thought.[9] Nevertheless, a long series of European armies bent on conquering both souls and territories, Bible in one hand and a sword in the other, might be seen a starting with the First Crusade.

For the Franks, the taking of Jerusalem was a special moment, and the devout Godfrey of Bouillon made sure that it was not lost. Though he was effectively the ruler of the kingdom of Jerusalem, he humbly refused to be crowned king, preferring the title of Defender of the Holy Sepulchre (*Advocatus Sancti Sepulchri*). His brother Baldwin had fewer qualms, however, and he gladly took the crown when his turn came in 1100.

THE MUSLIM COUNTEROFFENSIVE

In the Muslim camp, the reaction to the Frankish invasion was slow and unorganized. With few exceptions, not many understood that this was a holy war from their adversaries' perspective. The attitude of the barons and many of their actions were indeed not always holy. But when, in Damascus, a preacher named ʿAlī ibn Ṭāhir al-Sulamī tried to alert his fellow citizens to the fact that this was a holy war, and that they needed to respond accordingly by launching a jihad, he found little support. This was in 1105, and the time was not yet ripe for a full-fledged Muslim counteroffensive.

Things started to change in 1144, when ʿImād al-Dīn Zangī (or Zengī), the Seljuk atabeg of Aleppo and Mosul, besieged and took Edessa, signaling the beginning of the Muslim counteroffensive. This led to the Second Crusade, proclaimed in March 1146 by St. Bernard of Clairvaux in Vézelay in central France. First led by Conrad III, king of Germany, and then by the king of France, Louis VII, the Second Crusade was to prove a complete disaster, which further empowered Zangī and his successors. But it would fall to his son Nūr ad-Dīn to undertake the reunification of Islam, a process that would be continued with great success by one of his generals, Salāh ad-Dīn, better known in the West as Saladin, whose jihad would prove fatal to the Crusaders. "The advent of the Atabeg Zengî in Aleppo and his reign over the principalities of Aleppo-Mosul (1129–1146) signaled, from the Muslim perspective, the turning point of the history of the Crusades," René Grousset writes.[10]

In short, then, the jihad around which Saladin was to ultimately reunite a fragmented and beleaguered Muslim community came initially as a reaction to a population that felt under siege. The clash of civilizations that was to materialize before the end of the twelfth century was not, however, a reality during the First Crusade and it took three committed individuals, Zangī, Nūr ad-Dīn, and Saladin, to get a holy war under way. Although Saladin is the towering figure of this history, Nūr ad-Dīn (1118–74) is in many respects the one who put this history into motion.

The internal violence that had begun to undermine the cohesiveness of the Near East at the end of the eleventh century, thus facilitating the invasion of the crusading armies, had continued into the next century. Only now the internal strife was spreading to new areas. After Syria (which comprised the area of the current state of Syria as well as Lebanon, Israel, the Palestinian territories, and Jordan), Egypt was now also disintegrating. The Assassins, already active against the Turks, were targeting the Shiite Fatimids, killing the grand vizier in 1121 and the caliph in 1130. Another caliph was killed by his own vizier in 1154. Between 1153 and 1164, out of five viziers, four were assassinated and one was killed by the Franks after fleeing to Palestine. The spiral of violence kept spinning faster. Until Zangī took matters in his own hands, the Frankish menace had not been perceived as a hemorrhage that called for urgent attention.

For the most part, however, each Seljuk vassal bey merely tried to protect whatever territory he had, without trying to regain what had been lost to the Christians. If the latter (who at their most numerous numbered only 150,000 in the region, kept gaining territories—Tyre in 1024, and Ascalon in 1153), it was more because of Muslim weakness than by reason of their own strength. The first significant counterattack on the Franks was the battle of Ager Sanguinis (Field of Blood) in 1119, in which the army of the Turkmen atabeg Īlghāzī annihilated Roger of Salerno's and Roger himself was killed.

By 1144, Zangī had consolidated enough power in the region to be able to attack the Franks. He was the first to portray this war as a holy one, a jihad, but this found little echo in the Muslim world. Learning that Edessa had been left unguarded in Count Jocelyn II's absence, defended only by the unarmed clergy, Zangī moved in easily. Although the city had fallen without a proper fight, the takeover gave a formidable psychological boost to the Muslim community, which now conceived of the idea that the lost territories could be recovered after all and that Jerusalem could once again fall under Muslim control.

Much the way Urban II had orchestrated a full-throttle propaganda campaign around Jerusalem, Zangī's entourage was now doing likewise. In that part of the world and within a Muslim culture strongly marked by its Persian coloring, the most influential propagandists of the day were the poets, who now channeled their talents and inspiration around the Holy City, which became the focal point of a nascent Muslim holy war that, in many aspects, came to mirror the Christian one. In 1146, Zangī's was assassinated by one his slaves, a man of Frankish origin, but his son and successor, Nūr ad-Dīn, was to prove a worthy heir, determined to uphold his father's ambitions. In the process, he was helped by the ineptness of the Frankish army.

The strength of Nūr ad-Dīn and the key to his success was his deep understanding of jihad as being more than a military operation against the Christian invaders. A refined and subtle man, he first expanded his efforts in reconstructing the Muslim community around a core set of moral values in line with the teachings of Islam. This attitude was not just an intellectual exercise and he proceeded to further the arts and the sciences and to provide a potent social infrastructure, creating dozens of hospitals, libraries, and places of worship. Thus conceived, the jihad became a moral and social force in the Muslim community in addition to being a military struggle against the adversary of Islam. Foreseeing victory, Nūr ad-Dīn had a cabinetmaker in Aleppo carve an elaborate pulpit destined for the al-Aqsā Mosque in Jerusalem.[11]

The leaders of the Second Crusade had grandiose objectives. Judging Edessa to be too modest to command their efforts, they sought a bigger prize:

Damascus, then under the control of yet another Turkish dynasty, the Burids. This strategic decision proved a disastrous one. Repulsed at the gates and forced to flee, they paved the way for Nūr ad-Dīn's takeover of the city, which he celebrated with another victory, this time against the Franks of Antioch in June 1049, the severed head of their leader, Raymond of Poitiers, being sent as a gift to the caliph of Bagdad. Nūr ad-Dīn did not seek to take Antioch itself; he contented himself with controlling the surrounding territories.

The Christian unity that had enabled the Crusaders to take Jerusalem was breaking down, and there was now open enmity between the Franks and the Byzantines. The First Crusade had had two effects on the collective consciousness of the Europeans. On the one hand, it had reinforced the sense of a Christian community, of a spiritual, cultural, and geographic Christendom (*Christianitas*). On the other hand, it had created an irreparable rift between Western and Eastern Christians, one that would foster a durable disdain in the West for "Oriental" people and a deeply held belief that northern Europeans, raised in harsh, cold climates, were intrinsically superior to the effeminate, indolent, and lethargic peoples of the south. This notion remained potent throughout the Middle Ages and found its way into the political theories of the Enlightenment, most notably with Montesquieu. In due time, it would translate into the racial/racist theories of the nineteenth century, which would run parallel to, and then supplant, the religious fault lines around which Europeans had originally sourced their collective identities. This passage from William of Adam's treatise *How to Defeat the Saracens* gives an idea of the degree of mutual distrust that prevailed:

> The Fifth reason [why a crusade should begin in Constantinople] is that the army of the Lord can protect itself against the frauds and plots which the emperor of Greece [Byzantium] and his people are accustomed to make and devise against the sons of the Roman church. For since the emperor lacks confidence in his own power and is not armed with the prowess of soldiers and seeing that he has no defense against our men and no escape is possible, he turns to fraud and malicious deeds, and he devises any malice he can to harm us by some treacherous cunning. Being envious of us and full of the venom of hate, he does not want things to go well for us but wants bad things, and he wants and strives for good things for the Saracens more than for the Christians. This almost natural venom of bitterness against us has always originated with them, and this evil store still perseveres in their hearts. [. . .] The seventh reason, roused by the double cause of the stimulus of love and the zeal for revenge and hate, is that we have to fight the Greeks I do not say as much as but even more than the Saracens.[12]

By the middle of the twelfth century, the jihad launched by Zangī and pursued after him by Nūr ad-Dīn was gaining traction. The process was still a slow one, however, and it would take one more generation for all the parts to come together. For this to happen, it was imperative that Egypt fall into the right hands. Egypt, as it had been in the past, was an economic breadbasket and a key element of the strategic puzzle. Although it had been ruled by Shiites, the majority of the population was Sunni. Not only was it imperative for Nūr ad-Dīn to gain control of it in light of his quest for Muslim unity, it was just as crucial that it not fall into the hands of the Franks. Strategically, its conquest constituted a vital stage in the quest to recover Jerusalem.

The man entrusted with the task of conquering Egypt was Salāh ad-Dīn, whom the Franks called Saladin, a promising military officer of Kurdish origin whose father and uncle had fought loyally for Nūr ad-Dīn.

SALADIN'S JIHAD

We first hear of Saladin in 1164, at which time he participated in his first campaign in Egypt alongside his uncle, Shīrkūh. The Fatimid vizir Shāwar had been dismissed, and he had gone to Nūr ad-Dīn to help him regain his position, putting the fox in the hen house and thus precipitating the end of the Fatimid caliphate. By 1167, Shāwar had understood his mistake and sought help among the Franks of Jerusalem, thus bringing about a war between the Zengids and the king of Jerusalem, Amalric, in which Saladin played an active part. This first encounter between Saladin and the Franks ended with a truce and a civil meeting between Amalric and Saladin. Among the Franks in the Near East and Europeans in general, Saladin would from then on enjoy an excellent reputation, which has endured to this day, and many biographies of him that have appeared in the West, as compared to those written about other luminaries of the Muslim world.

In early 1169, events unfolded quickly, with Shāwar's assassination followed shortly by Shīrkūh's death (purportedly of "indigestion," which could have meant food poisoning or choking). Named head of the Syrian forces in Egypt by Nūr ad-Dīn and pushed to take over as vizier with the agreement of the Fatimid caliph, now devoid of any substantial power, Saladin was now fully in charge of Egyptian affairs. It was from there that he would build his power base and subsequently replace Nūr ad-Dīn at the head of the Zengid empire.[13]

Al-ʿĀdid, the last Fatimid caliph, died on September 13, 1171, eliminating one of the principal obstacles to Islamic unity. Egypt's largely Sunni population was not unhappy with this outcome, although Turkish rulers now replaced the Arabs. In Baghdad, thousands of Sunnis took to the streets to celebrate.

Saladin, being Kurdish, was himself in a neutral position with regard to the ethnic rivalry that ran parallel to the religious divide between Shiites and Sunnis. Though its role is difficult to assess, his ethnic neutrality may have played a significant role in Saladin's own rise to power. In any case, the Muslim world was not only divided on a religious axis but also on an ethnic/linguistic one. Islam sought to unify peoples of different cultural origins through religion, but this did not imply that ethnic rivalries, especially between the elites, evaporated. The Arab aristocracy, in particular, still felt a strong sense of entitlement as the originators of Islam and the driving force behind the historic Muslim conquests.

Alas, now accustomed to a life of luxury after several centuries in power, these urban Arabic elites were not altogether averse to leaving the dirty work of war to Turkic leaders and soldiers who were more versed in this art than they. The dynasties, be they Shiite or Sunni, that claimed a direct linkage to the Prophet retained a form of political and religious legitimacy and thus were somewhat protected from a complete takeover of power by the Turkic elites that now ran their armies and their governments. The system put in place forbade, at least for a time, the hereditary transmission of power.

In Egypt, Saladin now possessed a political base from which he was able to secure his own power and build on it. By the time of Nūr ad-Dīn's death in 1174, he was poised to take his place as leader of the jihad against the Franks. Moreover, he held much better cards than Nūr ad-Dīn ever had. Charismatic, morally beyond reproach, a devout Muslim, Saladin was able to mobilize the populations around the recovery of Jerusalem. Although not an Alexander or a Hannibal, he would prove the greatest general of his generation.

The meshing of politics and religion that is an inherent characteristic of governance in the Muslim world meant, for Saladin, that he needed the approval of the caliph in order to succeed Nūr ad-Dīn to the throne. To gain this approval, he organized a lobbying campaign that revolved around his active defense of Sunni orthodoxy, his opposition to the heretical Fatimids and rebels in Yemen, and his desire to repel the Franks. "We faced the sabers, and others aspired to the highest honors," he wrote in a letter to the caliph shortly after Nūr ad-Dīn's death. "There is no doubt that we are claiming our due in the name of justice,

FIGURE 5. Saladin monument in the Saladin Citadel, Cairo, Egypt.
Photo by Boda Art Works/ Shutterstock.com.

which restores what has been taken by force." [14] His correspondence with Caliph al-Mustadi (1170–80) focused on one line of argument: that he had served as the military hand of God in His quest to restore power to the Abbasid caliphate. Al-Mustadi's successor, Caliph al-Nāsir li-Dīn Allāh (1180–1225), would take this argument to heart and use it to reassert the Abbasids' religious authority over the Community of Believers. At the same time, Saladin installed a new form of government in Egypt, which would ultimately take shape as the redoubtable and enduring Mamluk military state perfected by Baibars a few decades later. But, before the dust settled, even for a brief period, Saladin channeled all his energies toward one goal: taking back Jerusalem.

This Saladin was able to do after eliminating the Zengid Turks from contention, a political purge he also undertook under the guise of Muslim reunification. The titles conferred to him by the caliph was clear: as *al-mujāhid* and *al-murābit*, Saladin was deemed the combatant of the jihad and the defender of the frontiers of the caliphate. In his earlier correspondence (1175) with Caliph al-Mustadi, Saladin had already evoked his determination to retake Jerusalem:

> The Franks know that, in us, they have an adversary that no calamity can take down before that day when they become discouraged, a leader who will not lay down his sword until they disarm. If our view gains the [caliph's] high approval, we will fight with a sword formidable even in its sheath, by the will of God we will achieve our desires. Believers will not even need to take their hands out of their mantles, and we will liberate the mosque where God transported his servant during the night.[15]

Although it would take a full decade before Saladin could take on the Franks, his long campaign to unify Egypt, Syria, and Upper Mesopotamia was undertaken and advertised as a jihad against the Christians. During this time, he communicated this ideal through a forceful propaganda that relentlessly portrayed him as the only individual capable of defeating the Franks and crushing their will to destroy Islam. Central to this propaganda was the idea that victory was impossible without unity, a justification based on a firm belief in the truth of this premise and also on the need to justify his wars against other Muslims, including Sunni Muslims like the Zengids.

According to his biographer Ibn Shaddad, "The Jihad, his love and passion for it, had taken a mighty hold on his heart and all his being, so much so that he talked of nothing else, thought of nothing but the means to pursue it, was concerned only with its manpower and had a fondness only for those who spoke of it and encouraged it." [16] So committed was Saladin to the jihad that his strategic decisions were sometimes guided by religious considerations, and he often extolled God's assistance in this struggle. Thus, he often launched his attacks on a Friday, usually during midday prayers, the best attended of the week, when most Muslims were participating. This, of course, was a double-edged sword, because a Friday defeat was more ominous than any other military setback. Jerusalem would be taken on a Friday, and Acre would be lost on a Friday. Both outcomes were interpreted in light of what God had in store for His combatants.

Saladin's grand strategy hinged on the recapturing of Jerusalem, hence his focus on conquering Syria, from which he would launch his attack. In making Jerusalem the centerpiece of his strategy, Saladin and his propagandists made the status of the city equivalent to that of Mecca, thereby justifying all the efforts that were put into retaking it from the Franks. This is one of many similarities with the actions earlier of Pope Urban II. Both Urban and Saladin sought to unify a religious community through the launching of a holy war centered on the recapturing of Jerusalem. Saladin's jihad, however, was in the end much more focused than Urban's crusade, chiefly because Saladin was at the same time architect, engineer, and project manager, whereas Urban confined himself to being only the architect. The result was that the pope's crusade relied on men whose motives were tainted by personal ambitions and aggrandizement while Saladin's goals remained pure to the end, or at least as pure as humanly possible in the context of ferocious political and military struggles.

Popular crusaders helped steer the struggle back toward Jerusalem during the First Crusade. With Saladin, no such popular movement was needed, as his unwavering authority and moral direction created a synergy that infused the jihad with great vigor. From a military perspective the Franks constituted a formidable force. The reorganization of the Frankish armies under Pepin and then Charlemagne had marked a military renaissance of sorts in the West. Further developments right through to the eleventh century provided the Western armies with a formidable weapon: the heavy cavalry. Although the reputation of the knight in his shining armor was to suffer a major setback during the Hundred Years' War, with the successive, humiliating defeats of French cavalry by English and Welsh longbowmen at Crécy (1346), Poitiers (1356), and Agincourt (1415), in the twelfth century, Frankish knights were capable of defeating the best armies of the day. There was also a new factor to take into account: the emergence of the warrior monk or monk soldier, a figure who would long play a pivotal role in religious wars, not only in the Middle East but later in Europe.

The monk soldier was a direct product of the First Crusade. Originally founded to provide medical and logistical assistance to crusaders and pilgrims, the various orders of "monks of war," as Desmond Seward calls them,[17] that were created in the twelfth century quickly began to play a role in combat too.[18] Other such orders, though not as well known or as powerful as the three main orders, the Hospitallers, Templars, and Teutonic Knights, also emerged in Spain and Portugal in the context of the Reconquista. The Hospitallers essentially remained committed to the noncombatant role that was initially theirs, while the Templars and Teutonic Knights fully embraced the Crusades and actively participated in their violence, becoming key players in the battles that pitted the Christians against the Muslims. After the Near Eastern Crusades, they would import religious violence back into Europe, where the Teutonic Knights in particular played a significant geopolitical role. In the Middle East, the monk soldiers came to form a military elite that was the core of the heavy cavalry of the Christian armies. The Templars and Teutonic Knights formed a caste of their own, which created its own power bases, thus adding to the tensions that already divided the various Latin kingdoms of the Middle East. Still, from a military standpoint, they were a vital asset to the Christian armies.

What we see emerging in the Middle East in the twelfth century, then, is a renewed struggle between, on one side, a Christian force that was both potent militarily and divided politically and, on the other, a steadily growing Muslim force that, under Saladin, demonstrated both military potency and political unity. Ultimately, though, the fate of Jerusalem hinged on the capacity, or lack thereof, of the leadership to defend the city. In this regard, the Christians did everything wrong, while Saladin did everything right.

Saladin's call for jihad merged the fight against insiders (heretics) and the fight against outsiders (infidels) into one struggle. With time, Christianity would follow suit. With Saladin's jihad, the concept of purity/purification, a focus of all Western religious and ideological wars, also took center stage. In this regard, most contemporary accounts of Saladin's retaking of Jerusalem testify to what almost seems like an obsession. Another important element seems to have pervaded this jihad: the concept of humiliation. This was the humiliation that Muslims suffered at the hands of the Franks, and that they sought to avenge, but it was also the humiliation they wanted to inflict upon their adversary. Humiliation, resentment, and vengeance would play a significant role in subsequent relations between the Muslim and the Christian worlds. But the fate of Jerusalem, the fate of the Middle East, and, in consequence, the fate of Europe was also to be marked by a series of accidents, disingenuous decisions, intrigue, and even romance—all culminating in a decisive battle that plunged the defeated party into chaos and for the victors created a renaissance of sorts, a tale central to the history of the Crusades.

MUSLIMS RETAKE JERUSALEM

The fate of Jerusalem might well have been sealed when a young boy contracted leprosy, for which there was no cure at the time. This child was the future king Baldwin IV of Jerusalem, who should have led the charge against Saladin. A remarkable political leader, strategist, and military commander, he was to show extraordinary courage, will, and resolve in the face of the personal tragedy that overtook him and his kingdom.

The years that followed Saladin's takeover of power from the Zengids were marked by increasing military activity on the part of the Franks. On November 23, 1177, three hundred mounted knights inflicted a humiliating defeat on several thousand troops (26,000 according to the chronicler William of Tyre, but this is surely an inflated number) under Saladin's command. This was to be his greatest defeat, from which he evidently learned his lesson, having barely escaped being captured by the enemy.

By that time, after being chaperoned by an able regent, Raymond III of Tripoli, after the death of his father, Amalric, Baldwin had taken control of the kingdom. His illness greatly impeded his actions, however, and the knowledge that he would never bear children generated an intense battle behind the scenes for his succession. His sister, Sybilla, was adamant about her right to take over, though according to Frankish Salian law, she could only do this via her spouse or child. The latter, also named Baldwin, was still very young, however, and her first husband, the capable William of Montferrat, had died of malaria a year after their marriage in 1176, so Sybilla married Guy of Lusignan—who would subsequently lose Jerusalem for the Christians.

Lusignan, portrayed unfavorably by all those who knew him, was an upstart who, with his brother Amalric of Lusignan (more highly judged than Guy by his contemporaries), had been forced by Richard Coeur de Lion to flee France. On his deathbed in 1185, Baldwin IV designated the younger Baldwin to succeed him, but the latter also died in 1186, and Sybilla managed to place Guy in a position of strength. Helped by the internal rivalries that pitted the various Frankish lords against each other, as well as the increasingly powerful warrior-monk orders, Sybilla and Guy managed to get their way. The result of this power struggle paved the way for the demise of Frankish Jerusalem, for Guy de Lusignan was to prove a poor strategist, an inept tactician, and a disastrous military commander.

The war between Guy and Saladin was instigated by a third party, Reynald of Châtillon, the master of Kerak Castle (which still stands, well preserved to this day, and can be visited on the way from Amman to Petra in Jordan), a brutal, greedy warlord who had come to prominence in a devastating raid on Cyprus. At this point, the Franks were very far from displaying a united front. The master of the Temple himself, Gerald of Ridefort, seemed all consumed by his personal animosity toward Raymond of Tripoli, to the point of convincing Guy of Lusignan to focus his war efforts against the latter rather than against Saladin. This situation had Raymond flip-flop his allegiances, moving back and forth between Guy and Saladin, which further convinced Saladin that his enemy was divided and vulnerable. This situation was a mirror copy of the First Crusade when a fairly united Christian front attacked a fragmented Muslim community. This time, however, the holy war was centered from beginning to end on a single individual with a single purpose—Saladin. Like many medieval wars, this one was decided by a decisive battle, the battle of Hattīn. Although there were to be six more crusades, Hattīn marked an irreversible shift in favor of the Muslims, which the Europeans were never quite able to reverse.

Before the battle, Saladin had managed to negotiate a truce with some of the Christian barons to ensure that they would not intervene, among them Bohemond III of Antioch, even though he had been a victim of Saladin's repeated raids. Saladin's call for an alliance with the Byzantine emperor had fallen on deaf ears, but the Byzantines eventually chose to stay out of the war, which was a victory of sorts for the Muslim commander. As with many such confrontations, chance played its part. Thus, it was by sheer coincidence that one of Saladin's armies encountered a contingent of Hospitallers and Templars sent by Guy to negotiate an alliance with Raymond of Tripoli, who, at that point, was siding with Saladin. This unforeseen clash quickly turned into a rout in favor of the Muslims. The two mighty orders had been completely caught flat-footed, so to speak, and had proven uncharacteristically ineffective. The Hospitallers' grand master, Roger des Moulins, perished in the battle.

To exploit this religiously charged victory over the Christian monk soldiers, Saladin had his soldiers parade with the severed heads of the knights atop their pikes. God, it was suggested, had sent a strong signal to the Muslim community: "This was a great victory, for the Templars and Hospitallers constituted the mightiest force of the Franks; the news of this victory was sent everywhere," ibn al-Athīr writes.[19] With the momentum clearly on his side,

Saladin was able to reunite all his troops north of Basra, totaling perhaps 20,000 men. Despite their accumulating problems, the Franks still could count on a significant force, including 3,500 knights and 10,000 foot soldiers (though very little was said about the latter in the various accounts of the battle).

The battle of Hattīn, fought on an excruciatingly hot day, July 4, 1187, was a textbook case of strategic entrapment. Drawn into a desert snare with no access to water, Saladin having cut the route to the nearby Lake Tiberias (the Sea of Galilee), the Frankish knights found themselves quickly depleted of the energy to resist the Muslim charge. Though poorly led, the Frankish troops were in fact well trained and experienced. The Templars, and to a certain extent the Hospitallers, were formidable combatants, though at this point, somewhat diminished physically and psychologically. The Crusaders fought a resolutely Western style of warfare with heavy frontal attacks and successive charges from the heavy cavalry, supported by the infantry and some light cavalry, in this instance Turkic *turcopoli* mercenaries. Saladin's army was more versatile and at this point in time, the Muslim armies offered a good mix of mobility and mass. In addition to deploying highly mobile mounted archers, they had learned the art of the heavy cavalry charge from their enemy. In the Muslim tradition, ruses were considered the highest form of strategy, and Saladin had become a master at this art. The Crusaders, in the Christian tradition, tried to refrain from such practices, which they deemed immoral and beneath them: God decided who was the more worthy of the two opponents and the fight had to be fair and square. A least, this was the idea, though these principles were not always applied diligently. However, at Hattīn at least, considering the unimaginative tactics of Lusignan, ruses were out of the question, whether on principle or by lack of foresight.

In this respect, the strategies adopted that day were in conformity with the different religious codes underpinning the two very different forms of warfare. Vastly superior to Saladin in all areas related to sieges, be they defensive or offensive, the Crusaders were taking risks fighting a pitched battle in the middle of the summer. With their heavy mail armor, they were likely to get dehydrated much more quickly than their lightly clad opponents. That being said, on that day, the Franks were far from displaying the best that the Western world had to offer in these matters. In sharp contrast to the hapless Lusignan, Saladin showed his military genius, exploiting the various elements that came into play, be they topographical, physiological, or other, to gain a decisive advantage over the enemy. Saladin made sure that all the preparations were made correctly before engaging his troops, and all the strategies and tactical scenarios had been studied long before Lusignan even thought about how he was going to overrun his adversary. Indeed, late into the night, Lusignan was still debating whether to listen to Raymond of Tripoli, who argued for delaying tactics, or the more aggressive barons, who were eager to attack immediately. An impressionable character, Lusignan listened to those who spoke last, and these were the barons, led by Châtillon, who waited for Tripoli to return to his tent before applying pressure on the king of Jerusalem.

So sure was Lusignan of his victory that he had brought with him the True Cross, so as to insist in the most dramatic way on the religious character of this engagement and, perhaps, motivate his troops to defend to the end the highest symbol of the Crusading movement and the physical link to Jesus Christ. As with most of his initiatives, this one was to prove catastrophic, and one wonders how his entourage could have let him make such a foolhardy decision. In effect, this was to be the last time the True Cross was ever seen.

Lusignan decided to take the initiative and he launched several charges at Saladin's center, but to no avail. Lusignan had walked into the trap set by Saladin. "The Saracens then [. . .] lit a fire all around the Christians so that they might suffer from the misfortune inflicted upon them from the heat of the fire and that of the sun," an eyewitness named Ernoul recounts.[20] The Franks, described another eyewitness, Imād ad-Dīn, "were now powerless, they were dislodged, pressed, hunted."[21] The Templars were the last to resist, and the battle ended with a handful of monk soldiers, sword in hand, desperately fighting off the enemy from the top of a small hill. Saladin's son, Al-Malik al-Afdal, who accompanied his father, described the last moments of the engagement: "I shouted again 'We have beaten them!' But my father turned around and said: 'Shut your mouth! We will have beaten them when their tent falls.' And as he was speaking, the tent fell. The sultan dismounted his horse, fell to the ground and thanked God as tears of joy fell on his cheeks."[22] The True Cross, kept in the tent, was then captured, as were the knights who had mounted the last stand, including Châtillon and Ridefort. "Since the time of their first assault on the shores of Syria the Franks had never endured such a defeat," al-Athīr writes.[23] Shortly thereafter, Saladin summoned the defeated dignitaries to his tent and offered a cup of sherbet to Lusignan, who passed it on to Châtillon. Saladin stopped Châtillon from drinking by beheading him with his sword, sparing Lusignan on the grounds that kings do not kill other kings.[24] "Twice have I vowed to kill him [Châtillon] if I had him in my power;

once when he wished to march on Mecca and Medina and again when he treacherously seized the caravan," Saladin is reported to have said.[25]

This decisive battle had ended in a most dramatic way after what had otherwise been a somewhat anticlimactic confrontation. The devastating news that the True Cross had been lost to the Muslims spread quickly among the Frankish community and throughout Europe. The Frankish resistance now completely shattered, and the cities held by the Franks fell one after the other like dominoes. On September 20, Saladin reached Jerusalem, which surrendered on October 2. The Great Cross (not to be confused with the True Cross) that the Crusaders had erected in Jerusalem was dismantled on the spot. A few places managed to resist, like Tyre, Tripoli and the Krak des Chevaliers, well defended by the Knights of Saint John. Conrad of Montferrat, whose arrival in the Near East on July 13, a few days after Hattīn, had given hope to the beleaguered Christians, was to become a central actor of the Third Crusade launched at the behest of Pope Gregory VIII. With the three major European heads of state participating, the Holy Roman Emperor Frederick Barbarossa, Richard Coeur de Lion, and Philip Augustus of France, this new holy war seemed destined for success. In the end, though, only Richard proved a lasting factor in the conflict and a worthy opponent of Saladin. Richard met with some significant successes and repossessed some of the territories lost after Hattīn.

Alas, even the pugnacious Coeur de Lion could not retake Jerusalem, and he and Saladin negotiated an agreement, finalized on September 2, 1192, whereby the Franks regained a foothold on the shoreline and were able to revive the kingdom of Jerusalem, but without Jerusalem itself, which remained in Muslim hands. Saladin guaranteed the safety of Christian pilgrims to the Holy City. Conrad of Montferrat, backed by the other Frankish lords who remained in the Near East, was elected king of Jerusalem in place of Guy of Lusignan, who by way of compensation was crowned king of Cyprus, recently conquered by Richard. Montferrat's ambitions for the region, however, were cut short when he was murdered by the sect of the Assassins on orders from their leader, Sinān. Inevitably, conspiracy theories around the assassination emerged that suggested that either Richard or Saladin were in cahoots with Sinān, but little or no evidence corroborates either scenario. In essence, Montferrat's disappearance complicated matters for both parties, and in the end, another French baron, Henry of Champagne, became "lord of Jerusalem," having refused the title of king.

Now threatened by his old ally turned adversary Philip Augustus, who was trying to undermine him in Europe, Richard Coeur de Lion was forced to accelerate the negotiations. Once again, the Christian front had fallen prey to personal and political rivalries. Saladin, on the other hand, despite having to face internal problems of his own, had managed to maintain unity and cohesion in his camp. His admirable example would serve future generations of would-be Muslim unifiers or reunifiers. From this point forward, the Crusaders continued to regress, and the Third Crusade was to prove the last truly worthy effort on the part of the Christians to reclaim the Holy City. Saladin, the great unifier of Islam, died on March 4, 1193. His son, al-Afdal, in a letter addressed to the caliph (written by Imād ad-Dīn) summarized his father's accomplishments, highlighting his father's commitment to jihad:

> Egypt—what am I saying? the whole world—was witness to his zeal for holy war; mountains and plains were all one where his actions were concerned. Jerusalem was one of his conquests, and the kingship of this world was one of the results of his resolution. . . . It was he who subjugated the infidel princes and placed a chain around their necks; it was he who captured the fiends of idolatry and bound them with heavy bonds; who subdued the worshippers of the Cross and broke their backs; who unified the Believers, preserved them, and put their affairs in order; who closed our borders, directing our affairs with a sure hand; humiliated every enemy outside your august House; and protected it from the arms of every impudent man.[26]

THE LAST CRUSADES

With Saladin dead, his sons and successors, including al-Afdal, fought one another, threatening the unity that their father had spent so much time and energy achieving. Less than a century after Saladin's death, another central figure emerged, the Mamluk sultan of Egypt Baibars, who would wage jihad of his own against the Franks and, more important, against a much more formidable threat: the Mongols. This jihad most probably saved Islam once again. Building on the much reinforced Mamluk system, Baibars ensured that the Muslim world possessed a core that preserved the whole from totally disintegrating with internal rivalries. Saladin and Baibars thus came to embody the jihadist spirit that generated and preserved Muslim unity. Later, with the erosion of the Mamluk system, the torch was taken over by the Ottomans, including Mehmet II, the conqueror of Constantinople, and Suleiman the Magnificent, who presided over the apogee of the Ottoman Empire in the sixteenth century.

FIGURE 6. *The Entry of the Crusaders into Constantinople*, oil on canvas by Eugène Delacroix (1840), Musée du Louvre.

Between the death of Saladin and the arrival of Baibars, the Franks launched several more crusades. The Fourth Crusade (1198–1204), called for by Pope Innocent III, was anything but innocent as the war effort geared toward Jerusalem was quickly redirected against Constantinople. The Crusade thus ended up pitting Christians against Christians when it was initially designed to seal an alliance between Catholics and Orthodox Christians. Against a backdrop of Byzantine intrigue and betrayals, the Crusaders took the city on April 13, 1204. After that point, the history of Byzantium became one of a slow agony artificially prolonged by the inroads made by the Mongols and then by Tamerlane, before the Ottomans finally occupied Constantinople in 1453.

Pope Innocent III's call for a crusade had been formulated in a radical fashion because he construed the appeal as coming directly from Christ in what amounted to a reenactment of the treachery and imprisonment that befell Jesus. In this light, the pope deemed any kind of refusal to participate in this holy war as an act of treason and betrayal of Christ, an attitude that came close to the Muslim doctrine of jihad.[27] "Pope Innocent (1198–1217) has been identified as marking the culmination of a process by which all barriers between religion and war in Latin Catholicism were removed," the historian Peter Partner writes.[28] It is ironic that this particular crusade ended, on their own account, in such disastrous fashion for the Christians.

After the sack of Constantinople, the near eastern crusades lost their momentum, as well as their symbolic force. By the Fifth Crusade (1215–21), Jerusalem was deemed by Rome less important than Egypt, meaning that geostrategic interests had by then superseded religious ones. Pope Honorius III's man in charge of operations, Pelagius, decided to forgo the capture of Jerusalem, at one point within the crusaders' grasp, so as not to jeopardize the conquest of Egypt. In the end, though, the crusaders were unable to take Egypt and, with this setback, lost any hope of reclaiming the Holy City.

The Sixth Crusade (1225–29) was possibly the strangest one of all, more bizarre still than the Fourth. The recently excommunicated Holy Roman Emperor Frederick II embarked on a "crusade" despite being shunned by Rome. Playing a weak hand, he banded together with the opportunistic sultan of Egypt, Malik al-Kāmil, who sought to eliminate a rival, the sultan of Damascus (his brother), who had allied himself with a Turkic warlord from Central Asia, Jalal ad-Dīn Mengübirti, driven out of Khwarazm by the Mongols, who had recently carved a kingdom out for himself between Armenia and Persia. Already, the geopolitics of the region were starting to feel the pressure from Genghis Khan and his Mongol armies. In exchange for Frederick's support, Malik al-Kāmil promised to cede some territories, including Bethlehem, Nazareth, and Jerusalem (aside from the Temple area). Upon his arrival, the Damascene sultan, al-Mouazzam, succumbed to a premature death, which meant that Frederick's services were no longer needed by the sultan of Egypt, who now found himself in a very difficult situation. Still, the sultan decided to keep his word, and Frederick was offered control of Jerusalem, as well as other territories, by the sultan: a "gift" that alienated both the Muslim community and the pope, Gregory IX. The gesture also showed how much Jerusalem's symbolic value had deflated, at least in the eyes of some, since the days of Saladin. Unhampered by religious considerations, Frederick's crusade had little about it that was holy, the Holy Roman Emperor's materialistic outlook was shocking to Christians and Muslims alike. In the end, with little local support and none from Rome, Frederick was forced to flee Jerusalem before a booing crowd and under a shower of rotten giblets thrown at him by the local butchers.

Christian control over Jerusalem was short-lived. To make matters worse, the new masters of Jerusalem switched alliances in support of Damascus against Egypt. As a result, an army of crusaders allied with dissident Muslim troops was completely demolished by Central Asian mercenaries hired by the Egyptian sultan. The battle, on October 17, 1244, saw several thousand allied soldiers perish.

Frederick's contempt for Jesus Christ and his disregard for religious sensibilities had doomed his efforts, indicating that such matters were still important in the region. The fact that Muslims were willing to ally themselves with infidels showed how the unity achieved by Saladin was also starting to weaken. Soon, the Mongol invasions would break the complicated geopolitics of the whole region wide open while giving the opportunity for some to rebuild a community anew. The Frankish presence in the Middle East looked to be reaching its last stages. Still, the West was able to launch one last worthy effort with the Seventh Crusade (1248–54), which, along with the First and Third Crusades, retained the initial spirit of a Christian Holy War.

This time, however, the impulse came not from Rome but from Paris, not from the pope but from the king of France, Louis IX, known as Saint Louis. This "Ideal Crusader," as Jacques le Goff described him, led what was essentially a French crusade that involved the greater part of the French nobility. As committed to the crusading spirit as any of the crusaders ever were, King Louis was intent on recovering the lost territories. At this point, however, Jerusalem was a distant objective and the crusader king preferred to focus on Egypt. Quickly, he scored a victory with the capture of Damietta in June 1249 and proceeded toward Cairo. But in the battle of Al-Mansūrah, on February 11, 1250, an impetuous commander, Count Robert of Artois, fatally exposed his small army of knights and Templars by pursuing the enemy inside the city, where his troops found themselves trapped. Louis and the bulk of the French forces were then stuck for several weeks, at which point they fell prey to scurvy and famine. Louis himself was captured in April 1250 and, after negotiating his release, stayed on, managing the kingdom of Acre with unrelenting energy and devotion for four years, while helping secure the fortresses of Jaffa, Sidon, and Caesarea. His devoted and selfless community work did considerably more to establish his reputation than his military actions.

In 1270, King Louis made an ultimate attempt at launching yet another crusade, known as the Eighth Crusade (1270–72) by negotiating a tenuous alliance with the Mongols. By then, however, Islam had found another unifying figure in Baibars, in many ways the new Saladin, who had managed to vanquish the Mongols on several occasions, most notably at Ayn Jalut, on September 3, 1260, a decisive battle that may very well, as Francis Fukuyama argues, have saved Islam from collapse.[29] Having turned back the Mongols, the newly empowered Mamluks possessed a formidable army, far superior to that mounted by the crusaders. The Mamluk system was a meritocracy, all its leaders rising through the ranks from forced slavery and conversion to Islam. The individuals that made up the Mamluk elite were bought or captured as children, usually in the Balkans or in Central Asia, and then received a rigorous military and religious education. Although some became rich and powerful, their power was confined to themselves, not their families, so that each generation produced a new crop of individuals in charge of political and military affairs. The system proved durable and incredibly efficient until cracks began to appear when the children of those in power inherited the power themselves. The Ottomans created a similar system with the janissaries, which ultimately superseded the Mamluks. Although eventually the Mamluks lost their luster, the institution remained in place, and, when Napoleon conquered Egypt at the end of the eighteenth century, he employed Mamluks in his army and amongst his entourage.

Saint Louis died of bubonic plague near Tunis on August 25, 1270, and King Edward of England, who took over, could do no more than secure a short truce. Before the end of the century, the remnants of what was essentially a scattered archipelago of small fortresses disappeared completely. Tripoli was taken in 1289 and Saint John of Acre, the main Christian base in the Near East since the Third Crusade, was overrun in May 1291. William of Beaujeu, grand master of the Templars, and Matthew of Clermont, marshal of the Hospitallers, perished during the final assault; the Templars fighting to the end before being crushed by the collapse of their fortress, a symbolic burial for those who came to embody the spirit of the Crusades. With all their continental territories now fallen into the hands of the Muslims, the Crusaders were left with Cyprus, from whence a glimmer of hope remained that a new effort might be organized with the help of the Mongols. In essence, though, the Near Eastern Crusades were all but over.

CHAPTER 6

The Crusading Spirit Lives On

Christ is risen!

—Teutonic battle cry

During the Council of Clermont in 1095, Spanish clergymen in attendance gave Pope Urban II a thorough assessment of the holy war that the Spaniards were conducting against the Moors. No doubt, this might have influenced Urban's decision to call on November 27 for the taking back of the Holy Land. The holy war in Spain was not a new phenomenon as it had been brewing for a while and was beginning to materialize in a big way. A century and a half prior, in 850, about fifty Christians from Córdoba had defied a religious ban enacted by the Muslim rulers and been put to death by the local authorities. Known as the Martyrs of Córdoba, their fate had profoundly shaken the rest of Europe and fueled a general sentiment in favor of, and an interest in, the support of a holy war to eject the Muslims from the Iberian Peninsula. With Christian armies making inroads in Spain and then taking over Jerusalem in 1099, Rome quickly envisioned both ventures as part of a single effort to overcome the Muslims everywhere.

THE POWER OF THE CLUNIAC ORDER

During centuries of conflicts against the Saracens, Spain had developed a very strong Christian identity. The discovery of relics of Saint James the Apostle in the Galician city of Compostela enhanced this sentiment, and Santiago de Compostela (Saint James of Compostela), as the city was now called, soon became one of the key centers of Christianity, along with Rome and Jerusalem, Constantinople, and Antioch. Along with that of the Virgin Mary, the cult of Saint James became a central theme of Spanish armies (Cortés's and Pizarro's *conquistadores* launched their attacks on the Aztecs and the Incas in the early part of the sixteenth century with the cry *¡Santiago y cierra, España!* [Saint James and attack, Spain!]). The whole of European Christianity was dumbfounded and profoundly indignant, even though the Muslims spared Saint James's relics, when Santiago de Compostela as sacked in 996–97 by the famous Muslim commander Almanzor (al-Mansūr), vizier of the Umayyad caliphate of Córdoba.

The strict Benedictine Abbey of Cluny in France, which plays a leading role in this history, decided to respond with its own means, and, under the leadership of its fifth abbot, Odilo (afterwards Saint Odilo of Cluny), exploited its vast network of support to encourage and develop a massive pilgrimage to Compostela. Much like the pilgrimage to Jerusalem that served as the pretext for the Near Eastern Crusades, this one quickly assumed a paramilitary aspect. It was claimed that Saint James appeared from time to time to guide the Christians in their pilgrimage; his first appearance dating to the battle of Clavijo (844). Henceforth, he was known as *Matamoros*, "killer of the Moors" or "Moor Slayer," a word that came to have a profound resonance in Spanish culture. From there, the sanctification of the conflict against the Arabs instilled the entire Peninsula with a crusading spirit that remained strong even after the Muslims were ousted from Europe.

In addition to being directly and indirectly supported by Rome in spiritual, psychological, and material ways, after the fall of the caliphate of Córdoba in 1009, the Iberian crusaders benefited, like their Near Eastern counterparts, from Muslim political fragmentation.[1] A twelfth-century sermon by Julian of Vézelay conveys the bellicose mood of Cluny, with its liturgy grounded on a "ritual aggression against the forces of evil":

> A terrible war assails us. Knights of Christ seize your arms. [. . .] Courage, Soldiers of Christ! [. . .] The Enemy is at our gates, there's not a moment to lose, we must fight immediately, hand to hand. Our enemies are so numerous and they throw flaming darts at us from every direction. If they discover that we are ill-prepared and defenceless they will only be more emboldened to brandish their arms, unsheathing their swords against us and launching more impetuous attacks. They are enemies with whom we can neither arrange a truce, however short it may be, nor conclude a peace treaty.[2]

Such talk undoubtedly had the effect of further bridging the gap between spiritual ideals and military expediency.

The Abbey of Cluny, in the heart of Burgundy, was probably the single most influential driving force behind the crusading movement. As a center of scholarly activity and a true meritocracy, it attracted the brightest minds of Europe. As its intellectual and spiritual influence grew, so did its political clout. The Burgundian nobility took interest in Cluny and began to funnel financial support to the abbey. The Cluniac monks, by all accounts great administrators and businessmen, were keen to share their talents with the whole of Christendom and the order spread throughout western Europe. Pope Urban II was a member of the order, and Pope Gregory, the great reformer, espoused its ideals. In Spain, the Cluniac monks, sometimes referred to as the "soldiers of Christ," served as administrators in the cities and territories taken from the Muslims. This was the case in Toledo, for example, where a monk by the name of Bernard of Sédirac overhauled the city's management with great diligence and religious zeal, transforming the local mosque into a cathedral, despite the treaties of tolerance that had been signed to protect the Muslim inhabitants. Following the actual soldiers, the Cluniac "soldiers of Christ" proved invaluable in securing the Christian hold on Spain and Portugal.

THE SURGE OF ISLAMIC FUNDAMENTALISM: THE ALMORAVIDS AND ALMOHADS

The Reconquista experienced two great surges, the first under the kingdom of León and Castile in the second half of the eleventh century, and the second in the twelfth century with the momentous victory of Alfonso III of Castile at Las Navas de Tolosa (1212), won with the support of Navarre and Aragon, as well as a small contingent of Knights Templar (who participated, albeit modestly, in the wars of the Reconquista). The first significant Christian victory was won at Coimbra in Portugal in 1068, followed by the capture of Toledo in 1085 with the active participation of German, French, and Italian Knights.[3] Burgundy, in particular, provided much-needed soldiers, who flocked to Spain. King Alfonso VI of León and Castile having married Constance, the daughter of Duke Robert I of Burgundy, in 1079, an alliance of sorts arose. Although this period predates the 1095 papal call for the liberation of the Holy Land, Rome was actively engaged in supporting the Reconquista. Western historiography has tended to treat the Reconquista and the Crusades separately, but, from the perspective of both the Catholic Church and the Frankish nobility, the two were part of the same struggle.

The first surge of the Reconquista provoked counterreactions from two Berber nations, the nomadic Moroccan Almoravids (1056–1147) and the Almohads (1140–1269), inhabitants of the Atlas mountain range. Both practiced a rigorous, one might even say extremist, form of Islam based on a strict observance of the Quran. Their venture into Spain was motivated in both cases by a call for a jihad to save Islam from Christian attacks and to uphold the faith that the inept *taïfas* were unable to defend. The two movements, and dynasties, although similar to one another, were also marked by intense rivalry.

The Almoravids were a confederation of Berber tribes who, inspired by a Moroccan theologian, Abd Allāh ibn Yasīn, undertook religious reforms before embarking on a war of conquest all the way to Algiers and then to Spain, where they fought a jihad against the Christian kings. Their leader, Yusuf ibn Tashfin, proclaimed himself "Commander of the Muslims," a grandiose title resembling that of the Commander of the Faithful, the Abbasid caliph, whom the Sunni Almoravids accepted as the supreme leader of the Muslim community. The victory of the Almoravids at Zalaca, near Badajoz, in 1086, stopped the Christians in their tracks, allowing the Almoravids to recreate a semblance of Muslim unity in the south of the Iberian Peninsula (their capital was Marrakech, Morocco). With the exception of Valencia, taken by the legendary Rodrigo Díaz de Vivar, *El Cid* (famously portrayed by Charlton Heston in the eponymous 1961 Hollywood film), the Almoravids regained control of most of Muslim Iberia before folding under the double pressure of the Christians in Spain and the Almohads in Morocco. The tide began to turn in 1118 with the fall of Saragossa, soon to be followed by the Almohad rebellion in 1125. By 1147, the latter had taken over Marrakech and overwhelmed the Almoravids just as the Christians were entering Lisbon.

The Almohads, meaning "those who affirm the unity of God," were more radical still than the Almoravids. Their ideology revolved around a strict understanding of the unity of God and a commitment to puritanical reform. They too had their ideologue, Ibn Tūmart, who gave the movement an intellectual impetus that fostered its unity, as noted by Ibn Khaldūn: "Many tribes could equal or surpass them in numbers and in esprit de corps in the Maghreb. But their religious unity galvanized the strength of their group feeling thanks to the clarity of their vision and their determination to fight to the death. [. . .] Hence, nothing could resist them."[4] But, as pointed out by Marshall Hodgson, the feeling was mutual, so to speak, and the tribal unity of the Almohads was what essentially kept the movement and the ideology afloat:

Ibn Tūmart went on to acquire a core of enthusiasts because of his wide religious and intellectual horizons [. . .] and a reputation among the people of the towns for opposing the luxuries of the Mûrabīt dynasty. All this was necessary, but the movement became politically significant and the religious reform effective only when the followers he had gained for his ideas became the nucleus of a power organization founded on the tribe with which he was identified. Then the ideas sustained the tribesmen in their independent course in spite of defeats; but it was the tribal solidarity that was able to carry them to victory.[5]

Although the Almohads quickly overran the Almoravids, their victories over the Christians—notably by Abū Yūsuf al-Mansūr at Alarcos in 1195—were short-lived, and in 1212, they were decisively defeated in the battle of Las Navas de Tolosa.[6] Like the Almoravids, the Almohads relied on a very small Berber minority ruling a largely Arab community. The Almohads proved brutal, especially to religious minorities, and the religious tolerance we generally associate with Andalusian Islam was by now only a dim memory. With time, the fundamentalist ideology that had given the Almohads their initial momentum waned, as illustrated by the fact that the intellectual movements generated by Ibn Tufayl and Averroës (Ibn Rushd) were able to thrive under the rule of the Almohads. Indeed, Averroës's influential writings on Aristotle and Plato were commissioned by the Caliph Yusuf I, Abū Yūsuf al-Mansūr's father.

The Almoravid–Almohad period, which coincided with a resurgent Christian push—both provoked by the fragmentation of Islamic Iberia—was thus characterized by a strong rise in religiously motivated violence from two rival parties that sought to establish or reestablish their hegemony on the entire peninsula. Given both the Christians' and the Muslims' commitment to holy war, this particular stage of the conflict took the form of a clash of religions that may have been even more pronounced than in the Middle East, where the Frankish crusaders were often distracted by considerations that had little to do with religion and holy war.

In this war, the infighting among the Islamic states, first between the *taïfas*, then between the Almoravids and the Almohads, proved as detrimental as it had for the feisty rulers of the Latin states who had bowed before the Muslim unity sowed by Nūr ad-Dīn and Saladin. In the Iberian Peninsula, Christian unity was equally decisive, and neither the Almoravids nor the Almohads were able to contain the adversary. After the fall of Lisbon, Córdoba was lost in 1236, Valencia in 1238, Murcia in 1243, Seville in 1246, and Cadiz in 1263. By then, only the kingdom of Granada remained in Muslim hands, which held on until 1492. The Jewish communities of Andalusia, already under fire with the arrival of the Berber jihadists were now forced by the Christian rulers to convert or to flee, many landing in the Ottoman Empire, where they thrived. Columbus's discoveries in the Americas channeled the energies of the centuries-old Reconquista into yet another holy war, now to win territory and converts for Christianity in the New World. After fighting barbarians from the east and infidels from the south, Christian holy warriors now headed west to conquer and convert another foe, the American savage, not yet perceived as noble. This time, however, their armies were led by adventurers for whom religion was a secondary motivation, though they were accompanied by clerics who, when they were not occupied enriching themselves, sought to convert their victims and sometimes even came to their defense, as in the case of the Dominican friar Bartolomé de las Casas (1474/84–1566), author of the influential *On the Destruction of the Indies*.[7]

THE EUROPEAN CRUSADES OF THE WARRIOR MONKS

The role of the knights of the Teutonic Order in the Near Eastern Crusades was neither as significant nor dramatic as those of the Hospitallers and Knights Templars, who were in the thick of things. After the Crusades ended in the Near East, however, the Teutonic Knights retreated to Europe where with the backing and active support of Rome they carved out a significant chunk of territory for themselves in central Europe in what would later become Prussia. From there, their power and influence grew dramatically and their geopolitical impact on the region was both great and durable. But if the Teutonic Knights lived by the sword, they also perished by the sword. At the battle of Grünwald-Tannenberg in 1410, they were improbably defeated by a Polish-Lithuanian coalition, and they were never able to regain their earlier status.

In many ways, the warrior monks embodied all the contradictions we find in the concept and practical application of Christian holy war. Some historians have contended that the true essence of the Crusades is to be found in the "popular Crusades" of Peter the Hermit and the like.[8] Others see the crusading spirit as an attempt by chivalry to realize its ideals, thus allowing, Alain Demurger writes, "the exteriorization of its religious consciousness."[9]

While the history of the Hospitallers is peculiar in its own right, in that an existing structure adapted itself to the circumstances brought upon it by the First Crusade and the capture of Jerusalem, the order of the Knights Templar is truly singular in that it was created specifically to meet the demands of the Crusades *after* Jerusalem fell into the hands of the Christian armies. In turn, the model and success of the Templars formed the basis for the creation of the Teutonic Order.

Pope Urban II's crusading appeal was based on the twin concepts of pilgrimage and holy war. Historians disagree as to whether pilgrimage to the Holy Sepulchre evolved into a holy war or, conversely, the holy war became a pilgrimage once Jerusalem was recovered. Because the First Crusade was such a complex event, consisting of so many different layers, it is difficult to decide one way or the other. What is clear, however, is that both ideas were in the air from the outset, and that both remained strong throughout the first Crusades. In this development, we also see the unlikely rapprochement of two key figures of the feudal order: the monk and the warrior, who forcefully displayed values at opposite ends from one another. For while the monk renounced all earthly pleasures and desires for an introspective spiritual quest, the warrior knight sought a life of travel and adventure that could end only in a glorious death on the battlefield or marriage to a noble lady of high birth.

Yet, through their commitment to a set of higher values and their religious devotion, the medieval monk and the knight in their own ways represent the spiritual and earthly lives that symbolize the dual nature of Christianity. Thus seen, they are the two faces of the same coin, which fuse together with the meshing of the actions that each one is undertaking respectively: pilgrimage and (holy) war. With the creation of the Order of the Temple, the fusion reaches its logical conclusion and the monk and the soldier become one in what amounts to spiritual osmosis. The Order of the Temple can thus be described, Demurger contends, as an institution "that permanently represents the model of the chivalry of Christ; a religious order that conciliates the irreconcilable by reuniting under the same roof [. . .] the monk and the knight, thus the monk and the soldier; an order, finally, that 'will embody permanently, and not just for a given period of time, as was the case for the crusaders, the ideology of the crusade.'"[10]

Created in 1119/20, the Order of the Temple was officially approved by the Council of Troyes ten years later. Its founder, Hugh of Payns, had left the Levant for three years to lobby for it with the clerical powers. Upon his return to Jerusalem after the Council, he had the guaranteed full support and blessing of the Catholic Church; he had secured significant funds from a variety of sources, and he had brought with him a number of individuals eager to join the order, and participate in the holy war.[11]

His mission had not been an easy one and, initially, his arguments had met with some skepticism on the part of church authorities. But Payns had managed to sway one person, Bernard of Clairvaux (the future Saint Bernard), the highest moral authority in all of Christendom. This was no mean feat and, in effect, Bernard's active support secured the future of the order and gave it the impetus it needed to thrive. Had it not been for this meeting, we might have never heard of the Templars, or, for that matter, of the Teutonic Knights.

What were Payns's arguments? Chiefly, that, practically speaking, the crusaders presented a temporary solution to the problem of maintaining control of the Latin states, including the kingdom of Jerusalem. The pilgrims that flocked to the Holy City needed protection, and the newly created states needed security. Crusaders tended to go back home once they had made the journey, and the lay rulers of the states could only be trusted up to a point, their personal interests often superseding their religious commitment. What was needed was a permanent army made up of individuals devoted to Christ and capable of handling a horse and a sword. Could the same individual be as committed to praying as he was to fighting and killing? The idea ran counter to the traditional church teachings, but the Gregorian reforms and Urban's call had broken a lot of mental barriers, even among the naturally conservative clergy. Payns's theological or ethical arguments were bolstered by current events in the Near East: the Franks' humbling defeat near Antioch in 1119 had reminded everyone that the region was far from secure, even before the enemy launched a proper counteroffensive. This event had pushed Baldwin II of Jerusalem to offer a sanctuary to the fledgling order in the form of the former Temple of Solomon—hence the name of the order—which had been rebuilt as a mosque by the Arabs (al-Aqsā). In his "Sermon of Exhortation to the Knights of the Temple," Bernard gave his blessings in a grand, and unequivocal manner:

> A new sort of knighthood, I say, unknown to the world, is fighting indefatigably a double fight against flesh and blood as well as against the immaterial forces of evil in the skies. [. . .] Truly the knight is without fear and totally without worries when he has clothed his body with the breastplate of iron and his mind with the breastplate of the faith. [. . .] So knights, go forth untroubled, and with fearless mind drive the enemies of the cross of Christ before you, certain in the knowledge that neither death nor life can separate you from the love of God that is in Christ

Jesus, as you say to yourself in every dangerous situation: "whether we live or die, we belong to the Lord." How glorious is the return of the victors in battle! How blessed is the death of the martyrs in battle![12]

Payns needed a blueprint for his order with clear objectives and, with Bernard of Clairvaux on the bandwagon, rules were adopted inspired by life in the monasteries. For the nobility, the order was a boon, with the highest chivalric ethos being put at the full service of the church. For the church, the creation of the order guaranteed that a permanent force was present in the Near East. Created to ensure the safety of Christians in the area, the Knights Templar were something like the United Nations' Blue Helmets. But with a Second Crusade looming, and then a Third, their role became central to the crusading effort, and their military skills served offensive strategies as well as defensive ones. Soon, also, they would be embroiled in the complex power struggles of the Christian rulers of the Near East. For the Muslims, these soldier monks embodied the best and the worst of what the enemy was throwing at them. The best, because their ethical standards and commitment to Christ and to their faith were deemed admirable, the worst because they were considered the most dangerous of the adversary's armed forces. When caught by the enemy, the Templars were massacred; the Muslim armies knew better than to release them in exchange for ransom, as they did with regular soldier prisoners.

At a time when armies rarely wore uniforms, the sight must have been daunting: mounted knights on their immense horses, a large cross on their tunics (the Hospitallers wore a black tunic with a white cross, the Templars a red cross on a white tunic, and the Teutonic Knights a white tunic and black cross), protected by their shiny chain mail, helmets, and arm and leg pieces. The Templars, Hospitallers, and Teutonic Knights were formidable soldiers, professional to the core: well-armed and well-equipped, generally well-trained and well-educated. Starting with nine French noblemen,[13] the Templars drew their recruits from the European aristocracy. Once integrated into the order, the knight gave all his wealth and belongings to the cause, to which he devoted himself until death. If greed and lust for power there was, it was collective and not individual. Warrior monks renounced property and personal wealth and vowed to remain celibate.

Military-religious orders in Spain and Portugal were attached to the royal armies, but those of the Near East were fully autonomous, which proved problematic once their members were forced to flee the region. Rich and powerful, particularly the Templars, the orders threatened the delicate balance of power that had emerged in Europe between the secular rulers and the church. In the end, a solution had to be found for each of the three Near Eastern orders. The Templars were eliminated outright, the Hospitallers found a sanctuary in the Mediterranean, and the Teutonic Knights were redirected by the Pope to Prussia, then inhabited by heathens, soon to be conquered and converted by the warrior monks, who, in time, would also challenge the local powers of Poland and Lithuania. In Spain, where military-religious orders had been integrated into the geopolitical system from the start, they never posed such problems, and the authorities never had to resort to such drastic solutions.

The autonomy granted the orders by the church came at a cost, inasmuch as the Near Eastern orders had to finance their own efforts. A prolonged war in a distant place is always costly, and the orders had to create their own economic organizations, procure matériel, and recruit troops and support personnel both in Europe and in the theater of operations. In addition to their intrinsic medical and military skills, members of the orders became master architects, building impregnable fortresses throughout the Near East and Europe, many of which are still standing today, including the greatest of them all, the Hospitallers' Krak des Chevaliers in Syria.

Starting from a blank slate in 1119, Hugh of Payns managed within a few years to secure vast amounts of money and property in Europe, on which the Templars built their economic and logistics base, as well as hundreds of Templar houses (commanderies) and fortresses. Through the Templars, the European aristocracy was able to contribute significantly to the effort, knowing that gifts would not be diverted to the empowerment or enrichment of local warlords. Donations came from all rungs of the nobility, as well as kings: Henry II of England gave a house and the king of Aragon a castle. Donations included rents and royalties: the powerful counts of Champagne (the region from whence the first Templars, including Hugh of Payns, came) gave the order a percentage of the proceeds generated by the famous Foire de Provins, which attracted merchants from all over Europe. Others, like Count Henri of Bar, underwrote a knight, much the way a wealthy donor might finance a chair at Yale or Harvard today. In Laon, also in northeastern France, from where the order drew much of its initial support, a group of wealthy bourgeois gave dozens of donations throughout the thirteenth century. By comparison, royal donations were modest; whereas in Spain, royal donations were essential, half the *commanderies* founded there being financed through royal generosity.[14]

The Templars in particular became very rich very quickly and their territories in Europe multiplied exponentially, even though their military focus remained to the end geared to the Near East. William of Tyre, writing in the 1170s, reported:

> Since then [their beginnings], their status and activities have increased immensely, so that now they have more than three hundred knights in their monastery, all wearing their white coats, not including the brother servants, whose number is almost infinite. It is rumored that they have immense properties, both in the land and overseas, and that there is not one province in the Christian world that did not assign them a portion of its wealth, so that their riches are, one has been assured, equal to those of kings.[15]

William of Tyre could not have used a better comparison, because this "equality" would rattle the French King to the breaking point.

Soon enough, stories and conspiracy theories started to emerge, some no doubt generated by the secular powers, chief among them the kingdom of France, for the Templars' wars in the Near East drastically enhanced their prestige and their power in Europe. The mystique and mystery surrounding them continued to grow, until finally, in 1312, in what was essentially a power struggle between King Philippe le Bel of France and the Catholic Church, the order was dissolved by Pope Clement V. Two years later the Templars' grand master, Jacques de Molay, and other leaders of the order were burned at the stake by order of King Philippe. The unsubstantiated, though entertaining, stories linking the Templars to the Holy Grail, to a secret treasure, and to the Assassins, among other things, have served to maintain an interest in their history, possibly to the detriment of their true accomplishments, which were remarkable.

When they faced Saladin at the battle of Montgisard in 1177, a handful of Templar Knights did sterling service routing a Muslim army that greatly outnumbered the Franks and included a large contingent of elite Mamluks.[16] Spurring on their horses as one, the Templars "charged without looking either right or left. Seeing Saladin's squadron, they headed straight to it, penetrating it immediately, hitting the enemy without interruption."[17] Saladin himself escaped capture with difficulty.

So humiliating a defeat would have undoubtedly destroyed a lesser man than Saladin, and Baldwin IV's glorious victory should have set the stage for a resounding Christian overtaking of the Muslims, but fate had other plans and the dysfunctional politics of the Christian kings that led to the battle of Hattīn reversed the momentum. The Templars played an important role in the Crusades that ensued, right down until their disappearance. After 1291, when they moved their headquarters to Cyprus, they sought an alliance with the Mongols in the hope of defeating the Mamluks, but this was thwarted by the Mongols' disadvantage in desert areas, where their dependence on food and water for their horses impeded their capabilities.

One of the Templars' greatest accomplishments was their capacity to ensure the security of two main roads, from Jaffa to Jerusalem, and from Jerusalem to the Jordan River, on which they controlled several fortified castles. They organized security patrols throughout the Latin states, and, with the Hospitallers, held a primary position in the entire security apparatus of the Christian areas. In battle, they usually formed the front or rear guard, alternating positions in this respect with the Hospitallers, who fought in similar fashion.

How did they rate as soldiers? The Templars may well have been the most highly professional army to come out of Europe since the demise of the Roman legions. After their brutal disappearance, however, their model did not really perpetuate itself, and the French knights who fought the British and repeatedly lost to them would have fared much better if they had retained the tactical know-how of the Templars against the archers. The Templars, as well as the Hospitallers and Teutonic Knights, were of the same mold as the European mounted knight, only better and more versatile. They employed shock tactics and favored pitched battles. But, having to face the Turks, who retained the tactics of the steppe, they had to be careful not to fall into their traps and be overwhelmed by archers or by the rapid movement of squadrons. For this, they had competent support troops, both infantry and light cavalry, including the *turcopoli*. Column formations allowed the mutual support between infantry and light and heavy cavalry. The infantry, consisting of foot archers, protected the cavalry with a barrage of arrows, and they were in turn protected by the lances of the cavalrymen.

The difficulty lay in bringing the adversary to fight a pitched battle, which Turkic commanders generally tried to avoid. All sources, Western and Muslim, cite the Templars cohesiveness and unflappability, which one could count on both in combat and also during difficult retreats, as at Damietta in 1219 or in Egypt a couple of years later.[18] As support troops as well as fighting ones, the orders were also in charge of protecting those who identified and buried the dead after battle, and they organized raids in enemy territory to procure food for the troops and the horses. With time, the Templars acquired the reputation of being first on the battlefield and last to leave.

How did they train and prepare for combat? In Europe, knights honed their skills through hunting parties and tournaments, but the orders were prohibited from engaging in those activities. Little is known, then, about the formal preparation of the warrior monks but, being almost constantly at war, they practiced their art frequently and at the highest level. Moreover, those who joined the orders as combatants were noblemen who had already received a thorough military training.

The Templars and the knights of the other orders sustained their commitment to religion from beginning to end, their higher ethical standards probably feeding their military ones. One episode, also during the siege of Damietta in 1219, is revealing: counting on the Christian troops sleeping during the early hours of the night, two hundred Muslim soldiers managed to penetrate the city with food for the civilians held hostage by the Christians. The intruders had not, however, realized that the Templars and Hospitallers were already up, celebrating mass, at that time, and the knights quickly dealt with them.[19]

The crusading armies did not always possess commanders equal to their task. More often than not these were given high responsibilities because of their family lineage rather than their military merits. Occasionally, as with Richard Coeur de Lion, a great commander would emerge and rise to the occasion. The Muslims, and more specifically the Turks, with their military meritocracies, managed on the other hand to produce a great general with each generation: Zengī, Nūr ad-Dīn, Saladin, Baibars, and later Bayezid, Tamerlane, Babur, and Suleiman.

The system developed by the religious fighting orders was simple and in truth not very original, but the very cohesion and discipline of the troops made these armies extremely potent and lethal. No doubt that the Mamluk system that emerged at the time was designed to generate the same type of professionalism and commitment displayed by the Christian military orders, which the Muslims admired and feared. But unlike the Mamluks, the warrior monks never constituted more than a small elite force that supplemented the armies of the Christian states of the Levant, under whose authority they fought. Designed to support the Christian effort in the Near East, they never sought, despite their wealth and their might, to take on a leading role, except perhaps at the very end, when the Templars and Hospitallers sought to launch a Crusade of their own with the help of the Mongols.

Shortly before the Templars' demise, a new impetus was given to the Mongol alliance with the nomination of Jacques de Molay as the head of the order in 1292. Starting in 1300, a year after the Mongols had beaten the Mamluks at Homs, the Templars and Hospitallers launched a naval operation against the Mamluks on the Egyptian coast, with the assurance that their Mongol ally Ghāzān (whose family had recently converted to Islam) would soon join them by land. But Ghāzān came too late, with too few troops, and, with his death in 1304 and Molay's subsequent clash with the French king, the alliance never fully materialized. Had the orders and the Mongols better coordinated their efforts, the alliance might possibly have overrun the Mamluks, and the Templars and Hospitallers might very well have retaken control of Jerusalem (Ghāzān had agreed that in case of victory, he would cede the Holy City to them). This, however, was not to be and within a decade, the Templars were no more, and the Hospitallers were on a new course, moving from one Mediterranean island to another.

"MASSACRE THEM, FOR THE LORD RECOGNIZES HIS OWN!": THE CRUSADE AGAINST THE ALBIGENSES (1209–44)

After the Crusaders were forced out of the Levant, a crusade at the beginning of the thirteenth century against the Albigenses, or Cathars (*katharoi*, or "pure ones"), a dualist sect in southern France, brought Catholic holy war to the heart of Christendom and expanded the Catholic Church's perception of just how far sanctified violence could go. In the long series of wars initiated and fought in the name of Christianity, the Albigensian Crusade occupies a special place. As the papacy's first holy war against a heretical movement, it set a precedent that would a later bear fruit in the proscription of the Templars, the Teutonic Crusades, and the Wars of Religion of the sixteenth and seventeenth centuries, in addition to giving rise to the notorious Holy Inquisition,[20] a baleful institution that would thereafter spread throughout Europe and to the New World.[21]

The Albigensian episode itself was short-lived and confined to a geographical area, Languedoc, from which it was never allowed to spread to other regions. The term "Albigensian" is in fact misleading, as it relates to one town,

Albi, whereas the Cathar movement flourished from beyond Toulouse in southwestern France all the way to Nîmes, on the border with Provence. While the Cathar movement was never allowed to reproduce itself, the Crusade against the Cathars provoked a revolution of sorts by expanding the idea of the crusade to include internal holy wars designed to purify Christianity from within.

Up until then, crusades had been directed either against pagans, whose cults were deemed irreligious, or against "infidels" who worshipped another "false" God. These were, by definition, exterior, non-Christian threats. Heretics, on the other hand, proclaimed themselves to be Christians, threatening the faith and its institutions from within. Movements such as Arianism had caused much turmoil earlier, and dissident movements had been very active during Saint Augustine's time. These groups and the havoc they wreaked had been duly publicized by Augustine and others, and, as a consequence, they left a profound negative imprint on people's minds. Such occurrences had all but disappeared, however, since the theological struggles of the early days waned once the Catholic Church asserted its authority in western Europe. If anything, the crusading movement against the Muslims reinforced the power and influence of the church. Prior to the Cathar episode, "heretical" manifestations had been witnessed here and there, inasmuch as trials against heretics had been conducted, some of which may have been fabricated for political purposes, as in Orléans in 1022 and Arras (in northern France) in 1025.[22] But these manifestations were sporadic, at least until the twelfth century, when the number of incidents increased dramatically: Soissons in 1120, Liège, Trier, and Utrecht in 1135, Cologne in 1143.

The word "Cathar," derived from the Greek for "pure," appeared at around that time in Germany to describe heretics (in France, they were then referred to as *tisserands*, or "weavers").[23] Prior to the Cathars, however, a movement of some significance had taken root in Bulgaria, that of the Bogomils ("Those loved by God"), which bore similarities, most notably belief in the dual nature of God, with the Albigensian sect and other "heretical" manifestations, including earlier ones such as the Gnostic movement (these were often described by their adversaries as "Manichaean," though the direct filiation with Manichaeism is unproven).

The Cathars believed in the duality of the spiritual, peace-loving New Testament God as opposed to the creator of the physical world of the Old Testament; they had their own sacraments; they adhered to a strict lifestyle marked by the essential obligation of all, including priests, engaging in manual labor; they displayed an unequivocal respect for life, including the life of animals (some of these characteristics have drawn comparisons with other religions such as Buddhism).[24] Even their adversaries noted their spiritual purity and ethical rigor and they were the first to manifest their dissatisfaction with the corruption of the Catholic Church, a common thread among future dissident religious movements, be they Hussite, Calvinist, or Lutheran. Aside from Languedoc, Cathar communities took root in northern Italy (Lombardy) and in the Balkans (Bosnia), though these were more modest.

Two elements made the Albigensian episode unique in relation to the other heretical movements, both during the period and before. The first relates to time and space, with the Cathars coming of age at the time of the Crusades, shortly after the loss of Jerusalem, and in a general area where the crusading spirit was particularly strong. The second element was an individual whom we have already encountered, Pope Innocent III, who became the driving force behind the anti-Cathar Crusade. Thus, this small-scale crusade against a heretic movement was in several ways directly linked to the greater crusade that was taking place at the same time in the Middle East. The violence it generated on the part of the anti-Cathar crusaders and the energy deployed by the pope to organize and support their efforts were totally disproportionate to the size of the movement itself, yet understandable when one considers the larger picture.

In the beginning, the measures taken against individuals accused of heresy were much more radical in northern Europe, where those condemned were often burned at the stake, than in the Languedoc region of southern France where the condemnations remained for a time largely symbolic. Until the Council of Tours (France) in 1163, the identification of heretics was solely based on accusations. At Tours, however, the first measures to conduct formal investigations into heretical behavior were undertaken. This was the first step toward the institutionalization of the war against heresy that was to mark the late Middle Ages, with the formal development of the Inquisition. For the Church, this struggle, to which it would devote increasing efforts and energies, was an integral part of its global strategy of fostering Christian unity.

During the years 1172–81, a pre-crusade of sorts was organized against the Cathars by Count Raymond V of Toulouse in response to an appeal from the archbishop of Narbonne, Pons d'Arsac, who declared: "The Catholic faith is severely threatened in our diocese, the boat of Saint Peter has been so beaten by the insults of the heretics that it is close to going under. May the arm of your zeal brandish the shield of the faith and the arms of justice, and may it come to the side of our Lord."[25] Raymond alerted the king of France, Louis VII, as well as the king of England, Henry II, and a fact-finding mission was organized. Around the same time, the pope, Alexander III, sent an envoy into Languedoc and, in 1181, a small army was levied by the cardinal of Albano, Henri of Marciac, who marched with a band of mounted knights against the "Synagogue of Satan."[26] The result, for the authorities, was encouraging: the two main individuals sought by Marciac pleaded guilty to their heretical activities and renounced their faith, both being rewarded with positions in the Catholic clergy. After the Third Lateran Council, presided over in 1179 by Pope Alexander, more steps were taken to fight heresies. The pressure on heresy was slowly mounting. Two decades after the Council of Tours, and five years after the Lateran Council, Pope Lucius III provided specific guidelines (Verona, 1184) for priests to conduct regular inquiries into heretical activities. In 1198, after the death of Celestin III (Lucius's successor), Innocent III took over. The Vatican had a new master, and a vindictive one at that. Less than ten years later, Pope Innocent was launching the first full-fledged Crusade against a home-grown heretical movement.

From what we can gather from the sporadic information that has come down to us, Catharism was solidly implanted in the Languedoc region at the turn of the thirteenth century with possibly more than a hundred towns and villages adhering to it. The local nobility had partaken in the effort and provided a good number of the Cathar leaders called the "Perfects" (*Parfaits*), who included both men and women.[27] Pierre des Vaux de Cernay, the biased chronicler of the Crusade, who backed his rival Simon de Montfort, depicts Count Raymond VI of Toulouse—whose father, Raymond V, had first alerted the Catholic authorities—as a devout Cathar,[28] and Pope Innocent himself thought Raymond too soft on the Cathars.

Innocent III's campaign against the Cathars occupied a great deal of his eighteen-year tenure as pope, and its early years were somewhat frustrating. Though Innocent wanted to take radical measures from the start, he had to content himself with half measures until he rallied adequate means and resources to quell the movement and eradicate its leaders and adherents. He began by promulgating a decree on March 25, 1199, proclaiming all those found guilty of heresy dispossessed of their property. Heresy being a special crime of the highest order, it warranted a special punishment. But signing a decree and enforcing it are two different things, as Innocent was soon to find out; both the local clergy and the local political authorities seemed reluctant to take on the Cathars, many of whom were close friends or relatives. As far as the clergy were concerned, Innocent could initiate a purge, which he did, but persuading lay rulers to undertake a war against their own proved more difficult.

By 1204, after being in office for five years, Innocent was growing weary of the lax attitude shown by the local political authorities. Dejected by his lack of result, he sent a letter, dated May 28, to the king of France, Philip Augustus, asking him to "confiscate the property of the counts, barons, and citizens who are not willing to eliminate heresy from their lands or who dare to cultivate it," adding that Philip Augustus should "attach their entire country to the royal domain."[29] At this point, however, the appeal fell to a deaf ear, Philip Augustus being seemingly uninterested in engaging his armies in this particular holy war. Innocent, however, was undeterred and he connected with a local clergyman, Arnaud Amaury, the abbot of Cîteaux, who was deploying a great deal of energy to convince the French authorities and others about the need for armed intervention. An effective public speaker, Amaury managed to gain the support of three powerful leaders: the duke of Burgundy, the count of Nevers, and the count of Saint-Pol. However, it was a fourth man whom Amaury solicited personally who would take over the mantle of the crusade: Simon de Montfort, fifth earl of Leicester in England.

Simon de Montfort had taken part in the Fourth Crusade, the one that had been diverted against Constantinople, but had quit it when it went astray. A man of fifty at the time, he had been frustrated by the turn of events that surrounded the Fourth Crusade, but the crusading fire was still burning in his bones. More so even than the other partakers in the campaign, Montfort was both a religious zealot and a seasoned warrior, thus combining in high fashion the two qualities sought by Innocent III and his man in Languedoc, Arnaud Amaury. The carrot dangled in front of Simon by the pope and the clergyman was not insignificant, being the vast chunk of territory in southern France that the crusaders sought to conquer and purge. "God put the land of the miscreant, heretic people in my hands," Montfort wrote. "Through the ministry of the crusaders, his servants, God has thus judged it legitimate to dispossess them [the Cathars] of the land itself. And upon the insistence of the barons of the army of our Lord, the officers of the law, and the priests who were present, I accept the charge and administration of this land with humility and devotion."[30] For his part, Innocent III reiterated the objective of the Crusade to Montfort: to preserve the peace and the faith, by violence if necessary.

Montfort's strategy essentially revolved around a series of cavalry raids, the same strategy that the Teutonic Knights would use to good effect against the pagan populations of Prussia. The Cathars, however—many of whom were highly educated, urbanized, well-organized, smart, and determined—proved a tough nut to crack. All Montfort's holy cavalry accomplished was to provoke a series of rebellions throughout the Languedoc. As in the Near Eastern Crusades, the participation of lay rulers and their armies merged their political/territorial ambitions and the pope's religious aims. Political alliances in the conflict sometimes created bizarre situations. The king of Aragon, for instance, who had just fought a Catholic holy war against the Muslims in Spain, now found himself on the side of Raymond of Toulouse lending a hand to the Cathars. The mix of religion and politics was, as always, an explosive one, especially since civilians were involved. Indeed, noncombatant populations became the primary targets of the so-called Militia Christi in a terror campaign designed to crush the spirit of the Albigenses.

Early on during the Albigensian Crusade, at Béziers, July 22, 1209, where twenty thousand people are reported to have been killed,[31] Amaury was asked by an officer how he should distinguish Catholics from heretics, to which he responded: "Massacre them, for the Lord recognizes his own! [Massacrez-les, car le Seigneur connaît les siens!]."

This terror strategy was commonly practiced at around the same time by the Mongol and Turkic armies of Central Asia. Even as Amaury and Montfort were conducting their raids, Genghis Khan was organizing his own, albeit on a much grander scale. However, it had until then been a rarity in western Europe, where wars were often confined to skirmishes between small armies. From this point on, however, civilian populations became increasingly involved in armed conflicts, to the point where they would be incorporated into Clausewitz's "trinity" of war, along with the state and the military forces.[32] If anything, the Albigensian Crusade sought "soft targets," as we now call them. "All the terrorizing tactics that had been practiced before the Crusades were intensified, but with a terrible twist: there was an unnerving new shamelessness among the combatants, who had come to understand that depredations against civilians were now central to all military campaigns," Caleb Carr writes.[33] It was a turning point in the history of warfare.

The horrors associated with this war between populations that were ethnically, linguistically, and culturally indistinguishable from one another certainly played a part in breaching the code of conduct around which feudal warfare revolved. It also brought into the conflict an emotional element that was largely absent from feudal wars. The emergence of resentment in war, which would play such a large role in the European wars of religion and in many other conflicts around the globe, was a major event. It is no coincidence that Saint Thomas Aquinas and others began around this time to revive the notion of the just war. Many of the rules that the church had for so long fought to impose on feudal warriors were completely obliterated by this conflict. The irony, of course, was that the Church itself was directly responsible for this state of affairs. Buoyed by the Crusades in the Holy Land and by the Reconquista, Innocent III probably never anticipated that a holy war fought against Christians in the heart of Europe might have very different consequences.

By the end of the summer of 1209, Montfort—who had come into the picture shortly after the Béziers massacre—seemed poised for total victory. Since this was a crusade, the pope proceeded to bless the apparent victory, which meant that the vanquished were dispossessed of their titles and territories, duly transferred to the victorious Catholic prince, Simon de Montfort. By choosing Montfort, who hailed from the Île de France (the region around and including Paris) but also happened to be the fifth earl of Leicester in England, Amaury had picked an outsider, indeed a "Frenchman" whose very presence irked the lords of the pays d'Oc in southern France, many of whom switched sides.

Despite the success of the early raids, by the end of the year, the anti-Cathar crusaders were reeling. Raymond of Toulouse, who was the principal victim of Montfort's territorial claims, was thus able to organize a counteroffensive. This was now a different type of war. What had looked to be a quick, victorious campaign became a long, deadly, protracted conflict that would last thirty-five years and bring foreign armies into the fray.

In the summer of 1212, Raymond sought assistance from the king of Aragon, Peter II, his cousin, who had routed the Almohads at Las Navas de Tolosa on July 16. The two men pleaded the pope to end the Crusade and to resolve the issue peacefully, including the matter of the Cathars. In January 1213, the pope effectively stopped the Crusade, but the diplomatic frenzy that ensued was interrupted by a major battle at Muret, a place on the Garonne, just south of Toulouse, on September 12, where the crusaders, though facing an army three times larger than theirs, won an improbable victory in which the king of Aragon was killed, along with seven to seventeen thousand soldiers (sources vary). Montfort was unable, however, to translate his military victory into political success. During the next period, the Occitanians were actually able to regain the upper hand. By now, the conflict had seen the emergence of a strong and potent ideology, Occitan nationalism,[34] which was more powerful than Catharism as a tool to mobilize the populations. In effect, while Rome was fighting a religious war, the Occitanians were now effectively engaged in a war of liberation that included, but also transcended, the Cathar element.

Against these rapidly evolving circumstances, the holy war initiated by Pope Innocent and first undertaken by Amaury and Simon de Montfort was losing ground and something needed to happen if the crusaders were to regain momentum. This happened on January 28, 1226, when King Louis VIII of France, "Le Lion," assumed the leadership of the crusade. Although politically motivated, Louis's strategy followed a religious agenda, each stage corresponding to a religious celebration, starting with the (re)launching of the crusade at Bourges in central France on Easter Day. Louis died that same year, however, after a short reign, and was succeeded by Louis IX (Saint Louis). The war, now dominated by the royal army, led to the Treaty of Paris of 1229 (also known as the Treaty of Meaux) and to inquisitorial exactions and massive persecution.

Still, the Cathars were able to organize an underground resistance movement that culminated with an ultimate and spectacular stand at Montségur, where forty-nine Perfects, including fifteen women, led the defense of a fortified castle against an army of besiegers. On March 16, 1244, after a heroic defense, Montségur fell, and with it the last of the Albigensian resistance. Those Cathars who were not condemned to death or forced to convert managed to migrate to Lombardy, where a community of Cathars survived for a while before the Inquisition disposed of them. The last Cathar community known to exist, in Bosnia, eventually dissolved in the Ottoman Empire after its last survivors converted to Islam. The brutality of the crusade against the Albigenses left open wounds that never fully healed among the populations of the Languedoc region, and Protestant communities emerged in the area during the Reformation.

The episode, long depicted as a parenthetical manifestation of religious violence, set a precedent as the first full-fledged crusade undertaken by the church authorities against Christian dissidents. With the anti-Cathar crusade, the genie was out of the bottle, and, at the beginning of the fifteenth century, it would unleash its wrath against another dissident movement, the Hussites of Bohemia.

With this new type of crusade, Pope Innocent III raised the level of violence that could be committed with the blessing of the Catholic Church to a new height. When the Teutonic Knights embarked on a crusade of their own against the pagan Old Prussians, the papacy encouraged another form of violence derived from the experience of the Near Eastern Crusades. Within a couple of centuries, the center of gravity of religious violence moved from the Mediterranean to central Europe, where the Teutonic, German, and Livonian military orders engaged in a protracted (though essentially, to use modern parlance, "low-intensity") warfare in the name of religion with the full backing and support of the Catholic Church. In parallel, the Inquisition took off, first principally in southern Europe and then in the Americas.

THE TEUTONIC KNIGHTS AND THE EUROPEAN CRUSADES

No less remarkable than the history of the Templars is that of the Teutonic Order, though it has suffered somewhat from the exploitation of it by German nationalist propaganda in the nineteenth century,[35] and, more damaging still, by the Nazis in the twentieth. Much like the Knights of Saint John, the Teutonic Knights emerged from the need to provide Christian pilgrims and fighters of the Near East with medical attention and protection. The order had humble beginnings: a small hospital in Acre, created around 1189–90, during the famous siege of the city, by merchants from Lübeck and Bremen,[36] to which was adjoined a small church and a cemetery. The order was officially founded about ten years later, in 1198—almost a full century after the conquest of Jerusalem by the crusaders—in grandiose fashion, before an assembly consisting of German princes and high-ranking Church authorities, as well as the grand masters of the Templars and Hospitallers. Its official code retained the rules of the Templars for its military activities, and of the Knights of Saint John for its community services, and both directives were approved by the pope on February 19, 1199.

The military dimension and purpose of the order were written into its first constitution, as they were with the Templars, though not with the Hospitallers. More striking perhaps is the fact that this was also the first order identified with a specific nation; neither the Templars, Hospitallers, nor even the Iberian orders of Santiago, Calatrava, and Alcántara were national. This decision would set a standard and have momentous consequences throughout the history of Prussia and modern Germany, which until the year 2000 based citizenship on descent (*jus sanguinis*) rather than the "right of soil" (*jus soli*) birthright criterion used in countries such as the United States and France. In effect, from the beginning, the names *Alamanorum* or *Teutonicorum* were associated with the order, though "nationalism" as a policy or an ideology would have made little sense then. Let us then avoid the trap of anachronism and take the German identity of the order for what it was: a practical undertaking to help fellow Germans in need in a faraway region and a hostile environment.

From a hospital, the Teutonic Order quickly transformed itself into an army, which conducted itself rather well at the siege of Damietta (1218–21). Under the energetic Hermann of Salza, who played a role similar to that of Hugh of Payns with the Templars, and with the unconditional support of the Holy Roman Emperor Frederick II (r. 1220–50), the Teutonic Knights rapidly gained a reputation similar to those enjoyed by the two older crusading orders. As latecomers, however, the German warrior monks arrived on the scene at a time when the Christian states of the Near East were irreversibly on the defensive. Notwithstanding this situation, Hermann of Salza, grand master from 1209 to 1239, ensured the legitimacy of the Teutonic Order during his long tenure, securing its territorial bases both in the Near East and in Europe, in Germany and Sicily (where Frederick II held court), where he obtained rich donations despite the fact that, after the disaster of the Fourth Crusade, popular support in Europe for the holy war was waning.

Greatly helped by their military exploits in Damietta and by the active support coming from both the Holy Roman Emperor and Pope Honorius III, the order was, by the middle of the thirteenth century, firmly established in the Near East. In Europe, starting in 1211, the king of Hungary had already expressed interest in the Teutonic Knights, offering them a territory at the frontier of the kingdom, so that they might counter the pagan assaults and form "a solid wall at the service of the kingdom."[37] In this instance, it was understood that their mission was not just military and that they were expected to pacify the area and convert the Cumans,[38] a Turkic tribe that roamed the area. The affair, however, turned sour, with the order, backed by Pope Honorius, clashing with the Hungarian authorities, both lay and clerical, which resulted in the Teutonic Knights being forced to leave in 1225. Salza retained the lesson, and subsequently the Teutonic Order systematically pursued a policy of absolute territorial independence and unfettered authority, guided by the idea of establishing itself firmly as *dominus terrae*, lord of the land. The constitution of the order was written around 1244–50, consisting of a set of rules of conduct (39 articles), institutions (45 articles) and customs (63 articles). Christianity offers few other documents, if any, that go this far in marrying religion and war in such an elaborate and practical fashion.

This constitution owed much to the Templar model and emulated Dominican practices in nonmilitary matters. The Teutonic Knights were modeled on the Hospitallers, but by 1250, they were much more like the Templars.[39] They were, above all, *milites Christi*. The Teutonic Knights were never numerous. Sylvain Gouguenheim suggests that 10,000 may have joined the ranks between 1198 and 1309.[40] In the mid-thirteenth century, the order had perhaps 1,600 knights, with a quarter of these stationed in the Near East and the rest in central and southern Europe. Surprisingly, a few women (*sorores*) joined the order, though not as combatants.[41] Though officially members could not join if they did not belong to the nobility, rules were somewhat flexible in that regard, due to difficulties in recruitment. Members were almost exclusively of German origin, barring a few exceptions, such as Italians and Poles.

But what the order lacked in numbers, it compensated for with superior organization and discipline, as well as shrewd politicking. Throughout its existence, the order greatly benefited from the unwavering support it received from the papacy. Rome had backed all the warring religious orders from the start, but, after the loss of the Holy Land and the disappearance of the Templars, it focused on the only active, independent military-religious order in Europe. Although the Crusades were effectively over, the *spirit* of the Crusades was intact, and who better than the Teutonic Knights to uphold the sword and the cross? In the Iberian Peninsula, the orders were tied to the lay authorities, whereas the Teutonic Knights fiercely defended their independence vis-à-vis local authorities, while asserting their allegiance to the papacy. In the perpetual battle that opposed church and state, the Teutonic Order gave Rome political leverage in central Europe, a volatile region where East and West often came into conflict.

The association of religion and politics in the various orders was an integral part of their makeup, and their military actions often coincided with liturgical celebrations. This was especially true of the Teutonic Order, as the *Chronic des Landes Preussen* (Chronicle of the Prussian Land) by Johann von Posilge and the *Chronicon Livoniale* (a history of the Livonian Crusade) by Hermann von Wartberge testify, with many examples. More often than not, campaigns were launched to coincide with Candlemas (February 2), the day of the Assumption (August 15), or the Virgin Mary's birthday (September 8). The religious, political, and military calendars thus coincided to the point of being indistinguishable from one another.

The spiritual dimension of the order was one of war through and through, relating both to the wars of the Old Testament and to those expected during the struggle of the end of time. This spirituality of war defined the ideals of the order (one could even say its ideology) and the set of norms through which it conducted itself and measured its worth and its success. Gouguenheim suggests that these norms, which gave the order its impetus in the beginning, also precipitated its downfall in the fifteenth century:

> In the fifteenth century, the moral values upon which the [Teutonic] Order founded its existence, monastic asceticism, the ethics and courage of chivalry, and the renouncement of earthly rewards, lost their appeal. If the order was finally destroyed by its Polish and Lithuanian enemies at this time, the causes may not only have been economic and military but also moral. Attached, riveted to a classic conception of spirituality, anchored in the justifications of another time, the German order also lost the war of words and ideas, which may have been as crucial as the clash of swords.[42]

The papal motivations behind the conquest of Prussia are hard to decipher with certainty. Was Rome eager to counter the Holy Roman Empire and block its inroads into Prussia? As appealing as it may be, this idea runs against the fact that, in the thirteenth century, the empire did not seem to have much interest in the region, at the time inhabited by the pagan people known as the Old Prussians. But then again, this interest might have arisen in the future, in which case, Rome's support for the Teutonic invasion of Prussia may have been preemptive. Whatever the motivation, Rome's interest in the region can be traced back to 1210, when Pope Honorius named an independent "bishop of the Old Prussians," whose mission was subsequently a failure. Next, Rome, now under the authority of Gregory IX, authorized the Teutonic Knights in September 1230 to occupy Prussia, but only until Christianity was firmly implanted in the region, and assigned the Dominicans the task of converting the Old Prussians, starting in 1232.

On August 3, 1234, Pope Gregory IX boldly declared Prussia a "property of Saint Peter" under the jurisdiction of the pope and the Teutonic Order, which had complete autonomy from any lay government. The papal bull *Pietati proximum*, called the Golden Bull of Rieti, asserted the papacy's authority over "those parts of the land that have been known to have been acquired by you with the help of the Christian army and the action of God," which would "remain perpetually under special protection from the Holy See and we will concede it to you and your house [i.e., the Teutonic Order] with all its rights and revenues, in free and perpetual possession, so that this land may never be submitted by you or by any other party, to the domination of any power, whatever that power may be." The document made several references to the fact that this conquest was undertaken "with the help of God."[43] To assert the fact that the Teutonic Order was in the dominion of the Church, it was stipulated that the Order would pay an (unspecified) sum to the Roman Church annually "in recognition of its domination and of the freedom it received from the Holy See." In short, any attempt at taking Prussia away from the Teutonic Order would be akin to attacking the Church.

With the Golden Bull of Rieti, the pope legitimized the action of the Teutonic Order as a main pillar of Rome's Christianization policy and gave the order unprecedented power and authority over a vast territory. In four short years (1230–34), the pope had made a temporary mission a permanent one. Hermann of Salza, however, needed further warranties and he obtained from the Holy Roman Emperor, Frederick II, the right to conquer Prussia and exercise the authority granted to the independent princes of the empire, as stipulated in the Golden Bull of Rimini (1226). Henceforth, with the blessings of the pope and of the Holy Roman Emperor, the Teutonic Knights were free to wage a colonial war of conversion on the pagan populations of Baltic Europe, later called the Northern Crusade.

THE TEUTONIC WARS OF CONQUEST

The wars of conquest of the Teutonic Knights were, militarily, similar to many such wars, including those conducted later by the English and French in Africa and Asia in the nineteenth century: protracted, low-intensity confrontations pitting small, efficient armies against elusive peasant militias.

Throughout their history, the Teutonic Knights retained the basic characteristics of the warrior-monk armies. Like the Templars and the Hospitallers, they possessed superior engineering capabilities that enabled them to construct a wide web of defensive fortresses. Offensively, they relied on their heavy cavalry. Their adversaries the Old Prussians occupied vast patches of territory, benefited from the support of the local populations, and showed greater flexibility than the mounted knights. Few in numbers, the latter had difficulty controlling territory and could rarely get the enemy to fight a pitched battle. Given these constraints, the Teutonic strategy mainly consisted in conducting raids on villages to break the will of the populations. The rigorous religious ethics that guided their lifestyle did not prevent them from committing horrific acts of brutality on the battlefield and elsewhere. Since the guerrilla tactics of the Old Prussians were aimed at deterring support for the Teutonic Knights, the civilian population found themselves between hammer and anvil. Their villages were burned, and they were often killed or reduced to servitude. As early as 1234, the Teutonic Knights were described as having in one instance massacred five thousand Old Prussians.[44]

The war against the Old Prussians lasted half a century. By 1300, the Old Prussian population, estimated to have been between 150,000 and 170,000 before the invasion, had dropped to around 90,000.[45] The English philosopher and Franciscan theologian Roger Bacon attributed the difficulty of Christianizing Prussia to the brutality of the Teutonic Knights, who sought to enslave the Old Prussian people, who were eager to convert peacefully, he claimed, based on the reports he had heard from fellow Franciscans and Dominicans.[46] In hindsight, one might wonder how much this war may have contributed subsequently to the ideologically motivated violence of the Hussite wars and the Thirty Years' War.

Notwithstanding their financial and technical superiority, the Teutonic Knights rarely could align more than a thousand combatants against an adversary that could mobilize vastly superior numbers. However, with the papacy actively supporting the Northern Crusade, the Teutonic Knights could count on a perpetual flow of recruits from the Holy Roman Empire, Poland, Bohemia, and Austria. Crusaders included not only princes from the smaller principalities but rulers like King Ottokar II of Bohemia (r. 1253–78), who in 1254 mustered an army of sixty thousand for the crusade and led it in a successful campaign. Pope Innocent IV praised Ottokar as a "vigorous athlete of Christ,"[47] and the Teutonic Knights built the fortress city of Königsberg (King's Mountain) at the top of a hill in his honor (later famous for its most celebrated citizen, the philosopher Immanuel Kant, who was never known to leave it).

The intensity of the fighting fluctuated. With the Golden Bull of Rimini, the emperor allotted each crusading army one year; crusaders were not allowed to enlist for longer. Thus, after a campaign in which they could count on tens of thousands of troops, the Teutonic Knights might find themselves short-handed the following year. The fact that campaigning seasons were short, owing to the harshness of the climate, also helps explain why the war against the Old Prussians took so long.

For the papacy, this crusade, officially fought as a *praelia domini*, a "combat of the Lord"—not, technically, a holy war—by *crucesignatus*, crusaders, was part of the universal crusade called for by Gregory IX and Innocent IV. On September 13, 1245, Pope Gregory asked that all clerics pray for both the crusade in the Holy Land and the crusade in Prussia.[48] The vocabulary used by the pope to describe the two crusades was identical. Furthermore, the papacy also encouraged the crusade launched in Livonia by the bishop of Riga, who in 1202 created a small order of warrior monks, the Livonian Brothers of the Sword.[49] In 1237, the Teutonic Knights and the Brothers of the Sword merged, the latter being effectively absorbed by the former as a branch of the Teutonic Knights in Livonia, now a province under Teutonic authority (after difficult negotiations with Denmark). Subsequent to the fall of Acre of 1291, where all the Teutonic Knights present were massacred, the Prussian crusade took a new turn, and the order's headquarters were transferred from the Holy Land, via Venice (1291–1309), to Marienburg, Prussia.

This shift, which meant that the Teutonic Knights had left the land that had witnessed their order's birth for good, also altered the mission of the order. Gradually, the landless order of warrior monks was becoming a state attached to a territory, Prussia.[50] The decision to conquer Pomerelia (Gdańsk Pomerania, now part of Poland), a Christian land, at around the same time that the headquarters were moved to Marienburg, meant that the order was now engaged in what was for the church an illegitimate, unjust war that deviated completely from its crusading mission to conquer pagan territories. With the annexation of Danzig/Gdańsk, the order showed its true colors: it was now a state, in fact, a nation-state, and it behaved as such. "The settlement of Prussia was the outstanding colonial achievement of the Middle Ages," Desmond Seward writes.[51]

With the refocusing on Prussia, the other two lesser branches of the order, the German branch and the Livonian branch, were marginalized, as illustrated by the fact that no grand master of the order would henceforth come out of the German branch, as had been the case in the past. Teutonic Prussia now presented characteristics that one associates with modern nation-states, including a centralized and efficient bureaucracy, a dynamic economy, and a permanent army. One could say, to use Marxist terminology, that the Teutonic Knights acted as an avant garde of sorts, with a politburo, an official ideological line, and an effective security force ready to quell any type of dissent. But Teutonic Prussia was still, in one respect, far removed from the modern secular state, since it retained its religious core, from which it derived all its political institutions. In essence, it remained a "religious corporation and an international order of warriors."[52] As before, during the years of conquest, religion served to legitimate its military actions. Born of the Golden Bulls of Rieti and Rimini, which conferred on it both ecclesiastical and secular sources of legitimacy, it had within the space of a century become a full-fledged ecclesiastical state with the powers of a secular state.

Religion, which had originally served to legitimate a war of conversion against a pagan people was now used to justify all types of wars, including wars against Christian states. With its newfound power, the Teutonic Order was now able to emancipate itself from the tutelage of Rome and make political decisions on its own. As a religious military order, it nevertheless retained the structure, organization, and customs that had made it so potent, as well as its monastic lifestyle. Now, however, it faced redoubtable competition from Poland and Lithuania in a classic struggle for regional hegemony among great powers, with other, less important actors, most of them principalities of the Holy Roman Empire, tilting the balance in favor now of the one, now of the other. "Speaking with the voice of Jesus Christ," the fourteenth-century mystic Bridget of Sweden (d. 1373, canonized in 1391 as Saint Bridget) declared:

> And I tell you now that these Crusaders, whom I placed at the frontiers of Christianity, should be like bees. But now, they fight me, they do not have a care for people's souls; they do not even try to guide the bodies of the converts from error to me and to the Catholic faith. They oppress them with drudgery, deprive them of freedom, fail to instruct them in the faith, deprive them of the sacraments and send them to hell with immense suffering as if they had remained attached to their paganism. Furthermore, they fight only for their own glory and to increase their wealth. This is why the time will come when their teeth will be broken, their right hand amputated, their right foot paralyzed.[53]

Bridget's prophecy was soon fulfilled, and the mighty knights would indeed brake their teeth fighting a craftier adversary. Faced with mounting criticism, the Teutonic Order produced a vast body of lengthy written statements to justify its action and silence the critics. One such plea, sent to the pope in 1335, is over six hundred pages long. It reiterates the religious vocation of the order and its active engagement in promoting and spreading the faith.[54] That the order took the time to write such pleas is indicative of how important papal support remained for it even after the conquest of Prussia. It also illustrates the fact that the Teutonic Knights, from the very beginning, also had critics within the papacy, which meant that any action of theirs that might be considered a moral breach was always taken seriously. Like all the other combatant religious orders, they were always at risk of committing acts deemed immoral or unacceptable by the church.

But another factor came into play that affected the relationship between Rome and Marienburg: the brewing conflict between the papacy and the Holy Roman Empire, which, given the order's allegiance to both, created recurring tensions and problems. In 1239, shortly after the death of Hermann of Salza, Pope Gregory IX summoned the Teutonic Knights to choose sides, threatening to abolish their privileges and to deprive them of indulgences if they supported the Holy Roman Emperor, Frederick II (at which point the Hospitallers, whose only allegiance was to the pope, tried to seize the opportunity to make inroads against Teutonic Knights' power and authority). All in all, the order's position between the Holy Roman Empire and Rome was an uncomfortable one, especially as the German branch of the order became increasingly involved in the politics of the empire. The nature of the relationships, too, was altogether different. With the Holy Roman Empire, this relationship generally followed the traditional laws of international politics, while the relationship with Rome was defined by political but also religious, spiritual, and moral issues that made it all the more complex.

Since the Teutonic Knights' wars of the fourteenth and fifteenth centuries were no longer crusades, the order had to find soldiers in secular ways, and it began to hire mercenaries, who are notoriously unreliable. The influx of foreign troops might have given the order the impetus to change its practices and adapt to the times, but the mercenaries were as entrenched in the old ways as the Teutonic Knights. "The military efficiency of the mercenary of the thirteenth century was, however, only a development of that of the ordinary feudal cavalier," Charles Oman observes. "Like the latter, he was a heavily armed horseman; his rise did not bring with it any radical change in the methods of war. Though he was a more practiced warrior, he still worked on the old system—or want of system—which characterized the cavalry tactics of the time."[55] Significantly, perhaps, at the battle of Tannenberg against a

Polish-Lithuanian army in 1410, a catastrophic defeat for the Teutonic Order, between 38 percent to 48 percent of its soldiers were mercenaries.[56]

By the fourteenth century, the art of war in Europe was starting to evolve away from the mounted knight. This was truer even in Russia and eastern Europe, where the passage of the Mongols had taught local armies a thing or two about the deadly effects of mounted archers and light cavalry. The Teutonic Knights, however, never really changed their approach to war, which consisted in defending their largely impregnable fortresses and conducting large-scale raids into enemy territory.[57] In this, they followed the western European model that had served as the strategic foundation of the Templars and Hospitallers. Medieval strategy typically resulted in "the very slow progress of the attackers, the obstinate defence of those attacked, limited operations both in time and distance, a war of attrition."[58]

The Teutonic Knights were nevertheless open to technical innovations, and they made ample use of crossbows and were among the first to embrace artillery. The Catholic Church, which had condemned the use of archery and crossbows at the Lateran Council of 1139—a condemnation that, for some, like Peter the Chanter, did not count in wars against infidels and heretics—had remained silent when it came to the use of gunpowder and cannon,[59] perhaps because the slow progress of this technology did not enable conservative clerics to anticipate how much it might revolutionize war. Arrows, on the other hand, especially the bolts of crossbows, had shown themselves to be a lethal weapon liable to render the mounted knight obsolete and, thus, to threaten the whole social structure built around the ethos of chivalry. Quarrels (*carrés*), as crossbow bolts are also called, could pierce mail, and their use accounts for the evolution of the armor that covered horseman and horse with metal plates (and increased the cost of equipping a knight), which hampered movement somewhat (though good armor was less cumbersome than might appear). Cannon, which were used for the first time during the middle of the fourteenth century, had yet to show their impact. True, as late as the early 1500s, even a savvy analyst like Machiavelli famously failed to anticipate these changes, though a few decades later Don Quixote, the fictional hero of the great Spanish novelist Cervantes (a military veteran himself), laments that gunpowder has ruined the spirit of chivalry.

The struggle between Poland and the Teutonic Order saw a gradual increase in the mutual animosity, the Poles accusing the order of not playing fair in encroaching on the Polish borders. As Christian states, Poland and Teutonic Prussia were nominally allies, and the natural political tensions that

brought them into conflict were often constrained by the religious responsibility to avoid a war between Christians. The annexation of Pomeralia by the
order was a source of resentment for the Poles, however, and, like all such
resentments, brewed to the boil over time. Still, one should not underestimate
the religious aspect of this relationship during a time when political realism
as we understand it today was heavily restrained by the influence of the church.
In effect, it is only when the Teutonic Order's leaders felt that they had lost
Rome's support, in the early years of the fifteenth century, that they unleashed
their wrath against fellow Christians. In a matter of years, after a long series
of regional conflicts, they were embroiled in an all-out war with Poland and
Lithuania, which by then was also a Christian state.

In 1242–53, on the grounds that he had allied himself with the pagan Old
Prussians, the Teutonic Knights attacked Duke Swantopolk of Pomeralia.
Soon, in 1260, the order was fighting skirmishes against Lithuania, whose
princes were not yet ready to convert. Their conversion in the fourteenth
century complicated matters greatly for the order, since Christian Lithuania
was deemed out of bounds to it by the papacy. When, in 1403, the pope suggested that the Teutonic Knights leave Lithuania alone, it appeared that Rome
was distancing itself from the order. The breakdown of diplomatic relations
between the order and Poland in the 1380s, the cooling of relations with the
papacy, and the union of Lithuania and Poland at this time all contributed to
the outbreak of war.

THE DECISIVE ENCOUNTER AT GRÜNWALD-TANNENBERG

The battle of Grünwald, or Tannenberg (also called the battle of Žalgiris by
the Lithuanians), on July 15, 1410, is the basis of one of the great founding
myths of the Polish nation, whose historians, painters, and writers it has
inspired.[60] Curiously for such a decisive battle, not much is known about it,
which probably explains why it hasn't gotten the attention from military
historians that it deserves. Only Prussian Teutonic Knights fought at Tannenberg, although a contingent of the Livonian Order came up after the battle.
On the other side, the Polish-Lithuanian coalition was led by the king of
Poland, Władysław II Jagiełło. Some accounts assert that as many as 500,000
men may have fought that day, a number that modern historiography has
reduced to about 12,000–15,000 for the Teutonic Order and 20,000–25,000
for the Polish-Lithuanian coalition.[61] The battle was fought in two distinct

stages. During the first phase, the Teutonic Knights either routed the Lithuanians or were led to believe that they had, and thus looked poised for victory.
However, success was denied them by a devastating Polish counteroffensive
backed by Cossack and Tatar irregulars.

At the end of the day, a third of the Teutonic Order's troops had been killed.
Marienburg was then unsuccessfully besieged by Jagiełło (July 21–September
21, 1410), but faced with the prospect of having to fight the Livonian Order, he
withdrew, and the ensuing Peace of Torun (February 1, 1411), was not too
unfavorable to the order. The Teutonic Knights thus came out of the episode
without excessive financial or territorial damage. However, their aura of
invincibility had been seriously tarnished and, devoid of any crusade to fight,
they lacked any reason to exist.[62] When their grand master, Heinrich Reuss
von Plauen, tried to launch new hostilities in 1423, he met with much popular
opposition from the Prussian cities and states that were asked to levy taxes
for a new war. This was the beginning of a growing movement of popular
opposition that weakened the order within Prussia.

But the order lost ground in another area too: the propaganda wars, where
Jagiełło proved a redoubtable combatant. After Tannenberg, Jagiełło lobbied
hard to portray his wars as just wars fought between the forces of good
(Poland) and the forces of evil (the Teutonic Knights), while blaming the
Lithuanians and the Tatars for any crimes attributed to his armies. In this
war of words, the Poles' armies of legal scholars proved particularly potent.
This theological battle came to a climax at the Council of Constance (1414–18),
each side arguing for the just character of its wars and how it had upheld the
Catholic faith against an enemy of religion. For the Poles, arguing against an
order that, until then, had benefited from the almost unconditional support
of the papacy was a delicate business, but the Polish lawyers were a crafty
bunch. Their leader, Paweł Włodkowic (Paulus Vladimiri), rector of the
Jagiellonian University in Kraków, was both effective and restrained, while
the man in charge of defending the cause of the Teutonic Knights, Johannes
Falkenberg, proved too emotional and too extreme for the members of the
Council, which condemned his writings; Falkenberg was sent to jail, where
he died a few years later.[63] One event, in particular, was used by both sides for
their argument: the fact that Jagiełło had delayed the engagement, to the point
where the Teutonic Knights had sent him two swords via messenger. Around
this anecdotal detail, the Teutonic Knights argued that they had done this to
inform the king of their intentions without taking him treacherously by

surprise. The Poles argued that the swords had been sent as an act of arrogance and defiance, and that Jagiełło had wanted to go to mass and pray before battle. One man, in particular, was beside himself when he heard the reports of the Council, Jan Hus, a Czech priest, who declared: "In reality, they [the Teutonic Knights] bowed their heads before those whom they tried to humiliate to the ground. Here are the two swords they held out: arrogance and contempt, and yet they lost thousands! Where are the swords, the steeds, the armor, the weapons in which they had placed their faith? Where are their innumerable florins and their treasures? In reality, they have lost everything!"[64]

And indeed they had. The internal crisis that opposed the Teutonic Order to the Prussian population developed into an armed conflict, the Thirteen Years' War, or War of the Cities, which led finally to the loss of Pomerelia in 1466, although the order retained some rights in Königsberg. In 1524, the order espoused Lutheranism and abandoned Catholicism, which put the final nail in the coffin.

With the fall of the order and the effective end of the Teutonic Crusades in Europe, a new type of religious conflict was about to erupt. But this time, neither infidels nor pagans were the target. This time, the war was launched against the ultimate religious authority, the Catholic Church. The key figures at the outset of these religious wars, which would ultimately engulf half of the European continent, were two men, Jan Hus and Jan Žižka. The former would soon inspire a religious revolution that the latter would transform into a war, in the process reinventing the art of warfare. From that point on, religious violence would poison European politics right until the middle of the seventeenth century, when, after the most violent of all religious conflicts, the emerging European superpowers would flush the Catholic Church out of politics and redefine the nature of international relations, with the help of the theologians who had revived Saint Augustine's just war doctrine, foremost among them the thirteenth-century *Doctor Angelicus*, Saint Thomas Aquinas.

Born in Roccasecca in southern Italy (kingdom of Sicily) in 1224 or 1225, Aquinas joined the Benedictine order and then studied and taught theology in Italy, France, and Germany where the well-known scholar Albertus Magnus (Albert the Great) was expounding and reinterpreting Aristotelian philosophy. For ten years, from 1265 until his death in 1274, Aquinas worked on his *Summa Theologia*, which was to lay the foundation for the Aristotelian revolution that was to mark a new direction in the intellectual history of Europe. Among other topics, Aquinas discussed the just war doctrine, which, refined by Spanish theologians of the sixteenth and seventeenth centuries, would eventually form one of the basic tenets of international law.

Thomas Aquinas's take on war was straightforward, and he built on Saint Augustine's theories without altering their significance.[65] Thus, its importance must be judged more in terms of its subsequent influence than its novelty. In his exposition, Aquinas discussed four issues: the lawfulness of war, the status of clerics in war, the lawfulness of ambushes, and the lawfulness of fighting on holy days. The latter two topics, dealt in cursory fashion, yielded positive answers. Regarding just war proper and the role of clerics, Aquinas's answers left no ambiguity. To the question of "Whether it is always sinful to wage war," he had this to say:

> In order for a war to be just, three things are necessary. First, the authority of the sovereign by whose command the war is to be waged. For it is not the business of a private individual to declare war, because he can seek for redress of his rights from the tribunal of his superior. Moreover it is not the business of a private individual to summon together the people, which has to be done in wartime.
>
> Secondly, a just cause is required, namely that those who are attacked, should be attacked because they deserve it on account of some fault.
>
> Thirdly, it is necessary that the belligerents should have a rightful intention, so that they intend the advancement of good, or the avoidance of evil.

Finally, to the question of "Whether it is lawful for clerics and bishops to fight" Aquinas responded:

> Now warlike pursuits are altogether incompatible with the duties of a bishop and a cleric, for two reasons. The first reason is a general one, because, to wit, warlike pursuits are full of unrest, so that they hinder the mind very much from the con-templation of Divine things, the praise of God, and prayers for the people, which belong to the duties of a cleric.
>
> The second reason is a special one, because, to wit, all the clerical Orders are directed to the ministry of the altar, on which the Passion of Christ is represented sacramentally. [. . .] Wherefore it is unbecoming for them to slay or shed blood, and it is more fitting that they should be ready to shed their own blood for Christ, so as to imitate in deed what they portray in their ministry.[66]

Authority (and legitimacy), just cause, and rightful intention: these three principles would constitute the basis of the *jus ad bellum* (war decision), one of the two parts, with the *jus in bello* (war conduct), that would come to form the core of modern just war doctrine.[67]

CHAPTER 7

From Holy War to All-Out Religious War

To get rid of such a demon [the papacy] would not harm the Church, but would be useful to it; in working for his destruction, the Church would be working solicitously for the cause of God.

—John Wycliffe

The most frequent praetext of Sedition, and Civill Warre, in Christian Commonwealths hath a long time proceeded from a difficulty, not yet sufficiently resolved, of obeying at once, both God, and Man, then when their Commandments are one contrary to the other.

—Thomas Hobbes, *Leviathan*

During the transition from the Middle Ages to the modern era, religious violence remained pervasive in Europe. In the Muslim world, power relationships were transformed by the conquests of the Mongols and, subsequently, of the Turcic-Mongolian armies led by Tamerlane (Timur the Lame). The main change in the Middle East was the ascendancy of the Ottoman Turks, who had migrated into Anatolia after being forced out of Khorasān by the Mongols. In the second half of the fourteenth century, the Ottoman Empire supplanted Mamluk Egypt as the regional superpower, and in 1516, the Ottoman sultan Selim I effectively ended the Mamluks' autonomy.

The Ottomans had developed, a military system that was almost identical to that of the Mamluks. The janissary system was a meritocracy that brought Christian and Turkish slaves from the Balkans and the steppes of Central Asia and raised them as soldiers and defenders of the faith. In 1396, at Nicopolis (Bulgaria), the Ottoman army of Sultan Bayezid I, nicknamed the Thunderbolt, which at the time included what was probably the best infantry in the world, inflicted a humiliating defeat on a formidable Christian army.

The events unfolded after the dramatic battle of Kosovo (1389), where Sultan Murad I routed an army led by the Serbian King Lazar (Murad himself was assassinated after the battle), thus establishing a durable Turkish presence in the Balkans. This was not good news for Rome, which saw the Muslim menace taking form again. Seven years after Kosovo, Pope Boniface IX proclaimed a crusade to roll back the Ottomans.

At the time, Bayezid, who had succeeded Murad, was occupied with the siege of Constantinople, which had begun in 1394. Informed that a Christian army was heading his way, he was forced to abandon his prey to counter the offensive, which was led by a key figure in the religious wars of the period, Sigismund, then king of Hungary, later Holy Roman Emperor, and as such, responsible for igniting the Hussite Wars.

For the hastily assembled crusaders, their offensive was to prove disastrous. Miscommunication among the Christian troops resulted in a contingent of French knights attacking the Ottomans in total isolation, a misguided move that led to Bayezid's victorious counteroffensive. As it was, Nicopolis effectively marked the end of the great anti-Muslim offensives devised by Rome, at least for a couple of centuries. In 1571, by which time the world had radically changed, another pope would organize a Christian League—the new terminology for "crusade"—against the same adversary. But, despite the psychological blow, Nicopolis did have a positive effect for Christians in the Mediterranean, since it had momentarily distracted Bayezid from Constantinople, whose siege had continued this whole time, though in lower-intensity mode. Soon, however, the Thunderbolt was himself routed by Tamerlane at the battle of Angora (Ankara), in 1402; at which point he was famously taken captive and, as legend has it, placed in a cage and taken to Samarkand. Bayezid's demise had the effect of giving Constantinople a reprieve of a half century, and it delayed any inclination the Ottomans might have had to push further into Europe. By the time the Ottoman Empire recovered, with Murad II (r. 1421 -51), Europe was on the ascendancy and was no longer as vulnerable as it might have been at the turn of the century. So much so that, in 1444, a crusading army was sent to relieve the intense pressure that was building up against Constantinople, thus showing that Christian solidarity between Catholics and Greek Orthodox was not completely dead. As in 1095, Constantinople was still considered the main bulwark against Muslim/Turkish inroads into Europe. But, in an episode reminiscent of Nicopolis, though less spectacular, the crusaders, led by the Hungarians, were defeated first at Varna, a port on the Black Sea in Bulgaria

FIGURE 7. *The Battle of Nicopolis* (1396), by Turkish miniaturist Nakkaş Osman, in the *Hünername* (1584–88), Topkapi Museum, Istanbul.

and again, in 1448, at the second Battle of Kosovo. Inevitably, Constantinople fell in 1453. It was a miracle that its demise had not occurred earlier.

THE OTTOMANS, CHAMPIONS OF MUSLIM ORTHODOXY

With the fall of Constantinople, the Ottomans were now steadily working their way into Europe. They were held at bay, not by Rome, but by the Habsburgs, who, both in Spain and Austria, saw themselves as the true champions of Catholicism.

In the greater Middle East, the Ottoman Empire's hegemony provided the Muslim world with the type of stability that the Roman Empire had given Europe for several centuries. During the Ottoman Empire's apogee, which lasted a couple of centuries, the struggle between Sunnis and Shiites was subdued, and it only resurfaced when Persia reemerged at the turn of the sixteenth century and adopted Shi'ism as its state religion (with Shah Ishmael I). Even then, the fact that the religious schism largely followed national boundaries prevented tensions from erupting into an all-out civil war. The geopolitical makeup of the greater Middle East of the sixteenth century remained practically unchanged until the nineteenth, when England, France, and Russia (which had driven the Ottomans out of Crimea and the Caucasus) started to make inroads into those areas previously controlled by the Ottoman Empire, which then became known as the "Sick Man of Europe." The sickness was an interminable one, however, and the Ottoman Empire only collapsed after World War I.

In essence, then, while Islam was witnessing a period of relative stability brought about by the imperial hegemony of the Ottoman Turks, Europe was about to embark on a period of unfettered expansion, while also falling victim to growing internal religious, as well as political, violence. In this context, the struggle between Islam and Christianity was essentially confined to the marches of southeastern Europe, at the frontiers between the Ottoman and Austrian empires. But these particular wars, though they retained a religious element, were essentially a clash between two hegemonic empires. Association with the Ottomans was now deemed more or less acceptable, though it might be duly criticized by one's adversaries, as illustrated by the alliance contracted by French King François I (r. 1515–47) in his quest to counter the Habsburgs' hegemony. The latter, in turn, were solicited by the Persian Safavids to help them fend off the Turks. At that point, the Ottomans were themselves eager to establish some sort of status quo in the east, since their clash with Persia was reaching its climax. With the defeat of the Mamluks in 1516 (Syria) and 1517 (Egypt), the Ottoman Empire had become, effectively, the official protector of the holy sites of Mecca, Medina, and Jerusalem. With Suleiman the Magnificent, the Turks reengaged their armies in Europe and in the Mediterranean, replete with a series of impressive victories: Belgrade in 1521, Rhodes in 1522, Mohács in 1526.

In 1529, Vienna was besieged by the Ottomans, but this was as far as they could ever go. The Ottomans never considered their defeat in the naval battle of Lepanto in 1571—the "Thirteenth Crusade"—decisive.[1] However, they were halted in the battle of Saint Gotthard in western Hungary in 1664 by one of the great commanders of the day, Raimondo Montecuccoli, an Italian serving the Habsburgs. Through his penetrating analysis of his campaigns against the Turks, Montecuccoli effectively invented modern strategy—or, if one prefers, modern strategic thought—as we know it today.[2] Later, at the end of the eighteenth century, another great commander, Russian this one, Alexander Suvorov, gave further proof that European armies were now superior. In the Horn of Africa, meanwhile, in the context of the Abyssinian-Adal War (1529–43), a Christian coalition consisting of Portuguese and Abyssinian troops defeated a Muslim army composed of Ottoman troops and soldiers from the Adal Sultanate (Battle of Wayna Daga, February 21, 1543) and led by an imam, Ahmad ibn Ibrahim al-Ghazi. The preceding year, at Wofla (August 28), al-Ghazi had repulsed a Portuguese expeditionary force of four hundred musketeers and killed its leader, Christopher da Gama, the son of the famous explorer Vasco da Gama. Although the intervention may have been construed as a crusade by the Portuguese, they were primarily motivated by their imperial grand design.

The victory of the Ottomans in the battle of Chaldiran (1514) did not end the conflict with Persia, which used a fifth column inside Anatolia, the Shiite sect of the Kizil Bash (Red Heads). With the two rivals exchanging victories during the course of the sixteenth century, borders were set between the two nations that remained essentially unchanged until the collapse of the Ottoman Empire. Tensions, political and religious, between Ottoman/modern Turkey and Iran have lasted to this day, with renewed vigor since the 1979 Iranian Revolution.

The Sunni/Shiite conflict that underpinned the confrontation between the Turks and the Persians witnessed a bizarre episode when Nader Shah (r. 1736–47), the great Persian commander of the early eighteenth century, later dubbed "The Persian Napoleon," attempted to reconcile the two creeds to become the leader of all Muslims, a prospect that did not sit well with the Ottomans, Nader Shah's principal adversaries and, more often than not, his principal victims.[3] Nader Shah suffered a megalomaniac mental breakdown, however, and his dream never materialized. The Shiite-Sunni wars were thus neatly confined, for centuries, to the rivalry between the Ottomans and the Persians, both before and during the period of European expansion and colonization.

THE SECOND COMING OF THE KNIGHTS HOSPITALLER

After the fall of Acre to the Mamluks in 1291 and the end of the Jerusalem crusades, European activity in the Mediterranean was essentially left to the seafaring merchant cities of Italy. The Hospitallers found sanctuary first on the island of Cyprus. Then, in the early fourteenth century, with the blessings of the Holy See, and in what was called a crusade, they invaded Rhodes, in alliance with Genoa, which supplied the necessary fleet. The invasion, under Fulk of Villaret, the order's grand master, included a few dozen Hospitaller knights but required bringing in additional troops from Italy. In 1310, the city of Rhodes fell to them, and the Hospitallers moved their headquarters there. In May 1312, the pope issued a bull that granted the Hospitallers a good portion of the Templars' former estates in Europe. This helped to finance their activities in the Mediterranean, where they became the primary defenders of the faith. They remained on Rhodes until 1523, when the Ottomans expelled them. The emperor Charles V thereupon offered them Malta as a base, which they held until Napoleon occupied the island on his way to Egypt and dispersed the knights.

Rhodes is about twelve miles off the Anatolian coast, and in 1310, the island had a population of about ten thousand. By 1356, the Hospitallers had fortified the island, and they encouraged immigration. To ensure the safety of trading vessels and the safe passage of pilgrims on their way to Jerusalem, the knights created a fleet of eight galleys commanded by warrior monks and rowed not by slaves but by free oarsmen. They were now the principal remaining representatives of the crusading spirit in the eastern Mediterranean, and as such they took part the Smyrniote crusades (1343–51), called for by Pope Clement VI, the fourth of the Avignon pontiffs. In 1402, Tamerlane expelled the Hospitallers from Smyrna, which they had held since 1344, but since the Ottomans had also been humiliatingly vanquished by him, the knights' prestige vis-à-vis their main adversaries did not suffer too greatly.

Nevertheless, the loss of Smyrna so soon after Sultan Bayezid's defeat of the Christians at Nicopolis reverberated deeply in Europe—the Muslim threat seemingly coming from all sides. Tamerlane's plundering had weakened the Hospitallers enemies, however, and the warrior monks of Saint John were able to hold of besiegers for more than a century, the Egyptians in the 1440s and the Ottomans in 1480. In the latter case, the knights resisted the siege with great courage and their victory resonated throughout Christianity. In 1522, however, when the Ottomans were at the height of their power, the

Hospitallers were forced out of Rhodes and evacuated to Malta (where the order is still officially based today).

Two centuries after the Templars had been obliterated and over a century after the Teutonic Knights' defeat at Grünwald-Tannenberg, the Hospitallers' defeat at the hands of Suleiman I marked the end of the crusading military orders. The Hospitallers remained active in Malta, as the German and Livonian Teutonic orders did in northern Europe, but the Reformation effectively deprived them of their territories and the properties in areas that espoused Protestantism. Weakened politically, defeated militarily, and economically smothered, the orders withered slowly into oblivion, to the point where their diminished power no longer mattered.

THE EMERGENCE OF THE HOLY LEAGUES

Devoid of the military arm constituted by the various military orders, the papacy sought other ways to uphold the crusading spirit. One of these was the creation of Christian "leagues," equivalent to what we now call collective security organizations. The main difference between the Crusades and the leagues was that the latter were generally formed of specific states or city-states, whereas the former were broad appeals made to states as well as individuals. As Jonathan Riley-Smith points out,

> A defining feature of crusades has always been that they were supranational, representing in theory, if not always in practice, the "Christian Republic". The leagues, on the other hand, never claimed to be representing the whole of Christendom. Called by one historian "frontier crusades", they were alliances of those front-line powers which felt themselves to be most threatened or whose rulers were most enthusiastic, but their campaigns were authorized by the popes and their forces were granted crusade privileges.[4]

The transition, though never clear-cut, from Crusades to Holy Leagues was effectively guided by several factors. These included the transformation of the Muslim threat from a rather vague religious menace into a specific political one in the form of the Ottoman Empire; the rise of powerful European states; and the great religious divide that separated Christian Europe into two entities, as a result of which crusading energies were from this point on increasingly focused on non-Catholic Christians, be they Hussites or Protestants. The shift from the open crusades to the closed leagues was almost imperceptible, and the Holy Leagues retained both the spirit and the language of the Crusades. The approach, however, was altogether different, since the initiative often came from the protagonists rather than from the pope, even though the papacy was inevitably involved in the process and indispensable when it came to giving its blessing to the enterprise and bestowing indulgences and spiritual rewards on those who partook. Still, the last of the great Holy Leagues, which was created in 1684 to fight the Turks, was drawn up at the instigation of a pope, Innocent XI.

The emergence of the Holy Leagues, however, is only one part of the story, since they only concerned interstate conflicts. In infrastate or suprastate conflicts, the crusading spirit remained alive. "The [French] wars of religion were, for the Catholics, crusading wars inasmuch as these were wars of the fear of the end of time," Denis Crouzet argues; conversely "Huguenot violence seem to have been a violence of reason, methodically planned in order to ensure the greatest glorification possible of God as the advent of the New Testament."[5] In 1584, the Catholics fighting the Huguenots in France would form an alliance to protect the Catholic faith known as the Catholic League (also called the Holy Union), which was animated by a violent crusading spirit. That spirit also characterized the Holy League created at around the same time in Spain along with the so-called Invincible Armada.

The first Holy League came about in 1322—about thirty years after the fall of Acre—with an initial agreement that involved Venice, Byzantium, and the Knights Hospitallers, later joined by Rome, Cyprus, France, and England. The pope was the principal engine behind the affair, so much so that when he died in 1324, the league fell apart. This was to be the first of a long list of such initiatives, some stillborn and some that bore fruit. The fourteenth century witnessed several attempts at forming leagues. The idea of retaking the Holy Land was still in the air. However, European wars, particularly between England and France, made the organization of a global crusade difficult. Moreover, from 1378 to 1417, the papacy was split into two and sometimes even three entities, and there were as many popes and antipopes. The Great Schism that rocked the papacy for about forty years even generated mini-crusades backing one pope or other.

In 1362, the king of Cyprus, Pierre I de Lusignan, proposed an expedition to retake Jerusalem in a circular letter to European heads of state, but this fell through.[6] Subsequently, in 1365, Pierre and the Hospitallers attacked Alexandria with ten thousand men.[7] The following year, inspired by this Alexandrian crusade, the count of Savoy led an army of four thousand against the Turks and then against the Bulgarians, but the strategic objectives were modest and far removed from the idea of recovering the Holy Land.

During the second half of the fourteenth century, the sudden rise of the Ottoman empire as a superpower put a damper on the idea of retaking the Holy Land. Still, despite the unfavorable odds, a couple of sizable crusades were mounted during that time, including the operation that led to the confrontation at Nicopolis. In 1390, the Genoese, who backed the Roman pope, Boniface IX, appealed to Charles VI of France, who supported the rival Avignon antipope, Clement VII, to launch a crusade against the Hafsid kingdom of Tunisia, which harbored pirates. Genoa's ulterior motives were pecuniary rather than spiritual, but the Genoese must have sensed that appealing to the faith might more easily lead to an alliance than sheer greed. The approach worked, although the French king restricted the number of French noblemen who could join to fifteen hundred, perhaps because he thought the crusade not important enough to warrant too large a loss. France, after all, had to fend off the English.

Under the captainship of Louis of Clermont, the crusade received the blessings of Clement VII, but it was no more successful than the Alexandrian crusade of 1365. The troops, who, aside from the French and Italians, came from various corners of Europe, including England, were repulsed by the Tunisians, and the Genoese quietly negotiated an accord with the enemy. It seems, however, that the initiative generated some kind of momentum and, soon, France, Burgundy, and England were corresponding with one another and with King Sigismund of Hungary, who appealed his fellow monarchs to launch a crusade from eastern Europe. Both the Roman pope and the Avignon antipope backed the project, which now took the form of a southern crusade against the Turks, possibly, in the minds of its architects, the first of a series of efforts that lead to forming a larger expeditionary force to retake Jerusalem, which the kings of France and England proposed to lead in person should it materialize. At this point, throwing caution to the winds, France came out strongly in support of the crusade, whose disastrous defeat at Nicopolis in 1396, definitively buried all impulses to reclaim the Holy Land.

THE HUSSITE WARS (1419–36) AND THE TRANSFORMATION OF RELIGIOUS CONFLICTS IN EUROPE

A painting by Jan Matejko entitled *The Battle of Grünwald* (1878), now in the National Museum in Warsaw, shows all the main characters of the eponymous confrontation that pitted the Teutonic Knights against the Polish-Lithuanian coalition in 1410 locked in violent combat. In the middle of the painting, next to the commanders mounted on their horses, stands a robust man about to hew down an enemy. The man is Jan Žižka, the main character of the Hussite wars, who reportedly also participated in the Grünwald-Tannenberg affair. His victim in the painting is Heinrich von Schwelborn, a Teutonic knight who has come down in Czech history as the epitome of Teutonic (as well as Prussian and German) arrogance. That he was killed by Žižka, whose precise role in the actual battle is unclear, is probably not true, but Žižka's presence in the center of the painting is testimony to his importance. Symbolically, the image is powerful, since it depicts the first of the modern captains in what was effectively the last great show of force of one of the remaining crusading military orders, at least in Europe (the Hospitallers had been driven out of Smyrna by Tamerlane only a few years prior to this).

Jan Žižka is one of the great figures of Czech history and he is arguably one of the greatest military commanders of all time. Though not very well known in the West, principally because his country is of relative unimportance in the greater scheme of global history, Žižka nonetheless broke new ground. He was the first truly modern military commander, in the sense that his outlook on war was thoroughly novel, not just from a strategic, tactical, and technical perspective, but also in terms of the ethical-ideological elements he instilled into the organization of his army. In many ways, Žižka anticipated the military revolution that was later implemented by the Dutch, Swedish, and Huguenot leaders of the Reformation who dominated European military theaters in the sixteenth and seventeenth centuries. He and other Protestant commanders reinvented the art of war in Europe. Though it benefited from the evolution of technology, their strategy was mainly guided by a novel intel-lectual perspective on war, based on strict ethical standards, combined with an understanding of warfare that was profoundly influenced by their reading of the Old Testament and their interest in Roman Stoic philosophy. This new ethic of war provided strict standards for the conduct of war. At the same time, the religious fanaticism that often accompanied it led to an unleashing of violence that was often self-justified by the sanctity of the cause.[8] Neverthe-less, most military historians tend to downplay the impact of religion on the evolution of war in Modern Europe.[9]

The Hussite rebellion, like many of the religious wars that would soon engulf Europe, had multiple causes, both religious and political. The violence that seemingly burst out of nowhere in Bohemia was a consequence of two

FIGURE 8. *Jan Žižka of Trocnov,* sandstone statue in Žižka
Square, Tábor, by Josef Strachovský (1884). Photo by iStock.com/
josefkubes.

elements that would also be at the center of the Reformation and the Thirty
Years' Wars: the corruption of the Catholic Church and the chronic instability of the Holy Roman Empire. Furthermore, the outburst of violence in
Bohemia was a symptom of a boiling tension that, already present during the
Teutonic-Polish wars, would increase, sometimes drastically, over the centuries: the conflict between the Slavs and the Germans. Hence, we can already
perceive at this early point the principal sources of the many conflicts that
would erupt almost uninterruptedly in that part of the world: namely, religion,

politics, and ethnicity, an explosive cocktail that was to wreak havoc for centuries.

Essentially, the Hussite Wars were predicated on the fundamental element that had precipitated the Albigensian Wars, and they solicited the same type of violent response from Church authorities. This element revolved around the deepening spiritual crisis that had befallen Europe, to which a despondent Rome had been increasingly unable and unwilling to respond. This spiritual crisis, fueled by apocalyptic predictions (corroborated by distressing events like the bubonic plagues), thus led to a moral crisis. Consequently, the ever-growing gap between the peoples of Europe and church authorities generated violent responses from both sides. The main difference between the Albigensian and Hussite episodes lay in the fact that the former was principally an urban response, whereas the latter was a rural one. The fact that the Hussite movement took root at the heart of a fragile multiethnic empire made it much more volatile than the Cathar revolt. All these elements would play out again a century later, and in much grander fashion.

The origins of the Hussite rebellion are complex. As with many of the religious conflicts that punctuate the history of Christianity, this one was predicated on what may appear to many of us today as an obscure point of theological or, more precisely, ecclesiological (pertaining to the structure of the church), detail. It seems a Czech student in Oxford had come across the writings of the English religious reformer John Wycliffe (1320–84), who had challenged the papacy's authority and its role in mediating the divine message.[10] Wycliffe, whose followers were opprobriously dubbed Lollards ("mumblers") by their enemies, was not the first to put forth such ideas: a former rector of the University of Paris, Marsilius of Padua (1275/80–1342), had done so before him.[11] But Wycliffe's views now suddenly resonated in Bohemia, notably with the rector of the University of Prague, Jan Hus.

Wycliffe had been strategically ignored by the English monarchy, but the Lollard movement had been swiftly dealt with. In 1401, a law titled *De heretico comburendo* authorized burning heretics, and even before it was adopted by Parliament, a parish priest named William Sawtrey, effectively the first Lollard martyr, went to the stake. Unable to generate any kind of political traction, the Lollard movement was all but wiped out within a generation (in 1414, a rebellion was quashed), though it had a revival of sorts at the turn of the sixteenth century, before it was absorbed by Protestantism.

In Prague, things shaped up very differently. With the University of Prague officially supporting the dissenters, the challenge to church authority was formally engaged by a state. As rector of the university, Jan Hus was at the center of the controversy, and he and his partisans were excommunicated in September 1410, a few weeks, incidentally, after the battle of Grünwald-Tannenberg. The conflict between the church and Hus came to a head over the issue of indulgences, much as it would with Martin Luther in 1517.

This issue had surfaced through the rivalry between Pope Gregory XII and the antipope (the opprobrious term subsequently used by the Catholic Church) John XXIII. This conflict escalated, and John issued indulgences to pay mercenaries. When the collectors of indulgences entered Prague in May 1412, their presence generated a violent popular reaction, and Jan Hus found himself at the center of an acrimonious debate around the issue at the university. Forced to flee Prague in 1412 as the conflict with the church authorities escalated, Hus published anti-establishment pamphlets. What distinguished Hus from Marsilius or Wycliffe was that his virulent attacks came during a tense period when the Catholic Church was trying hard to regain its lost unity. Moreover, the intransigent personality of Hus, who proclaimed everywhere that "Truth will vanquish"—which would become the Hussite slogan—was a source of great concern for the clergy.

The church authorities chose to confront the enemy in person, and Hus was invited to defend his views at the Council of Constance, which began in 1414, whose purpose was to put an end to the Schism and generate a new unity. Against the advice of his friends, Hus proceeded to travel to the Council. Predictably, the invitation was a trap, and Hus was swiftly put in jail, though not without being given the chance to express his views publicly: the church, as always, followed protocol, even in these matters. The authorities needed no more convincing that this man was the threat they feared and Hus was condemned to death, which made him a martyr and the spiritual figure behind the Hussite Rebellion. What the church authorities had not anticipated was that another figure, and a formidable one at that, would bring the revolt to a new level.

With Hus physically out of the picture, the fight was then taken up by Jan Žižka, a man with extraordinary political and military skills, who was poised to lead a holy war in the Czech lands (Bohemia and Moravia) and beyond. Faced with an unprecedented menace, that of an army of dangerous heretics far more powerful than the Cathars had ever been, the church answered in kind with its usual response: a crusade or, as it turned out, a series of crusades.[12] As they would soon find out, the Catholic authorities had not faced such a potent enemy since the wars against Arab and Turkish Muslim armies.

The hostilities began in Prague on July 30, 1419, when a furious Hussite mob killed seven members of the city council by throwing them out of a window in the town hall (the "first defenestration of Prague"), shock at which supposedly caused King Wenceslaus IV of Bohemia to suffer a fatal heart attack. Quickly, the country became engulfed in religious violence further fueled by political conflicts between exterior elements seeking to take advantage of the chaos. The Hussites were themselves divided into two main currents, a moderate urban group and a radical peasant movement. As often happens, the radicals, under the leadership of Jan Žižka, won over the moderates.

Žižka combined two qualities that would greatly enhance the success of the Hussites: charisma and extraordinary military skills. A religious zealot, he was convinced that God had entrusted him with a divine mission, and he had the arguments to convince his followers that this was the case. In many ways, his tactics anticipated those of the revolutionary wars of the twentieth century. Years spent fighting warlords in Bohemia on behalf of the king had given the young Žižka a good understanding of guerrilla warfare and an intimate knowledge of the Bohemian peasantry. As the Hussite leader, he put this knowledge to good use, undertaking propaganda campaigns to mobilize the masses and organizing local guerrillas to fight the authorities and then the crusaders. The defeat of the Teutonic Knights at Tannenberg, still fresh in the collective memory, had destroyed the aura of invincibility that previously surrounded them, and Žižka, who knew them well, was confident that ingenuity could go a long way against heavy cavalry. For Žižka, the real warriors of God were the Hussites, not the knights of the warrior-monk military orders, as illustrated by the Hussite battle song:

Ye who are the warriors of God
And of his law,
Pray for God's help
And believe in Him
So ye will with him always remain victorious.

Christ will reward ye for what thou lose,
He promises ye a hundred times more.
Whoever gives his life for Him

Will gain life eternal.
Blessed everyone who stands by the truth

This our Lord bids us not to fear
The destroyers of the flesh
If ye want to win the life
For the love of thy nearest.

Therefore Archers and lancers
Of knightly rank,
Pikesmen and flailsmen
Of the common people,
Do all keep in mind the generous Lord.

Never fear the enemies
Do not mind their great numbers,
Keep your Lord in thine hearts.
Fight for him and with him
And do not ever retreat before thine enemies![13]

What Žižka set out to do was to transpose the theological ideas of Jan Hus to the military theater. Jan Hus had effectively contested the authority of the church, encouraging the masses to communicate directly with God through the word of the Bible. Now Žižka was contesting the military authority of the orders. In doing so, he would contribute to the final downfall, not only of the Knights of the Cross (who were already reeling), but of the mounted knight in general. By showing the effectiveness of the infantry and the lethality of new weaponry, he would help precipitate a new era of warfare in Europe, a true revolution that the Protestants would later push to another dimension. Žižka's defensive strategy corresponded to the defensive ideals of the Hussites, which they had discussed in the winter of 1419–20 and written down in the form of decrees prescribing the type of conduct expected of the combatants and defending the legality of their wars. This was reiterated in a 1426 decree that proclaimed that the Hussites "intend to conduct an orderly and Christian form of war, based on and established in the law of the holy Gospel. Such a war arises not from one's own will but in response to oppression, when somebody is resolved to use violence to deter his victim from the pursuit of the good, and it proves impossible to make the oppressor desist by any other means."[14]

The Hussite military revolution affected strategy, tactics, and military technology. It was also a moral revolution that set new standards for the conduct of war. Žižka's strategy was based on the indirect approach, always keeping the initiative and attracting the enemy into a trap. Like all great captains, Žižka had a superior understanding of his own and the enemy's strengths and weaknesses. His troops were motivated and well-drilled, and he established efficient and reliable lines of communication. His great tactical innovation revolved around the use of the battle wagons, mobile fortresses forming a protective wall from behind which his men could fire their *pišťala* (the original pistols), harquebuses (hook guns), and short-barreled cannons they called *houfnice* (howitzers). The battle wagons proved incredibly effective against charging cavalry, allowing for deadly counterattacks. Žižka was also the first commander to use field artillery effectively. By proving that an army of peasants could repeatedly defeat mounted knights, he challenged the superiority of the aristocratic knight, on which the Western art of war had been predicated for centuries.

Žižka also introduced yet another element that would come to define war in the next centuries: the power of nationalism. Far from impeding the universal message of the Hussites, his appeal to Czech (messianic) nationalism helped rally his citizen soldiers against what was essentially a German army of crusaders. This appeal to nationalism was based in large part on the resentment the Czechs harbored against the Germans, especially the Teutonic Knights. This combination of a people's army, a universalistic ideology, and a nationalistic appeal born of resentment would become a staple of revolutionary armies around the world.

Žižka was also the first European general to hold a citizen army to the same type of moral standards as the elite religious-military orders. In essence, the Hussite wars displayed all the characteristics of religious warfare in Europe in the sixteenth and seventeenth centuries: the ideal of the crusade, sectarian apocalyptism, national messianism, and the defense of a reformed faith.[15] In a twelve-point document,[16] Žižka laid down rules of conduct for his troops and a strict ethical code of private and public behavior, saying: "We do not suffer among us faithless men, disobedient ones, liars, thieves, gamblers, robbers, plunderers, drunkards, blasphemers, lechers, adulterers, whores, adulteresses, or any manifest sinners, men or women; all these will we banish and chase away, or punish them with help of the holy trinity according to the Law of God" (art. 11).

The punishment was unequivocal and no one was above the law: "Brother Žižka, and other lords, captains, knights, squires, townsmen, craftsmen and peasants named above and all their communities, with the help of God and of the Commonwealth, will punish all such crimes by flogging, banishment, clubbing, decapitation, hanging, drowning, burning, and by all retributions which fit the crime according to God's law, excepting no one from whichever rank and sex" (art. 12)

There was a strong egalitarian thread to this social compact, with specific guidelines to redistribute wealth (from booty): "And herefor elders shall be from all communities, those of the Lords, the knights and townsmen and peasants, that they faithfully administer these things to the poor and the rich, and that the things be justly distributed and divided among them as is proper" (art. 7).

The justness of the cause was written into the statutes, and this fact was reiterated by frequent prayers: "Then, when they move out from some place and before they undertake or order some enterprise in the war, they shall first make a prayer to the Lord God, and kneeling down before the Body of God and before the Face of God, at the time when they want to leave an encampment or a town, pray that Lord God the Almighty deign to give His help, that they thus may wage His sacred war for the praise of His sacred name and for the enhancement of this beneficence, and for the salvation and help of the faithful" (art. 4).

The Catholic response to the Hussite uprising was swift. In the aftermath of the Nicopolis disaster, Rome had issued several appeals for a crusade against the Turks (1398, 1399, and 1400) to save Constantinople, but Tamerlane's defeat of them had temporarily quieted the Ottomans and relieved the pressure on the Europeans. Rome was thus able to concentrate all its attention on the Hussite threat. Between 1419 and 1431, it managed to organize no fewer than five crusades. So close were these to each other that some of them are almost undistinguishable from one another.[17] As with the wars against the Cathars, these were brutal, take-no-prisoners affairs. The Holy Roman Emperor Sigismund led an army of eighty thousand, with troops from no fewer than thirty-three nations in the crusades against the Hussites. Cardinal Branda of Castiglione, the archbishop-electors of Mainz, Trier, and Cologne, and other clergy, most of whom even commanded troops in the field, helped organize the second crusade.[18]

Žižka and his troops proved too smart and too strong for anything the crusaders were able to throw at them, and the Catholic armies suffered defeat upon defeat. Žižka's defensive strategy allowed him to secure his gains solidly before moving on.[19] Žižka, over sixty years old when the conflict reached its climax and completely blind, was both bold and prudent, and he devoted much effort to reinforce his social and economic base rather than squander all his resources in the war. But his military genius was a double-edged sword that gave the Hussites too much confidence. Convinced that they were aided by God in their quest, they were unable to sustain their successes once Žižka was gone. Yet, he, more than God, had been the real engine behind the Hussite armies' victories. Without Žižka to guide his troops and his people, the string of successes would soon come to a halt.

Prokop the Bald, who took over the Hussite army in 1426, a couple of years after Žižka's death (Vitold the Great of Lithuania led it in the interim), was confident and impetuous, but he lacked Žižka's strategic intelligence. Despite some success against the crusaders, as at Domažlice in 1431, Prokop's overdrawn offensive strategy, coupled with internal conflicts among the Hussites, ultimately killed the momentum and brought the Hussite revolution to an end.[20] The wound remained open among the Czechs, however, and resentment brewed over several decades. Religious violence erupted again in 1618 in Prague, and in similar fashion, with a defenestration. This time, however, the consequences would be far graver.

THE FALLOUT FROM THE FALL OF CONSTANTINOPLE

Despite the crusaders' pitiful showing during the Hussite wars, the enemy had been eradicated. Rome could now turn its attention once again to the south, where the Ottoman Turks had recovered from their defeat by Tamerlane. The threat to Constantinople had produced a rapprochement of sorts between the Catholic and Eastern Orthodox authorities, due in great measure to diplomatic efforts on the part of the papacy. In 1443, January 1, Pope Eugenius IV, made an official appeal to defend the Christian East. A naval force to support the Byzantines was put together by the papacy, the duke of Burgundy, and the cities of Venice and Ragusa, among others, and King Władysław III of Poland, Hungary, and Croatia; János Hunyadi, the voivode of Transylvania; and Mircea II, prince of Wallachia responded to the pope's call with a Christian army of some twenty thousand men, which traversed Bulgaria, entered Sofia, after disposing of a Turkish army, and besieged Varna on the

Black Sea coast. It was no match for Sultan Murad II's army, however, which defeated the Christians on November 10, 1444, killing both the papal legate and King Władysław.

The fall of Constantinople less than a decade later, on May 29, 1453, effectively ended Byzantium's thousand-year history. The loss of Constantinople to the Turks did not, however, in any way put an end to the Vatican's eagerness to go crusading against the Ottomans. In 1455, Pope Calixtus III declared a new crusade, with a departure date set for March 1 of the following year. John of Capistrano (subsequently St. John of Capestrano) preached for the crusade, and János Hunyadi again took part in the expedition. On July 22, an underpowered Christian army managed to repulse the Turks at Belgrade, thanks in part to the popular enthusiasm that characterized this effort, which mobilized the lower social classes in an episode reminiscent of Peter the Hermit during the First Crusade. This unlikely victory nevertheless failed to yield further results. The Ottoman Turks were by then on the ascendant, and they were too strong for the Christian armies. This newfound power on the part of the Ottomans was to prove both profound and durable. It kept growing well into the next century. During the greater part of the sixteenth century, Suleiman the Magnificent was too formidable a foe, and the West would have to wait until 1571 to once again successfully engage the Turks.

WAR, RELIGION, AND THE FALL OF MEXICO

During the fifteenth century, crusades against the Muslims met with better fortune in Spain, which witnessed renewed interest in the Reconquista after the Fall of Constantinople.[21] The *reyes católicos* Ferdinand and Isabella rolled up what was left of Muslim rule in Spain with great zeal. After Granada was taken on January 2, 1492, the Spanish monarchs sought to project their troops across the sea into North Africa, which they invaded in 1497, with the goal of creating a safe passage to the Holy Land. Authorized by the pope, this campaign yielded an impressive series of successes on the coast, with the Spaniards reaching Oran in 1509 and Tripoli in 1510. In a way, this was Spain's way of dealing with the anguish of Christianity after the fall of Constantinople.[22] The conquest of Granada and the expulsion of the Jews a few months later (on March 31) marked a new Christian empowerment, which translated into a policy of religious purification, coupled with what we might today call ethnic cleansing, aimed at achieving *limpieza de sangre* (purity of blood).[23]

This was the logical outcome of a long-held belief that the people of Spain had been commanded by God to extend the rule of Christianity beyond the Iberian Peninsula.[24] This would lead to the liberation of Jerusalem and the beginning of the universal reign of Jesus Christ. The history of Spain was clearly thought to follow the model of the Old Testament, as "the image of a chosen people that must consolidate its alliance with God through the rejection of all external impurity, a chosen people to be purified of all those around it that do not follow the true faith."[25]

The fall of Granada had been quickly followed, not coincidentally (it was the principal element that enabled Christopher Columbus to persuade the previously reluctant Spanish monarchs to fund his voyage), by the discovery of America, opening up a whole new theater of operations for many of the soldiers that had partaken in the Reconquista and its aftermath. Many of these seasoned warriors would enjoy a second life as conquistadors in the Americas, which offered a whole new perspective on the mission of establishing the reign of God on earth. These tough men brought the religious rituals, rhetoric, and general paraphernalia that characterized the final chapter of the Reconquista to the New World. They were accompanied by priests bent on saving the souls of the pagan populations they sought to subjugate, so the whole enterprise had clear religious overtones. Prayers would be offered before each battle, all of which were fought in the name of the Virgin Mary and launched with the battle cry "Santiago y cierra, España!". Each territory conquered or occupied quickly saw the erection of a church where all the soldiers could pray and be forgiven their sins.

And yet, while religion may have given these expeditions a veneer of respectability, the principal drivers behind these conquests were greed, personal ambition, and lust for power. For while the crown may have reaped the bulk of the benefits that resulted from these territorial acquisitions, the actual exploration and conquest were left to those individuals who could organize and finance an expedition with their own means.

The first of the great conquests, Mexico, opened the path to most of the other military expeditions in the central and southern parts of the continent. In the historical conundrum of war and religion, this was a bizarre and rare event, in which religion came to play a decisive role in paralyzing the stronger of the two protagonists to the point where it was completely crushed and annihilated. Although, through our anachronistic tendencies, we tend to attribute Cortés's victory to the supposedly intrinsic military superiority of

Western soldiers, a careful reading of the facts gives a totally different version of the events as they unfolded.[26]

Fortunately, the conquest of Mexico benefits from having inspired one the greatest war histories of all time, Bernal Díaz del Castillo's *The Conquest of New Spain*, as told by one of the men who partook in the events that led to the fall of the mighty Aztec empire.[27] This powerful, penetrating account makes clear, first, how close Cortés and his men came, on several occasions, to being quashed by the enemy, and, second, how the religious beliefs and practices of the Aztecs ultimately gave the Spaniards the second chances that allowed them to defeat the Mexicans. Nor is this only Bernal Díaz's perspective on the events, as it is corroborated by the accounts of the Mexicans themselves.[28]

The religious beliefs and practices of the Aztecs played out in two different ways. Firstly, the Aztec mythic worldview and one of its prophecies initially helped Cortés penetrate Mexico by the arrival of the Spaniards being mistaken for the return a vengeful Quetzalcoatl, the powerful god of the Aztec pantheon. The emperor Montezuma was himself particularly sensitive to these beliefs, and he systematically sought to interpret each event according to his mythic outlook on life. After the initial contacts had been made, though, the Mexicans quickly realized that these callous individuals were no gods, but mere humans. All told, comprising only a couple of hundred men and a few horses, the Spanish army had little chance of overcoming tens of thousands of Mexican troops. Though the Castilians wielded sharp and sturdy Toledan steel swords against the obsidian weapons of the Mexicans, this superiority in armaments is insufficient to explain their success. So why did the Spaniards ultimately win this war?

Aside from the technological explanations—essentially, the lethality of the Toledo swords—as well as Cortés's true strategic genius, the answer points directly or indirectly to religious factors. This is true, also, of the smallpox epidemic that decimated the Mexicans (the Spaniards were to a certain extent immune to it), whose physical effects were psychologically aggravated by the fact that it was portrayed and interpreted as a divine punishment. The Spanish victory, or rather the Mexican defeat, can also be explained by the sacrificial dimension of the Aztecs' religion. They made great use of human sacrifices as a way of "establishing a means of communication between the sacred and the profane worlds through the mediation of a victim, that is, of a thing that in the course of the ceremony is destroyed."[29] The Aztecs frequently raided neighboring peoples to meet their consumption of such mediators. This had two effects. For one thing, it deeply alienated those neighbors. Secondly, it generated an approach to war based on this belief. In its military application, this made for highly ritualistic confrontations, in which the commander was typically in the middle of the fray, very distinctively clad, and the goal was to take prisoners rather than to annihilate the opponent.

For the Spaniards, this had two vital effects, one political, the other military. The first thing Cortés astutely understood, thanks in part to his Mexican translator, the controversial Marina (La Malinche), was that the other peoples of Mexico that had been subjected to these raids were deeply resentful, and that he could easily turn them against the Aztecs, which he did. These alliances meant that Cortés's force was exponentially multiplied (he also received Spanish reinforcements, including troops sent by Diego Velázquez de Cuéllar, the governor of Cuba, to arrest him), and that he could confront the Aztec armies with a respectable, if still numerically inferior, force. On the military front, the Aztecs' art of war made them extremely vulnerable on the battlefield, where their commanders were easily targeted and either killed or captured by the Spaniards, who showed no respect for the Mexican rules of engagement that protected commanders from being harmed. More important, perhaps, the Mexicans' failure to pursue a policy of annihilating the enemy meant that they were never able to capitalize on victory (and they had their share of successes). Thus, Cortés was always able to bounce back and, learning from his mistakes and setbacks, launch increasingly effective attacks. By the time of the ultimate assault on Tenochtitlán (Mexico City) in the spring and summer of 1521, the Aztecs had been struck by the smallpox virus introduced to the country by the Spaniards (unwittingly, it appears, through one of the men aboard one of the ships sent by Diego Velázquez to arrest Cortés). The impact of the epidemic on the issue of the war has divided historians,[30] but its effects were multiplied by the Aztecs' interpretation of the epidemic, which was thought to be a punishment of the gods that required additional human sacrifices. As Victor Davis Hanson suggests,

> The real advantage of the smallpox epidemic to Cortés was not the reductions in Aztec numbers per se but its cultural and political consequences. Because the Spaniards did not die at the same rate as the Indians, there spread the notion— mostly forgotten for a time after the *Noche Triste*—that the Europeans were more than mortal [. . .] Smallpox enhanced the Spanish reputation for superhuman strength and solidified their support among native allies, despite the fact that the disease killed as many supporters as enemies—and thus had no real effect on the numerical parity between attackers and besieged.[31]

The Spaniards, on the other hand, had no such qualms, being convinced that God was on their side, and that theirs was a divine mission to be duly rewarded in the afterlife and, before that, on earth itself. In Bernal Díaz's words, these men were there "to serve God and His Majesty, to bring light to those who live in darkness and to become rich, as all men desire."[32]

In the Name of God

Religious Warfare In Europe, 1524–1700

These types of wars claim to be spiritual, but they are no more so than a combat between insects. In between two murders, we attend mass, we preach, or we engage in dialectics in order to cleanse our consciences, and all is said and done.

—Jean Giono

Roughly around the time when Cortés had the last Aztec emperor, Cuauhté- moc, executed (1525), Europe began to experience religious violence that would shock, rock, and transform the continent over the next one hundred and twenty-five years.[1] This violence would manifest itself in different ways in various places, but it would, in the end, leave millions dead and launch the Western world in a new dimension, transforming society and economics, as well as politics and geopolitics, and, in general, the dynamics of war and peace. Between 1520 and 1650 almost all the wars that erupted in Europe were, in one way or another, religious wars.[2] Although one can argue that the period was no more bellicose than the one that preceded it or than the one that followed, the nature of the wars themselves was as peculiar as it was violent. One can thus look at the period as either a specific one, marked essentially by the shock provoked by the Reformation, or as the culmination of a longer trend that reached its ultimate outcome in the sixteenth and seventeenth centuries. Over the centuries, historians have oscillated between the one view and the other, while attributing various causes to the conflicts.[3] Some historians have recently been looking more closely at the religious violence that followed the end of the Thirty Years' War, while others are now characterizing the ideological conflicts that followed as essentially religious wars under another name.[4]

At the end of the run, in 1648 (with only some lingering conflicts resolved in 1660), the modern secular state emerged and a new European order was established, with a fledgling system of international law. Religion, which had for so long played a major role in European politics, would now essentially be relegated to the private sphere. With Catholics, Lutherans, Calvinists, and Anglicans having dissolved any sense of Christian unity, Europe's divisions fostered a new form of identity: secular nationalism. The adoption in 1555, at the Peace of Augsburg, of the principle of "one prince, one religion" (*Cujus regio, ejus religio*) laid the basis for another principle, the indivisibility of sovereignty, which would come to define the modern state and modern international relations.

EUROPE UNDER STRESS

At the turn of the sixteenth century, Europe was undergoing major changes. The Catholic Church had not fully recovered from the Great Schism that splintered the papacy in the fourteenth century. At the time, many in Europe favored a greater role for local churches and clergymen, and the peasant masses were particularly receptive to such reforms. The Catholic Church may well have been genuinely open to some, albeit by no means radical, changes. However, as Tocqueville observes in *The Old Regime and the Revolution*—where he argues that the French Revolution, though political, had all the marks of a *religious revolution*—corruption and injustices seem all the more intolerable precisely when reforms are enacted.[5] Rome's efforts at reform were insufficient to rally the vast portions of the population that felt forgotten or betrayed by the church.

Europe was in a state of great stress. Amid eschatological expectations and deep anxieties, it was frightened by novelty and by the future. France "was bitten by this anguish of a plunge into the unknown," Crouzet writes. The French took any news as a "sign and reflection of human sin, not individual but collective, and thus as a sign that humanity has left the path willed by God and is now engaged in an un-chartered road towards evil."[6] The sixteenth century was a time of change, and new means of communication, notably the invention in 1436–39 and rapid spread, of the printing press, would completely alter society's relationship with knowledge, which until then had been primarily monopolized by the clergy.

For those living at the eastern edges of the Holy Roman Empire, the pressure exerted by the Ottoman Turks was physically palpable. When, on August

30, 1526, Suleiman the Magnificent obliterated a Hungarian army at the battle of Mohács, the news sent shock waves throughout Europe, especially in the central regions. The psychological impact of this defeat was not unlike that of the fall of Constantinople, and it logically helped keep the crusading flame alive. Hence, Europe felt a double strain. As Christendom, it was under threat from the infidels, but the very idea of Christendom was itself being challenged by growing inner tensions. All Christians shared in the idea that one could not be saved if one believed in and practiced religious errors. God had revealed a certain number of truths, and salvation was contingent upon these. The legitimacy of the religious and political leadership was dependent upon the manner by which it enforced and defended these truths. Political stability itself was understood to be contingent upon religious homogeneity. The modern idea, at the core of our liberal democratic ideal, that a stable society is possible where people agree to disagree, would only become current at the end of the eighteenth century. Thus, when people started opposing different truths, tensions quickly started to arise.

THE HABSBURGS FEEL THE PRESSURE

The Habsburg Empire, which comprised both Spain and the Holy Roman Empire, found itself in the thick of things: it felt the pressure from the Turks in Europe and in the Mediterranean, and it faced popular unrest at home. At the same time, it was successfully spreading the Catholic faith on other continents, sword in one hand, Bible in the other. Its hegemony in western Europe was challenged by France, which would find itself embroiled in a serious home-grown religious conflict of its own, and by Sweden. These two nations would emerge as the great continental powers of the second half of the seventeenth century, the United Provinces (the Netherlands) and England being the great sea powers.

Religious violence first flared up in the Holy Roman Empire in 1524 with the so-called Peasant Wars (1524–26), which left several thousand dead. Earlier, in 1517, Martin Luther had famously posted his ninety-five theses on the door of the church at Wittenberg, or so the legend goes (he may, less dramatically, have just delivered or mailed them), thus igniting the spark of what would be known as the Reformation. Luther's demands, unbeknown to him at the time (though he later was made aware of it),[7] were oddly similar to Jan Hus's a century or so before. "Without knowing it," he would tell a friend, "we are all

Hussites." In what appeared in hindsight to be a prophetic intuition, Hus himself had declared before dying, "You are now roasting a goose [*husa* = goose in Czech], but God will awaken a swan whom you will not burn or roast." Luther never displayed the grace of a swan, but he was never burned at the stake either, though reviled by the church and excommunicated. Although rebellion against the church had long been brewing, as the Hussite and Lollard episodes showed, triggering it required both Luther's formidable energy and Gutenberg's printing press—Luther's ninety-five theses only had an impact once they were printed, distributed, and read by a large public.

It seems safe to say that the main cause of the religious revolution was first and foremost . . . religion. This revolution and the conflicts it subsequently caused were induced by the defensive and volatile religious climate that prevailed at the time. The Catholic Church, enmeshed in its quarrels and contradictions, had proven incapable of responding to the spiritual anguish that gripped European Christendom. While popes like Alexander VI (1492–1503) conducted themselves like wealthy abusive princes, local clergy were essentially working on an economic shoestring. In consequence, the quality of the spiritual leadership was suffering to the point where a renewal was deeply felt needed. This need provoked both moderate responses, exemplified by Erasmus's Christian humanism, and radical upheavals such as those of Luther, John Calvin, and Ulrich Zwingli.

Martin Luther, himself suffering a deep spiritual crisis, responded by first criticizing the trade in indulgences, then by developing a doctrine that confronted the church head on. In many ways, Luther's demands and criticisms echoed those earlier voiced by Hus and others but Luther upped the ante, dismissing altogether, and in specific terms, the role of the church as the primary and indispensable go-between that allowed the individual to communicate with God. One immediate political consequence, which would have deep long-term ramifications, was that the imperial power of the Habsburg monarchy was singularly weakened within the continental empire. The emperor Charles V's quest to create a hegemonic universal Catholic monarchy on the scale of the European continent was ultimately derailed from inside by the deep religious and political crisis that resulted from Luther's reform. From then on, the authority of the monarchy declined as steadily as that of the Lutheran princes of the Holy Roman Empire rose. This decline was precipitated by internal power struggles within the Habsburg Empire between the descendants of Emperor Maximilian II (r. 1564–76) that followed the effective separation of the empire into two main entities (Spain and Austria, with the Holy Roman Empire already ceded to Ferdinand in 1521) after the abdication of Charles V in the mid 1550s (the process extended over time) and his death in 1558.

At the same time that the Habsburgs were dealing with their religious crisis, other European powers were undergoing their own religious revolutions— including Denmark and Sweden, which adopted Lutheranism; England, which, through the impulsive Henry VIII, abandoned Catholicism for Anglicanism; and France, which became the theater of a bitter war between Catholics and Calvinists that ended with the adoption of the Edict of Nantes in 1598[8] (later revoked by Louis XIV), which promulgated the toleration of Protestantism in a country that remained nominally Catholic. Thus, while the religious crisis generated by the Reformation did not significantly modify the geopolitical landscape per se—most of the larger states retained their borders—it completely altered the geostrategic balance of power of Europe in a durable, extensive way. This change, logically, did not come about through peaceful intervention but as the outcome of a series of extremely violent conflicts. In these wars, the religious tensions that often sparked the confrontations were generally accompanied, and frequently overtaken, by political rivalries. Such was the case with the war to end all religious wars, at least in Europe: the Thirty Years' War.

MARTIN LUTHER ON THE CRUSADES

Like Jan Hus, Luther did not condone violence indiscriminately. He was very critical of the violence of the Crusades, including those waged against the Muslims and, breaking with a centuries-old ecclesiastical attitude, took a very strong stand against holy war in general. This did not, needless to say, prevent Rome from making repeated appeals throughout the sixteenth century for crusades against the Turks, but it did set a new tone.

In light of the religious tensions that have surfaced in the twenty-first century, along with a global rise in religious violence, Luther's pamphlet *On War against the Turks* (1529) can be read in a new light. It is a remarkable document, especially as its author was keen to separate the topic of holy war from the issue of religious toleration. More specifically, Luther condemned religious violence in any shape or form, and while he criticized certain aspects of Islam, notably its treatment of women, he accepted the Muslim faith and went as far as to distinguish some of its more radical manifestations from other commendable "mainstream" practices. At the time, this attitude was progressive to say the least. For Luther, the Crusades were, first and foremost, an exercise in corruption and extortion:

> For the popes had never seriously intended to make war on the Turk, but used the Turkish war as a conjurer's hat, playing around in it, and robbing Germany of money by means of indulgences, whenever they took the notion. All the world knew it, but now it is forgotten. [. . .] If they had seriously wished to fight against the Turk, the pope and the cardinals would have had enough from the pallia [i.e., the sale of archbishoprics], annates [i.e., income due to bishops appropriated by the papacy], and other unmentionable sources of income, so that they would not have needed to practice such extortion and robbery in Germany.

The bulk of his argument, however, revolved around the message of Jesus Christ, even though he almost systematically substituted rants against Jews, Turks, and the papacy for Jesus's message of love:

> It did not please me, either, that the Christians and the princes were driven, urged, and irritated into attacking the Turk and making war on him, before they amended their own ways and lived like true Christians. These two points, or either separately, were enough reason to dissuade from war. For I shall never advise a heathen or a Turk, let alone a Christian, to attack another or begin war. That is nothing else than advising bloodshed and destruction, and it brings no good fortune in the end, as I have written in the book On Soldiers; and it never does any good when one knave punishes another without first becoming good himself.
>
> But what moved me most of all was this. They undertook to fight against the Turk under the name of Christ, and taught men and stirred them up to do this, as though our people were an army of Christians against the Turks, who were enemies of Christ; and this is straight against Christ's doctrine and name. It is against His doctrine, because He says that Christians shall not resist evil, shall not fight or quarrel, not take revenge or insist on rights. It is against His name, because in such an army there are scarcely five Christians, and perhaps worse people in the eyes of God than are the Turks; and yet they would all bear the name of Christ. This is the greatest of all sins and one that no Turk commits, for Christ's name is used for sin and shame and thus dishonored

Luther was not altogether against war, as long as it was undertaken for a just cause:

> It must be known that the man, whoever he is, who is going to make war against the Turk, must be sure that he has a commission from God and is doing right. He must not plunge in for the sake of revenge or have some other mad notion or

reason. He must be sure of this, so that, win or lose, he may be in a state of salvation and in a godly occupation. [. . .] What are we to do, then? Are we to fight against the pope, as well as the Turk, since the one is as godly as the other? Answer: Treat the one like the other and no one is wronged; like sin should receive like punishment. I mean that this way. If the pope and his followers were to attack the empire with the sword, as the Turk does, he should receive the same treatment as the Turk; and this is what was done to him by the army of Emperor Charles before Pavia. For there stands God's verdict, "He that takes the sword shall perish by the sword."[9]

In the same pamphlet, Luther urged his fellow Germans to refrain from engaging in war against the Turks, but his argument was a pragmatic one: the Turks were far too powerful at this juncture to be messed with. The assessment was based on sound judgment, since the Ottomans were then at the height of their power and likely to respond forcefully to any provocation.

Luther's was not the only voice to condemn the Crusades. Erasmus, more moderate in his speech than Luther, anticipated Luther's fierce criticism of the Crusades. In his *Institutio principis christiani* (1516), the Dutch humanist stated that "judging by the people who fight this kind of war nowadays, it is more likely that we shall turn into Turks than that our efforts will make them into Christians," adding, "Let us first make sure that we are truly Christians ourselves and then, if it seems appropriate, let us attack the Turks."[10]

LEPANTO AND THE REVIVAL OF HOLY WAR

The pro-crusade movement, generated by the growing violence between Protestants and Catholics, provoked a sudden revival of the spirit of holy war. Pope Pius V (r. 1566–72) became the guiding force behind the creation a powerful, though short-lived, Catholic Holy League meant to oppose the Ottomans on the high seas. Antonio Possevino (1533–1611), a Jesuit, produced a military manual entitled *Il soldato cristiano* (The Christian Soldier) that was distributed to the men who fought against the Turks in 1571. The "Thirteenth Crusade," culminated with the great naval battle of Lepanto in the Ionian Sea, off the coast of Greece. The main Christian force was a mighty fleet of galleys commanded by Don Juan (Johann) of Austria, an illegitimate son of the emperor Charles V, and manned by sailors and soldiers levied by Rome, Venice, and Spain. Pope Pius spared neither energy nor effort, diplomatic or financial, and he was the man who made it happen.

In the months and weeks preceding the decisive battle, an explosion of popular enthusiasm had gripped Spain and Italy (on the Turkish side, the attitude was much more subdued). On the day of the battle, October 7, 1571, the Christian soldiers and sailors took communion from Capuchin monks and shouted in unison: "Victory, and hail to Jesus Christ."[11] After the first ritual artillery salvo, the two fleets closed in on each other, and by evening, the Ottomans had been thoroughly defeated, with their commander Grand Admiral Ali Pasha himself killed and his head stuck on a pike to demoralize his men. Thirty or forty thousand Ottoman combatants, including thirty-four admirals and 120 galley commanders also perished, compared to 7,650 combatants of the Holy League.[12] In Europe, the battle was hailed as a historic victory for Christendom, comparable to the taking of Jerusalem in 1099, and long overdue revenge for the fall of Constantinople and other defeats at the hands of the Turks over the centuries. Rome made sure that the victory received the proper propaganda treatment, while the Ottomans for their part saw to it that it got as little publicity as possible. The Turks soon managed to rebuild their fleet, and geopolitically and geostrategically speaking, Lepanto brought little about. However, it seems to have had a profound psychological effect on both sides in the relationship between the Europeans and the Turks. In that sense, it was perhaps one of the most decisive battles in history. "T'was a fine naval battle that was gained under the command of Don John of Austria a few months since against the Turks; but it has also pleased God at other times to let us see as great victories at our own expense," Montaigne quipped at the time.[13]

Successful as this last crusade may have been, it was Rome's last great attempt to organize a holy war against a Muslim foe. The Vatican had achieved victory in both its first holy war in 1099 and its last one in 1571. Sandwiched between the two, however, was a long string of defeats and humiliations, with many deaths. None of this ever seems to have pushed the church to the brink of collapse or even to have encroached on its power and influence. Unlike that of secular authorities, the fate of the church was never contingent on its military successes or failures, for it could always find an explanation as to why God may have desired one outcome rather than another. The growing conflicts within Christendom would in any case prove much more troublesome for the church, and far from abating tensions between Catholics and Protestants, the victory at Lepanto gave the former newfound energy to fight for their faith.

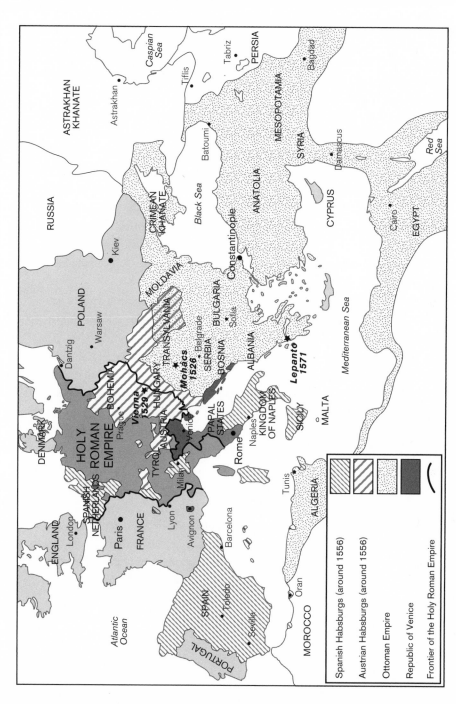

MAP 4. Europe and the Ottoman Empire in the sixteenth century

Spanish Habsburgs (around 1556)

Austrian Habsburgs (around 1556)

Ottoman Empire

Republic of Venice

Frontier of the Holy Roman Empire

MÜNSTER 1534 TO 1648

In Europe, the growing support for holy war, evident in the celebrations that followed the routing of the Turkish fleet, gave growing confidence to the Catholic factions determined to destroy heretics with all means necessary, much as they had annihilated the Turks in the Mediterranean. This led to the Saint Bartholomew's Day massacre (August 24–29, 1572), which left ten thousand people dead, most of them Protestant French Huguenots. Although the concept of "total war" dates from the nineteenth century, the wars of religion of the sixteenth and seventeenth centuries also involved entire societies. Everyone from the most disenfranchised peasant to the most powerful prince played a part, whether active or passive, in the confessional conflict, which first erupted in Germany with the Peasant Wars of 1524–26 and the Anabaptists' creation of a Protestant theocracy in Münster in Westphalia in 1534–35.[14]

The Peasant Wars that flared up in Germany and Austria starting in 1524 were only the latest manifestation of discontent to erupt in that part of the world. Among the probable immediate causes were two successive bad harvests in 1523 and 1524. Also, the peasants, priests, and other "commoners" who took up arms were now emboldened by the doctrines propagated by Martin Luther through the dissemination of easily accessible, and increasingly cheap, printed material. The 1520s had seen an upsurge in the production of German-language books, a good proportion of which were written by Luther. In fact, as compared to a total of 80 German books published in 1500, 570 came out in 1520, half of them by Luther. Three years later, out of 900 German books in circulation, 400 were Luther's.[15] This amazing acceleration of the circulation of ideas and information acted in much the same way as social media do today. Thus, what might earlier have remained isolated social grievances now presented themselves as a vast network of peasant armies driven by the same ideology and rhetoric. From the traditional "dispute" (*disputatio*) format initially chosen by Luther to present his case, his own voice had now escaped him to serve the thousands of rebels now fighting in his name.

The Peasant Wars started in the areas around the Lake of Constance and the Black Forest with a few peasants armed with farm tools. Within weeks, the rebels numbered forty thousand and the uprising spread to other regions. Unlike the Hussites, however, this force never produced a leader capable of harnessing its potential. As a consequence, the Great Swabian League (initially formed at the end of the fifteenth century in support of the Holy Roman Emperor against the Swiss Confederation) that rose to fight them—fielding fifteen hundred cavalrymen with seven thousand infantry and led by noblemen experienced in combat—had little difficulty in defeating the peasant armies. On April 4, 1525, at Leipheim, a thousand peasant soldiers were killed by the Swabians, while another five thousand were annihilated on May 12 in Böblingen, with three hundred of them beheaded in public as an example. A few days later, on May 24, twelve thousand peasants surrendered Freiburg, which they had briefly occupied.[16] To add insult to injury, Luther disavowed the peasants, telling them that "it is not for a Christian to appeal to law, or to fight, but rather to suffer wrong and endure evil." Despite its success on the battlefield, the Great Swabian League did not survive long, succumbing to internal dissension.

The growing religious tensions and conflicts drove Holy Roman Emperor Charles V to seek a negotiated settlement, as a result of which the Protestant movement earned its legitimacy. One of the first attempts at negotiation took place at the Diet of Ratisbon in 1530, at the instigation of the emperor, but the diversity of the opinions expressed quickly convinced Charles that the problem should be resolved by forcefully reinstating the unity of the church within the empire.

The Protestant Schmalkaldic League was born in the winter 1530–31 as a direct response to the emperor's attitude. On April 3, 1532, the League adopted a charter, the Constitution for the Defense, founding a union of the empire's Protestant states. Shortly before, on October 11, 1531, the Swiss reformer Ulrich Zwingli had been killed in the battle of Kappel, where the small army defending Zurich, which had adopted Zwingli's teachings, was unable to repulse the assault of the Forest Cantons. This had the effect of expanding the Schmalkaldic League's influence to Strasbourg and Switzerland. The League also benefited from the sudden rise of a radical and aggressive group of Anabaptists, a fringe movement that originated in Zurich with a former follower of Zwingli, Conrad Grebel, and had taken root in the Netherlands in the 1520s.

In 1534, the Anabaptists took over the city of Münster, where they attempted to create a theocracy, eliciting a forceful response from the Catholic bishop of Münster and the Lutheran prince of Hesse, who, together, routed them and executed their leaders. This political alliance between denominational rivals was a portent of things to come and the first sign that political expediency would dominate and direct many, if not all, of the religious conflicts in that part of the world during the course of the next century. Furthermore, it showed that Protestantism was neither a unitary movement nor resistant to alliances with Catholic forces. In this regard, shortly before the Münster episode, a precedent had already been set in a secret alliance negotiated by the Schmalkaldic League with King François I of France, who agreed to pay a third of the cost of the war to defend "German liberties." France would ultimately become the main ally of the Protestants against Catholic Austria and Spain, and would tilt the balance during the latter part of the Thirty Years' War.

From 1541 on, Charles V was on the upswing, trying through various means to undermine the Protestants and reaffirm the religious hegemony of the Catholic faith in the empire. At the time, the Schmalkaldic League had been weakened by a controversy surrounding the private life of its leader, Philip of Hesse, who had tried to legalize his union with his mistress though he was still married to his ailing wife. The fracas led to the defections of several members of the League, and Charles V thought the time was ripe to press the issue. In a letter to his sister Mary in June 1546, the monarch made no secret of his intentions: "If we failed to intervene now, all the Estates of Germany would be in danger of breaking with the faith. [. . .] After considering this and considering it again, I decided to embark on war against Hesse and Saxony as transgressors of the peace against the Duke of Brunswick and his territory. And although this pretext will not long disguise the fact that it is a matter of religion, yet it serves for the present to divide the renegades."[17] This may have been the first instance where a religious war "was no longer waged and justified as a crusade but as *Religionskrieg*, as the military solution to conflicts arising from the protection of confessional possessions or from confessional conquest."[18] It is interesting to note here that although Charles was fully conscious of this fact at this juncture, he sought to find a political pretext to the intervention. In his mind the only manner by which to resolve the religious issue was through a *political solution*. In other words, Charles did not seek to punish or enact any kind of revenge on people practicing another faith but, more practically, to bring the leaders of the League to the negotiating table and accept the primacy of Catholicism in the empire. This is the same attitude that Richelieu, Mazarin, and other negotiators would adopt a century later in their quest to end the Thirty Years' War.

The Schmalkaldic War, provoked by Charles V, saw the intervention of mercenary troops sent by the pope. The war lasted less than a year and ended with a Catholic victory at the battle of Mühlberg on April 24, 1547. The emperor, rather than trying to impose Catholicism on the empire, now looked to enact a Christian reform that would settle matters in a way that might bolster his own power, while avoiding a protracted conflict. At the Diet of Augsburg, where the negotiations were being held in 1547, Charles made sure to show who was in charge by encircling the town with Spanish troops. However, unable to impose his political will on the Protestant princes, he gradually lost faith in his ability to find a satisfactory compromise, and he abdicated in 1556, spending the last few years of his life in a monastery.

The result of the complex negotiations and arm twisting that went on for almost a decade was the Peace of Augsburg of 1555, a half-baked deal that satisfied no one and generated resentments that led to the war that erupted in 1618 and took three decades to resolve. Although it proved a failure in practice, the Peace of Augsburg was of cardinal importance historically in that it laid down some of the principles that would later form the foundational structure of the new European order. "No State may impose its religion on another, nor on its subjects," the Augsburg treaties stipulated.[19] This clause would constitute the basis for the principle of sovereignty, one of the main building blocks of the settlements of 1648, ironically leading to the total secularization of the modern state.

The accords stipulated that religious minorities were allowed to emigrate. But the fact that non-Lutheran Protestants, including Calvinists and Anabaptists, were excluded from the accords singularly weakened the already unsteady peace. After brewing for several decades, the whole deal exploded into uncontrollable violence, which ripped apart the Holy Roman Empire.

In the sixty-three years that separated the settlement of 1555 and the defenestration of Prague that ignited the Thirty Years War in 1618, the denominational geopolitics of Europe underwent a revolution, much of which was mired in violence. This revolution produced deep sectarian and political (as well as economic) changes, each country finding its own solution to the problem. In southern Europe, the Catholics tightened ranks, with the rise of the Inquisition being one of the more visible manifestations of this reaction. In northern Europe, Denmark and Sweden formally switched from the one faith to the other in a fairly smooth transition.

THE PECULIAR NATURE OF RELIGIOUS VIOLENCE IN ENGLAND

In England, Henry VIII's break with Rome and the creation of the Church of England led to clashes all over the country, including the Prayer Book

Rebellion of 1549, where thousands of Catholics were killed in battle or slaughtered when they revolted after the publication of the Book of Common Prayer, which introduced the ideas of the English Reformation. Some massacres were particularly gruesome: at Clyst Heath, nine hundred (Catholic) rebel prisoners were reportedly tied down and had their throats slit . . . all in a span of ten minutes.

The decisive moment came in 1558 when Henry VIII's daughter, by Ann Boleyn, Elizabeth I, succeeded her half-sister, Mary Tudor, on the throne of England. The half Spanish Mary Tudor (she was the daughter of Catherine of Aragon) had shown herself a staunch ally of the Catholics and to the Protestants, she was "Bloody Mary" after she quashed the popular uprising called Wyatt's Rebellion in 1554, in which Elizabeth was accused of participation. Aside from the 200 massacred during that particular episode, the Marian Persecutions, as they would be called, had 288 additional victims, many burned at the stake.

Mary died childless, opening the door to Elizabeth, who ruled England for nearly half a century and managed the denominational transition, although as Owen Chadwick observes, "Historians still argue whether, in making England Protestant during 1559, the queen [Elizabeth] and her advisors were pushing a reluctant Parliament or whether the House of Commons was pushing a reluctant queen."[20] Whatever the case, Elizabeth had to deal with another Mary around whom the tensions between Catholics and Protestants revolved—Mary, Queen of Scots.

The presence in the increasingly Protestant region of Scotland of the controversial Catholic Mary Stuart—a descendent on her mother's side of the House of Guise, the most powerful French Catholic family—was bound to create problems. To complicate matters, Mary was tied in one way or another to practically all the dynasties of Europe. Seen by some as a legitimate heir to the English throne, her derailment led to the Northern Rising of 1569, which pitted Catholic loyalists against Protestants. This conflict was characteristic of what was happening in England at the time: a boiling pot of religious hatreds, clan rivalries, and dynastic wars, with an international twist that gratified the world with the improbable defeat of the mighty Spanish Armada in 1588.

The Invincible Armada, created by King Philip II of Spain, was the result of an earlier appeal made by Pope Sixtus V in 1585 to launch a crusade against England in order to force it back to Catholicism. Though reluctant at first, Philip relented when Elizabeth I executed Mary Stuart in 1587. This was not

MAP 5. Religious divisions in Europe in the sixteenth century

just about religion: the disposal of Elizabeth would not only signify a major victory for the Counter-Reformation, it would also help the Spaniards in the Spanish Netherlands, where England was spoiling Madrid's efforts to keep control of its territory.

The brewing sectarian conflict between Catholic Spain and Protestant England was thus quickly escalating into an all-out war. The Spanish fleet, still basking in the glory of Lepanto, looked poised to conquer England despite the energy of the flamboyant privateer Sir Francis Drake, who managed among other things to destroy the supply of potable water meant to be transported on the Spanish warships, which subsequently led to the poisoning of their crews. Philip sought to use the fleet to protect and bolster an attack from the army of Flanders, which looked to invade England and depose Queen Elizabeth. Alas, in addition to Drake's harassment tactics, the combination of the Spaniards' poor strategy and extreme weather off the coast of Britain resulted in the complete annihilation of the fleet, a third of which never made it back to Spain. The humiliating defeat marked the beginning of the end for Spain, which, after this point, was to be relegated to secondary status among the European powers. France, the chief of these, however, was now the theater of a series of violent conflicts known simply as the Wars of Religion.

THE FRENCH WARS OF RELIGION

Religious tensions in France started to surface in the late 1520s. By the mid 1530s, a growing religious rebellion was crystallizing around the French-born Protestant theologian John Calvin (1509–64), based in Geneva, and his book defending his faith, the *Institutio Christianae Religionis* (1536), translated (much later) as *The Institutes of the Christian Religion*. Quickly, it became clear that all the efforts made by French authorities to avoid a religious breakup were yielding few results. Unlike in Germany, where the religious revolts had started from the bottom of the social ladder, in France the adherents of the new religion were educated urban dwellers, artisans, and intellectuals, the same types that had previously been seduced by Catharism. Soon, too, Calvinist Reformed recruitment was efficiently targeting the urban elites and the nobility, and by 1545, some prominent individuals and families had adopted it. Proselytizing by Calvinist missionaries from Geneva had created as many as two thousand Reformed communities by the early 1560s. This sudden explosion of Reformed activities was met by the formation of activist Catholic groups ready to use force to stop the hemorrhage. For Catholics, the religious disunion threatening the country was ominous, and it went beyond the religious disputes between the two parties: if not stopped, they believed, it was certain to unleash the wrath of God, with dire consequences for the country and its people.

After King Henri II's death in 1559 and the rise to power of the ultra-Catholic dukes of Guise under his son and successor, François II (who had married Mary, Queen of Scots, in 1558), the French monarchy took a harder line. The Guise were bent on destroying anyone who stood in their path, be they Protestant or Catholic. The fact that the Guise hailed from Lorraine, and thus had the status of *princes étrangers* (foreign princes), did not help ease the tensions. With the death of François II in 1560, the brewing crisis became an open one. In southwestern France, which had witnessed the rise and fall of the Cathars, emboldened Huguenots took to defacing and destroying religious images and symbols in churches and cultural buildings. This destructive violence was seen as a way to teach the Glory of God by restituting a Truth that had been buried by centuries of darkness. Essentially, these symbolic actions were meant to prove "that nothing could impede the true religion."[21]

By 1562, as many as two million people out of a population of about sixteen million may have converted to the new religion. Everywhere, Catholics, often with the encouragement and support of local authorities, took matters in their own hands, going into houses and killing Huguenots who might be engaging in hymn singing or in prayer. In April, a Catholic triumvirate who promised to restore religious unity to the country was formed by three prominent aristocrats: François de Lorraine, duc de Guise; Anne, duc de Montmorency (a man, Constable of France); and Jacques d'Albon de Saint-André (marshal of France and ambassador to England). At that point, the monarchy was still split as to which attitude to adopt, with the chancellor, Michel de L'Hôpital, and Catherine de Médicis, the queen mother, ready to make concessions while the newly crowned King Charles IX (December 1560) followed the duc de Guise's call for a radical response. The moderates seemed to win the day an edict on January17, 1562, but on March 1, François de Guise orchestrated the gruesome massacre of Huguenots in the town of Wassy, thus sparking a series of eight almost uninterrupted conflicts lasting thirty-six years.

The self-proclaimed leader of the Protestants, Louis I de Bourbon, prince of Condé, responded in kind, taking up arms to save the king and cleanse the monarchy of evildoers, chief among them the Guise family and their inner circle. Though Condé won a series of victories at the beginning of the war, the defeat of the Protestants at Dreux (December 19, 1562) led to the first negotiated peace with the edict of Amboise (March 19, 1563), which accorded Protestants "liberty of conscience."

The first truce was short lived. The Huguenots attempted to kidnap the king, in what was subsequently dubbed the "Surprise of Meaux" (September 28, 1567), leading to a second war, which ended with the Peace of Longjumeau (March 23, 1568). From there on, the confrontation was much tougher, with the monarchy now fully engaging in a hard-line strategy to eradicate the

Huguenots. Unable to win a military victory against the pugnacious Protestant commander Gaspard de Coligny, the king sought a compromise, the edict of Saint-Germain (August 8, 1570), which gave Protestants freedom of conscience and the liberty to exercise their faith in those areas where they practiced it before the war. An attempt to assassinate Admiral de Coligny (August 22), who escaped with a minor wound, reignited the war in a big way. An attack on the Huguenots, probably instigated by the king, and originally meant to target only a few Protestant commanders, started on Saint Bartholomew's Eve, 1572, and lasted several days.[22] From fifteen hundred to three thousand Huguenots were massacred in Paris.[23] Coligny himself was stabbed, defenestrated, and finally beheaded by Guise hirelings. The immediate consequence of the massacre was a weakening of the Protestants in northern France and the strengthening of the resistance in the South. On July 11, 1573, a new attempt was made at ending hostilities with the edict of Boulogne.

With the massacre, the Catholic radicals had crossed a threshold that would ultimately prove fateful, for moderate Catholics now began joining the Protestants to fight the radical Catholics and save the country. After the death of Charles IX, his brother and successor to the throne, Henri III, was challenged by a rival faction supported by German mercenaries. Forced to capitulate, the king promulgated the edict of Beaulieu (May 6, 1576), which gave Protestants freedom to practice their faith throughout France, except Paris and the royal residences, and rehabilitated the names of those massacred in 1572. The formation of a Catholic League eager to roll back the edict led to a sixth war, a new truce and another edict, promulgated in Poitiers (September 17, 1577), which now restricted the liberties guaranteed by the previous accords. The peace was as short lived as the previous ones, and a seventh war ensued on November 29, 1579, known as the "War of the Lovers," which lasted until the edict of Blois at the end of the following year. But the death of the king's brother, the duc d' Anjou, in 1584, added another layer of complexity to the conflict. Given that Henri III had no children, the next man in line was Henri of Navarre, a Protestant.

Faced with this prospect, Henri de Guise formed a radical Catholic faction of powerful noblemen, which concluded a secret alliance with Spain. In July 1585, the publication of the Treaty of Nemours, which banned Protestantism and deprived Henri of Navarre of his claim to the throne, triggered the eighth and final conflict of the French Wars of Religion, this one known as the "War of the Troubles of the League," which lasted thirteen years. This war was

FIGURE 9. The St. Bartholomew's Day Massacre (1572), detail from illustration, Bibliothèque nationale de France. Courtesy of iStock.com/Nastasic.

characterized by intense political rivalries within the Catholic league itself and between the League's leaders, the Guise brothers, and the King, Henri III. Due in part to the dire economic situation in France, the king proved incapable of dealing with the Protestant army, which, remarkably commanded by Henri of Navarre, was now in control of southwestern France and ready to move northward. Pressed further still by the Guise family, the king decided that he had had enough. In an about-face, he organized the assassination of the two Guise brothers (Henri and Louis) on December 23, 1588, in a brief moment of high drama that took place in Blois castle in the Loire Valley. Far from easing tensions, this caused Paris and other major cities such as Orléans, Lyon, and Marseille to take up arms against the king, while the Sorbonne officially declared that such a tyrant did not warrant obedience from his subjects. (The Catholic Church had officially denounced tyrannicide, the legitimate assassination of a dictator at the Council of Constance of 1415, but theologians and philosophers continued to debate the topic.)[24]

Too weak to fight the League alone, the king formed an alliance with Henri of Navarre in April 1589. But, as the two Henris organized the siege of Paris, a Benedictine monk, Jacques Clément, took the law into his own hands and murdered the king. Just before dying, on August 2, Henri III officially anointed Henri of Navarre as his successor. Two days later, Navarre made the promise to maintain the integrity of the Catholic religion in France. The Leaguers were not convinced, and they vowed to kill the new king, arguing that his heresy made him unfit to rule and rightful for any Christian to kill him "in the name of God." "The League derive[d] its power from the dream, still relevant and necessary, of a crusade, as relevant and necessary to the Catholic imagination as it had been at the beginning of the first unrest," Crouzet writes. "In their mind[s], the Leaguers march[ed] toward the celestial Jerusalem, behind Christ."[25]

The Leaguers were no match, however, for Henri of Navarre, who won the support of moderate Catholics by depicting himself as the providential savior of the monarchy. He abjured his faith, famously saying, "Paris is well worth a mass," was crowned at Chartres, and entered the capital in triumph on March 22, 1594.

The war was not over, however, for Spain entered the conflict in support of the League (January 1595). But any hopes the Leaguers may have entertained that Spain's intervention might tilt the balance in their favor were completely dashed when their leader, the duc de Mayenne, was forced to surrender. On May 2, 1598, peace with Spain was signed at Vervins, a few days after the promulgation of the edict of Nantes, which was based on the provisions already contained in the edicts of Beaulieu and Poitiers. Among other agreements, Protestant ministers were to be paid directly by the crown and all Protestants were allowed access to public and military employment. Pope Clement VIII had initially supported Spain against Henri of Navarre, but when the latter renounced his faith, Rome changed its policy in order to reconcile the French and Spanish monarchs and avoid further divisions among Catholics.[26]

How many had died as a result of these wars? Though no reliable numbers exist, perhaps 10 percent of the French population had perished as a result of the violence, the total decline hovering around 20 percent between 1580 and 1600, with climatic and economic factors also contributing to this drastic change.[27] Still, the demographic decline was smaller than what France had suffered in previous centuries with the One Hundred Years War and the Black Death, which were each responsible for the deaths of around a third of its people.

In the end, Henri of Navarre, now Henri IV, founder of the Bourbon dynasty (Henri III being the last of the Valois), became both the architect of a political revolution that projected France into the age of absolutism and the engineer of a new religious order that forced Catholics and Protestants to coexist. A century later, Louis XIV, the Sun King, would transport France even further into the golden age of absolutism while at the same time doing away with religious cohabitation by revoking the edict of Nantes in 1685 (edict of Fontainebleau), certainly one of his more distinctive decisions and, one might argue, one of his most unfortunate (200,000 Protestants left the country).

Henri IV, Henri le Grand, by crossing the denominational barrier, had transcended the religious violence that had taken hold of France and, by restoring the monarchy, had launched the country onto the path of secular modernity. When he fell at the hands of an assassin in 1610, his violent death served for generations as the poignant symbol of an era of extreme violence that his murder effectively brought to an end: "The mystical dream of a society united under God through its spiritual fulfillment came to a stop in 1610, after its ultimate spasm."[28] The popular wave of sympathy for the dead king and for his heirs that overcame the country surprised everyone. "Thus the union of the good people whom God had blessed found itself stronger than the league of evil men, whose numbers are not small in Paris: thus it was a good thing that God intervened as He had," the contemporary observer Pierre de L'Estoile said.[29]

Although it was entering a new era of durable political stability, France was an economic shambles.[30] Aided by the duc de Sully, a former Huguenot soldier, Henri IV had managed before his death to steer his country back in the right direction. France, the most powerful country in Europe, led the way into the age of absolutism, and the European monarchies that came to embody this period had one primary objective in mind: to avoid unrest and instability that might jeopardize their hold on power. For all of the sovereigns of Europe, great and small, it was clear that confessional conflicts were to be avoided at all costs. The French Wars of Religion were not, however, the last of the "wars of opinion," as they came to be called. Another, much more deadly, conflict was soon to engulf the greater part of Europe. It came to be known as the Thirty Years' War.

THE WAR TO END ALL RELIGIOUS WARS

The Thirty Years' War is generally considered by historians to be the most deadly conflict to have been fought before World War I and World War II, though this can be disputed. Even in the subcategory of religious conflicts, it is probably surpassed by the Taiping rebellion in the nineteenth century, in which twenty to one hundred million people died. Nevertheless, it was, as Pierre Chaunu says, "a catastrophe without equivalent."[31]

However much one would like to come up with reliable or even approximate casualty figures, the statistics are too fragmented to allow for it.[32] Demographic comparisons, however, give us an idea of the damage: the population of the Holy Roman Empire, estimated at twenty million at the turn of the seventeenth century, fell to about seven million in 1650 (it was back to twenty million a century later, in 1750).[33] In Pomerania and Mecklenburg in northern Germany, 65 percent of the population died as a result of the war. More reliable city registries show dramatic numbers: in Frankfurt an der Oder, the population fell from 13,000 to just 2,400 between 1618 and 1654.[34] In the Czech lands, Bohemia and Moravia, the population plunged from two and a half million inhabitants before the war to a little over one and a half million at the end of the conflict.[35]

Numbers, as always, only tell part of the story and the misery that befell millions of innocent victims was beyond anything one could imagine, even in a world that was used to hardship and wars. The heavy emotional toll of the conflict on millions of individuals is probably best captured by fictional accounts, and the best account of these may be Hans Jacob von Grimmelshausen's masterpiece *The Adventures of Simplicius Simplicissimus* (1669).[36] Midway through the war, its unbearable horrors reached a pinnacle of gratuitous violence in the sack of Magdeburg, which shocked the entire continent and marked the turning point of the war. On May 20, 1631, Catholic forces led by Count Tilly and Field Marshal Pappenheim entered the Protestant-held city and went on a rampage: looting, burning, raping, torturing, and killing. Pappenheim, who had encouraged his men to destroy the city and its inhabitants, saw the victory in biblical terms, and he had no remorse: "I believe," he wrote in his report of the events, "that over twenty thousand souls were lost. It is certain that no more terrible work and divine punishment has been seen since the destruction of Jerusalem. All of our soldiers became rich. God with us."[37]

The Thirty Years' War is very complicated to understand when one tries to observe it from up close. It is made up of layer upon layer of smaller and larger conflicts that mesh with one another in intricate ways, making it extremely difficult to follow the complex path of the war. But as one begins to distance oneself from the details that make up the conflict, things start to become a lot clearer. The main characteristic of the war is that it started as a religious conflict inside the Holy Roman Empire and gradually evolved into a struggle for power over European hegemony between the archaic Habsburg Empire (or Empires) and the emerging modern nation-states, France and Sweden foremost among them. Put differently, what was initially a localized religious conflict with political overtones became a global political conflict with religious undertones. The Thirty Years' War was an epoch-changing event, and it provoked a shift in terms both of how societies functioned and organized themselves and of how they engaged with each other. It changed the nature of war: why wars were fought and how they were conducted.

The stability of the Holy Roman Empire rested on the Peace of Augsburg of 1555. But what had seemed at the time a good compromise, owing to the ambiguity of its clauses, now lay at the root of the many tensions that rose to the surface. In effect, the Augsburg accords were testimony to the incapacity of the imperial monarchy to impose its authority on the Holy Roman Empire. Though the accords of 1555 seemed to reaffirm its hold on the empire, they had given the Protestant states both too little and too much for this unfinished peace to last. Their autonomy was too constrained for them to be durably content, and they were given too much independence and power for the central authorities to be able to control them. In 1608, a Protestant union had been formed by the elector of the Palatinate and the following year, a Catholic League was constituted by Maximilian I of Bavaria. Although these initiatives were theoretically defensive in nature, they both led to the creation of armed forces ready for combat. Given the denominational rivalries and resentments that underlay and fueled the political tensions between the states and the empire, violence was bound to erupt somewhere and spark a conflict in which many were ready to partake.

The spark was ignited in the exact same place that had seen the birth of the Hussite rebellion, and in the same manner. This was no coincidence; the act that started these catastrophic events was voluntarily charged with historical symbolism. On May 23, 1618, two Catholic noblemen representing the monarchy were hurled from the windows of Prague Castle by neo-Utraquist (Hussite) Protestants whose grievances touched upon recent religious decisions that had led to the closure of Protestant churches. The neo-Utraquists deemed these actions insulting and illegal, and they vented their anger by defenestrating two of the Catholic Lords Regent, Count Jaroslav Bořita of Martinice and Count Vilém Slavata of Chlumu, along with their secretary. Though the victims landed on soft ground (according to some accounts, a pile of manure) and managed to escape the scene unscathed, this act of defiance was an affront that the imperial authorities could not leave unpunished.

Soon the Protestant armies of the Elector Palatine of the Rhine Frederick V, who in 1619–20 at the invitation of the Protestant estates assumed the throne of Bohemia (which was 80 percent Protestant), with 21,000 men, faced 28,000 imperial troops dispatched to suppress them, commanded by Count Tilly, the Walloon general mentioned earlier. An embassy sent to Turkey to ask for the Ottomans' support had yielded no result, and the Protestants were outnumbered. On both sides, this battle was perceived as a confrontation between Protestants and Catholics. Set on Bila Hora, the White Mountain, on the outskirts of Prague, the battle, fought on a Sunday, November 8, 1620, proved disastrous for the Protestants. Frederick, nicknamed the *Winterkönig* (winter king) because of the shortness of his reign, was forced to flee, and what they called an "age of darkness" began for the people of Bohemia. Meanwhile, imperial propaganda hailed the victory as the greatest triumph of Catholicism since Lepanto.

Ferdinand II, set to exploit this victory to reassert his authority and reaffirm the Catholic character of the empire, decided to take a hard line. On June 21, 1621, twenty-seven men, including one Catholic—the former head of the royal palace guard—deemed responsible for the rebellion (or, in the case of the royal guardsman, of allowing it) were executed in a highly publicized display of imperial power, right in the middle of the old town in Prague (incidentally, on the very spot where the statue of Jan Hus was to be erected in 1915). Their severed heads were placed at the entries to the Charles Bridge, where they were left to rot in iron baskets for ten years. The tone was set, and it did little to temper the emotions. In hindsight, Ferdinand II effectively transformed a decisive military success into a Pyrrhic victory. Rather than bring unity, the executions provoked further divisions and fueled even deeper resentments.

By reaffirming the Catholic identity of the now reinvigorated imperial leadership, the battle of White Mountain made both the Protestant Scandinavian states and France more aware of the menace posed by the resurgence of the Habsburgs. Scandinavia was itself subject to political tensions between Denmark and Sweden. France, reeling from the Wars of Religion, was embroiled in a struggle against a resurgent Protestant force led by Henri of Rohan and the prince of Condé. Cardinal Richelieu, King Louis XIII's chief minister, took his religion seriously and adopted a tough stance. The fighting was largely confined, however, to a protracted siege of the Protestant stronghold, La Rochelle on the Atlantic coast, which finally surrendered in 1628.

For France, it was now imperative to break the stranglehold of the Habsburg pincer by weakening Spain in Flanders, where Madrid was challenged by the Dutch, and then by undermining the Austrians. In this sense, Paris's geopolitical imperatives clashed with its denominational allegiances, since its natural allies were all Protestant. In a memo written to Louis XIII in 1629, *Avis donné au Roi après la prise de La Rochelle pour le bien des affaires*, Richelieu displayed his Machiavellian character, asking the King to definitively crush the Protestant rebellion while stopping the progress of Spain. Soon after, France would seal its alliance with the northern Protestant States and throw all its weight into the battle against Austria, then the greatest champion of the Catholic Counter-Reformation. In doing so, Richelieu definitively broke the divide that may have separated European Christendom into two distinct entities, thereby realigning alliances through another criterion that would come to define the essence of modern international relations: the national interest.

The rulers of Protestant states in the Holy Roman Empire quickly felt the imperial pressure. Too weak to lead a successful fight against the emperor, they were in dire need of outside assistance. With time, everything fell into place, and the German Protestants first found support with the Scandinavians, then the French. At the same time, Spain lost its footing in northern Europe, where the independent Dutch United Provinces, motivated as they were to uphold and extend their political freedom, invented a new art of war that Protestant commanders put to the test with great success against the Spanish and Austrian armies.

In the first phase of the internationalization of the conflict, Denmark played a leading role. It was unable to sustain the effort, however, and its regional rival, Sweden, supplanted it. With financial and material support from France, the Swedes successfully fought the imperial armies of Count Tilly and Albrecht von Wallenstein, a Protestant who had converted to Catholicism and the most powerful war entrepreneur of his day. But after the death in battle of King Gustavus Adolphus of Sweden at Lützen in November 1632, followed by the assassination of Wallenstein, the war entered a new phase, in which France took the reins of the fight against Austria, its armies led by two remarkable generals, the Great Condé and Marshal Turenne, the latter educated in the Dutch art of war. Richelieu and his successor Cardinal Mazarin in turn took the lead in negotiating the Peace of Westphalia that ended the Thirty Years' War in 1648. Working hand in hand, Protestant generals and Catholic diplomats thus improbably produced the strategies of the war, the architecture of the peace, and the engineering of a new geopolitical order.

The Dutch theologian, jurist, and diplomat Hugo de Groot (1583–1645), best known to history by the Latin form of his name, Grotius, also played a significant role in this monumental shake up of European politics. Grotius synthesized the extensive work that Spanish theologians and others had devoted to the ethics of war and peace, and when it appeared in 1625, his massive legal treatise *De jure belli ac pacis* (*On the Law of War and Peace*), written in Paris and dedicated to the king of France, Louis XIII (its author had been embroiled in a theological controversy in Holland and forced to go into exile), became the blueprint for modern interstate interactions. Analyzing international relations, it established the basic elements of modern international law. Grotius was deeply steeped in the doctrine of the just war, which pervades his own legal doctrine, and the authors he cites most often are Cicero, Augustine, and Aquinas. Faced with the new ethical conundrum posed by the brutal conquest of America and the subjugation by Spain of entire peoples, the Spaniards, chief among them the Jesuits, had labored hard to modernize and further develop the classical doctrine, and Grotius built upon their findings to come up with a coherent, comprehensive legal reinterpretation. Though one may argue, as Carl Schmitt does, that Grotius's take on just war and other "all-important matters" is more hesitant than that of his predecessors, Francisco de Vitoria (1492–1546), Balthasar Ayala (1548–84), and the Italian Alberico Gentili (1552–1608), it was through him that their influence on international relations was felt.[38] And it was through them, Vitoria aside, that the doctrine of sovereignty developed by the French political theorist Jean Bodin (1530–96) came to form the core element of the geopolitical order that was put into practice after 1648.[39]

Put on paper early in the Thirty Years' War, Grotius's framework had time to be digested by the theologians, jurists, and diplomats who were engineering the peace in the 1640s. The man himself was well known in Paris, where he served as Sweden's diplomatic representative (1634–45). He was not always appreciated, as a diplomat at least, by the French authorities. King Gustavus Adolphus, on the other hand, took *De jure belli* with him on his campaigns. For Richelieu and Mazarin, the two cardinals successively at the helm of French diplomacy, the tone of the book, steeped in theological references, struck a chord, though they may not have liked its author.

Grotius's *De jure belli* was the ideal blueprint for a new European order that remained religious in spirit but was secular in its engineering. Although this new order was far from being governed by international laws, the geopolitical framework that came out of the Peace of Westphalia was based on a set of rules and norms designed to bring stability to the system or, more crudely, to stop things from getting out of hand. The rulers of Europe understood that civil wars were altogether a bad proposition that heightened tensions and invited foreign powers to meddle in other people's affairs. What was needed now was a global regime that preserved the geopolitical status quo and the integrity of its main components, namely, the dominant monarchical states. The idea was not to prevent wars, which were deemed inevitable, or to do away with the regular use of force, deemed necessary and understood to be a tool of policy, but to prevent certain *types* of wars, chief among them religious wars. This the architects of the peace did through two essential resolutions: by lining up national and religious identities (a broader interpretation of the "*Cujus regio, ejus religio*" principle of 1555) and by agreeing that no sovereign should ever interfere in the domestic politics of other nations (the principle of sovereignty). The rest was a matter of developing and setting up the right mechanisms to ensure the sustainability of the regime, the balance of power being one of those mechanisms.

In essence, this system, informally known as the Westphalian order or system,[40] was not conceived by men and women [Queen Christina of Sweden (r. 1632–54), was an advocate] who sought to flush religion out of public life but by devout Christians who understood that religion and politics did not always make for a happy marriage or a stable international regime. The new order was marked by the emergence of modern nation-states and the fading of age-old empires, including the Holy Roman Empire and the Ottoman Empire, which fought each other in one last significant military confrontation in 1683 (the battle of Vienna), where the Turks were repulsed by a coalition commanded by King Jan III Sobieski of Poland. Sweden, one of the big winners of the Westphalian peace, enjoyed its newfound status only for so long, since it suffered a humiliating defeat at the hands of Russia at the battle of Poltava in 1709, which forced the Swedish monarchy to scale back its geopolitical ambitions. With Austria and Sweden fading and Russia still far removed, France was now the main European continental superpower, though it would quickly be challenged by England.

More than a century of unrelenting religious wars had left millions of Europeans dead. Had religion not been a factor in the conflicts that plagued the continent, other wars would probably have erupted that may have killed just as many people. Be that as it may, religion had been a potent element that either generated or fueled the violence that overtook Europe during this period. Also ending was a longer period of almost one thousand years where religion had stirred up violence in Europe, in the Middle East, and beyond.

With Europeans now projecting their power around the world and imposing, wherever they could, their political and social models, the struggle for global hegemony that henceforth dominated international relations brought on wars that were no longer fought for God or salvation, but for power and territories, for resources and the protection of trade, and for lines of communication. For those at the receiving end, particularly the Muslim world, the invasion by European armies of their territories may have been envisioned as new crusades to be dealt with as such. True, a missionary element accompanied these campaigns, with priests and nuns often acting as educators, doctors, and social workers who instilled a dose of humanity into these otherwise ruthless endeavors. But the main objective of the governments that encouraged these aggressive policies, which inevitably led them to engage in

FIGURE 10. *The Peace of Westphalia (The Swearing of the Oath of the Ratification of the Treaty of Münster)*, oil on copper by Gerhard ter Borch (1648), National Gallery, London.

wars with their competitors and with those they sought to colonize, was to generate more wealth and power for themselves in relation to their adversaries. This was the dawning of the Age of Reason, which in political terms meant the primacy of "reasons of state," to use the phrase coined in 1589 by the Italian philosopher and one-time Jesuit Giovanni Botero (1544–1617) in his treatise *Della ragion di stato* (Of the Reason of State), which set the new standard for political engineers.

HOW PROTESTANT COMMANDERS CHANGED THE FACE OF WAR

This discussion of religion and war in modern Europe would be incomplete without a few words on Protestantism and the art of war. Thanks to the German sociologist Max Weber (1864–1920), the Protestants' impact on the evolution of economics and the development of capitalism has received the attention it deserves.[41] Less well known is the impact of Protestants on the evolution of war, though the effect was significant and had considerable ramifications on the development of European society, including its social and economic makeup.

The sixteenth, seventeenth, and eighteenth centuries, when military conflicts were prevalent, were a watershed in the history of war. The European military revolution gave Westerners a military superiority that lasted until 1905 (when the Japanese navy sank six Russian battleships and forced the surrender of the rest of Russian fleet at Tsushima). Most historians have attributed this revolution (inevitably, a debate ensued as to whether it was a revolution or an evolution) to technological and economic breakthroughs, perhaps because our own epoch is technologically and economically driven.[42] However, while technological and economic factors played their part, this revolution was primarily a revolution of minds. And the most fertile military minds of the time were those of the Dutch commanders who defeated Spain. With the odds stacked against them, the Dutch managed to create the model of the modern army that Protestant officers and commanders from other parts of Europe adopted and put to use.

In the Middle Ages, Central Asian armies had dominated all other military forces, be they Arab, European, Chinese, or Indian. One of the last great Central Asian armies was Babur's, which conquered northern India at the beginning of the sixteenth century (battle of Panipat, 1526), though the Ottoman Turks still retained some of the military features that had enabled them to conquer Anatolia in the first place. During the late fifteenth and sixteenth centuries, the Spanish *tercio* formations were the best infantry units in Europe, although the Swiss, Germans, and Czechs provided some of the best troops in the mercenary armies that still dominated the landscape. The Spanish general Gonzalo Fernández de Córdoba (1453–1515), aptly dubbed *el gran capitán*, was the model of the great commander, emulated among others by Cortés and Pizarro. Generally speaking, the best military formations were in southern Europe.

Things, however, were about to change. The instigator of the changes to come was Maurice (Maurits) of Nassau (1567–1625), prince of Orange, a great captain in his own right, who made a name for himself at the battles of Geertruidenberg (1593) and Nieuwpoort (1600). For Maurice, the question was how to defeat the best army in the world, and to do so with limited means and resources. Influenced by his friend the neo-Stoic philosopher Justus Lipsius, an admirer of Machiavelli (who had deplored mercenary armies), and by the mathematician and engineer Simon Stevin, Nassau was convinced that a permanent army was preferable to the mercenary forces on which he had been forced to rely. More important, he wanted to create an army that strongly adhered to the ethical principles laid out by the Reformed Church. In many ways, his systematic and innovative approach echoed Jan Žižka's, though Maurice did not display the same religious fanaticism that characterized the Czech commander. Maurice was a not a military thinker per se, and the Protestants did not really produce intellectual breakthroughs in this area such as Machiavelli's and, later, Montecuccoli's (though they did publish military manuals such as Henri of Rohan's *Parfait capitaine* [1631] and *Traité de la guerre* [1636]). These were practical men who were looking for solutions and who were convinced that the quality of an army rested in great part on the moral fiber of the men who were part of it. Still, Maurice was intellectually curious and, guided by Justus Lipsius, became acquainted with the classic treatises by the Roman writers Vegetius and Frontinus and the Byzantine emperors Maurice (Maurikios) and especially Leo VI, author of the *Taktika*, which Maurice particularly enjoyed and put to use for his military exercises. In practical terms, Maurice reduced the size of his army—but what he lost in numbers, he tried to make up in quality. He introduced new military exercises and drills, instilled discipline, and loyalty, and made sure that his soldiers were paid correctly and regularly.

The Dutch army, 12,000 strong, including 2,000 mounted soldiers, with an artillery force of fifty cannons, was organized around companies of 130 men deployed through battalions of 550 in Roman square formations. These were armies that had superior cohesion and great speed, both in and out of battle. Maurice also innovated in the area of logistics, securing elaborate chains of supply, using, among other things, waterways. He created a corps of engineers specifically designed to prepare sieges and provided them a higher pay than the soldiers who had previously, and reluctantly, assumed this task. The recruitment and advancement of officers and commanders was overhauled, and it followed a more democratic approach that did away, in part at least, with the old practices that favored birth rather than merit. Dedicated to the national cause, Maurice was also a Protestant to the core, and he invited young officers and commanders, both Lutherans and Calvinists, to study his reforms and his art of war and even participate alongside him or his entourage in his campaigns. He was not only the engineer of this revolution, but created a movement that outlived him, backed by the House of Orange-Nassau.

Among the many students of Maurice's art of war were some of the leading commanders of the seventeenth century, most notably Gustavus Adolphus and Turenne, who defeated the imperial armies during the Thirty Years' War and helped redefine the art of war in Europe. Gustavus Adolphus and Turenne were on Napoleon's short list of the greatest military commanders, and he considered Turenne, a Nassau on his mother's side of the family, to be the greatest of all (Napoleon devoted an entire treatise to Turenne's campaigns, the *Précis des guerres du Maréchal de Turenne*). The Swedish army of Gustavus Adolphus may have been the ultimate model of the new Protestant army, with troops devoting a considerable amount of time in prayer and reading passages from the Bible. But it was also a model for the national citizen armies that would come to dominate Europe and, in time, gradually see its religious aspirations diminish.

The ramifications of the Protestant military revolution were considerable, for these armies required greater governmental commitment and organization, which in turn demanded governmental and economic reforms. In France, such reforms were implemented, and all of Europe had to adapt in order to keep up with the French. The consequence was the exponential growth of military apparatuses and well-trained permanent armies became the norm. To sustain such armies, economic resources had to be pooled, also on a permanent basis.

The other effect of the Dutch military revolution was a more systematic usage of military technology, which had multiple consequences, among which were dependency on ammunition and the greater destruction done by artillery. In the eighteenth century, this had the effect of pushing armies to fight static wars around sieges—provoking a revolution in the science of fortification—though commanders like the duke of Marlborough and Frederic the Great fought wars of movement with great success. Artillery, which had evolved very slowly since its introduction in the fourteenth century, now became a fixture of war. The military revolution also signaled the demise of the great mercenary armies that had roamed the European continent for several centuries, generally wreaking havoc wherever they marched and fought. The disappearance, though not altogether complete, of the mercenary soldier, was conducive to greater economic stability, and this also contributed to the development of modern economies, and of national identities.

The Protestant ethic that carried this revolution did not eliminate the dark excesses that characterized the old armies, but it did help delineate which type of conduct was now deemed permissible and which type was not. Governments now had a better grip on their armies, and they generally had higher standards of discipline than before. The fact that soldiers usually got paid somewhat reduced their tendency to loot and massacre civilians.

In short, armies and wars were better controlled, and the danger of escalation was much diminished. The epitome of the eighteenth-century derivative of the Dutch revolution was the Prussian army of Frederick the Great, whose near obsession with drills and exercises elicited many a caustic comment from his one-time friend Voltaire.[43] Frederick never hesitated to appeal to the national (Prussian) and religious (Lutheran) fiber of his soldiers, and he managed to create what was probably the best army of its day. During the Seven Years' War (1757–63), his alliance with Britain against a coalition of Catholic countries may have given the impression that this was a war pitting Protestants against Catholics, but it was not. This was, for France, Britain, and Austria, a struggle for power and hegemony, and for Prussia, a means to gain recognition and play a role on equal terms with the big powers. In essence, this war planted the seeds of the modern German nation, created in 1870, and signaled the ascendance of Britain over France as the premier European power.

The modern armies that had emerged from the Thirty Years' War were, of course, also designed to perpetuate the international order that emerged from the Peace of Westphalia, and their objectives had to align with the informal agreement to uphold the general balance of power and status quo. France's decision in 1793 to create a "nation in arms" changed all that, as did Napoleon. By then, the relationship between war and religion had long been severed, at least in Europe.

POST-WESTPHALIAN RESIDUAL CONFLICTS

The Peace of Westphalia marked the end of the Thirty Years' War and the beginning of a new era for Europe and the world. It neither resolved all the conflicts of the day, of course, nor signaled the sudden end of religiously motivated violence.[44] Not all matters were solved in Westphalia, including the conflict between France and Spain, nor were the accords able to prevent religious tensions from resurfacing here and there. A rebellion by the so-called Camisards, involving some twenty thousand armed Protestant combatants, most of them artisans (52 percent) or peasants (42 percent), erupted in south-ern France in 1702, for example, and lasted eight years.[45] Their leader, Jean Cavalier (Joan Cavalièr in Occitan), was a baker's apprentice. The war, a guer-rilla operation, was focused on Catholic churches and clergy. By 1703, forty churches in the Cévennes region had been burned and a further three hundred abandoned. Initially, the Camisards met with some success, principally because royal troops were busy fighting the War of Spanish Succession (1701–14). But the local Catholics soon mounted a counterguerrilla force and applied a scorched-earth strategy to isolate the rebels. Ultimately, the Camis-ards surrendered when Cavalier accepted the terms offered to him by the royal authorities, which included the formal creation of a regiment of Camisards and his commission as a colonel. But Cavalier had negotiated as a soldier, not a rebel, and this provoked the wrath of his followers, who had never relin-quished their ideals and entrusted him to fight to the end to regain their liberty of conscience. In the end, Cavalier fled the country, offering his services to other nations and, with those who chose to stay alongside him, fought other wars in various European theaters, ending his career as a British major-general. This, the very last of the French wars of religion—which had started in 1562—may have been the most religious of all, and the least political.

Nearby Switzerland was also the theater of religious violence between Protestants and Catholics in 1656, with the Villmergen War, and again in 1712 with the Toggenburg (or Second Villmergen) War. Each war only lasted a couple of months before being settled on the battlefield, with the Catholics winning the first confrontation, the Protestants the second. In Britain, the Civil War (s) (1642–51), long regarded by some historians as the first of Euro-pean revolution, are now also interpreted as one of the last wars of religion, inasmuch as the Puritans fought against the Anglicanism promulgated as the state religion in the 1630s. Although the Civil War was "a defensive political operation, a defence of existing liberties against an arbitrary king, it was an aggressive religious operation, a challenge to the whole of the existing structure and practice," the British historian John Morrill writes.[46] Undoubtedly, it was marked by a heavy dose of religious discourse, propaganda, and symbolism, and Oliver Cromwell's demeanor was in many ways reminiscent of Jan Žižka's, as was the military genius he displayed on the battlefield.

Farther East, just as the Westphalian diplomats were drying the ink on their treaties, a formidable Cossack uprising (1648–54, known as the Khmel-nytsky Uprising, from the name of the Cossack leader), which opposed

Eastern Orthodox Zaporozhian Cossacks, allied on this occasion with Muslim Crimean Tatars, to a Polish-Lithuanian Catholic coalition, nearly brought the region, the epicenter being Ukraine and Belarus, to its knees. Though the ire of the Cossacks was directed at the Poles, it translated into anti-Catholic, and anti-Jewish, feelings, which resulted in particularly gruesome pogroms and many other massacres. The war led to the defeat of the Poles and helped Russia impose its hegemony on the region, thereby completely transforming its geostrategic dynamics.

In essence, then, religious violence lingered for a few decades after the treaties of Münster and Osnabrück that concluded the Thirty Years' War, as did the confrontation between Austria and the Ottoman Empire. In Europe, religious violence, which abated right after the end of the war in 1648, picked up again in the 1680s until around 1710, at which time government authorities seemed poised to control the situation and, more important, were determined to prevent such conflicts from escalating and spilling over into other regions. One explanation for the upsurge in violence during this short period might be that some of the religious conflicts were temporarily resolved by the simple exhaustion of the protagonists, after decades of war, before they resurfaced with the next generation. In any case, after this momentary resurgence, things calmed down significantly.

In the Muslim world, the sudden rise of Persia, which adopted Shi'ism as its state religion, fueled the underlying tensions between Shiites and Sunnis that the regional hegemony of the Ottomans had managed to keep below boiling temperature. The conquests of Persia's Nader Shah in the first half of the eighteenth century channeled all the energies of the region into the confrontation between Ottomans and Iranians. Nader Shah's avowed ambition of reuniting the Muslim faith under a single banner did not sit well with the Ottomans, and they did all they could to prevent him from achieving this goal. Ultimately, the matter was resolved by Nader's psychological breakdown, followed by his death.

In Europe, fear of religious violence took some time to disappear. Half a century after the end of the Thirty Years' War, and years after Cromwell's demise, the English writer Daniel Defoe, the author of *Robinson Crusoe*, echoed this sentiment. In 1701, Defoe wrote a pamphlet entitled *The Danger of the Protestant Religion Considered, from the Present Prospect of a Religious War in Europe* in which he shared his fear of a religious war gripping Europe once again. At the time, the signs were indeed ominous that a new outbreak of violence would erupt, and that Protestant minorities would find themselves at the mercy of powerful authorities ready to use force to quash them, the consequence being that isolated Protestant states might be overrun. Fifty years after the Peace of Westphalia, Defoe still saw the world of 1700 following the patterns of the past, as a majority of his contemporaries probably did too:

> I see no War can be Rais'd in *Europe*, but what will of Course run into a War of Religion: For if the *Popish* Princes agree in Interests, they can have nothing to quarrel about: And to confirm this, I appeal to a Review of the General History of *Europe:* In which I offer to make it appear, That setting aside the Quarrels between the *French* and the *Spaniards*, and between the *English* and the *Dutch*, almost all the Wars of *Europe* have been Wars of Religion.[47]

Given this pattern, Defoe's logical solution was to advocate a union of Protestant states which "seems to me to be the only possible Means to prevent the Union between the *Popish* Powers of *Europe*, and therein the Ruin of the *Protestants.*" Defoe did not, of course, grasp that power politics had overtaken sectarian allegiances. The commercial rivalry between the Netherlands and England; global rivalry between France and England; and the struggle of older multinational empires such as Austria to survive in a world of nation-states, above all, the rising kingdom of Prussia, now dominated Europe's geopolitics. By the end of the century, too, Europe's absolute monarchies were being challenged by democratic republics whose first order of business was the formal separation of church and state, starting with a country, the United States, that had been settled in large part by men and women who had fled Europe in order to practice their faith freely and escape religious persecution. The fact that the United States remained deeply religious in the nineteenth century became one of the central questions that Alexis de Tocqueville sought to answer in his penetrating analysis of democracy in America.[48] Still, in the minds of America's Founding Fathers, the issue was clear. "Our civil rights have no dependence on our religious opinions, any more than our opinions in physics and geometry," Thomas Jefferson succinctly argued. Freedom of religion was enacted into law by the state of Virginia in 1786.[49]

Religious Violence in a Secular World

Religions are not for separating men from one another; they are meant to bind them.

—Mahatma Gandhi

Islam is not only here to establish rules for acts of worship and morality but to regulate the affairs of society, especially financial and political affairs.

—Ayatollah Khomeini

Generally, the evolution of religion and war after the seventeenth century was shaped by the secularization of politics, the modernization of Western society and the Westernization of an increasingly interdependent global society.[1] This period witnessed the withering and quasi disappearance of religiously motivated conflicts, at least until the late 1970s when the Iranian Revolution and the subsequent state-sponsored terrorism of the Iranian regime suddenly reversed what was thought by many to be a forgone conclusion. Until this late reversal, it was not so much that religion disappeared from the political process as that, by and large, it ceased to be relevant. Frederick the Great's armies, for example, may have been molded to a degree by the strong Lutheran identity of its Prussian soldiers but, ultimately, these armies fought for Prussia and for its king, not for a religion, God, or, for that matter, Martin Luther.

Likewise, religion or the church may have been in the line of fire of French revolutionaries in the 1790s, or the target of Stalin and Hitler in the 1930s and 1940s, but in none of these cases were the totalitarian projects in question defined by their anticlerical attitudes and policies. Religion, especially its representatives and its symbols, was merely the collateral victim of those who sought to cleanse and purify society in order to reconstruct from scratch a new system of beliefs with its own icons, symbols, and ideals. These absolute dictators' attempts at legitimizing their power by appealing to some kind of secular god were often as pathetic as they were futile. Hannah Arendt's blunt comment on Robespierre illustrates the process, and its effects:

> The need for gods in the body politic of a republic appeared in the course of the French Revolution in Robespierre's desperate attempt at founding an entirely new cult, the cult of the Supreme Being. At the time Robespierre made his proposal, it seemed as though the cult's chief function was to arrest the revolution, which had run amok. As such, the great festival—this wretched and foredoomed substitution for the constitution which the revolution had been unable to produce— failed utterly; the new god, it turned out, was not even powerful enough to inspire the proclamation of a general amnesty and to show a minimum of clemency, let alone mercy. The ridiculousness of the enterprise was such that it must have been manifest to those who attended the initiating ceremonies as it was to later generations.[2]

For the most part, religious violence in the eighteenth, nineteenth, and twentieth centuries rarely met the conditions that might have provoked the types of explosions characteristic of the previous epoch. When religiously motivated violence did erupt, it was quickly superseded by secular elements. By the end of the eighteenth century, ideology became a much more potent factor of war than religion proper. For the most part, the Westphalian order pushed the more powerful European powers to export their territorial ambitions to other continents, where they built colonial empires. Colonization and empire building tended to downplay religion, inasmuch as the real motivations of the colonizing nations lay in gaining political and economic power and influence over their rivals. Much like the Pax Romana, the British, French, and Russian empires (we tend to forget about the latter) effectively put a lid on religious and ethnic conflicts among the peoples they subjugated. By the time the old Austrian and Turkish empires crumbled with World War I, and then the British and French colonial empires themselves after World War II, the claims and identities of the liberating forces were defined along ideological lines much more than on religious ones, as they might have been, for example, in the early nineteenth century. By the early twentieth century, secular ideologies had come of age as potent tools for radical change, and all the revolutionaries who sought to disrupt and annihilate the existing order turned to these ideologies and away from religion. Only in the second half of the twentieth century did religion make a comeback as an agent of political change—in the forms of Latin American liberation theology; the linkage of

Solidarność and the Polish Catholic Church; the struggle of the Afghan Mujahideen against the USSR; and the anti-Western theocratic revolution of the Iranian ayatollahs.

Still, although the major conflicts of the eighteenth, nineteenth, and twentieth centuries were mostly not powered by religion or even marked by strong religious undertones, religious violence occasionally flared up, at times dramatically. During the early eighteenth century, the struggle by many nations and peoples who tried to repulse the Europeans or, later, to unshackle themselves from their dominion, was inevitably marked by the religious identities and allegiances of those who fought Western colonialism. Considering that most Western colonization came at the expense of Muslim countries, from Algeria to Egypt, from Central Asia to the Arabian Peninsula, from northern Nigeria to northern India, one can see how many of the struggles against it may have been envisaged as jihads or defensive holy wars. In essence, when French troops fought Abd El Kader or Samori Touré in North and West Africa, their adversaries were fighting Christians as much as they were fighting France. Europeans, of course, did not see these wars as holy wars, but rather as clashes of civilizations. "Islam gave Samori's empire a veneer of ideological unity," Douglas Porch notes of Touré. "But the real solidity of Samori's dominion resided in his formidable military organization."[3] By the same token, when the British troops in India were fighting the Thugs in the early part of the nineteenth century, it was not so much that they were going after a religious sect as that they were trying to suppress a terrorist group that was impeding their colonizing efforts (the sect was quickly eradicated, and by 1848, it had ceased to exist).[4]

Secular Europe itself did not completely escape the religious conundrum during this period. The fight for the independence of Ireland, for example, seen today by many as a matter of religious antagonism between a Catholic minority and an Anglican majority in Ulster, dates back to the Battle of the Boyne in 1690, when James II was defeated by William of Orange, and before that to the incredibly brutal English colonization of Ireland under the Tudors in the sixteenth century, an enduring template for all later English colonial aggression (one notes that the UK's prime minister, Lord Salisbury, asserted as late as 1886 that the Irish were as incapable of self-rule as the Hottentots). After the independence of Ireland in 1921, the denominational conflict developed into a protracted war between the IRA and the British state, which led to a campaign of terror that claimed among its victims the last viceroy of India,

Lord Mountbatten (August 27, 1979). Still, although the conflict had deep-seated religious underpinnings, it ultimately proved to be a political struggle between an irredentist movement and a state that refused to yield to its demands.

RELIGIOUS VIOLENCE IN THE NINETEENTH AND EARLY TWENTIETH CENTURIES

Religion played a role in several important conflicts of the nineteenth and early twentieth centuries, including the Crimean War, the Taiping Rebellion in China (which directly and indirectly involved Western powers), and the genocide orchestrated by the Ottoman regime in 1915. After the restoration of the classical balance of power in Vienna in 1815, the monarchical system, which could not sustain the changes wrought by industrialization, modern ideologies, and the predatory engagements of the great powers, gradually disintegrated, and nationalism emerged everywhere to take its place, with religion as its subtext. ("Nationalism in France, at least, cannot begin to be understood properly without reference to religion," David A. Bell writes.)[5] This disintegration ultimately led to Sarajevo and World War I, and there religion played a marginal role at best—for example, the British agent T. E. Lawrence successfully played the Arabs against the Turks, notwithstanding that they were of the same faith.

The Crimean War (1853–56), one of the major wars of the nineteenth century, came to symbolize incompetent decisions leading to indiscriminate butchery. In many ways, it set up the intricate geopolitical alliance system that later came to cause World War I. Although the background to the war was essentially geostrategic—big power rivalry among ambitious European rivals—the immediate causes of the war were religious.

As in the days of the Crusades, the point of contention lay in the Holy City of Jerusalem, which had long been under the control of the Ottomans. The issue regarded the control of, and access to, the Christian holy sites, previously accorded to the Russian Orthodox Church by the Ottoman authorities. When a dispute arose in Constantinople between Catholic and Orthodox authorities over access to the shrines, Napoleon III of France decided to intervene and claim these rights for the Catholic Church. The French ambassador to Constantinople, Marquis Charles de La Valette, a fanatical Catholic and a *chevalier* of the Hospitaller Order of Saint John, persuaded the Sublime Porte to oblige without much arm-twisting. The rift inevitably led to diplomatic tensions between Russia and France, which escalated until finally formal hostilities were declared. The tsar, Nicholas I, was at this point keen to profit from the Ottoman Empire's rapid decline. Britain, like France, was eager to contain and roll back the Russians in the Black Sea and Mediterranean. Never mind that the local Orthodox and Catholic authorities managed to reach an agreement, the damage was done, and neither Paris nor Moscow was ready to back down. With England siding with France and the Ottomans tagging along (and later in 1855, the kingdom of Sardinia, which a few years after this moved its capital to Rome and changed its name to Italy), the Russians were overrun; the battle of Sebastopol constituting the decisive engagement of the war and one of Napoleon III's few military successes. Unlike the conflicts of the seventeenth century, this was not a religious war that had turned political, but a political (or geopolitical) war that was launched on a religious pretext. Still, this sloppy and costly effort produced at least two literary pieces of note, Tennyson's narrative poem "The Charge of the Light Brigade," inspired by the eponymous event during the siege of Sebastopol (battle of Balaclava) and Tolstoy's *Sebastopol Sketches* (Tolstoy participated in the war as an artillery officer; his experience and observations served as a basis for some of his masterpieces). Incidentally, this was also the first conflict to be photographed.

At around the same time, but further east, another violent war erupted, which takes us beyond the geographical scope of this book. But given the amplitude of the violence and the fact that it implicated a Western religion and drew in Western governments, troops, and commanders, the Taiping Rebellion (1852–64) deserves a brief mention here. This was to be the most lethal conflict of the nineteenth century, and one of the most devastating wars of all time, leaving at least twenty million dead—more than the Thirty Years' War or, for that matter, World War I (by comparison, the U.S. Civil War, considered by historians to be the first of the deadly wars of the industrial age, killed fewer than a million men). Taking the low estimate of twenty million, the Taiping Rebellion would thus rank second only to World War II, with its roughly fifty million casualties. Given the lack of reliable statistics and given China's demographics, it is possible, however, that the Taiping war may have killed even more people than World War II. A Chinese study published in 1999 put the number of deaths from the war at fifty-seven million for the hardest-hit regions, with projections for all the regions affected at seventy million dead from the war. Whatever the real numbers may be, they are astounding.[6]

This time, religion was the principal driver of the war and the one element that determined at various stages the direction of the conflict. This was not the only conflict with religious implications to hit China at around the same time.[7] The Muslim Dungan Revolt in western China (1862 –77), a confusing, aimless war that left several million dead, was also fraught with deep resentments fueled by sectarian antagonisms. However, like China's conflicts with Tibet, it was mainly brought about by Beijing's will to impose its authority on territories it considered part of China. The Panthay Rebellion in the Hunan province (1856–73), which involved both Muslim and non-Muslims, was not a religious conflict.

What is peculiar, then, about the Taiping Rebellion is not only that it was motivated by religious dogma, but that it was specifically directed at Confucianism; hence the violent nature of the conflict, which went to the heart of what it meant to be Chinese. The general background of the war lay in the destabilization of the country that had been caused in great part by the incursion of Western powers in China and the unequal treaty system they had imposed on the Chinese authorities. This had undermined the authority of the central government and its legitimacy in the eyes of the people. China, unlike Japan, was unable to foster an internal revolution influential enough to modernize the country to the point where it might respond to the Western menace. The ruling dynasty, the Qing (1644–1911/12), was of Manchu stock and origin, and thus had minority status vis-à-vis the Han majority. This situation was not unusual in Chinese history, but, as with the Yuan (Mongol) dynasty of Kublai Khan, the legitimacy of the ruling elite lay principally in its ability to project and exert its authority. Faced with the humiliation of being told what to do by France or England (now working together thanks to the Crimean War alliance), society started to break at the seams, and one war or rebellion led to another. The First Opium War (1839–42), caused by the forced sale of opium by the British, rocked the shaky Chinese foundations and invited more unrest.

If the social, economic, political, and geopolitical environment may have been ripe for civil unrest, the origins of the Taiping movement were very mundane, and utterly modest. It was launched by an obscure, severely distraught student who had failed to pass the governmental examinations that had for centuries been the staple of the Confucian order and its civil meritocracy. Falling sick and prey to a violent fever, the student, Hong Xiuquan, began to have visions leading him to believe that he was the new messiah, Jesus's little brother. Combined with his delirium, his reading of a Christian pamphlet that had recently landed in his hands provoked the Christian epiphany. Convinced that God had called upon him to fight the forces of evil, and bent on destroying the Confucian elite to fulfill God's command, Hong Xiuquan, along with a neighbor and a couple of cousins, embarked on a proselytizing mission that soon gained formidable traction among a segment of the underprivileged rural poor. Soon Hong Xiuquan and his partners were at the head of a powerful military force and were challenging the central government. Already overstretched, the beleaguered authorities barely managed to resist the onslaught, but with the help of Western powers, they managed with time to roll back the Taiping and destroy the so-called Heavenly Kingdom.

The decisive battle that put an end to the war in July 1864 (though rebel guerrilla groups remained active until 1871) came after a long series of violent encounters that saw the one side and then the other advance, only to be repelled in what became a perpetual back-and-forth cycle that never seemed poised to end. The ultimate encounter was as dramatic as the rest of the war. Thanks to powerful modern artillery, the Chinese (Hunan) army forced its way into Nanjing after a protracted siege. Faced with defeat, in a move reminiscent of Masada, thousands upon thousands of Taiping soldiers committed mass suicide to escape being massacred by the enemy. All told, one hundred thousand perished in the battle, which lasted three days. Notwithstanding the longer campaigns of the two world wars, this was and remains to this day, one of the deadliest battles in history.

The Manchus had survived, but not for long, since the war planted the seeds that would ultimately push the Qing to the brink: technological modernization, decentralization, and nationalism. As for the Taiping Heavenly Kingdom, it was completely obliterated. Though it anticipated in many ways the ideological conflicts that would define warfare in the twentieth century, this was the last large-scale war to be fought in the name of God, though not the last war directed against a faith. In China, the Boxer rebellion of 1900 began as a reaction to foreign Christian missionaries, though these were mere scapegoats, as a general xenophobic sentiment had gripped China after the military interventions of the West. Only fifteen years later, in the Ottoman Empire, another war was launched by the regime against another Christian community in what would constitute the first mass murder of the twentieth century orchestrated by state forces.

The Armenian Holocaust of 1915 is considered to be the first genocide of the twentieth century. It is often compared to the Jewish Holocaust, with individuals and communities being specifically targeted by a government to be exterminated as a people. Inasmuch as one can compare two such horrific events, the analogy may be partly skewed by our anachronistic interpretation of the first event in light of the second one. For the Young Turks who ruled the Ottoman Empire defined and conducted their radical nationalistic policies differently from the Nazi Germany of the late 1930s and 1940s. True, this nationalism revolved around the Turkish identity (pan-Turkism) and character of the Ottoman state, but also around its religious identity, which was Muslim, Islam having been from the start its official religion, which was still at this point, in 1915, a caliphate.

Thus, the extermination of the Armenians fell into the wider scheme of physically eliminating all the Christian minorities of the Ottoman Empire, a fact made all the more clear in that the government did not explicitly target non-Turkish Muslim minorities such as the Kurds. Hence the religious, anti-Christian element was essential in defining those people whom the Ottoman government sought to exterminate, which included Armenians, Assyro-Chaldeans, and Pontic Greeks. Although the exterminations are often treated as separate events or at least categorized differently (Armenian Genocide or Pontic Greek Genocide, for example), they were all part of the same policy of ethno-religious cleansing.

As testimony to this war against Christians, the massacre of individuals and communities was all along accompanied by the systematic destruction of churches or their conversion into mosques. The fact that the Turkish government may have privileged Turkish nationalism over Islam—though the two were linked—does not alter the fact that this particular war against its own people was at base a war against a religion, against those who adhered to it and against its symbols. Unlike the Nazi extermination policies, which were absolute and universal in character, the 1915 genocide (or genocides, which went beyond the year 1915) must be understood as an effort to cleanse a nation. More than a million Armenians, 120,000 Assyro-Chaldeans, and 350,000 Orthodox Pontic Greeks were killed in the process.[8]

HOLY TERROR: RELIGIOUS VIOLENCE AND TERRORISM

At around the same time that the Taiping were fighting their ultimate battle, a new form of violence was emerging in Russia and Europe. Terrorism, a term first coined during the state-sponsored terror of the French Revolution, was about to mean something entirely different than what the conservative Anglo-Irish thinker Edmund Burke, among others, had understood it to be during the dark days of the revolutionary *Terreur*.

The mid-1860s were a watershed for terrorism, with the convergence of the main elements that would resurrect an ancestral practice largely forgotten since the demise of the Assassins. The emergence of revolutionary and nihilist groups, along with anarchists, coincided with Alfred Nobel's invention of the dynamite (intended for public works). Armed with dynamite sticks and intent on lighting the spark that, in their mind, would make the existing order crumble, various terrorists and terrorist groups began to wreak havoc, killing heads of state, monarchs, government officials, military and security personnel, and a few civilians along the way. Convinced that actions spoke louder than words, their motto, as well as their modus operandi, was contained in a catchy formula: *propaganda by deed*. The psychological shock provoked by terrorist attacks was supposed to awaken the subdued masses and weaken governments through a strategy of chaos designed to set the revolutionary forces in motion. This was the first age of modern terror. Right until 1914, and then during the interwar years, 1918–39, and, after 1945, during the colonial and postcolonial periods, terrorism was essentially a nonreligious phenomenon, though a majority of terrorists adhered to some kind of ideology, be it anarchism, nationalism, fascism, or Marxism. But, as the latest iteration of terrorist activity petered out in the late 1970s through isolated radical postcolonial left-wing groups, two major events were about to change the whole dynamics of global politics, and bring about a dramatic resurgence of terrorist activity on a grand scale. Only this time, the violence was going to be perpetrated in the name of a God, and it was going to target the general population, in other words anonymous civilians, in an indiscriminate fashion. The two events, which took place in the same region but under vastly different circumstances, were the Iranian revolution and the Soviet invasion of Afghanistan.

The toppling of the pro-Western regime of the Shah in 1979 by the Ayatollah Khomeini was an extraordinary event with profound and complex consequences, in the Middle East and beyond. Not only did it eliminate one of America's, and the West's, main allies in the region, it completely transformed its geostrategic dynamics. Notwithstanding the influence it may have had on the 1980 U.S. presidential election, it put religion back on the political map in a big way. Iran became an Islamic theocracy (April 1, 1979) determined to export its revolution using all means necessary, including state-sponsored terrorism. Starting in the sixteenth century with the founder of the Safavid dynasty, Shah Ishmael I (r. 1502–24), Persia had been at the vanguard of a Shiite revival and it was, in essence, going back to its roots with an intransigent regime bent on enforcing Sharia law in the strictest manner, much as the Safavids had done four centuries earlier. This meant "war" against the West, but also against the Sunni majorities that comprised and continue to make up the bulk of the populations of neighboring Muslim states, with the exception of Iraq, which was then run with an iron grip by the Sunni minority under Saddam Hussein, against whom Teheran was soon to fight a long and bitter conflict.

Meanwhile, Teheran was crystallizing the regional tensions it had vastly contributed to exacerbating around the ancestral Shiite/Sunni antagonism. In the early 1980s in nearby Lebanon, a fragile mosaic of religious communities that had plunged into civil war in 1975, the Ayatollahs created Hezbollah, a radical Shiite movement not shy to employ terror tactics, which has served as a proxy in the confrontation that has opposed Israel and Iran. From there on, the stage was set for more religious conflicts to surface in the region, inasmuch as the regional powers, Saudi Arabia, Egypt, and Turkey, were also forced to react against the resurgence of a militant Iran. Saudi Arabia kept the pressure on its Shiite rival by expending huge amounts of money to erect and support madrasas and mosques around the world, some of which became breeding grounds for radical Islamists, with a few individuals joining terrorist cells.

The period saw Palestinian movements make a transition from Marxist-inspired secular ideologies of liberation toward Islamic radicalism, while right-wing Jewish groups engaged in a new dose of radical rhetoric, which was sometimes accompanied by violent deeds. Elsewhere in the region, Islamic groups were emboldened to take violent action, as they did against Egyptian president Anwar Sadat, who was killed by Islamic radicals in 1981. The individuals who had plotted the assassination were a fringe jihadist group, the Egyptian Islamic Jihad, that emanated from the Society of Muslim Brothers, which had been created several decades earlier, in 1928. One of the men involved in the plot, Ayman al-Zawahiri (who was arrested and later released by the Egyptian authorities) would become Osama bin Laden's right-hand man and, after his death, take over as Al-Quaeda's leader, which brings us to the second momentous event of 1979, the Soviet invasion of Afghanistan on December 24, launched to uphold the beleaguered communist regime in Kabul, the toppling of a Marxist-Leninist regime being unacceptable to the USSR.

At the time, the invasion seemed unlikely to do more than derail U.S. President Jimmy Carter's (p. 1976–80) efforts at détente or depreciate the 1980 Summer Olympics in Moscow, which Carter decided to boycott in retaliation. The consequences of the war would prove far-reaching, however, affecting in a negative way both the Soviet Union and the United States, both of which appeared embroiled in a protracted superpower rivalry that looked, at the time, set to last several more decades.

Much like the U.S. intervention in Vietnam, the Soviet intervention in Afghanistan, meant as a quick fix to what seemed to be a fairly straightforward political problem, gradually transformed itself into a military quagmire of unanticipated proportions. As the conflict started to drag on, draining funds and men, it gradually came to embody the increasingly visible weaknesses of the regime. By the mid to late 1980s, the Soviet Union was starting to show signs of fatigue, having been under pressure from various angles, including the weakening of its authority in the Warsaw Pact nations of eastern Europe, the perceived need to keep up an expensive arms race, and the morass that the invasion of Afghanistan came to be. In 1989, after a decade-long nightmare, the Soviet Union pulled out of Afghanistan. Two years later, the Soviet regime collapsed under its own weight.

The war had been a struggle between ill-trained Soviet conscripts with little motivation and a growing army of guerrilla warriors known as the Muja-hideen ("those who conduct a jihad"). The Afghan resistance, fought as a global jihad against the Soviet infidels, had attracted soldiers from all four corners of the Fertile Crescent. Well-funded by Saudi Arabia and the United States, the Mujahideen wore the Soviet troops out, winning a historic victory. In the process, the war produced the Taliban and a generation of experienced, battle-hardened jihadists looking to pursue their holy war against other opponents and in other theaters. Foreign jihadists returning home to Algeria and other places launched terror wars that targeted civilians, who were also victimized at times by government forces. One consequence of the spill-over was the Algerian Armed Islamic Group (AIG), an underground movement, compris-ing thousands of guerrillas trained in Afghanistan, which launched a violent terror campaign against the government after the annulment of the 1991 election results. Beyond Algeria, the AIG also organized terror attacks in France in the mid 1990s, in what became the first wave of jihadist terror to hit western Europe.

Meanwhile, from Afghanistan itself, another jihadist group was also starting to make waves. Al-Qaeda, "the Base," was a direct offshoot of the Mujahideen resistance movement. Taken over by the Saudi millionaire Osama bin Laden, it distinguished itself from the other groups that had emerged from the war in Afghanistan in that it had universal objectives and a global outreach. Like many revolutionary movements in history, it was puritanical, intransigent, and idealistic. Its leadership comprised both a master of organization and propaganda in the form of Bin Laden and an ideological strategist with Ayman al-Zawahiri. Well-funded, it also had something that very few revolutionary organizations can boast of: a sanctuary. Protected by the Taliban who now ruled Afghanistan, Al-Qaeda could in all tranquility train its soldiers, devise its strategies, and carefully put its plans into practice. Its objectives were as precise as they were grandiose: topple the West and Western allies and recreate the Great Caliphate (which had been abolished by Mustapha Kemal Atatürk after the disintegration of the Ottoman Empire that followed World War I).

Al-Qaeda made itself known in the 1990's with several gruesome attacks, though, for a while at least, its activities mainly drew the attention of a few counterterrorism experts. After the dramatic bombing of the U.S. embassies of Kenya and Tanzania, followed by the attack on a U.S. carrier off the coast of Yemen, it was clear, though, that Al-Qaeda had a global reach and the means to inflict serious damage. These attacks, however, paled in comparison with what was to come. In the morning of September 11, 2001, Al-Qaeda operatives, most of them Saudis, launched what became the most spectacular and lethal terrorist attack in history, killing nearly three thousand individuals in New York, Washington and Pennsylvania while the world watched the events unfold live on television.

The success of the attacks, from the perspective of the perpetrators, proved in the end to have been too great for Al-Qaeda, which, under intense pressure from U.S. armed forces lost its sanctuary in Afghanistan, much of its potency, and its historic leader Bin Laden (in 2011). Still, Al-Qaeda provided new generations of jihadists with a powerful ideology and a sense of belonging. Thousands of young men and women joined the numerous offshoots of Al-Qaeda that sprang up in a vast area from East Asia to sub-Saharan Africa, and which included, among others, ISIS (the so-called Islamic State of Iraq and Syria; also known by its Arabic acronym, Daesh) and Boko Haram in northeastern Nigeria and neighboring countries, the most lethal terrorist groups of the 2010s.

But despite some ill-conceived policies and strategies on the part of Western powers—the intervention in Iraq (2003) being one of these—the West did not crumble and, on the whole, it managed to contain the Islamic threat, despite sporadic attacks that claimed dozens of lives, particularly in western Europe, as compared to the thousands of victims claimed each year by terrorist attacks in Muslim countries.

How will the recent wave of jihadist terrorism fit into the broader history of war and religion? Although the jihadists themselves may construe their struggle as a continuation of the wars that pitted Christians against Muslims for more than a millennium (which from their perspective includes the colonial period), it is too early to tell whether and how future developments might substantiate this. As a vanguard revolutionary movement, however, modern jihadism has been far from producing the type of success that armed Marxist movements formerly enjoyed. And, against the Western liberal democratic model, which it loathes and combats, jihadism, should it establish itself as a viable political alternative in some countries like Yemen, still lacks the sine qua non of political success: the capacity to generate economic growth. In essence, it has shown little more than a capacity to disrupt and bring violence in Muslim societies, particularly in those countries that offer a political vacuum. Overall, it is but a pale, distorted imitation of the great jihadist movements of the Golden Age of Islam with their mutually reinforcing spiritual message and redoubtable military capacity. But however much one may doubt that modern jihadism will rekindle the holy war spirit of the Middle Ages, combining religion and violence is clearly not yet a thing of the past.[9]

Despite the fact that the magnitude and scope of religious violence is on a much smaller scale today than in the past, one cannot but be struck by the riveting similarities between conflicts in different countries, regions, or even continents, that might have occurred centuries or millennia ago. To be sure, strategies, tactics, and weapons vary extensively from one conflict to the next, all the more so when spatial and temporal gaps are taken into account, but the human accounts of the violence that takes place all too often yields the same tragic stories.[10] Much like the religious fanatics of the twenty-first century, their forebears sought to enact brutal justice of their own. Adhering to a primeval understanding of violence, even in the age of technologies of mass destruction, modern terrorists have systematically reverted to the most primitive means of terror. With the crude and horrific beheadings perpetrated by jihadist militants, these terrorist acts are having an impact on the collective conscience that would be hard to match with any weapon, no matter the lethal potential, and at a much smaller cost to those responsible for these deeds.

Then, as now, mixing religion with power, politics, hatred, and resentment yields tragically similar results, with violence taking very primal forms, even as weapons have espoused the spirit of the age in their futuristic technological sophistication, one that seeks to distinguish between "hard" and "soft" targets, between combatants and noncombatants, a distinction also made by modern day-crusaders, but with reverse effects, civilians becoming the targets of choice. Unlike "political" wars that purport to engage legitimate combatants, religiously motivated wars logically involve large swathes of civilian populations, which inevitably bear the brunt of the violence—often, in fact, directed specifically at them.

In the greater scheme of things, neither the Iranian revolution nor the radical jihadist movements that emerged from the war of Afghanistan have managed to alter the geopolitical status quo. Although both have benefited from the instabilities of the greater Middle East and from the loosening of the global geostrategic order that followed the end of the Cold War, they have yet to capitalize on the weaknesses of the Western model they seek to challenge and hope to destroy. Nothing, indeed, indicates that the Iranian model or the jihadist ideology have produced a political movement with sufficient traction to challenge the existing order.[11] If anything, both seem to be losing steam and although the nuclear gesticulations of the Iranian government and the sporadic terror attacks of radical jihadists regularly make headlines, they are marginal events compared to the sudden rise of China to superpower status and all that this implies. The idea that the world might be witnessing a new clash of civilizations along religious fault lines is, so far, largely unsubstantiated. The religious wars that the Iranian authorities, on the one hand, and the jihadists, on the other, have tried to instigate through the orchestration of terror campaigns have never materialized, and the world is still, politically and geopolitically speaking, a secular one, dominated by power and economic relationships that, for the most part, are largely untainted by religious, or for that matter, ideological, considerations. That religion might come back in full force to fill the moral and spiritual void apparently created by the excesses of consumerism is possible; that political leaders might use this religious revival to enhance their grip on power is not only probable but has already taken place in countries like Turkey, once a champion of secularism. Still, it will take significant change for religion once again to become a major political force capable of directing countries, regions, and continents toward war or peace, in the name of God, as it was under the emperor Constantine the Great and the Prophet Muhammad.

Epilogue

Of Gods and Men

Few cities in the world are as majestic as Samarkand, the capital of Uzbekistan, once a part of the Soviet Union but now an independent country. The Bibi-Khanym mosque, in particular, is a stunning piece of architecture that rivals the greatest monuments produced by Islamic culture. East of Samarkand, far into the steppes of Inner Asia, the city of Karakorum pales in comparison, and one would be hard pressed to see what was once the capital of a mighty empire in this remote area of the Övörkhangai province of modern-day Mongolia. The two individuals who once ruled over Samarkand and Karakorum, Tamerlane and Genghis Khan, were of the same mettle: men of steel driven by an unrelenting desire to carve out the greatest empire known to mankind. Both were formidable warriors; both were ruthless; each sought to leave his imprint on history. But where Genghis thought himself a living god, Tamerlane knew better, and, as he proceeded to subdue and plunder half the Eurasian landmass and massacre all those that stood on his path, he was also careful to spare the talented individuals who might help him build the only legacy that mattered to him: Samarkand, his personal tribute to Allah, whose magnificence he hoped would purify him of his many sins and wash off his evil deeds. Tamerlane's immense empire had completely disappeared within a generation after his death; but Samarkand remains, a formidable symbol of the Turkic conqueror's own contradictions, and a monument to the struggle between good and evil that is humankind's predicament.

As Genghis effectively demonstrated, and Julius Caesar before him, empire builders do not need religion to conquer territories and establish the rule of law over the populations they force into submission. Nor, for that matter, do religions need empires to conquer the hearts and minds of individuals and communities. But, as history illustrates in high fashion, religions, particularly those with a universal appeal, and empires, have yielded many a fruitful marriage. As with the Bibi-Khanym mosque, architectural deeds great and small have left a trail of evidence to illustrate the point. From Santiago de Chile to Arequipa in Peru, from Antigua in Guatemala to Mexico and California, the Catholic churches that dot the path of the Spanish conquistadores point to the strength and resilience of the word of God in a part of the world where Christianity is durably implanted among populations that, for the most part, forcefully reject their colonial past and still bear strong resentments against the Europeans who invaded the New World. Few of these, however, would question their faith or the message of Jesus. Elsewhere, the places of worship erected by once mighty colonial powers act as an odd reminder that a foreign people came and left, leaving little else to testify of their presence but the symbols of the gods they worshipped. St. Joseph's Cathedral in Hanoi, one of the very first buildings erected by the French—on the site of a Buddhist temple—after they took control of Indochina in 1886, is such a testament, planted in the center of a city where very few people can even understand the language of those who only yesterday considered themselves to be their masters. Córdoba's Great Mosque-Cathedral (or Mezquita de Córdoba) in southern Spain, now a major tourist attraction, signals that this region of the world, which has effectively been a stronghold of Christianity for the past five hundred years, was once an epicenter of Islamic culture and refinement. Today, Muslims are still strictly forbidden to pray inside the building, and the Moorish structure whose minaret now serves as the Cathedral's bell tower serves as a symbol that it was not just a people that were defeated here but, more important perhaps, a religion. Nowhere is the contrast between the resilience of religious dogma and the ephemeral condition of empires greater than in the city of Rome, where Vatican City, now as always the symbol of church authority and home of the pope, cohabits with the decrepit vestiges of an empire, mighty as it may have been, that has clearly come and gone. For centuries, from antiquity to the Age of Reason, empires were the principal movers and shakers of regional and global politics on the Eurasian continent and in the Middle East, the Americas, and parts of Africa. So why were empires so resilient? And why did they disappear? In great part, the answer to both questions can be found in one essential element: religion.

In order for an empire to function durably and not collapse, its rulers imperatively need to establish an efficient system of beliefs that gives the enterprise a sense of legitimacy, which in turn holds the structure together and enables it to survive, a difficult task given the inherent heterogeneity of an entity that typically includes diverse populations not always keen to cohabit with one another. Though sheer force and power may be sufficient to create an empire, they are insufficient in and of themselves to keep it from disintegrating. In short, for empires to endure, they need a founding myth that will indefinitely keep social forces in check. With Confucianism, the Chinese proved that an empire could function durably without a god. At the opposite end of the spectrum, the Romans rested their founding myth on a plethora of gods and goddesses. In their great majority, however, the various empires that sprang up in Eurasia and around the Mediterranean adopted monotheistic religions as the foundational belief structure upon which they built the legitimacy of their rule. With Constantine the Great, the Romans accomplished the rare feat of successfully switching from one foundational myth to another. In the process, the rapidly eroding Roman Empire found a new lease on life in Christianity. Three centuries after Constantine, the Prophet Muhammad established a founding myth of his own, albeit with Judeo-Christian precedents.

Both Christianity and Islam were irretrievably tied to the imperialistic designs of those who championed their causes. Inevitably, given their geographic proximity, both quickly found themselves in each other's path, and violence ensued. Over time, Islam proved better adapted than Christianity to the power struggles that pitted one empire against another, and, notwithstanding the Mongol invasions of the thirteenth century, it flourished in the medieval era, with Arab and later Turkic imperial dynasties providing the global Muslim community with an enduring sense of purpose and stability. The connection between faith and empire, both in the Muslim and Christian world, was extremely durable, with the last of the self-styled Christian empires falling in 1806, when Napoleon formally dismantled what was left of the Holy Roman Empire, while the last Muslim empire, the Ottoman, disappeared, in more dramatic fashion, after World War I.

After Europe made the transition from faith-based empires and kingdoms to secular nation-states in the seventeenth and eighteenth centuries, it brought down the last Islamic empires: the Mogul Empire of northern India and Ottoman Turkey. This time, there were no new empires to take up the mantle of

Islam. The West had not only done away with its own imperial ambitions, which petered out after 1945, it had also done away with the very idea of empire.[1]

In Europe, the marriage between religion and politics was never really a smooth one and the relationship between church authorities and lay rulers had been rocky from the beginning. Clovis, the first western European ruler to adopt Catholicism as a state religion, was long hesitant before taking the plunge, and perhaps he sensed that something wasn't quite right. This was, in essence, a marriage of convenience rather than of love, and at some point, a divorce seemed inevitable. When did the system start to break down? Probably after the Near Eastern crusades, when it became clear that the church's quest to create a true Christian community would never fully materialize. Then, as the institution of the church itself began to break down, the Habsburg Empire, which by the sixteenth century held the keys to the future of the old order, was unable to sustain itself after the Reformation. With the scientific revolution looming, a new set of beliefs based on the power of reason emerged that challenged the old theological belief system upon which the entire social construction rested. As a result, the whole edifice broke down in a series of religious conflicts that, for the most part, ended in 1648 with the Peace of Westphalia. As the Westphalian order took shape, God was no longer part of the political equation, and the modern secular nation-state was now the way of the future. After hijacking the French Revolution, Napoleon revived the imperial ideals of the past in high style, but even he, perhaps the most talented general of modern times, could not turn back the clock.

With the American and French Revolutions, a new set of universal norms imposed itself on the world stage. This new belief system now revolved around man rather than God, around the ideas of liberty and equality, which, unlike competing omnipotent deities, could potentially cohabit. All in all, while one may equate modern ideologies such as nationalism, liberalism, communism, or fascism with the monotheistic religions that defined the politics of the previous age, none of these ideologies really have the power to move an individual like the conviction that comes from one's devotion to a higher being and the desire to share this passion with others. Communism, once envisaged as the mightiest of the secular religions, was all but dead after a short run of seven decades, with tens of millions of innocent victims. Though it promised Heaven on earth, what it delivered looked a lot more like Hell. Fascism, which promised Heaven to some and Hell to all others, had an even shorter lifespan. Human beings, it seems, are not long fooled by men pretending to be gods.

So, what now? Notwithstanding a few beleaguered Islamic terrorist organizations, there is little today that foreshadows a revival of religion as the primary driver of world politics. But then, who, at the turn of the fourth century CE, would have predicted that the faith of a marginal, persecuted community in the Roman Empire would, within a few decades, shape the course of history for centuries to come? And who, at the beginning of the seventh century, would have foreseen that a religion that had yet to surface would, in the span of a generation, push an obscure people from the deserts of Arabia to overrun two long-standing superpowers and rewrite humanity's destiny?

NOTES

INTRODUCTION

1. Epigraph: Élie Barnavi, "Il faut défendre la laïcité," *La Vie*, special issue, *Les guerres de religion—Du XVIe siècle au djihadisme*, June 2016, 9. See also Barnavi, *Les religions meurtrières* (2006; Paris: Flammarion, 2016).

2. Yuval Noah Harari, *Sapiens: A Brief History of Humankind* (London: Vintage Books, 2011), 243.

3. Carl von Clausewitz, *On War*, ed. and trans. Michael Howard and Peter Paret (Princeton, NJ: Princeton University Press, 1976), 75.

4. James W. Laine, *Meta-Religion: Religion and Power in World History* (Oakland: University of California Press, 2014), 1.

5. In terms of percentages, the results depend on how one defines religion and war, and how one assesses the part played by faith in armed conflicts, all subjective matters. Two different studies looking at all recorded conflicts in history and the presence of religion in these conflicts yielded very different percentages, less than 10 percent and 40 percent. For an informed discussion of the issue and these numbers, see Ara Norenzayan, *Big Gods: How Religion Transformed Cooperation and Conflict* (Princeton, NJ: Princeton University Press, 2013), 155–69.

6. Norenzayan, *Big Gods*, 164.

7. As Karl Kautsky observes, however, what is recorded of the Anabaptists' beginnings was reported by writers profoundly hostile to them. "After it [Anabaptist Münster] was captured by the besieging forces, almost the whole population was massacred," he writes. "No defender of the Baptist cause escaped a bloody grave, who was in a position to give a literary account of the events of the siege. All the descriptions proceed from the enemies of the Anabaptists." See Kautsky, *Communism in Central Europe in the Time of the Reformation*, trans. J. L. Mulliken and E. G. Mulliken (London: T. Fisher Unwin, 1897; LaVergne, TN: Kessinger Reprint, 2009), 240–41, 248, 249n, 256, 271.

8. Antoine-Henri de Jomini, *The Art of War*, trans. G. H. Mendell and W. P. Craighill (1862; Rockville, MD: Arc Manor, 2007), 17.

9. Nathalie Wlodarczyk, "African Traditional Religion and Violence," in *The Oxford Handbook of Religion and Violence*, ed. Mark Juergensmeyer et al. (Oxford, Oxford University Press, 2013), 159.

10. See John Hall, "Religion and Violence from a Sociological Perspective," in *Oxford Handbook of Religion and Violence*, ed. Juergensmeyer et al., 269.

11. Here I paraphrase and summarize the definitions put forth in greater detail by Laine, *Meta-Religion*, 6.

12. Garth Fowden, *Empire to Commonwealth: Consequences of Monotheism in Late Antiquity* (Princeton, NJ: Princeton University Press, 1993), 7.

13. Laine, *Meta-Religion*, 7.

14. The classic exposition of this phenomenon is that of Jacob Burckhardt's *The Civilization of the Renaissance in Italy* (1860; London: Penguin Books, 1990). See in particular his chapter on the development of the individual, pp. 98–104.

15. *The Texts and Versions of John de Plano Carpini and William de Rubruquis*, ed. C. Raymond Beazley (London: Hakluyt Society, 1903).

16. Henri Pirenne, *Mohammed and Charlemagne* (1936; London: George Allen & Unwin, 1954), argued that Europe had been plunged into the Dark Ages principally because of the rise of Islam, not the barbarian invasions. See Emmet Scott, *Mohammed & Charlemagne Revisited: The History of a Controversy* (Nashville, TN: New English Review Press, 2012); Richard Hodges and David Whitehouse, *Mohammed, Charlemagne and the Origins of Europe: Archeology and the Pirenne Thesis* (Ithaca, NY: Cornell University Press, 1983).

17. Ernst Jünger, *Storm of Steel*, trans. Michael Hoffman (1961; New York: Penguin Books, 2004), 7.

18. Reuven Firestone, *Holy War in Judaism: The Fall and Rise of a Controversial Idea* (Oxford: Oxford University Press, 2012), 221–47.

19. Michael Walzer, "Exodus 32 and the Theory of Holy War: The History of a Citation," *Harvard Theological Review* 61 (1968): 1–14. The passage reads as follows:

> Moses stood in the entrance of the camp, and said, "Whoever is on the Lord's side—come to me!"And all the sons of Levi gathered themselves together to him. And he said to them, "Thus says the Lord God of Israel: 'Let every man put his sword on his side, and go in and out from entrance to entrance throughout the camp, and let every man kill his brother, every man his companion, and every man his neighbor.'" So the sons of Levi did according to the word of Moses. And about three thousand men of the people fell that day. (*Holy Bible: New King James Version* [Nashville, TN: Thomas Nelson, 1990], 84)

20. Jean Lévi, "Introduction," in Liu Ja, *Nouveaux principes de politique* (Paris: Zulma, 2003), 8. See also Aihe Wang, *Cosmology and Political Culture in Early China* (2000; Cambridge: Cambridge University Press, 2006), 145–47.

21. *The Bhagavadgītā in the Mahābhārata: Text and Translation*, trans. J. A. B. van Buitenen (Chicago: University of Chicago Press, 1981).

22. Meir Shahar, "Violence in Chinese Religious Traditions," in *Oxford Handbook of Religion and Violence*, ed. Juergensmeyer et al., 185.

23. See Serge Chakotin, *The Rape of the Masses: The Psychology of Totalitarian Political Propaganda* (1939; New York: Haskell House, 1971), and Hannah Arendt, *The Origins of Totalitarianism* (1951; San Diego: Harcourt Brace Jovanovich, 1979).

24. Roger Caillois, *Bellone ou la pente de la guerre* (1963; Paris: Flammarion, 2012), 151. To the best of my knowledge, this book has not been translated into English.

25. Roger Caillois, *L'homme et le sacré* (1939; Paris: Gallimard, 1950), trans. Meyer Barash as *Man and the Sacred* (1980; Urbana: University of Illinois Press, 2001), 166, 167–70.

26. Caillois, *Man and the Sacred*, 173.

27. Caillois, *Man and the Sacred*, 165.

CHAPTER 1. THE RISE OF THE MONOTHEISTIC RELIGIONS

1. Chapter epigraph: Jacob Burckhardt, *Reflections on History* (Indianapolis, IN: Liberty Classics, 1979), 84.

2. Adrian Goldsworthy, *Pax Romana: War, Peace and Conquest in the Roman World* (New Haven, CT: Yale University Press, 2016), 215.

3. Ron A. Hassner and Gideon Aran, "Religion and Violence in the Jewish Traditions," in *Oxford Handbook of Religion and Violence*, ed. Juergensmeyer et al., 86–87.

4. In a debate that centers mainly on what Josephus said and did not say, Morton Smith, "Zealots and Sicarii: Their Origins and Relation," *Harvard Theological Review* 64, no. 1 (January 1971): 1–19, makes a strong case for differentiating between them.

5. In *The Jewish War or The History of the Destruction of Jerusalem*, 7.8, Josephus mentions five different sources of such violence, perhaps in chronological order: the Sicarii, John of Gischala, Simon Ben Giora, the Idumaeans, and the Zealots. See *The New Complete Works of Josephus* (Grand Rapids, MI: Kregel, 1999), 926.

6. See Pierre Vidal-Naquet, "De l'Atlantide à Masada: Réflexion sur querelle, mythe, histoire et politique," 45–66, and Pierre Vidal-Naquet et Claude Vigée: Le mythe de Masada," 367–74, " in Sylvie Parizet, dir., *Lectures politiques des mythes littéraires au XXe siècle* (Nanterre: Presses universitaires de Paris-Ouest, 2009).

7. Pierre Vidal-Naquet, "Du bon usage de la trahison," in Flavius Josephus, *La guerre des Juifs* (Paris: Minuit, 1977), and *Flavius Josèphe et La guerre des Juifs* (Paris: Bayard, 2005).

8. Josephus, *Jewish War*, 749.

9. Vidal-Naquet, *Flavius Josèphe et La guerre des Juifs*, 9.

10. Adrian Goldworthy, *The Fall of Carthage* (London: Orion Books, 2000), 353.

11. Polybius, *On Roman Imperialism* (Lake Bluff, IL: Regnery Gateway), 510.

12. See Adrian Goldsworthy, *Pax Romana*, 63–86.

13. Josephus, *Jewish War*, 680.

14. Josephus, *Jewish War*, 933.

15. Fowden, *Empire to Commonwealth*, 69

16. See Fergus Millar, "Empire, Community and Culture in the Roman Near East: Greeks, Syrians, Jews and Arabs," *Journal of Jewish Studies* 38 (1987): 143–64.

17. Fowden, *Empire to Commonwealth*, p. 71.

18. Marshall Hodgson, *The Venture of Islam. Conscience and History in a World Civilization*, vol. 1: *The Classical Age of Islam* (Chicago: University of Chicago Press, 1977), 130.

19. Tourai Daryaee, *Sasanian Persia: The Rise and Fall of an Empire* (New York: I. B. Tauris, 2009), 70.

20. Fowden, *Empire to Commonwealth*, 76.

21. Roger Savory, *Iran under the Safavids* (Cambridge: Cambridge University Press, 1980).

CHAPTER 2. CHRISTIANITY BECOMES A STATE RELIGION

1. Philippe Contamine, *War in the Middle Ages* (New York: Basic Blackwell, 1986), 302.

2. Laine, *Meta-Religion*, 92.

3. Karen Armstrong, *Fields of Blood Religion and the History of Violence* (New York: Knopf, 2014), 138.

4. See Roland H. Bainton, *Christian Attitudes towards War and Peace: A Historical Survey and Critical Re-Evaluation* (1960; Nashville, TN: Abingdon Press, 1990), 69–74, and, by the same author, " The Early Church and War," *Harvard Theological Review* 39, 3 (July 1946): 189–212.

5. Bainton, *Christian Attitudes*, 44–45.

6. Deut. 20 (New King James Version).

7. Num. 31: 3–20 (New King James Version).

8. Ps. 68: 1–3 (New King James Version).

9. Bainton, *Christian Attitudes*, 44.

10. In particular, see Gerhard von Rad, *Holy War in Ancient Israel* (Grand Rapids, MI: Eerdmans, 1991).

11. Reuven Firestone, "Holy War Idea in the Biblical Tradition," in *Encyclopedia of War and Religion*, ed. Gabriel Palmer-Fernandez (London: Routledge, 2004), 183, and E. W. Conrad, *Fear Not Warrior: A Study of "al tîrā" Pericopes in the Hebrew Scriptures* (Chico, CA: Scholars Press, 1985).

12. Susan Niditch, *War in the Hebrew Bible: A Study in the Ethics of Violence* (Oxford: Oxford University Press, 1993), 28.

13. Judges 9: 56–57 (New King James Version).

14. Esther 9 (New King James Version).

15. Niditch, *War*, 154.

16. "The War Rule," in *The Dead Sea Scrolls in English*, trans. G. Vermes (Baltimore: Penguin Books,1962), 133–35.

17. See Philippe Buc, *Holy War, Martyrdom, and Terror: Christianity, Violence, and the West* (Philadelphia: University of Pennsylvania Press, 2015), 22.

18. Matt. 10:34 (New King James Version).

19. Luke 22:36 (New King James Version).

20. Buc, *Holy War*, 19.

21. Fowden, *Empire to Commonwealth*, 77.

22. Lenin, *Political Report of the Central Committee*, March 7, 1918, in *Selected Works*, vol. 27 (Moscow: Progress Publishers, 1974), 100.

23. Eusebius, *Life of Constantine*, trans. A. C. McGiffert et al. (New York: Christian Literature Publishing, 1890).

24. Lactantius, *On the Death of the Persecutors*, trans. W. Fletcher (Edinburgh: Ante-Nicene Library, 1871).

25. Fowden, *Empire to Commonwealth*, 82.

26. See Peter Brown, *The Rise of Christendom* (New York: Blackwell, 1997), 24.

27. Armstrong, *Fields of Blood*, 149.

28. Tertullian, *Apology and De Spectaculis* (Cambridge, MA: Harvard University Press, Loeb Classical Library, 1931), 183.

29. Goldsworthy, *Pax Romana*, 260.

30. Pierre Chuvin, "Le Christ règne en méditerranée," *L'Histoire*, no. 157 (July–August 1992): 40.

31. Chuvin, "Le Christ règne," 41.

32. Brown, *Rise of Christendom*, 32.

33. James Skedros, "Christianity, Early: Constantinian Movement," in *Encyclopedia of War and Religion*, ed. Palmer-Fernandez, 74.

34. Henry Chadwick, *The Early Church* (London: Penguin Books, 1993), 125.

35. The number of bishops at the council varies from one source to the next.

36. See Bainton, *Christian Attitudes*, 86–87.

37. Cited in Bainton, *Christian Attitudes*, 88.

38. Bainton, *Christian Attitudes*, 89.

39. See *Byzantine War Ideology between Roman Imperial Concept and Christian Religion*, ed. Johannes Koder and Ioannis Stouraitis (Vienna: Österreichischen Akademie der Wissenschaften2012); John Haldon, *Warfare, State and Society in the Byzantine World, 565–1204* (London: Routledge, 1999), 13–33; and Tia Kolbaba, "Fighting for Christianity: Holy War in the Byzantine Empire," *Byzantion* 68 (1998): 194–221.

40. Haldon, *Warfare, State and Society*, 32.

41. See Henri-Irénée Marrou, *Saint-Augustin et la fin de la culture antique* (Paris: De Broccard, 1958); Herbert Deane, *The Political and Social Ideas of St Augustine* (New York: Columbia University Press, 1963); and Markus A. Robert, "Saint-Augustine's Views on the 'Just War,'" in *The Church and War*, ed. W. J. Sheils (London: Basil Blackwell, 1983), 1–13.

42. Louis J. Swift, "St. Ambrose on Violence and War." *Transactions and Proceedings of the American Philological Association* 101 (1970): 533.

43. Michael Walzer, *Just and Unjust Wars* (New York: Basic Books, 1977), 21.

44. See Swift, "St. Ambrose," 535.

45. Swift, "St. Ambrose," 536.

46. Cited in Swift, "St. Ambrose," 537.

47. Ernest L. Fortin, "St. Augustine," in *A History of Political Philosophy*, 3rd ed., ed. Leo Strauss and Joseph Cropsey (Chicago: University of Chicago Press, 1987), 176.

48. Fortin, "St. Augustine," 203.

49. Francis Fukuyama, *The End of History and the Last Man* (New York: Free Press, 1992).

50. Fortin, "St Augustine," 183.

51. Fortin, "St Augustine," 200.

52. Cicero, *De officiis* (Cambridge, MA: Harvard University Press, Loeb Classical Library, 1913), 1.7.

53. Quoted by Bainton, *Christian Attitudes*, 93.

54. Bainton, *Christian Attitudes*, 95–96.

55. See Charles Irénée Castel de Saint-Pierre, *A Project for Settling an Everlasting Peace in Europe* (London: J. Watts, [1714]).

56. Bainton, *Christian Attitudes*, 97.

57. John Langan, "The Elements of St Augustine's Just War Theory," *Journal of Religious Ethics* 12, 1 (Spring 1984): 19–38.

58. See Willam V. O'Brien, *The Conduct of Just and Limited War* (New York: Praeger, 1983); Reinhold Niehbuhr, *Moral Man and Immoral Society: A Study in Ethics and Politics* (New York: Scribner, 1932); and J. Bryan Hehir, Michael Walzer et al., *Liberty and Power* (Washington, DC: Brookings Institution Press, 2004).

59. Chadwick, *Early Church*, 231.

60. "For the past 2500 years—even in the Dark Ages, well before the 'Military Revolution,' and not simply as a result of the Renaissance, the European discovery of the Americas, or the Industrial Revolution—there has been a peculiar practice of Western Warfare, a common foundation and continual way of fighting, that has made Europeans the most deadly soldiers in the history of civilization" (Victor Davis Hanson, *Carnage and Culture: Landmark Battles in the Rise of Western Power* [New York: Random House, 2001], 5]. See also Hanson, *The Western Way of War* (Berkeley: University of California Press, 2009).

61. Contamine, *War*, 3.

62. Contamine, *War*, 260.

63. Cited in Contamine, *War*, 260.

64. Franco Cardini, *La culture de guerre* (Paris: Gallimard, 1982), 19.

65. On the intermeshing of religion and the chivalrous ideal and its origins, see Richard W. Kaeuper, *Holy Warriors: The Religious Ideology of Chivalry* (Philadelphia: University of Pennsylvania Press, 2009), 1–36.

66. See Iaroslav Lebedynsky, *La campagne d'Attila en Gaule: 451 apr. J.-C.* (Clermont-Ferrand: Lemme, 2011), 57–62.

67. See Ian Wood, *The Merovingian Kingdoms, 450–751* (London: Routledge, 2014), 43–45.

68. See Laurent Theis, *Clovis: De l'histoire au mythe* (Brussels: Complexe, 1996)

69. Wood, *Merovingian Kingdoms*, 108–15.

CHAPTER 3. THE EMERGENCE OF ISLAM

1. Chapter epigraph: Ibn Khaldūn, *The Muqaddimah: An Introduction to History*, trans. Franz Rosenthal, ed. N. J. Dawood (Princeton, NJ: Princeton University Press, 1981), 183.

2. John Mearsheimer, *The Tragedy of Great Power Politics* (New York: Norton, 2014), 44–45.

3. Fernand Braudel, *Grammaire des civilisations* (Paris: Arthaud, 1987), 102.

4. Hodgson, *Venture of Islam*, 1: 71.

5. David Cook, *Understanding Jihad* (Oakland: University of California Press, 2015), 5.

6. This historical development was used as an argument by Christians to prove the illegitimacy of Islam. See Thomas Sizgorich, *Violence and Belief in Late Antiquity: Militant Devotion in Christianity and Islam* (Philadelphia: University of Pennsylvania Press, 2009), 2–3.

7. *The Koran*, trans. N. J. Dawood (London: Penguin Classics, 1990), 70, 131.

8. Bernard Lewis, *The Muslim Discovery of Europe* (New York: Norton, 1982), 171–72.

9. See Stephen J. Shoemaker, *Death of a Prophet: The End of Mohammed's Life and the Beginnings of Islam* (Philadelphia: University of Pennsylvania Press, 2011), 18–72.

10. See Peter Brown, *The Rise of Western Christianity: Triumph and Adversity, A.D. 200–1000* (Malden, MA: Wiley-Blackwell, 2013), 3, 267–94.

11. Hodgson, *Venture of Islam*, 125, cites the following religions as following this pattern to varying degrees: Christianity, Zoroastrian Mazdeism, Vaishnavism and Shaivism, Buddhist-influenced neo-Taoism, Jainism, rabbinical Judaism, and Manichaeism.

12. On the Quran and war, see now Reuven Firestone, *Jihad: The Origins of Holy War in Islam* (Oxford: Oxford University Press, 1999), 47–98.

13. *Koran*, trans. Dawood, 37.

14. *Koran*, trans. Dawood, 237–38.

15. *Koran*, trans. Dawood, 29.

16. This is the sura titled "Repentance," the only one that does not begin " In the name of God . . . " *Koran*, trans. Dawood, 133.

17. *Koran*, trans. Dawood, 137.

18. Jean Flori, *Guerre sainte, jihad, croisade: Violence et religion dans le christianisme et l'islam.* (Paris: Seuil, 2002), 82–83.

19. In Gérard Chaliand, *The Art of War in World History: From Antiquity to the Nuclear Age* (Berkeley: University of California Press, 1994), 447.

20. Ibn Khaldūn, *Muqaddimah*, 223–24.

21. *Koran*, trans. Dawood, 102

22. *Koran*, trans. Dawood, 187.

23. *Koran*, trans. Dawood, 196.

24. David Levering Lewis, *God's Crucible: Islam and the Making of Europe, 570 to 1215* (New York: Norton, 2008), xxii–xxiii.

25. Sylvain Gouguenheim, *Aristote au Mont Saint-Michel: Les racines grecques de l'Europe chrétienne* (Paris: Seuil, 2008).

26. Carole Hillenbrand, *The Crusades—Islamic Perspective* (Edinburgh: Edinburgh University Press, 1999).

27. Edward Gibbon, *The History of the Decline and Fall of the Roman Empire* (New York: Harper & Bros., 1837), 932.

28. See, e.g., Franco Cardini, *Europe and Islam* (Oxford: Blackwell, 2001), 3–6.

29. Walter E. Kaegi, *Heraclius, Emperor of Byzantium* (Cambridge: Cambridge University Press, 2003), 17.

30. For full "letter" by Rustam, see Abolqasem Ferdowsi, *Shahnameh*, The Persian Book of Kings, trans. Dick Davis (1997; New York: Viking, 2006), 833.

31. See Abdesselam Cheddadi, *Ibn Khaldûn: L'homme et le théoricien de la civilisation* (Paris: Gallimard, 2006), 299–315.

32. Ibn Khaldūn, *Muqaddimah*, 229.

33. The manuscript was rediscovered by a scholar who translated it and published it in French as *Le livre des ruses: La stratégie politique des Arabes*, trans. René R. Khawam (Paris: Phébus, 1976).

34. Ibn Khaldūn, *Muqaddimah*, 126.

35. Ibn Khaldūn, *Muqaddimah*, 126. The figures given by Ibn Khaldūn probably exaggerate the different size of the armies even if by all accounts the Arabs had a significant quantitative handicap relative to their adversaries.

36. Ibn Khaldūn, *Muqaddimah*, 95.

37. Ibn Khaldūn, *Muqaddimah*, 120.

38. Cardini, *Europe and Islam*, 53.

39. See Jean-Paul Charnay, *L'Islam et la guerre: De la guerre juste à la révolution sainte* (Paris: Fayard, 1986), esp. chap. 3.

40. Ibn Khaldūn, *Muqaddimah*, 224.

41. See *The Cambridge History of Iran*, vol. 4, ed. Richard Nelson Frye (Cambridge: Cambridge University Press, 1975), 11.

CHAPTER 4. TOWARD A CLASH OF CIVILIZATIONS

1. Henri Pirenne, *Mohammed and Charlemagne* (1939; Mineola, NY: Dover, 2001), 284–85.

2. E.g., Brian A. Catlos, *Infidel Kings and Unholy Warriors: Faith, Power, and Violence in the Age of the Crusade and Jihad* (New York: Farrar, Straus & Giroux, 2014), 4.

3. Catlos, *Infidel Kings*, 5.

4. See Peter B. Golden, "The Conversion of the Khazars to Judaism," in Golden, Haggai Ben-Shammai, and András Róna-Tas, *The World of the Khazars* (Leiden: Brill, 2007), 123–62.

5. *The Fathers of the Church. St. John of Damascus: Writings*, trans. Frederic H. Chase Jr. (Washington, DC: Catholic University of America Press, 1958), 153–60.

6. See Katherine Scarfe Beckett, *Anglo-Saxon Perceptions of the Islamic World* (Cambridge: Cambridge University Press, 2003), 44–48, 123–38.

7. Philippe Sénac, *Charlemagne et Mahomet en Espagne (VIIIe–IX siècles)* (Paris: Gallimard, 2015), 25.

8. Sénac, *Charlemagne et Mahomet*, 25.

9. Hugh Kennedy, *The Great Arab Conquests: How the Spread of Islam Changed the World We Live In* (Philadelphia: Da Capo Press, 2007), 329.

10. Kennedy, *Great Arab Conquests*, 330.

11. In Sénac, *Charlemagne et Mahomet*, 117.

12. Pope Leo III, letter to Charlemagne (813), in Sénac, *Charlemagne et Mahomet*, 292.

13. Kennedy, *Great Arab Conquests*, 335.

14. Ibn Khaldūn, *Muqaddimah*, 209–10

15. Jacques Le Goff, dir., *L'homme médiéval* (Paris: Seuil, 1989), 14.

16. In Flori, *Guerre sainte*, 295–96. "He will have died for the truth of the faith, the salvation of the homeland, and the defense of the Christians," another version states. "This is why, as a consequence, he will receive from him the aforementioned reward."

17. See Tomaž Mastnak, *Crusading Peace: Christendom, the Muslim World and Western Political Order* (Berkeley: University of California Press, 2002), 2–9. See, too, *The Peace of God: Social Violence and Religious Response in France around the Year 1000*, ed. Thomas Head and Richard Landes (Ithaca, NY: Cornell University Press, 1992).

18. Flori, *Guerre sainte*, 160–66.

19. H. E. J. Cowdrey, "The Peace and the Truce of God in the Eleventh Century," *Past and Present* 46, 1 (February 1, 1970): 42.

20. Contamine, *War in the Middle Ages*, 271.

21. Flori, *Guerre sainte*, 166–167.

22. Flori, *Guerre sainte*, 168.

23. The story is told by André de Fleury in *Miracula sancti Benedicti: Les miracles de saint Benoît écrits par Adrevald, Aimoin, André Raoul Tortaire et Hugues de Sainte-Marie, moines de Fleury*, ed. Eugène de Certain (Paris: Paris: Ve J. Renouard, 1858), 5.1–5.

24. Flori, *Guerre sainte*, 186.

25. Flori, *Guerre sainte*, 139.

26. Alessandro Barbero, *Charlemagne, Father of a Continent*, trans. Allan Cameron (Berkeley: University of California Press, 2004), 47.

27. Barbero, *Charlemagne*, 47.

28. Twelve years later, with the *capitulare Saxonicum*, Charlemagne eased up these punishments, and the death penalty was replaced by more lenient measures.

29. Barbero, *Charlemagne*, 261.

30. Contamine, *War in the Middle Ages*, 273.

31. Flori, *Guerre sainte*, 148.

32. Thomas Asbridge, *The First Crusade: A New History* (Oxford: Oxford University Press, 2004), 2.

33. See João Marques de Almeida "The Peace of Westphalia and the Idea of *Respublica Christiana*" (Lisbon: Instituto Português de Relações Internacionais, 2007), https://web.archive.org/web/20070107102904/http://www.ipri.pt:80/investiga-dores/artigo.php?idi=5&ida=29.

34. See Mark Mazower, *Governing the World: The History of an Idea, 1815 to the Present* (London: Penguin Books, 2012), 116–28; Stephen R. Weart, *Never at War: Why Democracies Will Not Fight One Another* (New Haven, CT: Yale University Press, 1998), 13–23; and Michael Doyle, "Liberalism and World Politics," *American Political Science Review* 80, 4 (December 1986), 1151–69.

35. Jonathan Riley-Smith, *The Crusades: A History* (New Haven, CT: Yale University Press, 2005), xxx.

36. See Vicki Tamir, *Bulgaria and Her Jews: The History of a Dubious Symbiosis* (New York: Sepher-Hermon Press for Yeshiva University Press, 1979).

37. See Michel Balard, *Les Latins en Orient, XIe–XVIe siècles* (Paris: Presses universitaires de France, 2006), and id., "Gênes, Amalfi, Venise: Le triomphe des républiques maritimes," *L'Histoire* 156 (July–August 1992): 64–69.

38. René Grousset, *L'épopée des croisades* (1929; Paris: Perrin, 2002), 18–20. Translated by Noël Lindsay as *The Epic of the Crusades* (New York: Orion Press, 1970).

39. See Lewis, *Muslim Discovery of Europe*, 59–69.

40. *The Chronicle of Ibn al-Athir for the Crusading Period from al-Khamil fi'l-Ta'rikh*, Part I, translated by D. S. Richards (2005; Burlington, VT: Ashgate, 2010), 13–14.

41. Cited by Flori, *Guerre sainte*, 308.

42. See Michel Balard, *Autour de la première croisade: Colloque de Clermont-Ferrand, 22–25 juin 1995* (Paris: La Sorbonne, 1996).

43. Cited by Riley-Smith, *Crusades*, xxxiii.

44. Contamine, *War in the Middle Ages*, 296.

45. This topic has been thoroughly examined by various historians and philosophers. See, e.g., Raymond Aron's remarkable *Introduction to the Philosophy of History: An Essay on the Limits of Historical Objectivity*, trans. G. J. Irwin (Boston: Beacon Press, 1961).

46. Ibn Khaldūn, *Muqaddimah*, 132. Emphasis in source.

47. See Max Scheler, *Ressentiment*, trans. William Holdheim (New York: Schocken Books, 1972).

48. Thomas Hobbes, *Leviathan* (London: Penguin Books, 1983), 186.

49. Gregory VII, *Registrum epistolarum*, 2: 37, Monumenta Germaniae Historica, *Epistolae selectae*, ed. E. Caspar, 5.1 (Turnhout: Brepols, 2010), 175.

50. Jay Rubenstein, *Armies of Heaven: The First Crusade and the Quest for Apocalypse* (New York: Basic Books, 2011), 1.

51. Foucher de Chartres, *Historia Hierosolymitana*, in Alain Demurger, *Les Templiers: Une chevalerie chrétienne au Moyen âge* (Paris: Seuil, 2014), 20.

52. For an analysis of the speech and a review of the various sources around it, see Jean Flori, *Pierre L'Ermite et la première croisade* (Paris: Fayard, 1999), 153–77.

53. In Rubenstein, *Armies of Heaven*, 27.

54. "Itinéraire de Bernard, moine franc," in *Croisades et pélerinages: Récits, Chroniques et voyages en terre sainte, XIIe –XVIe siècle*, ed. Danielle Régnier-Bohler (Paris: Robert Laffont, coll. Bouquins, 1997), 923.

55. Cited by Rubenstein, *Armies of Heaven*, 6–7.

CHAPTER 5. THE MIDDLE EASTERN CRUSADES

1. Nicholas Morton, "Was the First Crusade Really a War against Islam?" *History Today* 67, no. 3 (March 2017): 16; and id., *Encountering Islam on the First Crusade* (Cambridge: Cambridge University Press, 2016).

2. Bernard Lewis, *The Assassins: A Radical Sect in Islam* (New York: Basic Books, 2003), 134.

3. Ali ibn al-Athīr (1160–1233), *al-Kāmil fit-Tārīkh* (Complete History),10.185, cited in Francesco Gabrieli, *Chroniques arabes des croisades* (Paris: Actes Sud, 1996), 42–43.

4. Grousset, *L'épopée des croisades*, 18–20.

5. The account, written a few years after the fact, is from Albert of Aachen's *Historia Hyerosolimita*, cited in August Krey, *The First Crusade: The Accounts of Eyewitnesses and Participants* (Princeton, NJ: Princeton University Press, 1921), 55.

6. Rubenstein, *Armies of Heaven*, 49.

7. *The Chronicle of Ibn al-Athir for the Crusading Period*, 16–17.

8. Rubenstein, *Armies of Heaven*, 240.

9. Joshua Prawer, *The Latin Kingdom of Jerusalem: European Colonialism in the Middle Ages* (London: Weidenfeld & Nicholson, 1972).

10. Grousset, *L'épopée des croisades*, 116.

11. Anne-Marie Eddé, *Saladin*. Translated by Jane Marie Todd (Cambridge, MA: Belknap Press of Harvard University Press, 2010), 20–21.

12. William of Adam, *How to Defeat the Saracens*, trans. Giles Constable (Washington, DC: Dumbarton Oaks Research Library and Collection, 2012), 75, 77, 85. Written around 1315, after the Near Eastern Crusades had ended.

13. Saladin's accession to this post was not an easy affair, however and many negotiations took place behind the scenes before he was able to claim the prize. Many around Nūr ad-Dīn saw Saladin's rise as potentially dangerous, but Nūr ad-Dīn's own attitude is unclear. He may or may not have grown distrustful of Saladin, or of his father and uncle before that, depending on which historian or chronicler one reads. See Eddé, *Saladin*, 34–46.

14. Cited by Eddé, *Saladin*, 91.

15. In Eddé, *Saladin*, 169.

16. In Eddé, *Saladin*, 172.

17. Desmond Seward, *Monks of War: The Military Religious Orders* (London: Penguin Books, 1972).

18. The Templars and Teutonic Knights, however, were trained as soldiers. The Templars were officially created as an independent order in 1119–20, under the direct authority of Rome. The Order of the Teutonic Knights emerged a little later, around

1189, during the siege of Acre. The Hospitallers progressed from a small hospital to an independent order during the first half of the twelfth century. They have survived to this day as the Order of Malta.

19. Ibn al-Athīr in Gabrieli, *Chroniques*, 146.

20. *Chronique d'Ernoul et de Bernard le Trésorier* (Paris: Renouard, 1871), 469.

21. Gabrieli, *Chroniques*, 159.

22. Ibn al-Athīr in Gabrieli, *Chroniques*,151.

23. Ibn al-Athīr in Gabrieli, *Chroniques*,151.

24. There are various accounts of the dramatic scene, with Saladin either beheading Châtillon or cutting off his arm, or having a third party do it. What is certain is that Châtillon died either on the spot or quickly from the blow.

25. Ibn al-Athīr, *al-Kāmil fit-Tārīkh*, 2.324, in Gabrieli, *Chroniques*, 152.

26. Cited in Eddé, *Saladin*, 363.

27. Peter Partner, *God of Battles: Holy Wars of Christianity and Islam* (New York: Harper Collins, 1997), 112.

28. Partner, *God of Battles*, 112.

29. Francis Fukuyama, *The Origins of Political Order: From Prehuman Times to the French Revolution* (New York: Farrar, Straus & Giroux, 2011), 201–3.

CHAPTER 6. THE CRUSADING SPIRIT LIVES ON

1. The emirate of Córdoba reached its apogee in the tenth century under Abd al-Rahman III (912–61). In 929, following its separation from the Abbasid Caliphate, the it became a full-fledged caliphate. Córdoba, with 200,000 inhabitants and a vibrant economic and cultural life, was then Europe's most advanced city. By the beginning of the eleventh century, however, the caliphate disintegrated into a constellation of about twenty rival political entities, the Taïfas. This fragmentation opened the doors for the Christians to regain the territories lost to the Muslims.

2. Contamine, *War in the Middle Ages*, 297.

3. Count Henry of Burgundy fought alongside the Spaniards, married the king of León and Castile's daughter, and was appointed governor of the county of Portugal, then part of León, by his father-in-law. In 1139, his son Afonso Henriques became king of the new kingdom of Portugal.

4. Ibn Khaldūn, *Le livre des exemples* (Paris: Gallimard, Bibliothèque de la Pléiade, 2002), 1: 423.

5. Marshall G. Hodgson, *The Venture of Islam*, vol. 2: *The Expansion of Islam in the Middle Periods* (Chicago: University of Chicago Press, 1977), 483.

6. The Almohads were forced to retreat to North Africa where they were crushed by local rivals. Marrakech fell to the Marinids in 1269.

7. Bartolomé de las Casas, *A Short Account of the Destruction of the Indies* (London: Penguin Classics, 1999).

8. E.g., Paul Alphandéry and Alphonse Dupront, *La Chrétienté et l'idée de croisade* (1954–59; Paris: Albin Michel, 1995).

9. Demurger, *Templiers*, 45.

10. Demurger, *Templiers*, 45. Historians have tried to show that the model of the Templars may have been based or influenced by the "warrior-monk" model found in the Muslim world with the notion of the *ribāt* and the *murabitūn*, but there is little proof that a practice found in Spain may have migrated to the Near East, where the Templars were founded. See Elena Lourie, "The Confraternity of Belchite, the Ribāt, and the Temple," *Viator* 13 (1982): 159–78, and María-Milagros Rivera Garretas, "El origen de la idea de Orden Militar en la historiografía reciente," *Acta historica et archaeologica mediaevalia* (Barcelona), no. 1 (1990): 77–90.

11. On the creation of the order, see Malcolm Barber, *The New Knighthood: A History of the Order of the Temple* (Cambridge: Cambridge University Press, 2012), 1–37.

12. In *The Templars: Selected Sources*, trans. and ed. Malcolm Barber and Keith Bate (Manchester: Manchester University Press, 2002), 216–17.

13. William of Tyre, "Fondation de l'ordre des templiers," in *Chroniques*, bk. 12, ed. Régnier-Bohler, 557.

14. Demurger, *Templiers*, 273–88.

15. William of Tyre, "Fondation" (cited n. 13 above), in *Chroniques*, 557–558.

16. William of Tyre, "Le roi livre bataille vers Ramla avec peu de forces et remporte la victoire. Evocation des Mamelouks," in *Chroniques*, bk. 21, ed. Régnier-Bohler, 699–700.

17. William of Tyre, in Demurger, *Templiers*, 263.

18. Demurger, *Templiers*, 266–67.

19. Société de l'Orient latin, *Quinti belli sacri scriptores minores*, ed. Reinhold Röhricht (Geneva: Fick, 1879), 1: 110.

20. The story of the Inquisition runs parallel to that of the Crusades and can be traced back to Roman legal procedure. See Edward Peters, *Inquisition* (Berkeley: University of California Press, 1989).

21. See *The Cathars and the Albigensian Crusade: A Sourcebook*, ed. Catherine Léglu, Rebecca Rist, and Claire Taylor (London: Routledge, 2014), 32–72.

22. Michel Roquebert, *Histoire des Cathares: Hérésie, croisade, Inquisition du XIe au XIVe siècle* (Paris: Perrin, 2002), 51.

23. Roquebert, *Histoire*, 53.

24. Lawrence W. Marvin, *The Occitan War: A Military and Political History of the Albigensian Crusade, 1209–1218* (Cambridge: Cambridge University Press, 2008), 2.

25. In Roquebert, *Histoire*, 62. See also Michael Costen, *The Cathars and the Albigensian Crusade* (New York: Manchester University Press, 1997), 103.

26. The expression is from chronicler William of Puylaurens. Guillaume de Puylaurens, *Chronique: Chronika magistri Guillelmi de Podio Laurentii* (Paris: Centre National de la Recherche Scientifique, 1976).

27. Roquebert, *Histoire*, 77, contends, however, that the Cathars were probably fewer than half the population of the Languedoc region.

28. *The History of the Albigensian Crusade: Peter of les Vaux-de-Cernay's "Historia Albigensis,"* trans. W. A. and M. D. Sibly (Rochester, NY: Boydell Press, 2002).

29. Cited by Roquebert, *Histoire*, 113.

30. Quoted in Roquebert, *Histoire*, 143.

31. The number, unsubstantiated, may just mean that a lot of people were massacred. Roquebert, *Histoire*, 136.

32. Clausewitz, *On War*, 89.

33. Caleb Carr, *The Lessons of Terror: A History of Warfare against Civilians* (New York: Random House, 2003), 61–62.

34. Marvin, *Occitan War*, 308, stresses the importance of the territorial conflict that dominated the war, but cautions against overstating it.

35. Notably by Heinrich von Treitschke. See *Treitschke's Origins of Prussianism: The Teutonic Knights* (Abingdon, England: Routledge, 2013).

36. Sylvain Gouguenheim, *Les chevaliers teutoniques* (Paris: Tallandier, 2007, 2013) is the chief source for this used in this book; see 19–39 on the order's origins.

37. In Gouguenheim, *Chevaliers teutoniques*, 43.

38. The Cumans were part of the Cuman-Kipchak Federation and by association are sometimes also called Kipchaks.

39. Gouguenheim, *Chevaliers teutoniques*, 56.

40. Gouguenheim, *Chevaliers teutoniques*, 65.

41. Gouguenheim, *Chevaliers teutoniques*, 68.

42. Gouguenheim, *Chevaliers teutoniques*, 139.

43. The document is reproduced in Gouguenheim, *Chevaliers teutoniques*, 173–74.

44. Gouguenheim, *Chevaliers teutoniques*,208

45. By 1400, however, there were 140,000 Old Prussians. They were subsequently either Germanized or migrated east to Lithuania.

46. Roger Bacon, *Opus Majus*, ed. John Henry Bridges (Oxford: Clarendon Press, 1897–1900), 3: 13 and 7: 4. Gouguenheim, *Chevaliers teutoniques*, 475.

47. Gouguenheim, *Chevaliers teutoniques*,215.

48. Gouguenheim, *Chevaliers teutoniques*, 226.

49. On the Baltic Crusade, see Eric Christiansen, *The Northern Crusades: The Baltic and the Catholic Frontier, 1100–1525* (New York: Macmillan, 1980).

50. The Teutonic Knights were on the Prussian frontier as early as 1228. William Urban, *The Prussian Crusade* (Lanham, MD: University Press of America, 1980), 105.

51. Seward, *Monks of War*, 104.

52. Gouguenheim, *Chevaliers teutoniques*, 320.

53. In Gouguenheim, *Chevaliers teutoniques*, 411.

54. Gouguenheim, *Chevaliers teutoniques*, 413.

55. C. W. C. Oman, *The Art of War in the Middle Ages* (Ithaca, NY: Cornell University Press, 1953), 67.

56. A total of 5,751 hired soldiers were paid July 10, 1410, out of a total of 12,000 to 15,000, though not all were present on the battlefield. Gouguenheim, *Chevaliers teutoniques*, 475–77.

57. See Sven Ekdahl, "Horses and Crossbows: Two Important Warfare Advantages of the Teutonic Order in Prussia," in *The Military Orders*, vol. 2: *Welfare and Warfare*, ed. Helen Nicholson (Brookfield, VT: Ashgate, 1998), 119–51.

58. Contamine, *War in the Middle Ages*, 219.

59. Contamine, *War in the Middle Ages*, 274.

60. The battle is depicted in great fictional detail in Henryk Sienkiewicz's nineteenth-century novel *The Knights of the Cross*, also titled *The Teutonic Knights* (New York: Hippocrene Books, 1993).

61. Gouguenheim, *Chevaliers teutoniques*, 476.

62. Seward, *Monks of War*, 118.

63. Gouguenheim, *Chevaliers teutoniques*, 488–93.

64. Gouguenheim, *Chevaliers teutoniques*, 494.

65. See Gregory M. Reichbert, "Thomas Aquinas between Just War and Pacifism," *Journal of Religious Ethics* 38, no. 2 (June 2010): 219–41.

66. Thomas Aquinas, *The Summa Theologica*, trans. Fathers of the English Dominican province, vol. 2 (New York: Benzinger Brothers, 1947), chap. 40.

67. Gregory M. Reichbert, *Thomas Aquinas on War and Peace* (Cambridge: Cambridge University Press, 2017), 257–82.

CHAPTER 7. FROM HOLY WAR TO ALL-OUT RELIGIOUS WAR

1. Michel Lesure, *Lépante: La crise de l'Empire ottoman* (Paris: Gallimard, 2013), 31.

2. Raimondo Montecuccoli, *Mémoires de Montecuculi, generalissime des troupes de l'empereur* (Amsterdam: Wetstein, 1752). See also Hervé Coutau-Bégarie, *Traité de stratégie* (Paris: Economica, 1999), 168–69, and Martin Van Creveld, *The Art of War: War and Military Thought* (Washington, DC: Smithsonian Books/Collins, 2005), 75–79.

3. "I am one sent from God, to punish an iniquitous generation of men," Nader Shah once claimed. Michael Axworthy, *The Sword of Persia* (London: I. B. Tauris, 2006), 251.

4. Riley-Smith, *Crusades*, 267.

5. Denis Crouzet, *Les guerriers de Dieu: La violence au temps des troubles de religion, vers 1525–vers 1610* (Paris: Champ Vallon, 1990), 50–51.

6. The king of France, Jean le Bon, who had been taken prisoner by the English at the battle of Poitiers in 1356, six years earlier, but had been allowed to leave England in 1360 to raise the funds to pay for his ransom, while his son Louis took his place, responded to the appeal. However, Louis escaped in 1363, and King Jean chose to surrender himself to meet the terms of his parole, so he was unable to join the expedition Pierre de Lusignan had proposed to retake Jerusalem. Jean died in captivity in 1364 of unknown causes.

7. Riley-Smith, *Crusades*, 269.

8. Exemplified by Žižka's depiction of his wars as a religious quest in which he was divinely ordained to purify the world of its sins. See Victor Verney, *Warrior of God: Jan Žižka and the Hussite Revolution* (London: Frontline Books, 2009), 186.

9. William H. McNeill's *The Pursuit of Power: Technology, Armed Force, and Society since A.D. 1000* (Chicago: University of Chicago Press, 1982), e.g., has practically nothing to say about the impact of religion on the transformation of war.

10. Antoine Marès, *Histoire des Tchèques et des Slovaques* (Paris: Perrin, 2005), 107–8.

11. See Marsilius of Padua, "The Defender of the Peace," in *Medieval Political Philosophy*, ed. Ralph Lerner and Muhsin Mahdi (Ithaca, NY: Cornell University Press, 1991), 439–91.

12. See Thomas A. Fudge, *The Crusade against Heretics in Bohemia, 1418–1437: Sources and Documents for the Hussite Crusades* (Aldershot, England: Ashgate, 2002).

13. For full text, see http://verneyo.wixsite.com/victor-verney/hussite-battle-song.

14. Cited by Norman Housley, *Religious Warfare in Europe 1400–1536* (Oxford: Oxford University Press, 2009), 165.

15. See Housley, *Religious Warfare*, 191–93.

16. http://verneyo.wixsite.com/victor-verney/statutes-and-military-ordinance.

17. Housley, *Religious Warfare*, 34.

18. Verney, *Warrior of God*, 78.

19. See the official strategic blueprint "The Military Rule of Jan Žižka and the Hussite Armies" (Summer 1423), in Fudge, *Crusade*, 167–71.

20. Fudge, *Crusade*, 374–78.

21. See Seward, *Monks of War*, 133–147.

22. Denis Crouzet, *Dieu en ses royaumes* (Paris: Champ Vallon, 2008), 43.

23. Pierre Chaunu, *Colomb ou La logique de l'imprévisible* (Paris: F. Bourin, 1993), 104–6.

24. Crouzet, *Dieu en ses royaumes*, 44.

25. Cited by Crouzet, *Dieu en ses royaumes*, 43.

26. For a critical analysis of the events and of the various explanations for the Spanish victory, see Hanson, *Carnage and Culture*, 208–32.

27. Bernal Díaz del Castillo, *The Conquest of New Spain* (London: Penguin Classics, 1963).

28. For the two perspectives, see Gérard Chaliand, *Mirrors of a Disaster: The Spanish Military Conquest of the Americas* (Abingdon, England: Routledge, 2005), and Matthew Restall, *When Montezuma Met Cortés* (New York: Harper Collins, 2018).

29. Henri Hubert and Marcel Mauss, "Sacrifice: Its Nature and Function," in *Princeton Readings in Religion and Violence*, ed. Juergensmeyer and Kitts, 110.

30. Hanson, *Carnage and Culture*, 213–16.

31. Hanson, *Carnage and Culture*, 216.

32. Bernal Díaz del Castillo, *La Conquête du Mexique* (Arles: Actes Sud, 1996), 16.

CHAPTER 8. IN THE NAME OF GOD: RELIGIOUS WARFARE IN
EUROPE, 1524–1700

1. Chapter epigraph: Jean Giono, preface to Blaise de Montluc, *Commentaires, 1521–1576* (Paris: Gallimard, Bibliothèque de la Pléiade, 1964), ix (translated by the author).

2. Using a strict definition of religious war, the German historian Konrad Repgen suggests that between 1524 and 1689, between a dozen and a half to two dozen wars

can qualify as "religious wars." Konrad K. Repgen, "What Is a 'Religious War'?" in *Politics and Society in Reformation Europe*, ed. E. I. Kouri and T. Scott (London: Macmillan, 1987), 312.

3. See David El Kenz and Claire Gantet, *Guerres et paix de religion en Europe aux 16e–17e siècles* (Paris: Armand Colin, 2003), 4–5.

4. Yuval Noah Harari, e.g., regards modern secular ideologies as conforming to his definition of religion, meaning that many of the wars of the modern era also qualify as religious conflicts. Harari, *Sapiens*, 249–63.

5. Alexis de Tocqueville, *The Old Regime and the Revolution* (1856; New York: Doubleday, 1983), 10–14.

6. Crouzet, *Dieu en ses royaumes*, 77.

7. Preserved Smith, *The Life and Letters of Martin Luther* (1900; 2nd ed., Boston: Houghton Mifflin, 1968), 72.

8. The *Edict et Déclaration du Roy sur les precedens Edicts de pacification* was adopted on April 30, 1598. It resulted from almost ten years of difficult negotiations and was preceded by seven other texts, the first dating from 1562. See Bernard Cottret, *L'édit de Nantes: Pour en finir avec les guerres de religion* (1997; Paris: Perrin, 2016).

9. Martin Luther, *On War against the Turks*, in *Luther's Works*, vol. 46: *Christian in Society III*, ed. Helmut T. Lehmann and Robert C. Schutz (Philadephia: Fortress Press, 1967).

10. Erasmus, *Institutio principis christiani*, trans. N. M. Cheshire and J. M. Heath, ed. A. H. T. Levi, in *Collected Works of Erasmus: Literary and Educational Writings*, vol. 6 (Toronto: University of Toronto Press, 2016), *xxvii*, 287.

11. Lesure, *Lépante*, 166. See also Alessandro Barbero, *Lepanto: La bataglia dei tre imperi* (Rome: Editori Laterza, 2012).

12. Arnaud Blin, *Les batailles qui ont changé l'histoire* (Paris: Perrin, 2016), 294.

13. *Essays of Montaigne*, trans. Charles Cotton (London: Reeves & Turner, 1877), bk. 1, essay 31.

14. See *The Thirty Years' War*, ed. Geoffrey Parker (Abingdon, England: Routledge, 1987), 160–69.

15. El Kenz and Gantet, *Guerres et paix*, 16.

16. Cathal J. Nolan, ed., *The Age of Wars and Religion, 1500–1650. A Global Encyclopedia of Warfare and Civilization* (Westport, CT: Greenwood Press, 2006), 346–347.

17. Cited in Housley, *Religious Warfare*, 194.

18. Repgen, "What Is a 'Religious War'?" 323.

19. El Kenz and Gantet, *Guerres et paix*, 55.

20. Owen Chadwick, *The Reformation* (London: Penguin Books, 1990), 130.

21. Denis Crouzet, "Huit guerres en trente-six ans," *La Vie*, special issue, *Les guerres de religion—Du XVIe siècle au djihadisme*, June 2019, 30.

22. Mack P. Holt suggests that the king did not plan the massacre. Holt, *The French Wars of Religion, 1562–1629* (Cambridge: Cambridge University Press), 90.

23. See Denis Crouzet, *La nuit de la Saint-Barthélémy* (Paris: Fayard, 2012).

24. Gabriel Palmer-Fernandez, "Tyrranicide, Medieval Catholic Doctrine of," in *Encyclopedia of Religion and War*, ed. id., 433–36.

25. Crouzet, *Guerriers de Dieu*, 394.

26. Pierre Blet, "Le rôle du saint-Siège," in *Les Fondements de la Paix: Des origines au début du XVIIIe siècle*, ed. Pierre Chaunu (Paris: Presses universitaires de France, 1993), 126.

27. El Kenz and Gantet, *Guerres et paix*, 101.

28. El Kenz and Gantet, *Guerres et paix*, 601.

29. Pierre de L'Estoile, *Journal de L'Estoile pour le règne de Henri IV et le début du règne de Louis XIII, 1610–1611*, vol. 3 in *Œuvres diverses*, ed. Louis Raymond Lefèvre and André Martin (Paris: Gallimard, 1960), 82.

30. Holt, *French Wars of Religion*, 199–216.

31. Pierre Chaunu, *La civilisation de L'Europe classique* (Paris: Arthaud, 1970), 43.

32. See Georges Livet, *La guerre de Trente ans* (1963; Paris: Presses universitaires de France, 1994), 47–71.

33. Henry Bogdan, *La guerre de Trente ans* (Paris: Perrin, 1997), 276.

34. Bogdan, *Guerre de Trente ans*, 276–77.

35. Bogdan, *Guerre de Trente ans*, 278.

36. Hans Jacob Cristoffel von Grimmelshausen, *Simplicius Simplicissimus* (1668/69; London: John Calder, 1964)

37. Quoted in Lotte Jensen, *The Roots of Nationalism: National Identity Formation in Early Modern Europe, 1600–1815* (Amsterdam: Amsterdam University Press, 2016), 221.

38. Carl Schmitt, *The Nomos of the Earth in the International Law of the Jus Publicum Europaeum*, trans. G. L. Ulmen (New York: Telos Press, 2006), 160.

39. Jean Bodin, *Les six livres de la république* (Paris, 1576), abridged in English under the title *On Sovereignty: Four Chapters from Six Books on the Commonwealth*, ed. and trans. Julian H. Franklin (Cambridge: Cambridge University Press, 1992).

40. See Leo Gross, "The Peace of Westphalia, 1648–1948," *American Journal of International Law* 42, no. 1 (January 1948): 20–41.

41. See Max Weber, *The Protestant Ethic and the Spirit of Capitalism* (1905; London: Penguin Books, 2002).

42. See esp. Geoffrey Parker, *The Military Revolution: Military Innovation and the Rise of the West, 1500–1800* (Cambridge: Cambridge University Press, 1996), and John Nef, *War and Human Progress: An Essay on the Rise of Industrial Civilization* (New York: Norton, 1968). On the military revolution debate itself, see *The Military Revolution Debate: Readings on the Military Transformation of Early Modern Europe*, ed. Clifford J. Rogers (Boulder, CO: Westview Press, 1995).

43. E.g., in Voltaire, *Candide* (1759), chaps. 2 and 3.

44. See *War and Religion after Westphalia, 1648–1713*, ed. David Onnekink (London: Routledge, 2009), 7.

45. El Kenz and Gantet, *Guerres et paix*, 138.

46. John Morrill, *The Nature of the English Revolution* (Abingdon, England: Routledge, 2013), 14.

47. Daniel Defoe, *The Danger of the Protestant religion considered, from the present prospect of a religious war in Europe* (London, 1701).

48. Alexis de Tocqueville, *Democracy in America* (1835–40), trans. Arthur Goldhammer (New York: Library of America, 2004).

49. Thomas Jefferson, *Statute for Establishing Religious Freedom in Virginia*, drafted in 1777 and enacted into law on January 16, 1786.

CHAPTER 9. RELIGIOUS VIOLENCE IN A SECULAR WORLD

1. Chapter epigraph: Khomeini quoted in Roy Mottahedeh, *The Mantel and the Prophet: Religion and Politics in Iran* (New York: Pantheon Books, 1985), 243. On the development of secularism, see Charles Taylor, *A Secular Age* (Cambridge, MA: Harvard University Press, 2007).

2. Hannah Arendt, *On Revolution* (New York: Penguin Books, 1987), 184.

3. Douglas Porch, *Wars of Empire* (Washington, DC: Smithsonian Books, 2006), 148.

4. See George Bruce, *The Stranglers: The Cult of Thuggee and Its Overthrow in British India* (New York: Harcourt, Brace & World, 1969).

5. David A. Bell, *The Cult of the Nation in France: Inventing Nationalism, 1680—1800* (Cambridge, MA: Harvard University Press, 2001), 24.

6. Stephen R. Platt, *Autumn in the Heavenly Kingdom: China, the West, and the Epic Story of the Taiping Civil War* (New York: Knopf, 2012), 358.

7. For a good summary of the crises of the period, see Jonathan D. Spence, *The Search for Modern China* (New York: Norton, 1999), 165–93.

8. See Annette Becker, *Le génocide des Arméniens: Un siècle de recherche, 1915–2015* (Paris: Armand Colin, 2015), esp. chaps. 2 and 7; Ronald Grigor Suny, *"They can Live in the Desert but Nowhere Else": A History of the Armenian Genocide* (Princeton, NJ: Princeton University Press, 2015); Gérard Chaliand, *The Armenians: From Genocide to Resistance* (London: Zed Press, 1983).

9. See Emmanuel Sivan, *Radical Islam: Medieval Theology and Modern Politics* (New Haven, CT: Yale University Press, 1990).

10. ISIS and Boko Haram have targeted communities that live in the areas they control, or close by, including Christians, Yazidis, and other Muslims.

11. As Michael Cook demonstrates, however, religious identity is comparatively stronger in the Muslim world than in other regions like India and Latin America. Michael Cook, *Ancient Religions, Modern Politics: The Islamic Case in Comparative Perspective* (Princeton, NJ: Princeton University Press, 2014), 3–52.

CHAPTER 10. OF GODS AND MEN

1. See Rupert Emerson, *From Empire to Nation: The Rise to Self-assertion of Asian and African Peoples* (Cambridge, MA: Harvard University Press, 1960).

SUGGESTED READINGS

Adam, William of. *How to Defeat the Saracens.* Translated by Giles Constable. Washington, DC: Dumbarton Oaks Research Library and Collection, 2012.

Asbridge, Thomas. *The First Crusade: A New History.* Oxford: Oxford University Press, 2004.

Bainton, Roland H. *Christian Attitudes towards War and Peace: A Historical Survey and Critical Re-Evaluation.* Nashville, TN: Abingdon Press, 1960.

Barber, Malcolm. *The New Knighthood: A History of the Order of the Temple* Cambridge: Cambridge University Press, 2012.

Barbero, Alessandro. *Charlemagne, Father of a Continent.* Translated by Allan Cameron. Berkeley: University of California Press, 2004.

Brown, Peter. *The Rise of Christendom.* New York: Blackwell, 1997.

———. *The Rise of Western Christianity: Triumph and Adversity, A.D. 200–1000.* Chichester: John Wiley, 2013.

Buc, Philippe. *Holy War, Martyrdom, and Terror. Christianity, Violence and the West.* Philadelphia: University of Pennsylvania Press, 2015.

Cardini, Franco. *Europe and Islam.* Oxford: Blackwell, 2001.

———. *Quella antica festa crudele: Guerra e cultura della guerra dal Medioevo alla Rivoluzione francese.* Milan: Mondadori, 1997.

Catlos, Brian A. *Infidel Kings and Unholy Warriors: Faith, Power, and Violence in the Age of the Crusade and Jihad.* New York: Farrar, Straus & Giroux, 2014.

Chadwick, Henry. *The Early Church.* London: Penguin Books, 1993.

Chadwick, Owen. *The Reformation.* London: Penguin Books, 1990.

Chaliand, Gérard. *The Art of War in World History: From Antiquity to the Nuclear Age.* Berkeley: University of California Press, 1994.

Cicero, Marcus Tullius. *De officiis.* Cambridge, MA: Harvard University Press, Loeb Classical Library, 1913.

Clausewitz, Carl von. *On War*. Edited and translated by Michael Howard and Peter Paret. Princeton, NJ: Princeton University Press, 1976.

Contamine, Philippe. *War in the Middle Ages*. New York: Basil Blackwell, 1986.

Cook, David. *Understanding Jihad*. Oakland: University of California Press, 2015.

Cook, Michael. *Ancient Religions, Modern Politics: The Islamic Case in Comparative Perspective*. Princeton, NJ: Princeton University Press, 2014.

Crouzet, Denis. *Les guerriers de Dieu: La violence au temps des troubles de religion, vers 1525–vers 1610*. Paris: Champ Vallon, 1990.

The Dead Sea Scrolls in English. Translated by Géza Vermès. Baltimore: Penguin Books, 1962.

Deane, Herbert. *The Political and Social Ideas of St Augustine*. New York: Columbia University Press, 1963.

Defoe, Daniel. *The Danger of the Protestant Religion Considered from the Present Prospect of a Religious War in Europe*. London, 1701.

Demurger, Alain. *Les Templiers: Une chevalerie chrétienne au Moyen âge*. Paris: Seuil, 2014.

Eddé, Anne-Marie. *Saladin*. Cambridge, MA: Belknap Press of Harvard University Press, 2011.

Eusebius, bishop of Caesarea. *Life of Constantine*. Translated by A. C. McGiffert et al. New York: Christian Literature Publishing, 1890.

Reuven Firestone, *Holy War in Judaism. The Fall and Rise of a Controversial Idea*. Oxford: Oxford University Press, 2012.

Firestone, Reuven. *Jihad: The Origins of Holy War in Islam*. Oxford: Oxford University Press, 1999.

Flori, Jean. *Guerre sainte, jihad, croisade: Violence et religion dans le christianisme et l'islam*. Paris: Seuil, 2002.

Fowden, Garth. *Empire to Commonwealth: Consequences of Monotheism in Late Antiquity*. Princeton, NJ: Princeton University Press, 1993.

Fudge, Thomas A. *The Crusade against Heretics in Bohemia, 1418–1437* Aldershot, England: Ashgate, 2002.

Haldon, John. *Warfare, State and Society in the Byzantine World, 565–1204*. Abingdon England: Routledge, 1999.

Hanson, Victor Davis. *The Western Way of War*. Berkeley: University of California Press, 2009.

Hillenbrand, Carole. *The Crusades—Islamic Perspective*. Edinburgh: Edinburgh University Press, 1999.

Hodgson, Marshall. *The Venture of Islam: Conscience and History in a World Civilization*. Vol. 1, *The Classical Age of Islam*. Chicago: University of Chicago Press, 1977.

Holt, Mack P. *The French Wars of Religion, 1562–1629*. Cambridge: Cambridge University Press, 2005.

Josephus, Flavius. *The Jewish War*. In *The Complete Works of Josephus*. Grand Rapids, MI, Kregel, 1999.

Juergensmeyer, Mark. *Terror in the Mind of God: The Global Rise of Religious Violence.* Oakland: University of California Press, 2017.

Juergensmeyer, Mark, Margo Kitts and Michael Jerryson, eds. *The Oxford Handbook of Religion and Violence.* Oxford, Oxford University Press, 2013.

Jünger, Ernst. *Storm of Steel.* 1920. Translated by Michael Hofmann. 1961. New York: Penguin Books, 2004.

Kaegi, Walter E. *Heraclius, Emperor of Byzantium.* Cambridge: Cambridge University Press, 2003.

Kaeuper, Richard W. *Holy Warriors: The Religious Ideology of Chivalry.* Philadelphia: University of Pennsylvania Press, 2009.

Kennedy, Hugh. *The Great Arab Conquests: How the Spread of Islam Changed the World We Live In.* Philadelphia: Da Capo Press, 2007.

Ibn Khaldūn. *The Muqaddimah: An Introduction to History.* Translated by Franz Rosenthal. Edited and abridged by N. J. Dawood. Princeton, NJ: Princeton University Press, 1981.

Koder, Johannes, and Ioannis Stouraitis, eds. *Byzantine War Ideology between Roman Imperial Concept and Christian Religion. Akten des Internationalen Symposiums (Wien, 19.–21. Mai 2011).* Vienna: Österreichischen Akademie der Wissenschaften, 2012.

The Koran. Translated by N. J. Dawood. London: Penguin Classics, 1990.

Laine, James W. *Meta-Religion: Religion and Power in World History.* Oakland: University of California Press, 2014.

Léglu, Catherine, Rebecca Rist, and Claire Taylor. *The Cathars and the Albigensian Crusade: A Sourcebook.* London: Routledge, 2014.

Lewis, Bernard. *The Assassins: A Radical Sect in Islam.* New York: Basic Books, 2003.

Lewis, David Levering. *God's Crucible: Islam and the Making of Europe, 570 to 1215.* New York: Norton, 2008.

Lyons, Michael Cameron, and David E. P. Jackson. *Saladin: The Politics of the Holy War.* Cambridge: Cambridge University Press, 2001.

Marvin, Lawrence W. *The Occitan War: A Military and Political History of the Albigensian Crusade, 1209–1218.* Cambridge: Cambridge University Press, 2008.

Mastnak, Tomaž. *Crusading Peace: Christendom, the Muslim World, and Western Political Order.* Berkeley: University of California Press, 2002.

Niehbuhr, Reinhold. *Moral Man and Immoral Society: A Study in Ethics and Politics* New York: Scribner, 1932.

Niditch, Susan. *War in the Hebrew Bible: A Study in the Ethics of Violence.* Oxford: Oxford University Press, 1993.

David Onnekink, ed., *War and Religion after Westphalia, 1648–1713.* London: Routledge, 2009.

Oman, Charles W. C., Sir. *The Art of War in the Middle Ages.* 1923. Ithaca, NY: Cornell University Press, 1953.

Parker, Geoffrey, ed. *The Thirty Years' War.* Abingdon England: Routledge, 1987.

Peters, Edward. *Inquisition.* Berkeley: University of California Press, 1989.

Pirenne, Henri. *Mohammed and Charlemagne*. Translated by Bernard Miall. London: G. Allen & Unwin, 1939. Mineola, NY: Dover, 2001.

Prawer, Joshua. *The Latin Kingdom of Jerusalem: European Colonialism in the Middle Ages*. London: Weidenfeld & Nicholson, 1972,

Rad, Gerhard von. *Holy War in Ancient Israel*. Grand Rapids, MI: Eerdmans, 1991.

Reichbert, Gregory M. *Thomas Aquinas on War and Peace*. Cambridge: Cambridge University Press, 2017.

Riley-Smith, Jonathan. *The Crusades: A History*. New Haven, CT: Yale University Press, 2005.

Rubenstein, Jay. *Armies of Heaven: The First Crusade and the Quest for Apocalypse*. New York: Basic Books, 2011.

Seward, Desmond. *Monks of War: The Military Religious Orders*. London: Penguin Books, 1972.

Sivan, Emmanuel. *Radical Islam: Medieval Theology and Modern Politics*. New Haven, CT: Yale University Press, 1990.

Shoemaker, Stephen J. *Death of a Prophet: The End of Mohammed's Life and the Beginnings of Islam*. Philadelphia: University of Pennsylvania Press, 2011.

Sizgorich, Thomas. *Violence and Belief in Late Antiquity: Militant Devotion in Christianity and Islam*. Philadelphia: University of Pennsylvania Press, 2009.

Swift, Louis J. "St. Ambrose on Violence and War." *Transactions and Proceedings of the American Philological Association* 101 (1970): 533–43.

Taylor, Charles. *A Secular Age*. Cambridge, MA: Harvard University Press, 2007.

The Templars: Selected Sources. Translated and annotated by Malcolm Barber and Keith Bate. Manchester: Manchester University Press, 2002.

Tertullian. *Apology and De Spectaculis*. Cambridge, MA: Harvard University Press, Loeb Classical Library, 1931.

Urban, William L. *The Prussian Crusade*. Lanham, MD: University Press of America, 1980.

Verney, Victor. *Warrior of God: Jan Žižka and the Hussite Revolution*. London: Frontline Books, 2009.

Walzer, Michael. "Exodus 32 and the Theory of Holy War: The History of a Citation." *Harvard Theological Review* 61 (1968): 1–14.

———. *Just and Unjust Wars*. New York: Basic Books, 1977.

Wood, Ian. *The Merovingian Kingdoms, 450–751*. London: Routledge, 2014.

INDEX